COMPARATIVE
SOCIAL RESEARCH

Volume 2 • 1979

COMPARATIVE SOCIAL RESEARCH

An Annual Publication

Editor: RICHARD F. TOMASSON
Department of Sociology
The University of New Mexico

VOLUME 2 • 1979

 JAI PRESS INC.
Greenwich, Connecticut

Volume 1 published as COMPARATIVE STUDIES IN SOCIOLOGY

CONTENTS

THEORIES IN COMPARATIVE STUDIES

INTRODUCTION

Volume 2 of *Comparative Social Research* differs in several minor ways from Volume 1. Most obvious is the change in title from *Comparative Studies in Sociology*. This was done to emphasize the central concern of this Annual with *comparative* social research, not only that done by sociologists. The contributors to this volume are somewhat less diverse in their formal academic affiliations than are those in Volume 1. Of the 17 authors, 13 are sociologists and four are political scientists. However, except in one or two cases, I defy anyone to distinguish the work of the political scientists from that of the sociologists, or the other way around. Only one of the contributors had a non-North American academic affiliation at the time of writing, but it is noteworthy that seven of the 16 remaining contributors were foreign-born, an observation that supports my contention that the foreign-born have a greater proclivity to do comparative social research than do the native-born.

As in Volume 1 and all subsequent volumes of *Comparative Social Research*, all contributions are strictly comparative in that they compare two or more, and sometimes all, cases of a particular type. None of the contributions here are only "materials for comparative study." As I noted in the Introduction to Volume 1 of this series, the amount of sociological effort that goes into comparative study is not great. At the 1977 Annual Meetings of the American Sociological Association something less than 4 percent of all papers presented were of the strictly comparative sort. These are listed in the Appendix. The number of such papers was 23 compared with 24 at the 1976 Annual Meetings, 22 at the 1966 Meetings, but only 2 at the 1956 Meetings. (See Introduction to Volume 1.)

The 13 papers in this volume are divided into three *ad hoc* categories. The first consists of six papers dealing with the developing societies. Nonethnocentrically, only two of these papers deal at all with the North American societies. The emphasis is heavily on the countries of western Europe. Coughlin's chapter deals with attitudes toward social welfare in eight rich nations based on coverage of a great deal of survey research material. He finds, quite surprisingly I think, that the citizens of the affluent societies are brothers (and sisters) under the skin in their general attitudes toward the different kinds of social welfare. Lüschen shows, based on data from five nations, that comprehensive schools do not seem to have the egalitarian consequences that school reformers had hoped for. Slater compares the class consciousness that has developed among Southern Italian migrants in the factories of Milan, and the reasons for it, with the fragmented organization of Southern European and North African immigrants in French factories. Björn demonstrates that political variables are more important than the rate of economic growth in predicting income redistribution in five capitalist democracies. Stephens deals with the relations between politics and religion in the three secular political systems of Sweden, Norway, and Britain. Merkl studies the underlying attitudes, ideological beliefs, and topical positions of 415 West German and Italian Socialists and Christian Democrats. He shows that nationality differences are often greater than party differences.

The three papers that focus on the underdeveloped world are of a different sort. Ragin and Delacroix conclude their study of the relationship between imperialism and underdevelopment with the suggestion that it is wise to separate these two often confounded issues. Marsh, in his study of the latecomer developing nations, concludes on the basis of world-wide evidence that a democratic polity appears to hinder economic development in poor nations. Among the significant conclusions that Kennedy and Pindas arrive at in their study of the knowledge of population facts among the elites of five Third World countries is that there is little relation between their knowledge and the seriousness with which they perceive the problem of population growth.

Four papers seemed appropriate to place under the rubric of "theories in comparative study." Tilton shows that Toqueville's interpretations of nineteenth century liberal society form a strikingly sophisticated, dynamic, and modern functional theory, one that has frequently been misinterpreted. Williamson and Weiss support the view that the curvilinear interpretation of the convergence theory is useful for describing the relationship between level of development and social welfare effort, albeit not as a single factor theory. Sinden finds a strong correlation to exist between conflict and land inequality in the modernizing nations and between *both* land and income inequality and conflict in the modern societies. Taraki and Westby conclude Volume 2 with a study of the radically different assumptions underlying Western and Maoist theories of interorganizational relations; the former focus on the autonomous actor (organization), the latter on interorganizational integration.

Again let me express my appreciation to colleagues, near and far, who have allowed me to impose on them for their opinions and suggestions on a number of papers.

Richard F. Tomasson

APPENDIX

STRICTLY COMPARATIVE PAPERS PRESENTED AT THE 1977 ANNUAL MEETINGS OF THE AMERICAN SOCIOLOGICAL ASSOCIATION

1. Diversity and Scientific Performance: Results from USA and Six European Nations. (Frank M. Andrews)
2. War and the Territorial Power of States. (Randall Collins)
3. The Utilization of Dynamic Models for the Comparative Analysis of Military Institutions. (G. David Curry)
4. Do Population Dispersal Policies Work? The Case of the Netherlands and Great Britain. (Gordon F. DeJong)
5. Methods of World Systems Analysis: A Critical Appraisal. (Nancy Esteb)
6. Dependency, Inequality, and the Tertiary Sector. (Peter Evans and Michael Timberlake)
7. National Policy and Urban Development. (Susan S. Fainstein and Norman I. Fainstein)
8. Toward More Effective and Ethical Carrying-Out of Applied Research Across Cultural or Class Lines. (Charles D. Kleymeyer and William E. Bertrand)
9. The Politics of Migration Policies: The New Reality in Europe. (Daniel Kubat and Jean Leonard Elliott)
10. Family Egalitarianism in Japan and America. (Fumie Kumagai and Gearoid O'Donoghue)
11. Social Equality and the Impact of Education in West Europe. (Günther Lüshen)

COMPARATIVE
SOCIAL RESEARCH

Volume 2 • 1979

PART I

THE DEVELOPED
SOCIETIES

SOCIAL POLICY AND IDEOLOGY: PUBLIC OPINION IN EIGHT RICH NATIONS*

Richard M. Coughlin

INTRODUCTION

Disparate Research Traditions
As a central concern of students of modern society, the comparative study of social welfare institutions is relatively recent. The study of mass attitudes, on the other hand, has been established for some time as a subject of political science and sociological research. Despite the increasing attention directed at the "welfare state" as an important institution of

Comparative Social Research, Vol. 2, pp. 3–40.
Volume 1 published as Comparative Studies in Sociology
Copyright © 1979 by JAI Press, Inc.
All rights of reproduction in any form reserved.
ISBN 0-89232-112-1

modern society, and despite the continuing proliferation of opinion surveys and attitudinal studies across a broad front, these two lines of research have rarely intersected. This study aims to bridge the gap between
these research traditions by exploring the relationship between social
policy and mass ideology among eight nations.[1] The principal questions it
addresses are: (1) To what extent do mass attitudes toward key aspects of
social policy converge or diverge across a sample of rich nations? and (2)
In what ways are these attitudes related to attributes of social structure?

CONVERGENCE THEORY: FROM SOCIAL STRUCTURE TO IDEOLOGY

The essence of convergence theory is the notion that advanced industrial
societies come to resemble one another in a number of important respects. In its most extreme form (and one which is largely discredited), it
holds that nations converge toward a common condition, impelled by the
requirements of a technologically advanced, complex economy (see, e.g.,
Galbraith, 1967, pp. 396–398; Giddens, 1973, pp. 19–22). Other aspects of
national experience, from political systems to cultural forms, are rele-
gated to a secondary, even epiphenomenal role; they are seen either as
adapting to the exigencies of economic life, or enduring as quaint vestiges
neither useful to nor threatening the new order. More recently, revised
versions of convergence theory have toned down or abandoned these
assumptions. The search for a rigid mold to which all modern societies
conform has given way to less sweeping and more empirically grounded
efforts probing the dualities of similarity and difference, convergence and
divergence in specific institutional areas of some or all of the twenty or so
"rich" (or "advanced" or "post-industrial") nations of the world.

Social policy is one such area in which hypotheses derived from revised
theories of convergence have been fruitfully developed and tested (Pryor,
1968; Wilensky, 1975). Most research thus far has focused on the sources
and structure of social welfare institutions, including program inaugura-
tion and development, organization and administration, financing and the
politics of the budgetary process, and so on. From the standpoint of
predictions of convergence, the results have been mixed. For example,
while there is little doubt that the development of social welfare institutions is related to level of economic development (i.e., significant effort is

*Richard M. Coughlin is Assistant Professor of Sociology at the University of New
Mexico. He is working on an expanded version of "Social Policy and Ideology" for mono-
graphic publication, and is engaged in collaborative projects on bureaucratic responses to the
"tax-welfare backlash" and on public opinion and the "fiscal crisis" of modern "capitalist"
nations.

possible only when a minimum level of national resources has been accumulated), there is nevertheless considerable variation among rich nations in such things as percentage of Gross National Product devoted to social welfare programs, coverage of the population against various risks, and generosity of benefits (Wilensky, 1975, pp. 15–28; Cutright, 1965; Galenson, 1968). Such differences are hardly trivial, but they do not refute the convergence hypothesis. Rather, they indicate the ways in which broadly similar development is mediated by a host of pre-existing and nonconverging factors which impinge on the social–policy-making process in different nations (cf. Taira and Kilby, 1969; Wilensky, 1975, pp. 50–69; Heclo, 1974, pp. 2–9). Indeed, to reject the possibility of such variations would be to revert to the "uniform mold" concept of convergence.

The Role of Ideology. The role of ideology in modern social development, including the formation of social policy, is problematic. It is often assumed to be among the persistent points of differentiation among modern nations; as we shall see, this assumption ought not to go unchallenged (cf. Galbraith, 1967, pp. 18–19). And its relationship to social policy is a matter of controversy. Part of the problem is the confusion over the term itself (e.g., elite rhetoric versus mass attitude and belief systems), but most of the disagreement is explicable in terms of the ambiguous place of ideology in most versions of convergence theory (where the emphasis is on *social structure*) (cf. Putnam, 1973; Geertz, 1964).

Heclo (1974, pp. 290–293), on one side of this debate, discounts almost entirely the impact of mass attitudes on the formation of social policy in Britain and Sweden during the late nineteenth and early twentieth centuries. While he recognizes the existence of a diffuse mass demand for services and benefits, he argues that its effects on social policy have historically been inconsistent. Similarly, he suggests that elite ideology has not counted for much, insofar as social policy has been created by "men who could learn and whose viewpoints could change" in a larger ongoing process he terms "policy learning" (pp. 321–322).

In contrast, Rimlinger (1971, pp. 8–10) places special emphasis on the "role of ideas" (by which he means dominant currents in social-philosophical thought) in shaping the development of social welfare in the industrializing nations of Europe, as well as in America and Russia, during about the same period studied by Heclo. While he does not ignore the effects of economic, political, and social-structural forces, he describes social welfare systems in terms of ideology: thus the United States is "out of the Liberal mold," Germany "out of the patriarchal tradition," and Russia "from patriarchalism to collectivism" (pp. 8–9). Further, Rimlinger stresses the continuing influence of ideas on social policy, as shown by the "major shift in public attitude" brought about in the United States by the Social Security Act of 1935. This nevertheless left intact "dominant individualistic values" which continued to delay social legislation in, for example, the area of national health insurance (Rimlinger, 1971, p. 243). While in Germany, he adds, highly favorable public attitudes toward cradle-to-grave social insurance continue to facilitate further development of social welfare institutions there.

Somewhere between these positions is the approach taken by Wilensky (1975, pp. 28–49). In his study of the welfare state and equality, he gives greatest attention to the structural roots of social policy development. Although he rejects elite ideology as having no consistent effect, he does allow for the influence of popular values and beliefs, especially as sources of resistance to the continued growth of social programs—the "welfare backlash." This is no trivial or evanescent phenomenon, he argues further, since the roots of backlash are also among the principal attributes shared by all modern societies; mass resistance may not halt rising public expenditures for social welfare, but it can impede program development and interfere with efficient program administration (pp. 39–42). Finally, Wilensky (1975, p. 39) notes that "countries vary in the size of the universal gap between ideology and practice. . . . The failure to separate official rhetoric and popular sentiment from welfare practice creates great confusion in discussion of the welfare state."

One major purpose of this study will be to test these viewpoints, extending the convergence paradigm from social structure to the study of ideology, or, to be more precise, the structure of public opinion. In focusing on this particular aspect of ideology, I pay special attention to developing the empirical base upon which the ongoing theoretical debate can rely, and subtracting, I hope, from the "great confusion" that has gone before.

Paths and Pitfalls of Attitudinal Measurement.   Even more troublesome than the debate over the importance of ideology for social policy are the previous attempts to define, locate, and measure mass ideology using survey techniques. The first and best known of these is the Campbell *et al.* (1960, p. 195) "domestic social welfare scale." Based on a rather fuzzy notion of what constitutes social welfare, the scale consists of five items pertaining to issues ranging from aid to education and public versus private production of electricity and housing, to government-guaranteed employment and medical care. On the basis of analysis of responses to these items, the authors (pp. 192–197) conclude that mass attitudes are only loosely structured, do not correspond to conventional ideological categories, and tap a dimension of individual self-interest rather than support for social welfare. These conclusions, it should be noted, strongly influenced many social scientists' conception of mass political attitudes, at least through the 1950s and 60s (cf. Lipset, 1960; Converse, 1964).

Less heralded but similar in methodology is the Opinion Research Corporation's (1960) "attitude toward government scale." Yet in spite of the similarities, responses to the items in this scale led the ORC researchers to conclude that there exists "broad support for government action" among Americans, or in other words, that there exists a de facto "liberalism."

An important step toward resolving this apparent discrepancy is the typology developed by Free and Cantril (1968, p. 32), which distinguishes between "operational" and "ideological" attitudes. Leaving aside for the moment objections to the conceptual validity of this distinction, whose limitations I will deal with later, Free and Cantril identify an important—and paradoxical—trend in American public opinion: in two national probability samples, they found that about two-thirds chose the "liberal" (i.e., pro-welfare) position on items related to the operation of particular programs ("operational" items), whereas about the same proportion picked the "conservative" (i.e., anti-welfare) position on items relating to general policy ("ideological" items). Americans, they conclude (pp. 25–26, 32–33), are "operational liberals" and "ideological conservatives." More important than these labels is the recognition that a simplistic, unidimensional "scale" of mass ideology does not suffice to capture the intricacies of public opinion.

Thus far, the most acceptable attempt to deal with the multiple dimensions intersecting mass attitudes is the concept of "ideological complexity" developed by Litwak, Hooyman, and Warren (1973). Although they limit its application to the "multi-causal belief system" of the upper working and lower middle class—i.e., blaming the very rich and blacks for their problems—I find the concept useful in understanding the apparent contradictions found in attitudes in virtually all strata and locales of modern society (even among elite ideologues; see, for example, Rusher, 1976).[2] As we shall see in the next section, the contrary demands for both security and mobility, for equality and freedom, which mark the modern world establish within nations and even within individuals conditions incompatible with simplistic ideological conceptions.

IDEOLOGICAL CLIMATE

Principles of Social Policy

There is surprisingly little agreement among scholars and laymen alike concerning the precise meaning of the term "social policy" (or "social welfare") (cf. Heclo, 1974, pp. 1–5; Wedderburn, 1965; Feagin, 1973.)

Still the broad outlines of a generally acceptable definition are clear enough. It is reasonable to begin with the assumption that social policy originates in government intervention in social and economic affairs in order to mitigate the effects of the "free market" on individuals and families. The actual forms that this intervention can take are varied—as are, of course, the possible consequences—but underlying the diversity of particular strategies are some characteristics which, taken together, constitute the essence of modern social policy. Briefly, these are (1) the guarantee of minimum standards of living (employment, income, health, housing, etc.) for all citizens as political rights; (2) the assumption of collective responsibility for attaining or maintaining these standards; and (3) the implementation of this collective responsibility through government action, involving obligatory participation of all (or most) individuals. The full expression of these principles in public policy coincides with what is generally identified as the "welfare state."

The extent to which such government intervention is approved or disapproved of by the populace is the principal dimension of "ideological climate" in this study. Up to a point, this usage is compatible with conventional ideological categories (i.e., "liberal," "conservative"), but it also takes into account the complex, changing, and sometimes contradictory systems of values, beliefs, and opinions found in modern societies. Thus, while the eight sample nations included in this study show considerable variation in aggregate levels of public support for social policy principles, they simultaneously evidence striking similarities in the ideological crosscurrents surrounding these issues (e.g., ranging from the sweeping concerns of "socialism" and the question of absolute equality of income and lifestyle, to the residual debate over preserving individual freedom and work-related incentives). I speak of ideological climate in order to suggest that these dimensions can be fruitfully explored, measured, and analyzed, but without the implication that they are ultimately reducible to points along a simple continuum.

COLLECTIVIST AND INDIVIDUALIST COMPONENTS OF MASS ATTITUDINAL SYSTEMS

People Like the Idea of Social Guarantees. A mass of survey evidence gathered under diverse circumstances over the past thirty years or so indicates a strongly favorable attitude in all eight nations toward minimum social standards guaranteed by government. Although there is variance in the wording and structure of questions put to samples in the eight nations, the conclusion that there exists everywhere a strong collectivist component in majority attitudes is inescapable. But, equally clearly, the commitment to collectivism is more robust in some nations that in others.

In numerous surveys done in the United States in the 1950s and early 60s, approximate two-thirds majorities were found to support government employment guarantees (at least when presented in an agree/disagree format), action to combat poverty, and provisions for medical care[3] (Survey Research Center, 1956, 1960). However, in subsequent surveys done in the late 1960s and early 70s, when confronted with the *choice* between government-guaranteed employment and a "good standard of living" for all, and an alternative proposal that each person "be allowed to get ahead on his own," the "collectivist" majority disappeared (Survey Research Center, 1964, 1968; Center for Political Studies, 1972). Yet, in the same surveys, a similar forced-choice alternative did not seriously undercut majority support for government guarantees in the area of medical care.[4]

On items virtually identical to those appearing in American surveys, Canadians appear a bit more receptive to the idea of employment guarantees: in 1947 and again in 1954, Schwartz (1967, pp. 99–104) reports an even split among Canadians in choosing between such guarantees and a "free mobility" alternative. On the question of collective provisions for health care, Canadian attitudes during the 1940s and 50s were about the same as those of Americans—that is, strongly favorable.

In the United Kingdom, West Germany, and Denmark, surveys done between 1947 and 1971 establish a pattern of even heavier endorsement of collectivist principles. On items roughly comparable in structure and wording to those from American and Canadian surveys, levels of support in these three nations run on the average about 20 points higher than in Canada, 30 points higher than in the United States (Social Surveys Limited, 1961; Danish Election Survey, 1971). The German surveys display the strongest trend in this direction: from virtual unanimity (96 percent of the total sample) on the perceived importance of "equal medical are for all," to an equally impressive proportion actually *choosing* high taxes and "state provisions for social security" *over* a situation where "the State helps only in cases of real distress" by a margin of 79 to 14 percent, respectively (Noelle and Neumann, 1967, p. 388; Institut für Demoskopie, 1965).

Data for Sweden, France, and Australia are less comparable—in that they do not pose the question of "government intervention" in quite the same way as surveys from the other nations—but are still useful as indicators of collectivist sentiment. In France, several surveys (Institut Français, 1966, 1967) done during the 1960s uncovered a strong demand for more government spending in the areas of social welfare and health, and housing, with only tiny numbers expressing the desire to see expenditures in these areas cut back. In addition, a majority of the French (and two-thirds of those with opinions) characterized as "rather a good thing" increasing State intervention in the economic life of the nation. In Sweden, a 1960 election-study survey (Särlvik, 1960) found high levels of agreement to proposals to "strive for more equality . . . in regard to income, working hours, and vacations" (77 percent of the total), and to maintain "State resources sufficient to give (sic) social security [and] full employment" (66 percent). Finally, in Australia (Stokes and Aitkin, 1967), a large proportion of a 1967 election-study sample chose greater government spending for "pensions and social services" over holding the line on expenditures (79 versus 17 percent, respectively), a figure only slightly dented (to 67 percent) in a follow-up question on the same survey tying increased taxes to increased spending.

What is most striking in all of these findings is the absence of a substantial expression of hard-core, unreconstructed laissez faire ideology in public opinion in *any* of the eight nations. This generalization includes the United States (Coughlin, 1977, pp. 87–89), where less than one-fifth of the 1968 election-study sample rejected *both* government employment *and* health care guarantees. Active government involvement in providing for the well-being of individuals and families is everywhere a matter of majority public acceptance; in most nations, the data suggest, it is strongly preferred over laissez faire alternatives. That this widespread demand for social and economic security mandated by government action is, in effect, an endorsement of collectivist principles is hardly debatable; however, as we shall see in the next section, the degree to which the full elaboration of these principles is embraced by modern populations is another matter altogether.

People Want Freedom and Mobility Too.   The entrenchment of collectivism in mass attitudes in the eight sample nations is matched by what might be termed the retrenchment of individualism. Nowhere is this seen more clearly than in the United States. Alongside the previously noted favorable attitudes toward certain types of social guarantees, one finds much evidence of the hardiness of traditional values and beliefs emphasizing the "success ideology," individual achievement and free mobility, and the ideal of minimum government. Often the tug-and-pull of these contrary tendencies can be glimpsed in a single survey, a fact that has inspired much confusion among interpreters of American public opinion (Free and Cantril, 1968; Etzioni, 1970). The surveys suggest that government intervention to assure minimum standards is attractive to Americans—or at minimum tolerable—only insofar as it poses no outright threat to the celebration of cherished individualist values and beliefs. When juxtaposed to these articles of individualist faith, the welfare state fares poorly indeed. The friction of residual—retrenched—individualism has meant that the expansion of the scope of protection or raising of the level of benefits of social programs has had to proceed defensively, if at all, with ritual obeisance to the "American" values of independence, self-reliance, individual initiative, hard work, and success.

Abroad, the situation may differ in the extent to which ideological cross-currents find expression, but there can be little doubt that they *are* expressed. We have already seen some evidence of this in the Canadian surveys cited above. The roughly equal proportions choosing collectivist and individualist options for employment/standard-of-living guarantees (in contrast to the large majority in favor of health-care guarantees) is reminiscent of the trend in American opinion, although the magnitude of the Canadian turnabout is not as great. Also, several students of Canadian politics (Schwartz, 1967, p. 103; Key, 1961, pp. 425 ff.; Lamontagne, 1954) have suggested that the division between these opposing tendencies is not as emotionally charged as the ideological conflict found on the American scene. In the same vein, although the survey evidence is not as solid, the persistence of values emphasizing individual achievement and mobility, and resisting the broad thrust of socialist policies, is evident among large segments of the population in Britain and Australia (Schwartz, 1967, p. 105; *Economist,* 1973; Kewley, 1973, p. 7).

In Denmark and Sweden in the same surveys (Danish Election Survey, 1971; Särlvik, 1960) which uncovered large majorities favoring various types of social guarantees, equally large majorities decisively rejected government ownership of industry (in Denmark, 86 percent of the total sample), or control of private enterprise (76 percent in Sweden); and, in both nations, equally large proportions agreed with proposals to decrease the amount of government "interference" in private affairs. Here we find clear examples of "wanting the welfare state and freedom too."

The evidence of public dissent from the collectivist demands of social policy is less striking in France and West Germany than in the other nations discussed up to this point. For example, a 1970 French survey (Institut Français, 1970a) found a distinct public preference for the existing "liberal" economic system over an "entirely planned" socialist economy. However, one can hardly resist noting that the variety of "liberalism" endorsed by the French is not the sort envisaged by economists and philosophers of the nineteenth century. Moreover, the French more than any other nationality in this study demonstrate the ability to demand ever more in the way of government services while simultaneously resisting efforts to pay for them. (See, for example, Institut Français, 1970b, 1972.) The lively tradition of tax avoidance and revolt in France, which Ehrmann terms *incivisme,* is beyond the scope of this study; but, however one chooses to label them, these stirrings of resistance to the fiscal requirements of social policy are incongruous with its collectivist spirit (Ehrmann, 1971, pp. 31–78; Schorr, 1967, pp. 220–237; Aron, 1962, p. 62).

Less conspicuously, but just as certainly, limits to the support for collectivism can be detected among West Germans. A survey in 1962 (Institut für Demoskopie, 1966–1967) demonstrated that the idea of absolute equality of income and lifestyle lacked majority appeal: when asked if they would "like to live in a country" where such conditions existed, 38 percent replied that they would, while 44 percent declined. More revealing are the results of a 1966 survey which found little public sympathy for a young worker who states that "the most important thing is that I have social security in my old age . . . and that I need not exert myself too much in my job." By a ratio of better than two to one, Germans endorsed the contrasting attitude of another worker, which stressed hard work and individual achievement. The work ethic, it seems, is alive and well.

These German data show that values affirming individual success need not collide head-on with a simultaneous public demand for broad social protection. An ideological climate of stable equilibrium, although rare, is possible as long as the egalitarian thrust of social policy stops short of demanding rigid equality, and to the extent that individualism abandons the theology of the "free market."

In sum: Americans are not alone in their sanctification of individualist values. Similar tendencies can be detected in Sweden, Denmark, West Germany, and the other "welfare leaders" of Western Europe. Conversely, support for the collectivist principles of social policy is not restricted to nations with strong social democratic traditions. Americans—and Canadians too—pay their respects to the values of security, social protection, and collective risk-sharing.

IDEOLOGY AND SOCIAL STRUCTURE

Social Location of Attitudes.   Thus far, the discussion has focused on aggregate comparisons, and has not addressed the penetration of ideological components among different segments of the population. Among the five nations for which disaggregated data are available, a roughly similar pattern is evident in four: the United States, the United Kingdom, Canada, and Sweden. Lower social status is associated with higher levels of support for government intervention, greater social equality, and other collectivist positions. In the fifth nation, West Germany, there is a notable absence of any significant within-nation variations on a number of items tapping mass ideology. But even where the general relationship holds, the magnitude and structure of within-nation differences vary greatly. In Britain and Sweden, sharp cleavages across broad social class categories can be found, with percentage differences of up to 50 points on various items. In contrast, the association of attitudes with income, occupation, and education in the United States and Canada is more gradual, with fewer cleavages. (The exception here is race in the United States; even controlling for other stratification variables, the cleavage between blacks and whites is as wide and deep as any divisions found in Britain or Sweden.)

This mixed picture confirms what a number of students of modern society have suggested: that the structural props for mass ideologies are complex, and that explanations based solely on crude self-/or class-interest are not very useful in sorting out the relationship between ideology and social structure. (See, for example, Wilensky, 1975, pp. 54–69; Giddens, 1973, pp. 99–112.) Taking account also of the West German "exception," it is clear that an adequate explanation of the anchoring of ideological elements in different social locations must address not only the variations among advanced industrial societies in their stratification systems, but also the historical and cultural contexts (e.g., slavery in the United States; economic collapse in Germany after both World Wars) which are likely mediators of attitudinal formation. This is a large and formidable task toward which this research marks only a point of departure.

The Development of Social Welfare Institutions. Although public opinion in all eight nations is similar in its ideologically complex structure, the relative proportions of the mix of collectivism and individualism are not constant, and appear to be correlated with a number of "objective" measures of social-policy development. As shown in Table 1, where social welfare institutions are most developed (in terms of relative budgetary effort, program coverage, or duration of program) the collectivist components of mass ideology predominate. Conversely, where institutional development lags, individualism and collectivism are either equally balanced (as in Canada), or individualism is dominant (as in the United States).[5]

The overall validity as well as the details of this relationship obviously need to be explored using a more rigorously comparative survey methodology before firm conclusions are reached. However, even at the present tentative stage of the research, it is the implications of this relationship that raise the most sociologically interesting questions. At issue are such questions as: Are mass attitudes changing over time? If so, does this change mirror developments in the social welfare institutions? Do mass attitudes constitute a "push" for social rights in modern society, or are they "pulled along" by the consequences of elite commitment? We cannot, of course, provide definitive answers to these questions at this

Table 1. Ideological climate and the development of social welfare institutions.

Relative Level of Public Support for Social-Policy Principles[a]	Social Security Spending as a Percent of GNP (1965)[b]	Years of Program Experience (through 1965)[c]	Percent of Relevant Population Covered (1965 or nearest year)[d]		
			Old-Age Pensions	Health Care	Family Allowances
Highest:					
West Germany	16.8	295	93	87	28[e]
France	15.6	252	100	88	83[f]
High, but lower than above:					
Sweden	14.6	239	100	100	100
Denmark	12.2	276	100	94	100
Australia	8.3	155	55[g]	73[h]	100
United Kingdom	12.4	255	84	100	52
Medium:					
Canada	10.1	95	100	95[i]	100
Low to Medium:					
United States	7.0	119	86	20[j]	—

[a]Approximate ranking, centered on the mid-1960s, and based on the review of available survey data.

[b]International Labour Office, 1972, pp. 324-330.

[c]U.S. Social Security Administration, 1971. The figure reported is the total of years of operative programs (i.e., from inception to 1965) in the area of pensions, employment injury, health care, family allowances, and unemployment.

[d]Unless otherwise noted, source of data is International Labour Office, 1972, pp. 385-393, 416-429.

[e]European Communities, 1974, pp. 232-233. Figure shown is coverage in 1969.

[f]European Communities, 1974, pp. 232-233, also for 1969.

[g]Kewley, 1973, p. 366. Figure shown is percentage of total population participating in voluntary national health insurance *circa* 1964.

[h]Kewley, 1973, p. 442. Figure shown is percentage of the aged who actually received pensions *circa* 1965.

[i]U.S. Social Security Administration, 1971, p. 30.

[j]Medicare and Medicaid only.

time, especially given the limitations of data. However, we can cast some light on these matters, especially as they pertain to the convergence hypothesis.

First, those time-series survey data that we do have (for the United States, Canada, and West Germany, covering roughly twenty-year periods) provide little evidence of any appreciable net changes in the structure of mass ideology. Certainly the rank order of nations shown in

Table 1 has not changed. The stability of established patterns in surveys done during the post-World War II period is striking.

Second, if we look backward beyond the relatively recent era of systematic polling, a similar—albeit largely qualitative—conclusion emerges. Numerous studies of nineteenth-century social thought concur in the judgment that prevailing *elite* ideologies varied substantially throughout Western Europe and the New World, especially concerning the relative influence of feudal, aristocratic traditions vis-à-vis the "liberal" economic and political philosophy associated with rising industrialism (See Heclo, 1974; Rimlinger, 1971, Wilensky and Lebeaux, 1965, pp. 27–86; Dicey, 1953; Hofstader, 1945; Hartz, 1955; Beer, 1966; Samuelsson, 1968; Miller, 1969). Taken together, these assessments of trends in *elite* ideology in the nineteenth century correspond remarkably well with the pattern of *mass ideology* in the mid-twentieth century shown in Table 1. More precisely, where elite philosophies stressing individualism and laissez faire flourished during the nineteenth century, contemporary mass attitudes toward social policy are most ambivalent (e.g., in the United States). Where nineteenth century liberalism had the least impact, current mass ideology is more consistently collectivist (e.g., in Germany). This very broad generalization is not, of course, entirely without qualification, but the correlational pattern is strong enough to warrant serious consideration.

In both of these findings we see evidence of the persistence of cultural differences among rich nations. Beliefs, attitudes, philosophies do not instantaneously transform, nor do their effects on social, economic, and political life suddenly change as nations become modern, or as modern nations become "post-industrial." In social policy, such differences are reflected in the structure of mass attitudinal systems, reinforced, we have good reason to believe, by elite ideology and its consequences for the development of social welfare institutions. Thus, if it is to move forward, any putative process of convergence must be expected to move slowly.

PROGRAM CONSENSUS: A UNIVERSAL DIMENSION OF SUPPORT?

A Different Frame of Reference

Up to a point, the core questions of the "ideological" debate over social policy have been settled in favor of ever greater levels of government intervention. Successive increments of legislation during the past seventy years or so have established the welfare state as a permanent fixture of modern society. The commitments that have been made—in old-age pensions, national health-care schemes, and other areas—are virtually irreversible. No nation is likely to embark on a retroactive campaign to restore the status quo ante. But this does not mean that the controversy over social policy has subsided; it obviously has not. The focus of concern has, however, passed from the question of *whether* to the issue of *how* the State should provide for the social and economic well-being of the citizenry, and the presumed secondary consequences of different levels and types of action. The ideological debate recurs, but it does so increasingly in terms of the equity of social programs and the implications of high levels of taxation for economic health and political stability (Kaltefleiter, 1974; *Dunn's Review,* 1976).

This changing frame of reference of the public debate has important consequences for public opinion. For one thing, specific social welfare programs, compared to abstract ideological issues, are more immediately rooted in the experience of ordinary individuals. Participation in a pension program, the seeking of medical care (and concern about how to pay for it), or the receipt of a family allowance benefit may inspire some people to contemplate broad questions of political and social philosophy, but for the majority of the population these activities are more likely simply regarded as the "way things are." Also, opinion leadership—as practiced by politicians and public relations people—has often served to reinforce this segmented apperception of social policy. A classic example of this was the publicity campaign mounted by the AFL-CIO in 1975: in nationwide television spots, Americans were helpfully informed that "Food stamps are not welfare, they are help for people in need."

Such definitional twists and turns, as we shall see, are not peculiar to the United States.

PUBLIC OPINION IN FIVE PROGRAM AREAS

Old-Age Pensions: Public Generosity Toward the Elderly.   In the winning of public acceptance, government-sponsored old-age pension programs enjoy a favored position. This generalization stretches across all nations for which data are available, and subsumes an enormous variability in the structure and operation of different national schemes.

In the United States, many public opinion surveys dating back to the mid-1930s affirm the extraordinary support accorded to the old-age pension part of the Social Security Act. From 1936 to 1945, in various surveys utilizing slightly different item formats and wordings, approval rates ranged from 68 to 97 percent (Schiltz, 1970, p. 36). Nor was this approval half-hearted: in 1941 81 percent of a Gallup sample (p. 44) expressed a willingness to pay an additional three percent tax on income to finance the public pension program.[6] Evidence from more recent surveys show that the charm has not worn off. A typical example is a 1961 Survey Research Center (University of Michigan) study which found that "help for older people" was ranked first in priority by the public as a target for increased government spending (p. 117). Even more recently, legislation dramatically raising the ceiling for Social Security contributions to forestall the much publicized "impending bankruptcy" of the trust funds passed without evoking as much as a murmur of public protest. Despite heavy criticism from politicians on both the right and left, public opinion has remained unperturbed. Nor is there much reason to expect a sudden public outcry when the new taxes take effect. As late as August of 1977, long after the initial disclosure of the pension fund's problems and in the midst of the political flap over what to do about it, an astounding 87 percent of a Harris Survey sample characterized a one-third cutback in government spending for Social Security as a "very serious loss," and another 9 percent labeled it a "moderate loss" (Harris Survey, 1977). For the overwhelming majority of Americans, it is clear, old-age pensions are not considered a manifestation of gratuitous meddling into something which ought to be left to individual responsibility. Indeed, probably more than any other single type of governmental activity, the old-age pension aspect of Social Security has achieved almost unanimous public regard as an American "birthright."

In Canada public enthusiasm for old-age pensions started early and held up over time. When asked in 1950 if they would favor a government-sponsored plan, about two-thirds of Canadians replied that they would. A year later, fully 81 percent expressed approval for a more specific proposal to give every person 70 years of age or older a minimum monthly pension. In both 1957 and 1970, nearly identical proportions (78 and 73 percent, respectively) characterized the current level of benefits as "too low" (Schwartz, 1967, pp. 99–100; Canadian Institute, 1970b).

Like Americans, Canadians managed to reconcile highly favorable attitudes toward public pensions with more ambivalent feelings about the broader ideological themes.

In the other sample nations, survey results provide evidence of similarly solid public support. The data are diverse in quantity and quality, but all point toward a universal popularity of old-age pensions as a type of government activity: in Britain consistent public approval from the 1950s through the early 70s for increasing public spending and benefit levels for pensions (e.g., Social Surveys, 1957, 1959, 1967c, 1971); in Australia 80 percent or more in favor of raising benefit levels (Australian Gallup, 1963a, 1967a); in Sweden, over 75 percent opposing the repeal of a supplementary pension program (Särlvik, 1960); in West Germany, Denmark, and France, scattered surveys showing a deep public sympathy for the economic and social plight of the aged (Konrad Adenauer Foundation, 1973a, 1973b; Institut für Demoskopie, 1967; Institut Français, 1964b; Halck and Østergaard, 1964, pp. 8–21; *Markedsanalyse, 1970*).

The general conclusion that old-age pensions are universally popular, whatever their form of financing or payout, is warranted by these data, but it needs some elaboration to be completely accurate. Beneath the consensual surface, there are a few exceptions of note. For instance, surveys dating from the 1930s and 40s in the United States have shown that old-age pensions evoke even greater public support when the criterion of individual "neediness" is attached as a condition of eligibility (Schiltz, 1970, pp. 48–49). In addition, several British surveys have uncovered a good deal of public dissatisfaction with the way the government handles the old-age pension program, as well as a substantial number for whom "contracting out" of the public system is attractive (Social Surveys, 1958; National Opinion Polls, 1969a; Harris and Seldon, 1965, 1970).

National Health Care: Opinions Both Favorable and Malleable. In cross-national perspective, government-sponsored health care schemes vary greatly in their organization, scope of coverage, methods of financing, and conditions under which the "benefit" is conferred. Contrast the current limited insurance plan for older Americans to the unique British National Health Service (NHS), or either to the decentralized West German *Krankenkassen*. In view of this diversity, it is surprising to learn that none of these characteristics appears to be related in any systematic way to relative levels of public support for the different health-care schemes in force across nations. They have all gained widespread acceptance among the public.

Even in the United States, which of course does not yet (in 1978) have a comprehensive scheme, a long history of surveys documents the receptiveness of the public to the idea. What is most striking about the American survey findings is the combined stability and nonspecificity of opinion over nearly a forty-year period. National health insurance may well be an idea whose time has finally come, but both the idea and the public willingness to see it implemented have been around for a long time (Fuchs, 1974, pp. 127–142; Marmor, 1973, pp. 1–14).

Beginning with the early 1940s, surveys produced a confusing picture of public opinion on the question of instituting a government-sponsored national health insurance plan: on the one hand, widespread appeal for such a plan seemed to exist; but on the other hand, private or voluntary schemes attracted as much or more support. Depending upon whom one listened to during the 1940s (and sadly, often who was paying for the survey), the American public either favored national health insurance by a decisive margin, or only a tiny—and presumably subversive—minority were behind the push for "socialized" medicine (Schiltz, 1970, pp. 124–134).

An admirable research effort by the Opinion Research Corporation managed to cut through the confusing and contradictory findings of previous surveys. In 1945, among a single sample, ORC found overlapping support of about 70 percent for *both* government health insurance and for a privately organized plan. When pressed to decide which strategy was "better," the sample split into three groups of nearly equal size: 35 percent in favor of the government plan, 31 percent choosing the private alternative, and 34 percent who had no preference or who were unable to decide (Schiltz, 1970, pp. 132–133, 148–149). The American people indeed "wanted something done" about health care, but they were uncertain or unspecific about precisely what this "something" should be.

During the late-1950s and early 60s, the proposed Medicare scheme evoked a similar response pattern. Most of those surveyed generally favored the idea of helping the aged meet the costs of medical care. Even under the threat of higher taxes, approval for Medicare ranged between 58 and 67 percent. But once again, when asked to choose between entrusting the provision of aid to the Federal government or to a private, voluntary fund, the pro-health-insurance majority split down the middle (p. 140).

The debate in the 1970s over national health insurance finds Americans, with few exceptions, circling in the same rut carved thirty years ago. Compare the results of a 1976 national election study survey with the 1945 ORC effort: given the choice between national (i.e., government) health insurance and a plan organized by private insurance companies, the 1976 sample was evenly divided. But of the 42 percent who chose the national health insurance plan, only 26 percent expressed a strong preference, and for the private plan the results were similar (24 percent strong support out of a total of 41 percent) (Center for Political Studies, 1976). The remainder of the sample either expressed weak or medium preferences for one or the other alternatives, or were undecided. In these as in earlier surveys there is no compelling mandate for any specific action. The prospect of national health insurance continues to be generally attractive to many Americans, but public opinion remains too diffuse to serve as a guide for policy formulation.[7]

Abroad, the United Kingdom presents one of the most instructive comparisons with the United States, both because the National Health Service (NHS) is so vastly different from any system of national health care likely to be adopted in the United States and because of some important parallels in public opinion that can be seen in the two nations. The British public, as many surveys over the period 1946 to 1971 well document, has always accorded a high level of support to the NHS. A consistently high level of satisfaction with the care rendered under the scheme has been accompanied by a general willingness to see public funds devoted to it[8] (Social Surveys, 1946, 1948, 1960a, 1963, 1968; National Opinion Polls, 1971). Furthermore, majorities of samples both in 1965 and 1967 soundly rejected proposals to introduce a "fee-for-service" charge, and to require additional payments for medical care of individuals "who can afford it" (Social Surveys, 1965, 1967d).

These results indicate a strong public commitment to the universalistic and egalitarian aspects of the NHS. Yet there also exists another side to British attitudes, specifically centering on the question of "voluntarism"—some would say "freedom"—in obtaining medical care outside the rubric of the public system. For example, a National Opinion Polls (1969b) survey found virtual unanimity (84 percent of the total) in agreement that individuals should be allowed to join private health plans. Other surveys, sponsored by a "free enterprise"-oriented institute, found that of three alternatives presented to samples (quota samples, mainly consisting of employed males), the one most often chosen was "to continue present service (sic), but allow individuals to 'contract out' and pay less taxes" (Harris and Seldon, 1965, 1970).

A similar diffuseness can be observed in Australian attitudes. While several surveys (Australian Gallup, 1965, 1967b) in the mid-1960s (done before the universal system named Medibank was launched) found "free health services" ranked first among a group of goals (including "better education" and "pensions without a means test") for which respondents indicated they would be willing to pay higher taxes, other surveys showed majority resistance to replacing the then voluntary health insurance system with a compulsory one.

Survey data for the other sample nations—Canada, West Germany, and France—confirm the conclusion that national health care schemes are widely popular (Schwartz, 1967, pp. 99–100; Noelle and Neumann, 1967, p. 387; Canadian Institute, 1970a; Institut Français, 1964a). In both Canada and France, the level of satisfaction expressed with the operation of the respective health insurance schemes is remarkably high. Unfortunately, these data provide little information about attitudes toward voluntary or supplementary coverage, but it is a fair guess that undercurrents similar to those observed in other nations are present in these also (see Galant, 1955).

To sum up briefly: the bitterness of the elite controversy over government involvement in providing for medical care (particularly in the United States, Canada, and Australia) does not have an analog in public opinion (Harris and Seldon, 1970; Corning, 1969; *Facts on File*, 1962; Grattan, 1975). Despite persistence of strong, occasionally even majority, preferences for voluntary alternatives in national health care schemes, the overall thrust of public opinion in all the nations for which we have data is much more favorable than unfavorable. While there is no sign of any mass-based health-care "backlash," neither is there a concerted push for expanded government intervention.

Family Allowances: A British Exception to a Uniform Trend.   Despite the multiplicity of connotations commonly attached to family allowances—ranging from a limited form of guaranteed income to conscious pronatalism—the programs which serve to confer benefits on families with children have managed to win the approval of large majorities of the public in four of the five nations for which we have data[9] (Titmuss, 1958; Moynihan, 1973, pp. 44–49).

Survey results from Australia, Canada, and Sweden provide the most compelling evidence of this favorable reception. Among Australians surveyed in 1957, 90 percent expressed confidence in the "child endowment" program, versus only 7 percent who wanted to see it abolished (Australian Gallup, 1957). Six years later, another survey found 68 percent in favor of *increasing* the level of benefits provided under the program (Australian Gallup, 1963b). In Canada and Sweden, the figures are only slightly less impressive: between 75 and 84 percent (in 1948 and 1950, respectively) of Canadians agreed that "family allowances are proving to be a good thing" (Schwartz, 1967, pp. 97–104) and 69 percent of the Swedish electorate opposed the abolition of the "child allowance" program in 1960 (Särlvik, 1960).

The French results present some ambiguities, mainly attributable to the content and structure of available survey items, but have been interpreted by at least one leading student of French social policy as reflecting a generally high level of public satisfaction with the intricate system of family subsidies (Ehrmann, 1971, p. 235).

The fifth nation, the United Kingdom, is on the surface an exception to this cross-national trend. For instance, nearly half the public disapproved of a proposal made in a 1960 Gallup survey to increase public spending in the area of family allowances, while simultaneously backing by a large margin increased spending for the NHS and old-age pensions (Social Surveys, 1960a). Later, in two separate surveys, only a tiny fraction of respondents approved of replacing the existing family allowance program with a comprehensive and generous plan (Social Surveys, 1966, 1967a). This rejection is more plausibly interpreted as resistance to family allowances generally than as affection for the existing system.

The nature of the British "exception" is not easily explicable either in terms of the comparative structure of family allowance programs across the five nations, or relative benefit levels, or even the effects of broad cultural differences concerning attitudes toward children and the family.

The key to understanding, as the final bits of evidence show, resides in the perception of "need" among the British public related to the receipt of family allowances benefits. A National Opinion Polls (1968) survey found that more than 75 percent of the public favored restricting benefits to those families of demonstrable "need"; an earlier survey in 1967 (Social Surveys, 1967b) had shown that once provided with an explicit restriction of eligibility, fully 61 percent could be induced to approve of increasing the level of benefits paid under the plan. Thus, British support for the family allowance program is not absent, but it is reluctant.

Unemployment Compensation: The Problematic Public Perception of Paying People Who Don't Work ("Variations on a 'Doleful' Theme").   The question of perceived "need" is one which troubles not only the British in their contemplation of family allowances, but Americans and Canadians, as well as Britons, in their attitudes toward unemployment compensation.[10] The American data are the most extensive, and reveal the perception of "need" to be both an explicit and implicit determinant of the direction of public opinion. The explicit effects can be seen in a series of questions appearing on Gallup surveys during the 1930s and 40s. The surveys done at the beginning of this period specifically mentioned that unemployment benefits would go to "needy" people; in response, public approval ranged between 58 and 68 percent (Schiltz, 1970, p. 98). Subsequent surveys made no direct mention of need in conjunction with the program, and public approval was not nearly as hearty. Reaction to President Truman's proposal to provide unemployed workers with a $25 per week allowance exemplifies this difference: five surveys done from May to October of 1945 failed in each case to produce anything approaching majority approval for more comprehensive coverage, and the introduction of higher taxes as a condition of the reform further depressed support to a meager 34 percent (pp. 102–109).

The lack of public enthusiasm for comprehensive and generous unemployment benefits during the 1940s developed into outright contempt by the 1960s. A 1961 Survey Research Center (University of Michigan) study found a scant 29 percent of Americans willing to support increased government spending in the area of unemployment compensation (versus 70 percent who approved of stepped-up efforts "to help older people," and 54 percent for "hospital and medical care") (Schiltz, 1970, p. 117). The reason for this majority hostility is suggested by the results of two surveys done in 1965. In response to the question "Do you think many people collect unemployment benefits even though they could find work?" 75 percent of a Gallup Poll (1965b) sample answered yes. Similarly, Free and Cantril (1968) report about the same level of agreement with the assertion that "any able-bodied person who really wants to work in this country can find a job and earn a living."

Consistent with these findings is the long-standing popularity that work relief programs have had among Americans. Surveys from the 1930s up to the present have repeatedly found a heavy preference for such programs over the payment of cash benefits to the unemployed (Schiltz, 1970, pp. 114–117; Gallup, 1969, pp. 20–21). Here the element of "need" is implicit: if an individual is willing to go to work to collect unemployment benefits, it is reasoned, then he must really need help, and is not simply opting out of employment at the taxpayers' expense. The message conveyed by American public opinion can be succinctly summarized as follows: tighten up the rules, restrict the benefits, and put the unemployed to work.

With only slight alterations, this summary accurately describes the state of Canadian and British public opinion as well. An intensive study of Canadian attitudes in 1968 found that the most frequently endorsed proposal for reforming the unemployment insurance system was to reduce the possibility of cheating by recipients (65 percent approved of this). Additionally, an overwhelming proportion of the large national sample (about 6,500 respondents) alleged that the system was frequently subject to at least one kind of abuse, and many respondents cited multiple abuses (Lanphier, Portis, and Golden, 1970, pp. 36–38). The thematic convergence of these results with those of American surveys is striking, from widespread suspicion that recipients of unemployment benefits do not attempt to find work, to allegations of various types of outright fraud such as under- or nonreporting of income, and drawing benefits while working (Adams, 1971, pp. 14–34).

Among the British, public attitudes are informed by the same kinds of suspicions. As reported by Klein (1974, p. 412), the results of a 1968 Opinion Research Corporation survey suggest that they may be even more extreme: 87 percent agreement that "too many people take advantage of unemployment and sickness benefits by taking time off from work"; 89 percent agreement that "too many people don't bother to work because they can live well enough on the dole;" and 78 percent agreement that "we have so many Social Services that people work less hard than they used to."

For the remaining sample nations no relevant survey data could be found, an obvious impediment to generalizing our inferences about the problematic character of unemployment compensation. One likely contributing factor to the underdevelopment of the survey-data base is the relatively low levels of unemployment that most of the nations in Western Europe have experienced until recent years, and the tiny unemployment compensation expenditures that they have made in consequence (cf. International Labour Office, 1972). Only in the economic crunch of the mid-1970s have rates of unemployment risen to substantial levels, and the reactions to this new predicament suggest that the pattern of Anglo-American opinion may not be unique. In Denmark, unemployment soared to nearly ten percent of the labor force in 1974, and with this unprecedented situation came new rumors of abuse of the unemployment compensation system, including stories of alleged "commuter" flights operating between Mediterraenean resorts and Danish cities where benefits could be collected every two weeks (Vinocur, 1975). In West Germany and Sweden, where the problem of unemployment was not so acute, the response by political leaders was nevertheless cautious. The Germans acted—as they had in earlier economic slowdowns—to "export" part of their unemployment by tightening restrictions on foreign worker residency, and maintained a low-profile domestic cash-benefit program for unemployed workers (Janssen, 1975). The Swedes have long shielded the operation of the unemployment compensation program from the spotlight of public attention by burying it in compehensive labor-market policies. Although in the absence of direct survey evidence we must speculate on the motives for these elite strategies, there appears to be little interest in either of these nations to publicize the operation of a program which pays people who don't work.

Public Assistance: What Do the Poor Deserve?   In the United States, it is well known that the poor have been "rediscovered" and the attention devoted to "welfare" (i.e., public assistance) programs and the "welfare mess" exceeds their importance in terms of numbers of recipients and/or relative cost (compared, for example, to old-age pensions). In contrast, in much of Western Europe the problem of poverty has been overlooked, and the role of public assistance programs downplayed. Coupled with these differential perceptions of poverty and its amelioration is the enormous noncomparability across nations in programs aimed at the poor. Together these conditions have produced serious obstacles to comparative attitudinal research. Thus, the exploratory comparisons which follow below must be interpreted cautiously. They yield some thematic similarities, some apparent differences, but leave much still uncertain or unspecified.

a. Suspicions of abuse.   Numerous surveys have documented the negative components of American public attitudes toward "welfare." Included here is the pervasive belief that "relief rolls are loaded with chiselers" (66 percent agreement), that public assistance programs serve as work disincentives (60 percent agreement), and that eligibility rules for "welfare" programs need to be tightened (about 75 percent agreement, depending on the wording of the question (Free and Cantril, 1968; Ogren, 1973; Gallup, 1961). These sentiments have been repeatedly reinforced by well-publicized "welfare scandals" and by the political campaigns of anti-welfare candidates such as Ronald Reagan and George Wallace (see Ritz, 1966; Wilensky, 1976; Rein and Heclo, 1973). It is easy to seize on these trends, and to ignore the paradoxically positive face of American opinion. For example, while they may mistrust the motives of the poor, a vast majority of Americans agree that welfare programs are needed "to insure that no one goes without the necessities of life" (86 percent agreement), that the Federal government has a responsibility to try to do away with poverty (76 percent), and that children of the poor should be provided with benefits, even if this entails supporting their "unworthy" parents (76 percent)[11] (Free and Cantril, 1968; Ogren, 1973).

To summarize American attitudes toward welfare as ambivalent understates the degree of underlying conflict in these divergent trends—conflict between humanitarian impulses and cynical skepticism, between a desire to help the materially disadvantaged and a fear of rampant welfare abuse. A surprising number of people seem to be consciously aware of this contradiction: when asked in a 1965 Gallup survey to characterize their overall reaction to welfare and relief programs, only 6 percent replied that the programs ought to be done away with altogether, 43 percent expressed favorable attitudes, and the remaining plurality of 45 percent admitted to "mixed feelings" (Gallup, 1965a; cf. Gallup, 1977b).

In Britain and Canada the situation appears much the same, although the survey evidence is not as complete. In Canada, public attitudes toward government spending for "welfare" are equally, or even more, negative than in the United States (Canadian Institute, 1971; cf. Gallup, 1965a). Furthermore, the imagery of the "welfare bum" is not unknown to Canadians (Lewis, 1972, for a different usage of this term). British attitudes toward the "dole," mentioned in the previous section, apply equally well to public assistance as well as to the unemployment compensation program ("dole" commonly refers to either or both). Other surveys have indicated that concern with "scrounging" and "sponging" (i.e., abuse) runs high among the British public, and that "coloured" immigrants (West Indians, Indians, and Pakistanis) are frequently suspected of being culpable of such acts (Abrams and Hall, undated, pp. 16–17; Rose, 1969, pp. 566–572). A Royal Commission appointed in the early 1970s to investigate abuse of public assistance programs described the situation as follows:

> Public opinion in relation to the control of abuse is volatile. Strong feelings of indignation can be provoked by descriptions . . . of men working and earning large sums

whilst drawing benefit, or living on supplementary benefit when they could be working.

However, the report hastens to add that

[E]qually strong feelings of sympathy can be aroused for unmarried or deserted women who are subjected to investigation. . . . The public, whilst ready to condemn abuse when it is established, is equally ready to condemn what it regards as excessive intrusion on individuals during the investigation of suspected abuse (Secretary of State for Social Services, 1973, p. 12).

Is this fascination with the myriad possibilities of "welfare" abuse peculiar to the Anglo-American nations?[12] Without denying the possible explanatory value of the common cultural inheritance (see below), the phenomenon appears to span diverse cultures. A case in point is the finding of a Danish Gallup Poll in 1974 *(Berlingske Tidende)* that over one quarter of the Danish public cited "youth, drug addicts, and 'social sponges'" as symptoms of the failings of the modern welfare state. Elsewhere it is reasonable to expect that at least the potential for similar expressions exists; why they remain less visible than in the United States or Britain is not easily explained.

   b. Causes of poverty.   Logic suggests that attitudes toward public assistance programs should be influenced by beliefs about the causes of poverty; indeed, at least for the United States, there is some empirical support for this hypothesis (Alston and Dean, 1972, p. 21). Although we lack survey data on attitudes toward public assitance programs other than those of the United States, Britain, and Canada, the question of public perception of poverty was the recent subject of a rare comparative survey effort, sponsored by the Commission of the European Communities (EC). Added to previous studies for the United States and Canada, the cross-national comparisons provide a basis upon which to draw some inferences about attitudes toward public assitance programs in West Germany, France, and Denmark.
   The most salient finding of the EC survey is that the British stand alone among the Common Market nations in near-majority attribution of the causes of poverty to "individual laziness and lack of willpower." In contrast, French and West German samples emphasized the role of "social injustice" as the principal cause of poverty, while the Danes focused on the fatalistic elements of "bad luck" and "inevitability" (Riffault and Rabier, 1977, pp. 71–72).
   Earlier surveys in the United States and Canada, covering the same subject but with different precoded categories, found that Americans

placed the blame for poverty more frequently on "lack of individual effort" than on "circumstances beyond individual control" (by a margin of two to fifteen points, in two different surveys), while Canadians did just the opposite (by a margin of four points) (Alston and Dean, 1972; Canadian Institute, 1964; Gallup, 1965c). But both American and Canadian beliefs about poverty more closely resemble those of the British than those of the West Germans, French, or Danes.

A second item on the EC survey tapped attitudes toward government activity to "combat poverty." It is important to note that this is *not* conceptually identical to attitudes toward public assistance programs, but, once again, it does provide us with a basis for some rough comparisons. Consistent with their modal belief that poverty is the result of social injustice, the French expressed a majority willingness to see government activity to combat poverty *increased* over present levels, followed, at some distance, by the West Germans. As might be expected from previous survey results, British support for this type of activity was fairly low, and 20 percent of the British sample responded that the government had already done too much in this area. But even further back were the Danes, who showed the least support among the four nations for increased government efforts, and who, like the British, also expressed significant resistance to current efforts (10 percent thought the government had gone too far already) (Riffault and Rabier, 1977, pp. 76–77). This lack of support for combating poverty in Denmark is only ambiguously related to Danish attitudes toward poverty, but it does fit in with the finding that "social sponges" and other undeserving beneficiaries of social programs are a focal point of public dissatisfaction with social policy there.

SIMILARITIES BENEATH THE IDEOLOGICAL SKIN

Assembling the bits and pieces of survey data discussed in this section, and condensing the major trends in public attitudes into approximate ordinal categories, we find that beneath the ideological skin program-specific opinions are strikingly similar across this sample of nations. As shown in Table 2, this is most true for old-age pension and national health-care schemes. For these two types of programs, neither ideological climate nor administrative structure, extent of coverage, type of financing, and type or level of benefits are related to the levels of public support across nations. While all of these factors vary considerably over the sample, public opinion is uniformly favorable. For family allowances, the cross-national convergence of public opinion embraces four of the five nations for which we have data, with Britain the sole exception (and then only when no mention of "need" is made). For unemployment compensa-

Table 2. Across variable ideological climates
there is a consensus of program-specific opinion.

Ordinal Ranking of Public Support for Programs[b]

Relative Level of Public Support for Social Policy Principles[a]	Old-Age Pensions	National Health Schemes	Family Allowances	Unemployment Compensation	Public Assistance
Highest:					
West Germany	High	High	na	na	(Medium)
France	High	(High)	(High)	na	(High)
High, but lower than above:					
Sweden	High	na	High	na	na
Denmark	High	na	na	na	(Low)
Australia	High	High	High	na	na
United Kingdom	High	High	Low	(Low)	Low
Medium:					
Canada	High	High	High	Medium to Low	Low
Low to Medium:					
United States	High	Medium to High	—	Low	Low

[a]See notes to Table 1.

[b]Rankings in parentheses should be interpreted with caution, since they are based on ambiguous or incomplete data. The abbreviation "na" signifies missing data.

tion and public assistance programs, the similarities are more complicated, with low-to-medium levels of support in three nations, four if Denmark is included, with a common concern with benefit abuse. Here France, and possibly West Germany, appear to be exceptions, at least in terms of beliefs about the causes of poverty and attitudes toward programs aimed at the poor. Just how "different" these nations are in this respect, however, remains an open question that will require more comparable, detailed survey data to answer (see below).

Tentatively, the cross-national similarities of program-specific opinion outweigh the differences in Table 2, and therefore, the convergence hypothesis is at least partly confirmed. It remains to explore the dynamics of this "universal dimension" of support, as well as to consider the nature and significance of the possible exceptions to it.

Ideologies Do Not Disappear, but Their Effects Are Uneven. The argument that modern societies reach an "end of ideology" is not persuasive, at least insofar as this implies the disappearance of conflict between alternative value and belief systems. Ideological currents persist, but, as can be observed in numerous surveys, their relation to public opinion on substantive questions of social policy is not strong. The broad similarities among nations in the aggregate level of popular support for different categories of social programs provides partial evidence of the weak net effects of ideology. Additional evidence is found in the weak or entirely absent social cleavages that obtain on program-specific questions.

a. Programs Differentially Tap Ideologies. To conceive of the convergence of public opinion as "pragmatic" is misleading, since this implies the existence of a neutral, eclectic orientation. It is more useful, I think, to interpret this trend in terms of the superimposition of divergent ideological systems, which form a matrix of intersecting and sometimes contradictory elements. It is in this matrix that particular programs are located, and that program popularity is determined. For example, the universal popularity of old-age pension and health-care programs can be understood as tapping the collectivist component of mass ideology, and almost entirely circumventing competing individualist values. While it is possible to argue that principles of self-reliance and individual initiative ought to be extended to pensions and health care, few would push this to the point of denying the aged their monthly allowance or the sick their medical care. The expressions of individualist ideology are limited in practice to a rear-guard fight for voluntarism within the workings of public programs.

In the case of unemployment compensation and public assistance, collectivism and individualism are more closely matched in competition to provide the definitional framework by which the programs are judged. In the United States, the surveys (and civic lore) teach that traditional values of individualism, hard work, and success provide the dominant frame of reference. The programs must respond defensively to these in order to win public acceptance. Often, of course, they fail. The influence of collectivism is not absent, but it must parade in the guise of "deservedness" and "need" in order to sway public opinion. And sometimes it succeeds. In other nations the interplay of conflicting ideologies may be less dramatic, but the dynamics are probably similar.

Thus, I interpret the uniformity of program-specific opinion to be a reflection of ideological complexity, as this concept was developed earlier in this analysis. To the extent that both collectivist and individualist components can be detected in the value and belief systems of modern populations, social welfare programs (and other policy-related issues) are able to tap differentially each dimension (and related "ideologies"), with the result that no single ideology dominates the content of public opinion. The process of public opinion formation, and attempts to influence it, can be understood as the construction of the matrix of competing ideologies, each of which seeks to legitimate its own definition of the social, economic, and political order.

b. *Attenuation of Social Cleavages.* The distribution of opinion on social welfare programs mirrors in most cases the pattern of "ideological" cleavage, but in a muted form. Moreover, on some issues (e.g., old-age pensions) there is virtual uniformity across all groups and strata within nations for which breakdowns are available. Even where cleavages do persist, for example between blacks and whites in the United States on questions of unemployment insurance abuse and attitudes toward "welfare," the gap is not nearly as large as on broader ideological issues, and on many points there is no gap at all (Ogren, 1973, pp. 104–106; Kallen and Miller, 1971, pp. 86–87). Similarly, attitudes toward the NHS in Britain or child allowances in Sweden are nowhere near as sharply divided along lines of social class as are ideological attitudes.

The consensus within as well as across nations lends further support to the "universal dimension" hypothesis. If mass ideologies only imperfectly reflect individual and group (or class) interests and aspirations, program-specific opinions do so not at at all. The relative absence of opinion anchoring may result from the self-canceling effects of competing ideologies described above. To verify this and understand why it is so, we need to devote much more study to the "reality structuring" function of beliefs and opinions (Glock and Piazza, undated). At present, this area of research is badly underdeveloped.

Possible Exceptions and Their Significance. The cases which appear not to conform to the convergence hypothesis are France and West Germany (in aggregate support for government efforts to combat poverty), and Britain (in attitudes toward family allowances). The British case presents no real threat to the hypothesis, since it can be understood as simply another variation on the theme of "neediness." The pattern of reluctant public support, lured only by the promise that benefits will go only to families who "really need" them, is similar to that found for unemployment compensation and public assitance, and can be explained in the same terms. Of course, why family allowances are regarded in this way in Britain and not, for example, in Canada is still a mystery, since Canadians no less than the British are disposed to become embroiled in questions of deservedness and abuse. This remains a question for future study.

The problem of French and German attitudes toward antipoverty programs (and beliefs about the causes of poverty) is stickier. Because both nations exhibit strongest support for social policy among the eight nations, it is plausible to make the connection between this favorable ideological climate and a greater willingness than is found elsewhere to support public assistance programs. However, the directness of this connection cannot be assumed, since evidence from the United States demonstrates that significant support for fighting poverty can coexist with unfavorable attitudes toward public assistance programs. The paradoxical results of American surveys should serve as a warning against hasty conclusions. It may well be that what appears at first glance to be a consequence of strong collectivist ideology is really only a difference of operational definitions of who among the "poor" are deserving of public aid. Specifically, we need to examine public opinion data on attitudes toward foreign worker populations in France and West Germany, and public readiness to include the families of these highly visible minorities in the scope of public generosity, before reaching any firm conclusions.

In short, the exceptions to the universal dimension hypothesis are neither so numerous, nor striking, nor as yet empirically established to overshadow the broad convergence of program-specific opinion.

CONCLUSIONS AND IMPLICATIONS OF THE RESEARCH

As we have seen, the structure of public attitudes, beliefs, and opinions concerning the principles and programs of social policy is broadly similar across the nations covered by this research. This convergence is clearest on levels of aggregate support for old-age pension and national health care programs, and appears to extend—with the exceptions noted above—to other program areas. Even when significant diversity can be found, as in the integration of collectivist and individualist elements into complex mass ideologies, the differences across nations tend to be of degree, measured in the proportions of the ideological mix, rather than of kind. To this extent, it makes sense to speak of modern social-policy development in terms of mass ideological as well as structural convergence.

Although we lack at the present time a comparative data base broad enough to encompass the full range of rich nations, much less the nations currently entering the modern world, enough evidence exists to lend credibility to the notion of a distinctively "modern" system of attitudes and opinions associated with social policy. The characteristics of this system include widespread public acceptance of the principle of the "social rights of citizenship," and with it the endorsement of positive government efforts to ensure the social security of individuals and families. Yet there remains simultaneously strong allegiance to individual freedom, private enterprise, and individual responsibility for success or failure in a competitive economic order. In addition, our data establish that some types of social welfare programs are invariably popular while others may be universally problematic.

How surprising is this evidence of the convergence of public opinion? The answer depends on one's initial perspective. If one assumes that nations are by nature culturally diverse, and that this diversity leads inevitably to vastly different world views across cultures, then the findings of this research pose considerable difficulties. If, however, one takes the initial position that nations tend to move toward one or more points of convergence as they respond to the functional demands of modern society, our findings hold less of a surprise. But they also serve as a warning to overly enthusiastic proponents of uniformity: in a number of important respects modern "welfare states" vary and so do the mass ideologies associated with them. Put another way, this research has identified some communalities of modern societies having to do with prevailing attitudes and opinions, but they are neither themselves immutable nor independent of other powerful forces at work in each nation. Like Almond and Verba's (1963) "civic culture," Inkeles' (1974) concept of "individual modernity," and Wilensky's (1975) study of the welfare state, this research has afforded a glimpse at an emergent set of characteristics shared to some extent by all the nations under study, but which are not shared equally by all and which are certainly not locked into a single socio-cultural form.

This leads to the second major implication of this research: where cross-national differences in the content, structure, and distribution of social-policy attitudes are found, the search for the sources of these variations must go beyond the study of social welfare institutions themselves, to the exploration of the historical, political, and economic factors that have mediated the formation and development of public opinion. "Cultural diversity" will not suffice as a residual explanatory category, the search must begin to unravel the sources of diversity (cf. Taira and Kilby, 1969, pp. 150–153). The following questions are directly implied by this research; they are only a few of the many possible directions in which future research should proceed:

● *West Germany as an exceptional case.* In the strong and socially uniform support for social policy (including, it seems, programs aimed at the poor) the German case is atypical. Can this pattern be attributed solely to the peculiarities of twentieth-century German experience, particularly the economic devastation that followed each of the two World Wars? Or are there alternative explanations unrelated to the vicissitudes of historical events? Possible strategies for unraveling this puzzle range from an intensive case study of the social base of support and resistance to German social-policy development from its origins under Bismarck to the postwar reconstruction, to a comparison between Germany and other nations suffering similar devastation (Japan is a likely candidate for such a comparison).

• *Minority group relations.* The strong support among American blacks for collectivist social and economic policy seems clearly linked to the subordinate position that they have occupied in American society dating back to the time of slavery. Other American minorities who have suffered discrimination also appear more receptive to government-guaranteed minimum standards. The question of whether this pattern extends to racial or ethnic minorities in other nations who have occupied a similar "out-group" status remains open. It is conceivable that increasing demands for cultural or regional autonomy in nations such as France, Canada, and the United Kingdom may undermine such support, supplanting it with a growing hostility toward central government control embodied in the welfare state. As separatist movements gain momentum, existing survey data will not suffice to answer this question.

• *Effects of social mobility.* We have some evidence that where social mobility ideology has been strong (e.g., in the United States and Canada), public support for collectivist social guarantees is lower and undercut by the "success ideology" to a greater degree than where social class boundaries have historically been more rigid. Australia seems to be an exception to this rule. However, it still remains to be seen whether beliefs about the openness of the opportunity structure and, even more important, the actual mobility experience of individuals are consistent predictors of attitudes toward the welfare state (cf. Wilensky, 1975, pp. 54–58; Rytina, Form, and Pease, 1970).

• *Elite opinion leadership.* The task of tracing the linkages between elite and mass attitudes has challenged political scientists and sociologists for decades (cf. Key, 1961, pp. 411–457; Luttbeg, 1966). The fruits of these labors have not been particularly rich, but reconfirm our sense that elite attitudes and rhetoric should not be ignored as an important force shaping public opinion. Research by McClosky, Hoffman, and O'Hara (1960) in the early 1960s showed Republican leaders out on an ideological limb, at odds not only with Democratic leaders and followers on such issues as "social security" and "slum clearance," but also out of step with Republican followers. In contrast, Barton's (1974) analysis of elite attitudes in the 1970s indicates an "ideological complexity" among both Democratic and Republican leaders not unlike the paradoxical pattern of American public opinion. Abroad, the evidence is even more mixed. For example, while some observers have remarked on the "pragmatic" normative convergence among British political elites, public opinion polls over the past twenty years have uncovered a consistent dissensus among Labour and Conservative party followers on a number of key social-policy issues (Christoph, 1965; Abrams and Rose, 1960, pp. 19–23, 38–41, 60–75; Alt, Särlvik, and Crewe, 1976). In Sweden, separate studies by Särlvik (1967) and Molin (1965, pp. 189–198) of the pension reform issue of the late 1950s both found convincing evidence of a developing elite-mass congruence over the course of the public debate. Yet in Denmark, Siune and Borre's study (1975, p. 73) of the 1971 national election concluded that "Danish politicians are not representative of the Danish public in their emphases on political issues."

In view of this apparent diversity among nations in the relationship between elite and mass attitudes, the problem of determining the character, extent, and effects of elite-mass linkage will require painstaking effort in the years to come. The importance of this task is matched by its difficulty.

● *Future trends in social policy.* Although the limited time-series data currently available show little evidence of systematic change in public opinion concerning most (if not all) aspects of social policy, this should not prompt the unthinking assumption that change is not possible. We must remain sensitive to the reaction of public opinion to—as well as its role in—the development of social policy over the next ten to twenty-five years. During this time it is likely that an ever increasing convergence in the structure and coverage of welfare-state programs will occur in rich nations. The United States will undoubtedly institute some form of national health insurance, and all nations may move further toward a system of universal minimum income maintenance. It remains to be seen whether this increased structural convergence will be paralleled by a growing similarity of mass ideologies, or whether existing differences will persist.

FOOTNOTES

*This study is part of the Welfare State and Equality project (National Science Foundation grant #SOC77-13265) directed by Harold L. Wilensky. I am grateful to Professor Wilensky for initial inspiration for this study, as well as for intellectual guidance through all phases of the research (including a careful critical reading of this article), and to Charles Y. Glock for his helpful comments on analysis of survey data. I am grateful for financial support provided by the National Science Foundation, the Institute of International Studies, the Chancellor's Patent Fund, and the Graduate Division, University of California, Berkeley.

1. United States, Canada, United Kingdom, Australia, France, West Germany, Denmark, and Sweden. Depending on survey data availability, the actual number of nations for which comparisons are possible ranges from three to all eight.

2. The thesis that the structural differentiation of modern society requires a concomitant ideological complexity is not original to Litwak, Hooyman, and Warren, 1973. For an earlier statement on the ideological paradox of the modern welfare state, see Wilensky and

Lebeaux, 1965. For more recent elaborations of this idea, see Wilensky, 1975, and Huber and Form, 1973.

3. Unless otherwise noted, all survey data come from national probability sample surveys, and all figures represent percentages of total sample.

4. Comparing responses to the agree-disagree format items from the 1960 survey to the forced-choice alternative items from the 1968 survey, support for employment and standard of living guarantees drops 31 points while support for health care guarantees drops only 10 points (in both years, of those respondents with opinions). In 1972 and later years, the content of the health-care item changed from a choice between broadly stated alternatives of government intervention and laissez faire, to a more specific choice between national health insurance and a private insurance alternative. As the focus became more specific, public support dropped off slightly, but remained a majority of those with opinions. See later discussion.

5. The ranking in Table 1 represents an attempt to compress a multidimensional phenomenon ("ideological climate") into a single measure ("relative support for social-policy principles"). The purpose of this "reduction" is heuristic: to facilitate comparisons and to permit the cross-tabulation by indicators of welfare-institutional development. As I emphasize above, all nations exhibit the effects of both individualist and collectivist ideologies (which categories in themselves oversimplify diverse cultural and philosophical traditions, e.g., "work ethic," "patriarchalism," "humanitarianism," etc.). For a more detailed discussion of this problem, see Coughlin, 1977, pp. 36–56.

6. Results of surveys conducted prior to about 1945 need to interpreted with caution, due to distortions produced by faulty survey designs. For example, Schiltz, 1970, reports a substantial overrepresentation of males in Gallup survey samples from 1935 to 1940, with somewhat erratic patterns from 1941 to 1945. Presumably these sampling distortions are indicative of the deeper methodological difficulties which plagued survey research in its early years. However, in the case of old-age pensions, as in other areas, early results are generally replicated by later, methodologically more sophisticated studies.

7. Despite intensification of talk about the "health care crisis" in the past few years, public opinion has remained quite stable both over the long (1940s to present) and short term. Evidence of the latter stability comes from two sources. The first is the ongoing national election-study surveys: repeat items on the 1972 and 1976 surveys (Center for Political Studies, 1972, 1976) concerning the choice (on a seven-point differential scale) between national health insurance and a private plan show *no* statistically significant changes over the four year period. A similar time series, based on identical items asked on Gallup surveys in 1972 and 1976, requiring respondents to choose from among *three* alternative proposals for national health policy, found a slight increase (six percent) in support for a "universal system of health insurance" along with a proportional drop (5 percent) for maintaining the "present system of voluntary care." These slight shifts did little to alter the indecisive pattern of opinion found in surveys in both years (Gallup, 1977a).

8. These figures will probably be regarded with as much surprise as displeasure by critics of "socialized" medicine, but the survey evidence is unmistakable. Perhaps even more surprising to the critics is the apparent high degree of physician commitment to the system. A 1956 survey of the members of the British Medical Association asked physicians how they would vote on the NHS if they could go back ten years to the time before the system began operation. Two-thirds replied that they would vote *in favor* of the system, about one-third said they would vote against it, and a tiny number had no opinion (Social Surveys, 1956). Emigration and periodic labor-management disputes aside, the NHS is hardly the moribund creature often depicted by American opponents of government regulation of health care industry.

9. If we include the positive public reaction to Nixon's Family Assistance Plan (FAP), the

proportion jumps to five out of six. However, because the discussion of FAP is inextricable from the operation of various public assistance programs it was meant to replace (e.g., Aid to Families with Dependent Children), it has not been included in this section. Below I discuss survey findings on attitudes toward a national guaranteed income versus work-relief programs.

10. These are the only nations for which public opinion data could be located.

11. Percentages relating to the "work disincentive" and "unworthy parents" items are based on a sample of adults living in the two largest urban areas of California (San Francisco Bay Area and Los Angeles).

12. We should not overlook the "bludger" (Australian cousin to the "scrounger" and "chiseler"), although we have no survey data for Australia with which to make comparisons to the other nations.

REFERENCES

Abrams, Mark and John Hall (undated) "The Condition of the British People." London: Survey Unit of the Social Science Research Council. (Mineograph.)
——— and Richard Rose (1960) *Must Labour Lose?* Baltimore: Penguin.
Adams, Leonard P. (1971) *Public Attitudes Toward Unemployment Insurance*. Kalamazoo, MI: W. E. Upjohn Institute for Employment Research (December).
Almond, Gabriel and Sidney Verba (1963) *The Civic Culture*. Princeton, NJ: Princeton University Press.
Alston, John P. and K. Imogene Dean (1972) "Socioeconomic Factors Associated with Attitudes Toward Welfare Recipients." *Social Service Review* 46 (March): 12–23.
Alt, James E., Bo Särlvik, and Ivor Crewe (1976) "Partisanship and Policy Choice: Issue Preferences in the British Electorate." *British Journal of Political Science* 6 (July): 273–290.
Aron, Raymond (1962) *France, Steadfast and Changing*. Cambridge, MA: Harvard University Press.
Australian Gallup Poll (1957) Survey 123 (September 2).
——— (1963a) Survey 162 (April 5).
——— (1963b) Survey 165 (October 11).
——— (1965) *Polls* 1 (Spring): 14–15.
——— (1967a) *Polls* 2 (Spring): 36.
——— (1967b) *Polls* 3 (Autumn): 17.
Barton, Allen H. (1974) "The Limits of Consensus Among American Leaders." New York: Bureau of Applied Social Research, Columbia University (August 15). Mimeograph.
Beer, Samuel H. (1966) *British Politics in the Collectivist Age*. New York: Knopf.
Berlingske Tidende (1974) "Gallup: Det går den gale vej, siger befolkningen." (April 28.)
Campbell, Angus *et al.* (1960) *The American Voter*. New York: Wiley.
Canadian Institute of Public Opinion (Gallup Poll) (1964) Set 308 (August).
——— (1970a) Set 339 (January).
——— (1970b) Set 341 (May).
——— (1971) Set 350 (November).
Center for Political Studies (1972) *The 1972 American National Election Study*. Ann Arbor, MI: Institute for Social Research.
——— (1976) *The 1976 American National Election Study*. Ann Arbor, MI: Institute for Social Research.

Christoph, James B. (1965) "Consensus and Cleavage in British Political Ideology." *American Political Science Review* 59 (September): 629–642.

Converse, Philip E. (1964) "The Nature of Belief Systems in Mass Publics." Pages 206–261 in David Apter (ed.), *Ideology and Discontent*. New York: Free Press.

Corning, Peter A. (1969) *The Evolution of Medicare: From Idea to Law*. Washington, DC: Government Printing Office.

Coughlin, Richard M. (1977) "Ideology and Social Policy: A Comparative Study of the Structure of Public Opinion in Eight Rich Nations." Unpublished doctoral dissertation. Berkeley: University of California.

Cutright, Phillips (1965) "Political Structure, Economic Development, and National Social Security Programs." *American Journal of Sociology* 70 (March): 537–550.

Danish Election Survey (1971) *Bulletin No. 1: Questionnaires August and October 1971*. Aarhus: Institute of Political Science, University of Aarhus. (English version; data from untitled supplement in Danish.)

Dicey, A. V. (1953) *Law and Opinion in England*. London: Macmillan.

Dunn's Review (1976) "The New Conservative Idea Men." 107 (April): 39ff.

Economist (1973) "Survey." 247 (June 23): 51.

Ehrmann, Henry W. (1971) *Politics in France*. Boston: Little, Brown.

Etzioni, Amitai (1970) "A Swing to the Right?" *Trans-Action* 7 (September): 12–18, 77.

European Communities (1974). *Report on the Development of the Social Situation in the Community in 1973*. Brussels-Luxembourg: European Communities.

Facts on File (1962) (July).

Feagin, Joe R. (1973) "Issues in Welfare Research: A Critical Overview." *Social Science Quarterly* 54 (September): 321–335.

Free, Lloyd A. and Hadley Cantril (1968) *The Political Beliefs of Americans*. New York: Simon and Schuster.

Fuchs, Victor R. (1974) *Who Shall Live?* New York: Basic Books.

Galant, Henry C. (1955) *Histoire Politique de la Sécurité Sociale Française 1945–1952*. Cahiers de la Fondation Nationale des Sciences Politiques, Paris: Librairie Armand Colin (No. 76).

Galbraith, John Kenneth (1967) *The New Industrial State*. Boston: Houghton Mifflin.

Galenson, Walter (1968) "Social Security and Economic Development: A Quantitative Approach." *Industrial and Labor Relations Review* 21 (June): 559–569.

Gallup Poll (1961) "The Newburgh Story." *Gallup Opinion Index*. Report No. 3.

——— (1965a) Press Release (January 24).

——— (1965b) *Washington Post* (September 16): F3.

——— (1965c) Survey 718 (October).

——— (1969) *Gallup Opinion Index*. Report No. 43 (January): 20–21.

——— (1977a) *Current Opinion* 5 (April): 40.

——— (1977b) *Current Opinion* 5 (August): 89.

Geertz, Clifford (1964) "Ideology as a Cultural System." Pages 48–76 in David Apter (ed.), *Ideology and Discontent*. New York: Free Press.

Giddens, Anthony (1973) *The Class Structure of Advanced Societies*. New York: Harper and Row.

Glock, Charles Y. and Thomas Piazza (undated) "Explorations in the Structuring of Reality." Berkeley: Survey Research Center, University of California. Mimeograph.

Grattan, Michelle (1975) "The Scheme Is Here to Stay." *Age* (Melbourne) *Guide to Medibank* (April 14): 3.

Halck, Niels and Fred Østergaard (1964) *Omkring den almindelige folke pension*. Copenhagen: Teknisk Forlag.

Harris, Ralph and Arthur Seldon (1965) *Choice in Welfare 1965*. London: Institute of Economic Affairs.
––––––– (1970) *Choice in Welfare 1970*. London: Institute of Economic Affairs.
Harris Survey (1977) *Current Opinion* 5 (October): 118.
Hartz, Louis (1955) *The Liberal Tradition in America*. New York: Harcourt, Brace & World.
Heclo, Hugh (1974) *Modern Social Politics in Britain and Sweden*. New Haven: Yale University Press.
Hofstader, Richard (1945) *Social Darwinism in American Thought, 1860–1915*. Philadelphia: University of Pennsylvania Press.
Huber, Joan and William Form (1973) *Income and Ideology*. New York: Free Press.
Inkeles, Alex and David H. Smith (1974) *Becoming Modern*. Cambridge, MA: Harvard University Press.
Institut Français d'Opinion Publique (1964a) Survey ER 105–S. 5.731 (February 12).
––––––– (1964b) Survey ER 109–S. 5.541 (April).
––––––– (1966) *Polls* 1 (Spring): 89–90.
––––––– (1967) *Polls* 3 (Winter): 25.
––––––– (1970a) Survey G. 971–EP 266 (April).
––––––– (1970b) Survey H. 981–EP 278 (September).
––––––– (1972) Survey N. 491–EP 324 (June).
Institut für Demoskopie (1965) Survey 1098I (February).
––––––– (1966–67) *Polls* 2 (Winter): 29.
––––––– (1967) Survey 2034 (December).
International Labour Office (1972) *The Cost of Social Security*. Geneva: ILO
Janssen, Richard F. (1975) "In Europe, The Jobless Get Special Treatment to Minimize Unrest." *Wall Street Journal* (March 28): 1, 29.
Kallen, David J. and Dorothy Miller (1971) "Public Attitudes Toward Welfare." *Social Work* 16 (July): 83–90.
Kaltefleiter, Werner (1974) "Geht die Demokratie an zuviel Wohlfahrsstaat zugrunde?" *Welt am Sonntag* (March 24).
Kewley, T. H. (1973) *Social Security in Austalia 1900–72*. Sydney: Sydney University Press.
Key, Vladimar O. (1961) *Public Opinion and American Democracy*. New York: Knopf.
Klein, Rudolph (1974) "The Case for Elitism: Public Opinion and Public Policy." *Political Quarterly* 45 (October–December): 406–417.
Konrad Adenauer Foundation (1973a). Data from research files (October 26).
––––––– (1973b). Data from research files (November 19).
Lamontagne, Maurice (1954) "The Role of Government." Pages 117–152 in G.P. Gilmour (ed.), *Canada's Tomorrow*. Toronto: Macmillan.
Lanphier, C. Michael, Bernard M. Portis, and Malcolm Golden (1970) *An Analysis of Attitudes Toward Unemployment Insurance*. Toronto: Institute for Behavioral Sciences, York University (July).
Lewis, David (1972) *Louder Voices: The Corporate Welfare Bums*. Toronto: James Lewis and Samuel.
Lipset, Seymour M. (1960) *Political Man*. New York: Doubleday.
Litwak, Eugene, Nancy Hooyman, and Donald Warren (1973) "Ideological Complexity and Middle-American Rationality." *Public Opinion Quarterly* 37 (Fall): 317–332.
Luttbeg, Norman R. (ed.) *Public Opinion and Public Policy*. Homewood, IL: Dorsey Press.
Markedsanalyse (Gallup) (1970) Survey 0970 (September).
Marmor, Theodore R. (1973) *The Politics of Medicare*. Chicago: Aldine.
McClosky, Herbert, Paul J. Hoffman, and Rosemary O'Hara (1960) "Issue Conflict and

Consensus Among Party Leaders and Followers." *American Political Science Review* 54 (June): 406–427.

Miller, Kenneth E. (1968) *Government and Politics in Denmark.* Boston: Houghton Mifflin.

Molin, Björn (1965) *Tjänstepensionsfrågan.* Göteborg: Elanders Boktryckeri Aktiebolag. (Summary in English.)

Moynihan, Daniel Patrick (1973) *The Politics of a Guaranteed Income.* New York: Random House.

National Opinion Polls (1968) *NOP Political Bulletin* (January): 10.

——— (1969a) *NOP Political Bulletin.* Special Supplement I (February).

——— (1969b) *NOP Political Bulletin* (December): 10–11.

——— (1971) *NOP Political Bulletin* (February): 14.

Noelle, Elisabeth and Erich Peter Neumann (ed.) (1967) *The Germans: Public Opinion Polls 1947–1966.* Allensbach and Bonn: Verlag für Demoskopie.

Ogren, Evelyn H. (1973) "Public Opinion about Public Welfare." *Social Work* 18 (January): 101–107.

Opinion Research Corporation (1960) *The Initiators.* Princeton, NJ: Opinion Research Corporation.

Pryor, Frederic L. (1968) *Public Expenditures in Communist and Capitalist Nations.* Homewood, II.: Irwin.

Putnam, Robert D. (1973) *The Beliefs of Politicians.* New Haven: Yale University Press.

Rein, Martin and Hugh Heclo (1973) "What Welfare Crisis?—A Comparison among the United States, Britain, and Sweden." *Public Interest* 33 (Fall): 61–83.

Riffault, Hélène and Jacques-René Rabier (1977) *The Perception of Poverty in Europe.* Brussels: Commission of the European Communities (March).

Rimlinger, Gaston V. (1971) *Welfare Policy and Industrialization in Europe, America, and Russia.* New York: Wiley.

Ritz, Joseph P. (1966) *The Despised Poor.* Boston: Beacon Press.

Rose, Eliot J. B. (1969) *Colour and Citizenship.* London: Institute of Race Relations, by Oxford University Press.

Rusher, William (1976) "Can We Have Jobs for Everyone?" Syndicated column appearing in the San Francisco *Sunday Examiner and Chronicle* (March 7).

Rytina, Joan, William H. Form, and John Pease (1970) "Income and Stratification Ideology." *American Journal of Sociology* 75 (January): 703–716.

Samuelsson, Kurt (1968) *From Great Power to Welfare State.* London: George Allen and Unwin.

Särlvik, Bo (1960) *The 1960 Swedish Election Study Codebook.* Göteborg: Institute of Political Science, University of Göteborg in collaboration with the National Bureau of Statistics. (Data obtained from Inter-University Consortium for Political Research, Ann Arbor, MI).

——— (1967) "Party Politics and Electoral Opinion Formation." *Scandanavian Political Studies* 2: 167–201.

Schiltz, Michael E. (1970) *Public Attitudes Toward Social Security 1935–1965.* Washington, DC: Government Printing Office.

Schorr, Alvin (1967) *Explorations in Social Policy.* New York: Basic Books.

Schwartz, Mildred (1967) *Public Opinion and Canadian Identity.* Berkeley: University of California Press.

Secretary of State for Social Services (1973) *Report of the Committee on Abuse of Social Security Benefits.* London: Her Majesty's Stationery Office (March).

Siune, Karen and Ole Borre (1975) "Setting the Agenda for a Danish Election." *Journal of Communication* 25 (Winter): 65–73.

Social Surveys Limited (Gallup Poll) (1946) Survey 132 (April).

———— (1948) Survey 162 (February).
———— (1956) "British Medical Association Conference, Brighton, July 1956." *News Chronicle*. London (July 5).
———— (1957) Survey CQ 40 (September).
———— (1958) Survey CQ 89 (October).
———— (1959) Survey CQ 99 (January).
———— (1960a) Survey CQ 153 (February).
———— (1960b) Survey CQ 153B (February).
———— (1961) Survey CQ 249 (December).
———— (1963) Survey CQ 311 (March).
———— (1965) Survey CQ 434 (July).
———— (1966) Survey CQ 505 (December).
———— (1967a) Survey CQ 519 (March).
———— (1967b) Survey CQ 527 (May).
———— (1967c) Survey CQ 533 (July).
———— (1967d) Survey CQ 537 (August).
———— (1968) Survey CQ 593 (August).
———— (1971) Survey CQ 740 (April).
Stokes, Donald B. and Donald Aitkin (1967) *The 1967 Australian National Election*. Ann Arbor, MI: Inter-University Consortium for Political Research.
Survey Research Center (1956) *The 1956 American National Election Study*. Ann Arbor, MI: Survey Research Center.
———— (1960) *The 1960 American National Election Study*. Ann Arbor, MI: Survey Research Center.
———— (1964) *The 1964 American National Election Study*. Ann Arbor, MI: Survey Research Center.
———— (1968) *The 1968 American National Election Study*. Ann Arbor, MI: Survey Research Center.
Taira, Koji and Peter Kilby (1969) "Differences in Social Security Development in Selected Countries." *International Social Security Review* 22 (Spring): 139–153.
Titmuss, Richard (1958) *Essays on 'The Welfare State.'* London: George Allen and Unwin.
U.S. Social Security Administration (1971) *Social Security Programs Throughout the World*. Washington, DC: Government Printing Office.
Vinocur, John (1975) "Denmark's Charter Escapes to the Sun." San Francisco *Sunday Examiner and Chronicle* (September 14): 13.
Wedderburn, Dorothy (1965) "Facts and Theories of the Welfare State." Pages 127–146 in Ralph Miliband and John Saville (eds.), *The Socialist Register 1965*. London: Merlin Press.
Wilensky, Harold L. (1975) *The Welfare State and Equality*. Berkeley: University of California Press.
———— (1976) "The Welfare Mess." *Society* 13 (May-June): 12–16, 64.
———— and Charles N. Lebeaux (1965) *Industrial Society and Social Welfare. New York: Free Press*.

SOCIAL EQUALITY AND THE IMPACT OF EDUCATION IN WESTERN EUROPE*

Günther Lüschen*

THEORETICAL CONSIDERATIONS AND STATEMENT OF THE PROBLEM

The use of education as an instrument for changing systems of social stratification or altering the life chances of individuals in terms of their social status has a long history. In theory at least, attempts to overcome social inequality by means of education can be traced back to Rousseau and Marx. In educational practice, the introduction of compulsory education is an early attempt at reform. Here the emphasis was on overcoming existing inequality. But there were also attempts to reinforce existing

Comparative Social Research, Vol. 2, pp. 41–69.
Volume 1 published as Comparative Studies in Sociology

patterns of inequality and privilege through education as well, the English public school system being a notable example. In all these attempts, there is an assumption that education and schools can have a major impact on systems of social stratification and on social change in general. This assumption is at the heart of educational policies introduced into the countries of Western Europe during the past thirty years. These policies range from the 1944 Education Act in England to the Swedish School System's going comprehensive and to the discussions in the French Ministry of Education concerning opportunities for lower-class pupils in a school system known for high quality and academic excellence. While the policies may have had the same goals, in the specifics of their enactment they differ substantially by country. For example, the goal of overcoming differential language competence led the French Ministry to introduce special language training for teachers in all subjects, while the State of Hesse in Germany sought to decree lower-class colloquial language in the teaching process.

At the general level of educational policy making there was the strong expectation in all of the five countries that more "education for all" and the advancement of a growing number of students to higher education would overcome the seemingly unjust structure of social stratification. Policies were carried out accordingly, as indicated by growing numbers of secondary students and increased educational expenditures. OECD figures (1973) show that from 1950 to 1970 students in secondary schools increased 72 percent in England, 230 percent in France, 254 percent in Italy, 59 percent in Sweden, and 20 percent in West Germany. Of course, some of these increases are accounted for by population and age cohort increases. Nevertheless the increase in students in higher education over the same period ranges from 100 percent in England to 375 percent in France. One should note that such intra-country comparisons refer most often to the post-1945 period, with the assumption that the long-range pattern is one of linear increase. In fact, patterns of school attendance and educational expenditure may be curvilinear. For example, France in 1906 had a school population relatively higher than in 1921, 1936, and 1946 (*Statistiques des Enseignments,* 1973, p. 3), and England in 1910 spent more of Central Government Revenue (9.8 percent) on education than at any time up to very recently, and even with local contributions added,

*Günther Lüschen, 1974 recipient of the Noel-Baker Award (UNESCO), is a Professor of Sociology at the University of Illinois, Urbana-Champaign. During the spring semester 1978, he was a Visiting Professor at the University of Cologne. Since 1970 he has been Chairman of the International Sociological Association's Committee for the Sociology of Sports. His primary interests are in stratification, family, sport, and sociological theory.

more than at any time up to the 1930s (Report of Ministry of Education, 1950).

By now, the educational system has become firmly established in Western democracies as a major instrument for providing equality of citizens' rights. Formerly such rights were provided through the legal, political, and welfare systems. These societies also seem to use educational reform policies to legitimize their existing systems of social stratification. Equal educational opportunity for all is a major principle of equality of rights, supposedly giving each citizen the feeling that he/she has had his/her chances, and that whatever inequality remains is therefore the result of differential talent and individual performance.

With respect to the actual impact of education on social inequality, opinion is divided. Previous research and discussion show two main lines of argument. On the one hand, a positive impact is assumed, while more detailed research often shows the limitations of the system.

Denison's international comparisons in *Why Growth Rates Differ* (1967) assume a strong impact of education on national economic growth. Years of schooling was used as an indicator of differential education. Ten years ago Denison forecast substantial economic gains for Italy and economic problems for Germany, directly relating them to expansion and relative nonexpansion of education in the two countries. The recent situation fails to confirm his predictions. The question arises whether this is the result of factors outside of education not subject to control, whether an indicator in terms of years of schooling is sufficient, whether education has only a minor impact on economic growth, or whether the potential impact of education has to be seen less in the economic or class dimension than elsewhere in the system of social stratification.

Jencks (1972) comes to quite different conclusions for the potential of schools and education. Dealing with a variable of social class, namely, income, Jencks finds that education has little impact compared with family background and heredity. The same holds for cognitive skills. It should be noted, however, that Jencks's statistics and statistical manipulations may not altogether confirm his conclusions. He did warn against thinking of education only in terms of impact on the system of social stratification, i.e., the social-class dimension. But only one major reviewer (Sewell, 1973) acknowledged Jencks's suggestions that schools should rather be seen in terms of fun and family culture. Of course, his inferences remained theoretically rather vague. In retrospect these suggestions may be as newsworthy as the major theme of the book, the impact of education on individual income distribution. A leading consequence of Jencks's work was, and is, to discourage policy makers and teachers from utilizing the schools for increasing social equality. Particularly in Western Europe

Jencks's conclusions were used by educational policy makers as a rationalization for investing less in education. To say the least, the dissemination of news items from the book dampened hopes for a positive impact of education on equality.

Actually the two lines of argument as well as the number of conflicting results should have led to a reconsideration of the theory implied. Lipset makes exactly this point in a preface to Boudon (1973). To raise but one such theoretical issue: With Max Weber's concepts of social stratification one may suggest that education and schools have their major impact on social status *(Stand)* and life style, whereas most of the research and discussion involves education's impact on class and marketable resources, Jencks's references to school as family culture being one of the few exceptions. Of course educational reform has implicitly responded to the predicament between class and status, opting in recent years for a vocationally oriented reform of secondary schools which makes market forces and manpower needs the determinant of curricula and school structure. In Western democracies, the OECD promotes such reform of schooling. But such market-oriented reform can be introduced in the public school system only to a limited degree, and manpower forecasts for tomorrow's economy have consistently run into problems. The UNESCO Commission on Education (Faure *et al.*, 1972) has thus rejected such consideration outright. In Sweden the establishment of high schools on the same level with different curricula (theoretical vs. practical) has, according to Swedish policy makers, resulted in student recruitment that seems again to be based on the traditional stratification system.

In one of the few theoretical considerations, Boudon distinguishes between educational and social opportunity (1973). In this connection, he also points to collective educational attainment and differential fertility rates by social class as major obstacles in reaping a higher occupational status from more education intergenerationally. This would explain the apparent paradox of more education's possibly meaning even less social opportunity. Moreover; Boudon's discussion and data analysis show that, even under conditions of more educational attainment, controlling for the above factors, advancement is in general likely only when social opportunities are enhanced as well.

But educational reforms have not been uniformly accompanied by general social reform. Reforms such as the general expansion of the school system or the introduction of comprehensive schooling have been brought about by and large without regard for other changes in society and its system of stratification. Such policies resulted in more years of education and more equality of education, but such policies could actually result in a weakening of education's impact on social equality. Indeed, Galtung

(1976), suggests that economic growth is accompanied by both educational growth and educational disparity, thus questioning the very basis of equality of education. Furthermore, he reports that on an international scale countries with a low level of educational disparity show a lesser impact of education on an individual's social status and the dimension of social stratification in general. Such results would be acceptable if one were interested in integrating society by equalizing life styles and the status dimension. Actually, the hopes of those trying to equalize educational opportunity and attainment by providing a similar level of education for all are, however, directed toward a change of the class dimension. Boudon's distinction between educational and social opportunity, as two related dimensions, should sound a note of caution. As early as the 1910s and 20s, Paul Oestreich, a noted socialist reformer of education, stated that educational reform would be futile if society as a whole had not been reformed as well (cf. Dietrich, 1966, p. 175).

MAJOR RESEARCH QUESTIONS, SOURCES OF DATA AND ANALYSIS

To investigate issues of equality and education raises complex problems of social science research. Social indicators speaking to system qualities and changes, such as those mentioned above on schooling, are generally vague in their theoretical meaning; they also require observation over longer periods of time. And the use of factual data and demographic variables in rigid statistical analysis necessarily limits the scope of argument in placing reliability and concept validity over general theoretical validity. Another means of investigation is to question a select number of individuals in the system. The following report and discussion is based on such an approach. We have investigated those who are intimately involved in major decisions and who also qualify as experts on the issues (policy makers), those who are most intimately involved in the explicit and implicit carrying out of policies (teachers), and those upon whom policies, in this case the implementation of comprehensive schooling, are enacted (students). In a way, this project pursues broad and important questions at the expense of rigid precision. Part of such a predicament is, however, overcome by a specific analysis of a fundamental and limited research problem, namely, whether a policy such as the implementation of the comprehensive school, which in Western Europe is perhaps the most valid indicator for equality and education, does indeed raise the prospects for more equality and opportunity in occupational aspiration.

Overall the following analysis and discussion will address these questions:

1. To what degree do the leading policy makers in education and the teachers see problems of equality as a policy issue?

2. To what degree do they see education making a contribution to greater social equality?

3. Does the implementation of a specific educational reform—the creation of the comprehensive school—influence occupational and mobility expectations of students?

4. To what degree does the comprehensive school, as compared to the traditional types of school, influence the students' perception of social stratification?

Data for the analysis were collected as part of a comparative project, "Educational Policy Making in Industrialized Countries (EPIC)" from 1974 to 1976 in five Western European countries in the following three subprojects:

1. A half-standardized interview of leading policy makers in England, France, Italy, Sweden, and West Germany. This study focused on the perception of the leading politicians and educational administrators of major policy issues and their solution.

2. A standardized questionnaire study of randomly selected teachers in four rural and metropolitain districts in each of the five countries. With return rates of 80 percent for Italy, 55 percent for Germany, 48 percent for Sweden, 42 percent for England, and 21 percent for France, this study took up issues of the first subproject and investigated teachers' perception of policy issues and their own impact on policy making.

3. A study of two partially industrialized counties/communities in England and West Germany, where a comprehensive school had been introduced. A standardized questionnaire, administered in the classroom to ninth graders 4th form, investigated occupational aspirations, perception of stratified society, and general attitudes toward school in different school types. This was in part a replication of a study by Ford (1969).

Data analysis for the study of policy makers and teachers will provide contingency tables and descriptive statistics on the above questions. The data for students will be analyzed descriptively as well as by regression analysis, in order to provide for necessary controls such as social class of family for predicting occupational career aspirations by type of school. Further details will be provided subsequently.

It should be mentioned that the rather low return rate for teachers in France was caused by severe friction within unions and toward the government, where social science investigations were a major issue of concern. The high rate for Italy is the consequence of investigators' bringing the questionnaires directly to the schools, while in England, France, Sweden and Germany questionnaires and two reminders were mailed.

SOCIAL EQUALITY IN THE EDUCATION SYSTEM AND THE POSITION OF POLICY MAKERS AND TEACHERS.

England, France, Italy, Sweden, and West Germany differ to a considerable degree in terms of educational systems stratified along lines of social class. Sweden has opted for the integrated comprehensive school system; England allows different school systems, including the comprehensive system, to coexist; Germany has essentially a three-class school system that allows a comprehensive system only on an experimental basis. Italy has a comprehensive system from ages 10 to 14, and France has none at all. The class bias of these systems of education and their differences in this regard became particularly apparent when family background of university students was analyzed. The working class was underrepresented in each of the countries among university students with the lowest (about 5) percent being for West Germany (Dahrendorf, 1965). For the early 1960s the relative chance of lower versus upper strata to enter higher education was 1 to 48 for West Germany, 1 to 26 for Sweden, 1 to 8 for England (OECD, 1971). Although comparability is problematical, in part because of the differences in the organization of higher education, data from the United States for approximately the same time period give a ratio of 1 to 4 (Sewell, 1971). Obviously there is a more rigid system of stratification with a greater impact on the educational system in Western European societies, with West Germany and France being by far the most rigid. Such figures and their meaning became public knowledge in the 1960s and resulted in tremendous pressure from public opinion and expert commissions on the government and educational policy makers to equalize educational opportunity and limit class bias in education. It is worth noting that the discussion centered around the issue of limiting social class impacts in education. The greater emphasis, resulting for West Germany in an increase to 15 percent for university students with lower-class background (Bundesministerium, 1977, p. 90), was on equal educational opportunity. It was to a lesser degree on educational equality, and hardly at all on the impact of education on social equality. Indeed, the latter issue, which would have had to be discussed in societal prospects beyond the system of education, was not a salient public problem in the 1960s. In terms of our previous discussion, the emphasis was on retaining the role of the educational system in legitimizing the existing order of social stratification. Of course, educational specialists and some policy makers wanted more and saw the potential role of education in enhancing social equality as well (cf. Husén, 1969).

At the time of our interviews with policy makers in 1974 the initial euphoria about education and equality was seemingly subdued, partly by the impact of Jencks's book, partly as a result of the general economic recession and concomitant fiscal contraints. Yet the issue was still alive among the policy makers.

Table 1 gives the opinions of policy makers and teachers of the problems facing education in the several countries. It should be mentioned that policy makers cited up to four problems in their answers, whereas teachers were restricted to one. Moreover, the categories are groups of more specific items; thus, within one category more than one answer could be given. Consequently, figures based on percentages can add up to more than 100 for policy makers.

The general result in Table 1 indicates a number of country-specific problems. The English policy makers are most concerned with the methods and structure of policy making, the Swedes see student achievement and discipline as their major problem, while German and Italian policy makers cite school structure and organization. Teachers by and large seem to agree with the policy makers in the relative position of problems. The issue of educational and social equality, also expressed in such slogans as "education for all," receives notable mention in France where it is the second most often mentioned item. Also, the comprehensive school as a particular policy to effect social and educational equality receives a rather strong consideration in England and Germany. Everywhere policy makers address education society relations and teachers raise the issue of equality to a lesser extent. Indeed, the principle as such is almost anathema among English teachers. It should be added that some of the other issues may well imply a consideration of social/educational equality. The response of German policy makers and teachers that school structure and organization is the major problem may be a reaction to the means level, which could be related to the equality problem. Except for French policy makers, the issue as such and also the related comprehensive school reform appear to be somewhat subdued in light of a situation where equality of educational opportunity was the major policy problem in the late 1960s. The concern expressed for equality and the comprehensive school very often also implies a negative attitude toward such policies.

When policy makers were asked in subsequent questions what they considered to be a major function of education, responses that referred to social equality were mentioned by 11 percent of German policy makers, by 10 percent in France, 6 percent in Italy, 4 percent in Sweden, while English policy makers did not mention it at all. This may reflect, particu-

Table 1. The "most serious problem facing education in England, France, Italy, Sweden, West Germany today" as seen by policy makers (up to 4 items) and teachers (1 item), 1974.
(Percentages)

Policy Maker	England		France		Italy		West Germany		Sweden	
	Policy Maker	Teacher	Policy Maker	Teacher	Policy Maker	Teacher	Policy Maker	Teacher	Policy Maker	Teacher
Student problems	16.5	5.9	22.4	28.5	4.0	1.3	3.0	1.2	122.5	16.6
Teacher's status training	23.3	5.8	34.8	11.9	48.8	14.8	25.8	10.7	11.8	7.2
Curriculum/method	19.8	4.5	29.0	17.3	14.3	5.3	38.6	14.3	41.2	12.0
School structure organization	36.6	19.5	136.8	2.4	81.5	22.7	127.1	31.1	21.1	4.7
Promotion, guidance	39.9	13.5	27.2	6.3	20.7	6.1	33.9	4.6	13.0	4.2
Opening system	6.6	1.4	19.3	4.0	15.3	1.3	9.0	1.8	15.3	2.4
Equality (ed./soc.)	16.6	.8	45.2	2.4	23.6	1.1	27.9	10.3	22.2	1.4
Relation education society	19.8	4.8	53.3	4.7	26.1	4.2	21.0	5.7	23.3	6.5
Finances, resources	63.4	20.7	15.6	6.3	63.5	15.5	16.6	11.9	6.0	9.2
Policy-making structure	91.9	12.2	24.5	2.4	52.0	2.5	17.0	9.6	15.4	10.1
Miscellaneous, other	—	1.3	—	—	1.0	6.8	—	.2	—	3.0
No answer/not ascertained	—	8.3	1.0	14.2	1.0	18.4	5.0	9.2	—	22.6
N	(30)	(374)	(104)	(127)	(127)	(472)	(101)	(533)	(86)	(446)

49

Table 2. The degree to which policy makers and teachers in England, France, Italy, Sweden and West Germany want the education system to promote greater social equality, 1974.
(Percentages)

Policy Maker	England		France		Italy		Sweden		West Germany	
	Policy Maker	Teacher	Policy Maker	Teacher	Policy Maker	Teacher	Policy Maker	Teacher	Policy Maker	Teacher
Very much	20.0	42.2	87.5	81.9	52.0	66.0	69.8	54.5	42.0	69.8
Much										
Moderately	20.0	39.3	5.8	10.2	18.1	16.0	16.3	32.9	26.2	22.9
Some										
Slightly	16.7	13.1	1.0	3.1	11.8	7.4	11.6	4.8	18.8	4.3
Not at all	3.3	5.3	1.9	4.7	12.6	10.2	1.2	7.8	7.0	3.0
No answer/not ascertained	40.0		3.8		5.5		1.2		6.0	
N	(30)	(374)	(104)	(127)	(127)	(472)	(86)	(446)	(101)	(533)

larly for England, a recognition that schools can do little about social equality. A specific question directed toward teachers and policy makers alike (Table 2) asked to what degree education should be concerned with "promoting social equality" and how "effective the education system" was in reducing inequality.

Results in Table 2 show that teachers and policy makers alike are in favor of using the educational system for the promotion of equality. Surprising is the figure for French policy makers, who obviously respond to the relatively unjust system of social stratification in France. More than anybody else, they want to use the educational system to rectify conditions. Again, the responses of English policy makers are rather subdued. Teachers show rates comparable to those of policy makers; in the three countries that are not exclusively comprehensive (England, Italy, and West Germany) teachers are, however, more in favor of using the school system than are policy makers.

Subsequently policy makers were asked for their expert opinion on "how effective the [country's] educational system could be in reducing social inequality." Their answers show that their trust in the system is none too high; only 15.4 percent in France, 23 percent in Italy, 14 percent in Sweden, 3.3 percent in England, and 6.9 percent in West Germany responded "very effective," while the majority expected only a moderate or slight impact. In order to investigate what is actually being done about social equality in the system, teachers were asked to evaluate what their schools and they themselves were doing to promote social equality.

Table 3 shows that teachers think that they themselves do more about social equality than do their own schools. Teachers in England indicate that schools and they themselves do not do as much as is done in other countries. Indeed, the rate for those saying "nothing at all" is rather high comparatively. The rather high rate for "much" in Italy and the high rate for no answers may indicate that the issue is more controversial there than in other countries. Overall, schools and teachers alike are everywhere concerned about equality, and in practice the promotion of social equality is a policy of the educational system.

In order to test more exactly how far teachers were willing to go in their efforts to use the educational system for promoting social equality, the problem of so-called "positive discrimination," i.e. giving special advantages to lower-class students, was addressed in a closed question (see Table 4). Positive discrimination has of course always been used by many teachers in their daily educational practice; as a specific policy it was discussed recently in England. It appears that an overwhelming majority of teachers in each of the four countries favor different forms of assistance to provide equal educational opportunity, but, with the exception of a marked proportion among Italian teachers, only a minority favor "posi-

Table 3. The degree to which, according to teachers' opinion
in England, France, Italy, Sweden and West Germany, their own schools and they
as teachers themselves promote social equality, 1974.
(Percentages)

	England		France		Italy		Sweden		West Germany	
	School	Teachers	School	Teachers	School	Teachers	School	Teachers	School	Teachers
Much	15.2	20.3	22.8	55.1	53.4	60.6	44.4	45.2	29.8	44.3
Some	52.9	48.9	23.6	26.8	19.9	16.5	40.8	40.7	49.9	41.1
None at all	24.9	22.7	40.2	6.3	4.4	3.0	7.0	6.3	13.5	9.0
No answer	7.0	8.0	13.4	11.8	22.2	19.9	7.8	7.7	6.8	5.6
N	(374)		(127)		(472)		(446)		(533)	

Table 4. Teachers' responses to the question, "Children who are at a disadvantage in school because of the social and educational background of their parents should . . ." 1974.

(Percentages)

	England	Italy	Sweden	West Germany
Be given special help and held to lower standards	11.5	32.6	17.7	5.3
Be given special help but held to same standards	78.3	62.7	77.4	91.0
Be given no special help and held to same standards	2.7	2.5	1.8	1.3
No answer	7.5	2.1	3.1	2.4
N	(374)	(472)	(446)	(533)

tive discrimination.'' In Germany, the idea appears to be almost rejected.

With regard to the theoretical concerns expressed above, some indication as to the understanding of the policy makers of the system of social stratification and the issue of social equality is provided by an open-ended question that was part of the German project only. After the equality issue had been pursued, policy makers were finally asked, ''How do you understand social equality in society anyway?'' (Table 5). Typical answers were:

> Equality of social chances yes, not as a societal orientation.
> This is a matter of self-esteem not of equality of income (although I don't reject that either).
> Equality of opportunity.
> There will always be people who do better. Equality is not primarily a matter of wealth and income. It is a matter of equal participation in state and society.
> Social equality means integration.
> Social equality means realization of equal opportunity as much as possible. And it means the suppression of handicaps, such as family background.

These remarks are the essence of what were at times rather lengthy discussions.

In general, few ideological statements came forth. Overall, there was an emphasis on pragmatic policy guidelines and hardly any theoretical reflection in terms of class, status, or the difference between educational and social opportunity. Moreover, one could detect a certain tendency to debate the issue in terms of individual independence from system constraints. The above results are most certainly in line with the general conception in modern Western democracies that equality is a matter of citizens' rights. For many, this implies equality of opportunity, but there

Table 5. German policy makers' responses to the question,
"How do you understand social equality, anyway?"

Equality is favored in every respect	5.0
Equality of chance in education and elsewhere in society	35.6
Equality is a matter of (citizen) rights, not of income and/or other factors	38.7
Society is stratified, but some change for equality is justified	18.8
Equality in society is a utopia	5.0
Miscellaneous other	4.0
No answer	11.9
N	(101)
	(19% are classified under two categories)

is little concern for genuine equality. Indeed, the small proportion of those advocating policies in that direction is balanced by an equally small proportion who declare the equality issue to be utopian. Breakdowns of party affiliation (or party leaning) show no strong differences between socialists (SPD) and conservatives (CDU). Actually, those few advocating the most wide-ranging reforms are from both parties. This is another indication that the liberal (socialist)- conservative dichotomy does not always work in the analysis of the German political scene. It is no surprise that the faction of socialists within the CDU based on the Catholic social ethic would also be represented among these educational policy makers.

THE POTENTIAL IMPACT OF SCHOOL REFORM ON SOCIAL EQUALITY — A COMPARATIVE ANALYSIS OF COMPREHENSIVE SCHOOLING

The comprehensive school can be identified as one of the major organizational reform programs for promoting equality in education and society alike. The American high school is a clear reflection of equal rights and the promotion of equal educational opportunity. And the comprehensive school has a rather long history in Europe as well. Socialists have long advocated what in Germany became known as the *Einheitsschule* (unity school). But the recent popularity of this form of schooling is probably as much a response to the American scene as it is in line with earlier discussions in Europe as a whole. Thus, the comprehensive school is not only defined in terms of equality but as a school oriented toward achievement as well (Sander *et al.*, 1971). At present, this type of school has been in existence just long enough to evaluate its effectiveness and impact. Ford (1969), a socialist by conviction, had earlier investigated the impact of comprehensive schools on occupational aspirations and social class integration within the school. Her results were not favorable to the comprehensive school, but rather indicated social class segregation within schools and a lesser chance for those going to comprehensive schools to become upwardly mobile. Of a number of studies in Germany, one by Fend *et al.* (1976) compares students in comprehensive schools with students in all the rest of schools for occupational and educational expectations. They find for students in comprehensive schools what they call an *Aspirationsschub* (aspiration advancement). While this study used a number of specific questions, the later statistical analysis casts doubt on the overall favorable results for the comprehensive school.

As Part 3 of the EPIC-project, the present study sought an answer to the question of whether comprehensive schools, as compared with the traditional types, enhance the mobility expectations of students and whether they influence the perceptions of social stratification. It should be said at once that the implied causality can be investigated only to a limited degree as the process of recruitment to the different types of school cannot be measured in the present study. One county/community each in England and Germany was selected for this comparative project. In both cases the availability of other forms of school within those communities allowed for controls by type of school. The following discussion is based on a questionnaire study of ninth-graders. They were given a questionnaire in their classroom which asked:

1.   father's and mother's occupation
2.   their own occupational expectations in terms of what they:
     (a) would like to do
     (b) probably would do when leaving school
     (c) what they would be doing at 25 years of age, and
     (d) what kind of work they would take if they could get "any type of work in the whole world."

They were also questioned on seven items referring to the possible perception of social stratification. These questions were taken from the study by Ford (1969) and translated into German by native speakers. Both questionnaires were slightly altered after pretesting. Because of the age level of the population to be investigated (14–15 years), the questions are worded accordingly. Certain items that in general would have been desirable to investigate, such as education of parents, were not included. The ninth grade was chosen as it was the last grade of compulsory schooling in both countries. A substantial proportion of the students would leave school after completion of that school year. In processing the data on occupation, Treiman's (1977) Standard International Occupational Prestige Scale (SIOPS) was used. While there are arguments concerning the comparability of occupational prestige across nations, such arguments carry less weight in the comparison of systems similar in structure, such as England and Germany. Moreover, whatever differences there are, for practical purposes of a study like this, can be disregarded. Treiman reports correlations of .956 for England and .916 for Germany between SIOPS and prestige scores from these two countries. Scores for SIOPS range from about 15 to 90 for Chief of State. For the analysis, a combined variable of family status was created by giving .50 weight to both father's and mother's occupation if the mother was working. In all other cases the occupation of head of household (father or mother) indicated family status. For the identification of social class, the first digit of the SIOPS was used as an indicator in a seven-class model. Thus, students whose father as head of household scored 35 as a telephone installer were classified upper-lower class in family background; a digit of 4, lower-middle class; 5 middle-middle, 6 upper-middle, 7 upper. Data are presented in part in the form of contingency tables. However, the prospective occupational aspirations of students by type of school cannot be evaluated only in terms of descriptive statistics. In a regression analysis, investigating type of school, family status and number of siblings were controlled for.

COMPREHENSIVE AND OTHER SCHOOLS IN ENGLAND AND GERMANY: SOME DESCRIPTIVE DATA ON CLASS AND MOBILITY EXPECTATIONS

The sample of students in both the English community and the German county represents a totality of all the students in the ninth grade who were present on the day of investigation. A total of 535 respondents come from one comprehensive school, one grammar school each for boys and girls, and one Catholic high school for girls in an English community of approximately 130,000 population. A total of 684 respondents from one comprehensive school, two *Hauptschulen* (main schools), one *Realschule,* two coed *gymnasia,* and two Catholic *gymnasia,* one for boys and one for girls, represents the students in the southern portion of a German county of some 240,000 population. Both areas are partly industrialized and in their education system have the reputation of being "progressive" and reform-oriented. The location of the two comprehensive schools affords the students the opportunity to attend them. In the English community the school is located in a neighborhood adjacent to a university, whereas alternative schools within the community are at quite a distance. School administrators have put in considerable effort to bolster this school in terms of reputation and genuine acceptance. In the German county, the school presents the only form of secondary schooling in a town of 9,000 people; other secondary schools are at a distance and students have to go there by bus. This school has received considerable support from within the community as well as from the state. It is one of the prime examples of comprehensive schools in Germany. For the local community it was the fulfillment of a long-nourished dream to have an advanced type of secondary school for the children. Thus, in both cases the so-called "creaming off" effect, i.e., the recruitment of prospective students for the comprehensive school by other schools (such as the grammar school or the *gymnasium*) are somewhat minimized.

Note from Table 6 that students in comprehensive schools are recruited largely from lower-class backgrounds (indicated here by occupation of head of household). The German comprehensive school shows a composition of students comparable to the class background of students in the

Table 6. Social class background of students in
England and Germany by type of school, 1974.
(Percentages)

	England		Germany			
	Compre- hensive	Gram- mar	Compre- hensive	Gymna- sium	Real- schule	Haupt- schule
Lower-lower	1.0	.4	–	.4	–	–
Middle-lower	12.4	1.4	12.8	.7	–	8.5
Upper-lower	44.8	6.0	44.1	16.9	36.4	54.6
Lower-middle	16.2	13.9	30.9	34.5	41.8	23.1
Middle-middle	16.7	30.6	7.4	27.0	9.1	6.2
Upper-middle	6.2	27.0	3.2	16.5	12.7	4.6
Upper class	–	16.7	–	44.0	–	–
No answer/unclear	12.7	8.0	2.6	–	1.0	5.0
N	(235)	(300)	(201)	(282)	(61)	(140)

Hauptschule. The relatively high proportion of upper-class students in English grammar schools is mainly due to a girls' school that is rather elitist in the family background of its students. At the same time this school, through its former headmistress, has made special efforts to recruit lower-class students.

On the basis of the class background of students by type of school and the occupation that students expect to follow at age 25 from Table 6, one may see a first indication of the mobility potential by type of school. Table 7 shows differences in means of family class background versus expected class, indicated by occupation. These means are the result of computing averages giving a weight of 0 to lower-lower class and up to 6 for upper class, multiplied by the percentages for each class. A difference in the mean of 1 would thus indicate that students in such a school would advance by one full class (based on the above 7-class model).

These results would seem to show a substantial advantage for students in comprehensive schools over those in all other types of school. However, there are a few puzzling observations. The German *Hauptschule* has rather high values as well. This is a result of a system of prestige

Table 7. Mean of expected class mobility (head of household vs. son/daughter) at age 25 for type of school in England and Germany, 1974.

England		Germany			
Compre- hensive	Gram- mar	Compre- hensive	Gymna- sium	Real- schule	Haupt- schule
.52	.03	1.09	.80	.47	.75

scores that by design favors positive results for those that are placed low to begin with. Furthermore, with one exception, all of the German schools show higher values than the two English schools. The national differences are a clear indication of total system influences on the data. When asked what they expected their first occupation to be, 35 percent of English students gave no answer; for German students 23 percent. English students often reflected upon the genuinely bad economic situation of the country. What is recorded as "Don't know" were often responses such as, "I am going on the dole"; "I'll be a government sponger"; "I'll collect unemployment benefits"; "None—jobs are so scarce"; "I can't say, with the job situation what it is today." German students instead expressed a high level of confidence, when they knew what they wanted to do. There were no responses such as that one would be on welfare or collect from the government. Under the circumstances cross-national comparisons in terms of impact of school on occupational aspiration should be made with caution, and the above means should be adjusted as well. Family status as well as number of siblings are factors that can be controlled for, when the effect of type of school is to be evaluated. Furthermore, comparisons within a given country may generate comparable indicators. And, finally, it appears necessary to distinguish between boys and girls.

TYPE OF SCHOOL AND ITS IMPACT ON OCCUPATIONAL ASPIRATION

In order to analyze the actual impact of type of school on occupational aspiration, variables that supposedly explain part of the variance need to be controlled for in the analysis. Thus, following the model in Figure 1, a regression analysis introduced family status as a value of SIOPS and the number of siblings. For the intermediate variable "type of school" dummy variables were created and students in grammar schools or *gymnasia* were used as a reference category. Since it was expected that the Catholic schools in both countries might produce different results, they

Figure 1. Model of occupational aspirations controlling for family status, siblings and type of school.

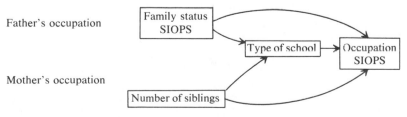

Table 8. English students by sex; regression analysis by type of school, controlling for family status and number of siblings, predicting first occupational position they would *like* to have, they will *probably* get, occupation expected *at 25 years of age, any kind of work* in the world, 1974.

	B	Beta	R^2	N=
Girls:				
First they would like to have				
Comprehensive School	-13.8	-.56†		
Catholic High	-2.6	-.11	.28	(259)
First they will probably get				
Comprehensive School	-13.8	-.54†		
Catholic High	-1.8	-.07	.3	(199)
Occupation at age 25				
Comprehensive School	-14.1	-.56†		
Catholic High	-7.1	-.03	.33	(172)
Any kind of work				
Comprehensive School	-3.9	-.14		
Catholic High	.6	.02	.03	(266)
Boys:				
First they would like to have				
Comprehensive School	-10.3	-.34**	.34	(161)
First they will probably get				
Comprehensive School	-7.4	-.24*	11	(130)

60

Occupation at age 25
Comprehensive School   -1.8   -.06   .08   (141)

Any kind of work
Comprehensive School   -2.8   -.1   .11   (179)

In the analyses done separately for girls and boys a Grammar School was used as a reference category and was thus omitted in the section of dummy variables.

* significant at .05 level
** significant at .01 level
† significant at .001 level

were separated from the regular grammar school or the *gymnasium,* respectively. The analysis was performed separately for country as well as for sex and produced the results given in Tables 8 and 9. As can be seen in the differences of the N's, a number of cases were lost in each step of the analysis. This was particularly high for English girls. Although these are not random samples, levels of significance are listed in order to indicate the strength of relationship between occupational aspiration and type of school.

A few general observations may be made first. Type of school does not predict much for "any kind of work in the world." This appears to be quite logical as an outcome. Interpretations about an imagined dream occupation may thus not be made in terms of schooling. Predictions for the occupation at age 25 by type of school are uneven for different groups. School type and the other factors included in the analysis explain little for English boys and German girls, while the explained variance for English girls and German boys is relatively high. The differences are difficult to explain. For the English girls they may be a result of the dismal economic situation, i.e., many have no idea under the circumstances, but those that do rely more on the type of school as a qualifying factor. The low explained variance for German girls at age 25 may be a result of the more traditional role of the German woman, who at this time would be greatly dependent on her husband. These are guesses that would need further exploration. The explained variance for the first occupational position, the one students would like to have and the one that they would probably get, is fairly standard across the groups, although German girls show lower values and English boys are particularly low for the first job they will probably get. The latter may again be a reflection of the difficult economic situation and job shortage they face in England.

As to the impact of school type on occupational aspiration, the main result is that students in the comprehensive school show a comparatively lower mobility potential than those in the grammar school in England or the *gymnasium* in Germany. Beta weights are high and thus are significantly different. Comparatively, values are worse for the English comprehensive school. In Germany the comprehensive school does comparatively somewhat better than its English counterpart, but the startling result is that its values are worse than those of the *Realschule,* a type of secondary school that trains for clerical positions. The German results indicate that students in the most traditional school type namely, those in Catholic *gymnasia,* are the most aspiring and seem to find in their school the most positive support for their occupational plans. The implications for a causal process are of course supportable to only a limited degree, since self-recruitment to type of school or active recruitment of prospec-

Table 9. German students by sex; regression analysis by type of school; controlling for family status and number of siblings, predicting first occupational position they would *like* to have, they will *probably* get, occupation expected *at 25 years* of age and *any kind of work* in the world, 1974.

Girls:	B	Beta	R^2	N=
First they would *like* to have				
Comprehensive School	-7.5	-.32†		
Realschule	4.8	-.11		
Catholic *Gymnasium*	.53	.02		
Hauptschule	-11.2	-.43†	.20	(283)
First they will *probably* get				
Comprehensive School	-7.3	-.33†		
Realschule	-3.7	-.09		
Catholic *Gymnasium*	.64	.02		
Hauptschule	-11.2	-.45†	.21	(247)
Occupation at age 25				
Comprehensive School	-2.4	-.08		
Realschule	-5.0	-.10		
Catholic *Gymnasium*	2.8	.08		
Hauptschule	-7.7	-.24**	.09	(225)
Any kind of work in the world				
Comprehensive School	-3.6	-.12		
Realschule	-2.6	-.05		
Catholic *Gymnasium*	.43	.01		
Hauptschule	-7.0	-.21†	.06	(298)
Boys:				
First they would *like* to have				
Comprehensive School	-8.5	-.31†		
Realschule	-6.9	-.15**		
Catholic *Gymnasium*	4.6	.12		
Hauptschule	-12.1	-.37	.32	(263)
First they will *probably* get				
Comprehensive School	-8.3	-.33†		
Realschule	-6.6	-.39**		
Catholic *Gymnasium*	.42	.01		
Hauptschule	-11.3	-.39†	.33	(246)
Occupation at *age 25*				
Comprehensive School	-5.9	-.23**		
Realschule	-3.0	-.08		
Catholic *Gymnasium*	4.0	.11		
Hauptschule	-6.2	-.21	.25	(241)
Any kind of work in the world				
Comprehensive School	-3.5	-.12		
Realschule	-.9	-.01		
Catholic *Gymnasium*	4.3	.1		
Hauptschule	.23	.01	.09	(263)

In the separate analyses for boys and girls the *Gymnasium* was used as a reference category and was thus omitted in the creation of dummy variables. *significant at .05 level, **significant at .01 level, †significant at .001 level.

tively mobile students from the lower classes, as in the English grammar school for girls, may be yet another cause other than school subculture.

In general the above results support those of Ford (1969, p. 46) that lower-class students aspiring to become socially mobile would be better off in a traditional school like a grammar school. The conclusion of Fend *et al.* (p. 141) about an *Aspirationsschub* for comprehensive school students is not supported, particularly when family status is controlled for. His crude analysis in which comprehensive schools were pitted against the totality of all others, represented to a high degree by students from the *Hauptschule,* biased his results, although they already indicated a subdued aspiration for occupational over educational goals (p. 174). Of course, his data would still allow the argument that comprehensive school students are motivated and prepared better when compared to those in a *Hauptschule,* where otherwise most of them would have enrolled. Our results indicate that there is not much difference between the comprehensive school and the *Hauptschule,.* Indeed, in terms of prospects at age 25 boys in the German *Hauptschule* and comprehensive school produce practically the same result.

PERCEPTION OF SOCIAL STRATIFICATION SYSTEM BY STUDENTS

Students in each school were asked in a closed question with seven items about their perception of social stratification in their country. These items can be classified in terms of recognition of collective class identity (three items):

    1. It is easy to tell whether someone belongs to the working class or to the middle class;

    2. People who work with their hands are completely different from people who work in an office;

    3. Workers can improve their lot only by uniting against their employers;

and in terms of classlessness and individualism (four items):

    4. If someone is smart and decisive enough, he can always get ahead in life;

    5. Everyone here in Britain (Germany) is middle class;

    6. There aren't any classes anymore;

    7. Life is a race and the best man wins;

as major modes of orientation in society. The above items had to be rated on a scale as being true, somewhat true, and untrue. A mean was computed by assigning values from 0 to 2 to the scale (Table 10).

The results in Table 10 show that in both societies there is a somewhat stronger recognition that society is structured along social class lines than that society is classless. But the difference is small for Germany. Differences by type of school are small. In both England and Germany students at grammar Schools/*Gymnasia* score the lowest for a perception that there is a classless society. Overall the differences are rather by country than by type of school. Relatively speaking, if one disregards the lower scores on the scale in general, English students seem more prone to recognize social classes versus a classless system. One could probably find evidence that differences between classes are more obvious in England than in Germany. However, the worse economic situation may again have its impact upon lowering scores for items that stress individual independence. The German students indeed score significantly higher on items 4 and 7, which stress individual achievement and advancement. They average 1.47 as against 1.06 for the English students and are thus more of the opinion that "someone smart and decisive enough will get ahead" or that "Life is a race and the best man wins."

If different types of schools are only modestly related to differential conceptions of social class or an awareness of social stratification as such, then their potential impact for a genuine revision of the existing system of social stratification may be limited. Such a conclusion is also suggested from the experiences in the German comprehensive school, which was created as a reform-oriented system in a conservative community of predominantly upper-lower and lower-middle-class people. The school attracted a corps of teachers of whom some were radically left. In its curriculum and substantive teaching the school was to a degree also working with an essentially Marxist conception of class and a crude application of

Table 10. Means of perception of class-structured and classless society by students in different types of school in England and Germany, 1974.

	England			Germany				
	Comprehensive	Grammar	Total	Comprehensive	Gymnasium	Realschule	Hauptschule	Total
Class								
Society	.82	.82	.81	.92	.99	1.1	1.0	.98
Classless	.74	.66	.70	.96	.86	.97	1.07	.94

such concepts in the analysis of present society and the community itself. To be sure, the majority of teachers in their subject areas and in personal position were modest if not indifferent to such teachings. Yet there were a number of substantive attempts in instruction to lay open the corrupt structure of modern society, the exploitation and suppression of workers, with the implicit understanding that this had to be changed, by revolution if necessary. This ultimately resulted in a number of conflicts within the school, with the higher school administration, and most of all with the community itself. The reaction was such that workers in the community took exception to the assertion that they were exploited and suppressed, that middle-class families moved their children out of the school, and that the school and higher administration ultimately removed some of the teachers from the school. These removals, though suggested earlier by community groups, occurred only after it became apparent that a hard core of the teachers were of the opinion that the comprehensive school was to be interpreted as the attempt of class society to conceal its actual structure and to use the comprehensive school as a mechanism of adjustment to the existing class system. In retrospect, and in light of the above results these teachers may not have been altogether wrong, because our results indicate that mobility chances for individuals are subdued in a comprehensive system and, according to the perception of social stratification by students, the system is not providing an ideological potential for change that is different from that in other schools.

SUMMARY AND DISCUSSION

In Western European education there is a feeling of resignation concerning the equality issue caused by such factors as limited resources after an era of expansion, the wide dissemination of the results of the Jencks's study, and a desire to consolidate schools and education after a period of rapid reform. Yet, the issue of equality in connection with education is still viable in Western Europe. In considering the potential impact of education on equality, the problems are, however, far from being resolved and understood. This realization may also contribute to the diminished expectation of immediate social change through education, though intentions in this direction have by no means been abandoned. National differences may refer to differential experiences; the English teachers and policy makers, after their experiences with the 1944 Education Act, expect and desire the least change in social stratification through education, and the French expect and desire the most. Hidden behind this may also be the methodological problem presented by differences in collective national attitudes and temperaments which may distort response rates. Finally, the uneven responses to the equality issue as such may be symptomatic of the abstractness of this policy, resulting under different circumstances in quite diversified rates.

Contrary to the conclusions of Jencks, but in line with some cautious observations by Kerckhoff about "formal sponsorship built into the British system" (1975, p. 1436), education in England and Germany makes a difference in aspirations and expectations toward occupational status. While descriptive statistics and contingency tables do not provide such information, regression analysis by type of school clearly indicates the differential impact by type of school. The comprehensive schools, which were intended to enhance mobility chances of lower-class students show much less than the desired results. These European findings suggest that the uniform school system in the United States may be the reason why, according to Jencks, education explains so little of the variance for income and occupation. Advocates of the comprehensive school have constantly pointed to the high social price that is being paid in more selective school systems (Husén, 1969). This is indeed a serious issue in such countries as France or Germany, where, among other problems, the dropout rate in secondary schools is particularly high for lower-class students. But the push for the comprehensive type in school organization brings its own predicaments. Their large size and anonymity may well be the cause of the large number of student problems reported in Sweden and experienced also in American schools. In terms of social stratification this type of school may lead to segregation rather than integration, making class differences more apparent. In this respect, Landecker's (1970) distinguishing between two levels of analysis would hold that under conditions of high class crystallization division will occur in interpersonal relations. His theory may well provide a useful theoretical insight. Furthermore, the establishment of comprehensive schools, through which educational disparities are being decreased, seems in fact to produce a collective educational mobility without commensurate social and economic opportunity.

Even within educational systems, opportunities are not necessarily developed on all levels. In West Germany one of the most serious policy problems, erupting in the summer of 1977 in renewed student protests, was that the number of *Abiturienten* (*Gymnasium* graduates) greatly exceeded the available capacities of the universities. Policy makers had already noted this as a most serious problem for education in 1974. Here, as well as in other areas of society, new opportunities would have had to be provided in order to absorb the increased number of people with advanced educational attainment. Instead, the expansion of the educational system resulted in considerable frustrations for those that were motivated to invest in education. This was not only a matter of unrealized reforms in society, but also a matter of eroding resources. Since the arguments and expectations were strongly linked to advancement on the class dimension, economic recessions such as that in the late 1960s and 1970s had to have a definite impact. If, however, education were to be seen more as a matter of status advancement and of life style, the predicament would be less problematic and actually produce a more egalitarian and humane society. This is implicit in the minds of some reformers. Against this background, discrepancies between educational attainment and income would be more easily accepted and a uniformly comprehensive school system could provide in the status dimension that amount of equality and system integration which reformers now yearn for in the class dimension. In this regard, the high investments for education that the public seems to reject at this time could receive a new legitimization. Moreover, a stronger budgetary consideration of education, based on better public understanding and support of the field, would potentially shift consideration of stratification away from economic determinism.

These are highly speculative suggestions. Yet, they need to be introduced into future policies. And they also need to be introduced into specific empirical studies. To mention just one example, the emphasis on single-factor studies has produced many findings about the class bias of teachers which result in a weakening of their professional impact for greater justice and equality. Their belief, expressed in the present study, that they themselves do more about equality than do their schools, may well indicate that education as a rule is served well through professionally responsible teachers and that other factors in the system may be more problematic. While the distinction between educational and social opportunity is only marginally adhered to among West Europeans, this distinction will help to provide for more rationality with regard to the equality issue in future educational policy making. Weber's distinction between the dimension of class and status is another such powerful analytic guideline.

FOOTNOTE

*This project (co-directors: Myron Atkin, Fred Coombs, Günther Lüschen, Richard Merritt, and Alan Purves) was supported by the Ford Foundation, the Volkswagen Foundation, and the Research Board of the University of Illinois. Dorothy and Austin Carley, Donald Dixon, Barbara Ekkers, Richard Howe, Robert Leonardi, Nancy Morrison, Gert Richertzhagen, Glenna Spitze, E. Svensson assisted in the project. Special thanks are due the administrators and teachers in the ministries and schools.

REFERENCES

Boudon, Raymond (1974) *Education, Opportunity, and Social Inequality*. New York: Wiley.

Bundesminister für Bildung (1977) *Grund- ud Strukturdaten*. Bonn

Coombs, Fred and Günther Lüschen (1976) "System Performance and Policymaking in West European Education." *International Review of Education*. 22 (2):133–154.

Dahrendorf, Ralf (1965) *Gesellschaft und Demokratie in Deutschland*, Munich: R. Piper Verlag.

Denison, Edward F. (1967) *Why Growth Rates Differ*. Washington, DC: Brookings Institution.

Dietrich, Theo (1966) *Sozialistische Pädagogik*. Bad Heilbrunn: Klinkhardt.

Faure, Edgar *et al.* (1972) *Apprendre à être*. Paris: Fayard.

Fend, Helmut *et al.* (1976) *Gesamtschule und dreigliedriges Schulsystem*. Stuttgart: Klett.

Ford, Julienne (1969) *Social Class and the Comprehensive School*. London: Routledge and Kegan Paul.

Galtung, Johan H, Christian Beck, and Johannes Jaastad (1976) *Educational Growth and Educational Disparity*. Oslo: University of Oslo (mimeographed).

Hauser, Richard (1969) "Schools and the Stratification Process." *American Journal of Sociology* 74 (6): 587–611.

Husén, Torsten (1969) "Productivity of Comprehensive and Selective School Systems." Pages 155–168 in M. A. Matthijsen and C. E. Vervoort (eds.), *European Seminar on Education*. The Hague: Mouton.

Jencks, Christopher *et al.* (1972) *Inequality*. New York: Basic Books.

Kerckhoff, Alan C. (1975), "Patterns of Educational Attainment in Great Britain," *American Journal of Sociology* 80 (6): 1428–1437.

Landecker, Werner S. (1970), "Status Congruence, Class Crystallization and Status Cleavage." *Sociology and Social Research* 54 (3): 343–355.

OECD (1971) *Group Disparities in Educational Participation and Achievement*. Paris: OECD.

——— (1973) *Educational Statistics and Indicators*, Vols. I and II. Paris: OECD (mimeographed).

Sander, Theodor *et al.* (1967) *Die demokratische Leistungsschule*. Hannover: Schroedel.

Sewell, William H. (1971) "Inequality of Opportunity for Higher Education," *American Sociological Review* 36 (5): 793–801.

——— (1973) Review of Jencks. *American Journal of Sociology* 78 (6): 1532–1540.

Statistiques des Enseignments (1973). *Année scolaire 1970/71*. Paris 15. (January).

Treiman, Donald (1977) *Occupational Prestige in Comparative Perspective*. New York: Academic Press.

——— and Kermit Terrell (1975) "Status Attainment in the United States and in Great Britain." *American Journal of Sociology* 81 (3): 563–583.

MIGRATION AND WORKERS' CONFLICTS IN WESTERN EUROPE*

Martin Slater

INTRODUCTION

Interest in industrial conflict is reawakened every few years by the political repercussions of major factory conflicts. In Western Europe, recent conflicts have shaken and even toppled national governments.[1] Since the late 1960s, when Western Europe's working class first showed signs of increasing militancy, the factory gate has come to be seen as a central arena of national politics. In explaining the waves of militancy in the work place, changes in the social structure of the labor market have largely

Comparative Social Research, Vol. 2, pp. 71–92.
Volume 1 published as Comparative Studies in Sociology

been ignored. Yet, it is precisely in this area that some of the most far-reaching changes have occurred. Through the mass immigration of foreign workers, the social and ethnic composition of Europe's industrial proletariat has changed almost beyond recognition. What effect have these new migrants had on industrial conflict? The following pages provide one answer to this question by contrasting the experiences of Paris, where migrants are foreign, with Milan, where migrants are internal.

Before 1945, the most important foreign migrations affecting Western Europe had been away from Europe to the Americas. In the past twenty years, the picture has changed dramatically. Millions of low-skilled workers, principally from the Mediterranean regions, have converged on the industrial heartlands of Europe. In the latter part of the 1960s foreign migrants arrived at the rate of over one million per year (Castles and Kosack, 1973, ch. 1). The major countries of immigration were France, West Germany, Britain, Sweden, Switzerland, and the Benelux nations. By the early 1970s, there were almost twelve million foreign workers in these countries, making up about 7 percent of the total population, and 12 percent of the labor force. Within each country, migrants have been concentrated in the industrial regions. Thus, of the four million foreign migrants in France in 1973, one-third were in the Paris region, making up more than 12 percent of the local population, compared to a figure of 7 percent for foreign migrants in the total French population (*Ministere du Travail*, 1973). In contrast to France, the industrial regions in Italy have not depended on foreign migration for their labor supply. There, a vast internal migration has taken place, involving the movement of millions of workers from the underdeveloped southern regions to the northern industrial regions (*Giunta Regionale Lombarda*, 1974). The cultural differences between northern and southern Italians make this internal migration very similar to the foreign migrations in France. Certainly, in the industrial regions of both France and northern Italy, the vast scale of migration has profoundly transformed the social composition of the industrial work force.

While migrants flowed into the factories, the latter were, toward the end of the 1960s and during the early 1970s, the scene of increasingly sharp conflicts between workers and management. The militancy of the working class, combined with an emerging egalitarianism in the ideology of many strikers, appeared to many observers to be the expression of new

*Martin Slater is in the Department of Government at the University of Essex in Colchester, England. He recently completed his doctoral dissertation at MIT on the impact of migration on industrial conflict in France and Italy. He is currently working on the effect of return migration on economic development in the labor-exporting countries.

class consciousness. The most interesting phenomenon, however, was the increasingly prominent role which many migrants appeared to be playing in labor disputes. This prominence was first noticeable in northern Italy. There, southern migrants played a major role in the wildcat strikes of 1968, and substantially contributed to the increased level of industrial conflict of the next few years. They are best remembered for the part they played in the "hot autumn" of 1969, which saw the renewal of the metal workers' contract after prolonged and bitter conflict (Pizzorno, 1974–1976; Bianchi *et al.*, 1970). By 1973, foreign migrants in other European nations had followed the lead of internal migrants in Italy. In Cologne, Turkish *Gastarbeiter* at the Ford factory initiated a series of wildcat strikes. In France, one of the first major strikes by foreign migrants was at the Renault-Billancourt factory in the Paris region. It took place in April 1973, and was soon followed by migrants' strikes in factories throughout France.

The action of migrants in the factories encouraged the political left, and especially the revolutionary fringe, to believe that migrants offered a potential base for revolutionary conflict. Governments were apparently of a similar mind. They faced the dilemma that, on the one hand, migration provided the labor supply for millions of necessary but unpleasant industrial jobs that had been vacated by the indigenous population. On the other hand, it was increasingly apparent that migration incurred significant social and political costs. Where migrants were foreign, as in France and Germany, governments tackled this problem by tightening controls on the internal movement of migrants and imposing restrictions of further immigration. At the same time, programs were set up to attract indigenous workers back into the types of jobs held by migrants. In pursuing these policies, the high unemployment of indigenous workers caused by the recent recession served as a handy justification.

Is it correct to view migrants as a potentially revolutionary force? Despite the current popularity of this view, the evidence is contradictory. Just a few years ago, the opposite view was equally popular. Studies of migrants' political behavior showed that migrants were less likely to participate in political or any other form of collective activity than indigenous workers (Alberoni and Baglioni, 1965; Cesareo, 1966; Fofi, 1964; Minces, 1973). Migrants, at best, played only a peripheral role in politics. To employers and the disinterested scholars alike, migrants appeared to be docile workers. Eager to earn a living and save money for the return to their homeland, migrants worked hard, met overtime requirements, and tolerated working conditions long deemed unacceptable by most indigenous workers. Furthermore, migrants, with their low skill levels, seemed content with their position at the bottom of the industrial hierarchy. Ex-

perience had shown that overqualified indigenous workers in such positions would soon turn into discontents.

How can the apparent paradox regarding migrants' political behavior be
explained? There is no doubt that many migrants were actively militant by
the late 1960s. But how widespread among them was this militancy, and
what caused the change? My own research focused on the participation of
migrants in industrial conflict in the automobile and construction industries. Both industries are among the heaviest employers of migrant labor,
but differ in that the levels of workers' militancy, measured by the level of
strike activity, political and union activity, and the level of unionization,
have traditionally been far higher in the former industry than in the latter.
Through in-depth interviews with workers' and management representatives in selected factories and work shifts, it emerged that growing social
cohesion among migrants had led to their increased participation in
work-place conflicts. This participation was more evident among the internal migrants in Milan than among the foreign migrants in Paris. The
fuller integration of migrants in Milan had also brought about a pattern of
conflict based on class rather than on ethnic relationships. At the same
time, in both France and Italy, the degree and precise pattern of work-
place conflict appeared to depend in large measure on the work environment. Indeed, the involvement of migrants in conflict differed widely
between the automobile and construction industries.

The influence on migrants' behavior in the work place can accordingly
be grouped in the following three categories: (a) migrants' own socio-
cultural background; (b) their work environment; and (c) their socio-legal
environment. Variations in these three influences affect both the *degree*
and *pattern* of migrants' participation in collective action at the work
place.

THE SOCIO-CULTURAL BACKGROUND OF MIGRANTS AND ITS EFFECT ON THEIR PARTICIPATION IN INDUSTRIAL CONFLICT

Migrants in Paris and Milan originate from regions where cultural traditions and social structure differ widely from those of an advanced industrial society. In Paris, migrants are drawn from a wide variety of ethnic
and national backgrounds. Most major immigration groups have had their
period of numerical dominance in terms of new arrivals. According to the
figures of the ONI (Office Nationale d'Immigration), the Italians and
Algerians were dominant during the 1950s, followed by the Spanish in the
early 1960s, and the Portuguese in the late 1960s. In recent years, the
major migration flows have been from Morocco, Tunisia, Yugoslavia, and
black Africa. As one source of migration has dried up, it has immediately

been replaced by another where labor reserves are still relatively un-exploited. In practice, this has meant that new migrants come from ever more distant and less developed regions. In Milan, a similar process has taken place involving internal migrants. By the late 1950s, southern Italians had replaced northern and central Italians as the principal immigration group. By 1970, 98 percent of net immigration to Milan was from the south (Giunta Regionale Lombarda, 1974, see pp. 271ff.). Despite the differences in the origin of migrants in Paris and Milan, a unifying feature of all migrant groups is their rural origin.

The ethnic and rural origins of migrants are the major barriers to participation in industrial conflict and the development of class-consciousness. First, the values of newly arrived migrants tend toward political passivity and the individual resolution of personal problems. Second, ignorance of the new industrial environment and of the host society initially deter the migrant from participating in industrial conflict. When he does begin to participate, it is directed toward specific work-place grievances, rather than general strikes protesting government policy. Third, the cultural differences between migrants and indigenous workers and among migrants themselves cause the social isolation of migrants and discourage their participation in collective action. Social cohession necessary for collective action is likely to develop only within individual ethnic groups. Only in Milan has the integration of migrants developed to the point where class consciousness replaces ethnic solidarity.

Unionists, seeking to recruit new migrants, are quick to note migrants' lack of radical traditions. At Renault-Billancourt, the secretary of the CFDT (Confederation Française Democratique du Travail) section noted:

There is no tradition of struggle among migrant groups. Many, when they first arrive, have a "wait and see" attitude towards the unions . . . (Interview with Algerian union secretary, CFDT, Renault-Billancurt, November 26, 1974).

Somewhat surprising was the uniformity of this characteristic among all migrant groups, even those of seemingly very different social origins. At Renault-Billancourt, for instance, Yugoslav migrants from a socialist state were scarcely more politicized than Moroccans from a traditional monarchy. In Milan, southern Italians in both the automobile and construction industries spoke proudly of the traditions of struggle of southern farm laborers (*braccianti*). For most migrants, however, it was pride in a tradition in which they had not participated. A union delegate at Alfa Romeo claimed:

... most of the workers who came here had not been involved in the struggles of
southern Italy; and they certainly did not know how to express themselves politically
when they arrived here (Interview with southern foundry delegate, CGT, Alfa Romeo,
Arese, May 7, 1975).

A very small number of migrants in both Paris and Milan could be described as politicized before their arrival. A southern union delegate at
Alfa Romeo had been brought up a Communist. He blamed his not finding
a job in the south on political discrimination. Obliged to migrate to the
north, he found work at Alfa Romeo, joined the factory's Communist
Party section, and became a union delegate. In Paris, some newly arrived
migrants also showed signs of prior politicization. A number of Portuguese and Spanish migrants viewed themselves as refugees from their
home countries. On arrival they tended to gravitate toward the Communist union, since the Communist Party had always been viewed as an
enemy of repression in their own countries. A few Algerians were also
politicized through having participated in their country's liberation
movement (the FLN). Although few in number, the politicized migrants
have been important in encouraging other migrants to participate in union
activity and strike action.

Combined with migrants' general lack of radical traditions is an individual or clientelistic approach to the resolution of problems. A case in
point is migrants' expectations regarding the nature and services of trade
unions. Unionists were irritated because many migrants looked upon the
unions only as a source of jobs and housing or aid in personal problems,
rather than as organizations defending the collective interests of workers.

... [they] sometimes expect the union to be some kind of social-work agency, regulating their personal problems. Because unions are unable to resolve these problems,
immigrants tend to lose interest ... others may first join two unions because they see
it as giving them double insurance. But then they lose interest later (Inteview with
union delegate, CFDT, Renault-Billancourt, October 7, 1974).

Migrants' individualism is also reflected in their attitude toward work,
being prepared to meet overtime requirements in their endeavor to save
money for their individual advancement.

The values that migrants bring with them are only one side of the coin.
On the other side, their attachment to prior values becomes an ignorance
of and unfamiliarity with the social norms and politics of industrial society. The majority of newly-arrived migrants are ill-informed about the
functions and ideologies of political and union organizations. There are
various manifestations of this ignorance. On one construction site visited
in Milan, migrants had chosen the chief foreman to be their union rep-

resentative. Fofi, writing of southern migrants in Turin in the early 1960s, noted migrants' confusion between management and union representatives (Fofi, 1964). In the large firms, where unions are active, such a scale of ignorance is not found. But, even there, a conscious choice is rarely made by migrants regarding union membership. Most migrants join the first union whose representative approaches them. They may, as noted earlier, join the second and third union as well.

Despite the political passivity and ignorance of migrants regarding the host society, there is no evidence that they consciously acted as strike breakers when industrial action was called for. Before the advent of migrants' strikes in the late 1960s, migrants in both Paris and Milan had followed the lead of indigenous workers. The participation of migrants, for instance, was important to the success of strikes at Alfa Romeo in 1966 and at Renault-Billancourt in 1968. The readiness of migrants to follow the lead of indigenous workers during the 1960s might be explained in terms of the thesis of Alberoni and Baglioni (1965). These two Italian sociologists, in a study of the attitudes of southern migrants in Milan during the early 1960s, argued that migrants underwent a process of anticipatory socialization. Essentially, this process meant that migrants were eager and willing to accept the values of the host society.

Perhaps more important than any process of anticipatory socialization of migrants is the length of time they spend in the host society. It is the newly arrived migrant who is most inclined toward political passivity. It seems no accident that the least militant migrants are to be found in the construction industry. It is this industry above all others that serves as the point of integration for new migrants into industrial society. Typically, the new migrant first finds work in the construction industry, and only later manages to find more secure factory employment (Fofi, 1964; Paci, 1974).

In the succession of migrants' strikes during the late 1960s and early 1970s, the legacy of migrants' ignorance of or lack of integration into the host society remained. In particular, it affected the type of strikes in which migrants participated. Grievances were directed toward the immediate work environment. At Renault-Billancourt, for instance, trade unionists during 1973 and 1974 worried about the excessive enthusiasm of migrants to engage in conflicts over shop-floor issues. The Communist-backed CGT (Confederation Generale du Travail) worried particularly about how factory unrest might affect the chances of the left at the national elections. At the same time, in November 1974, unionists failed to bring migrants out for a general strike protesting French government policy. One union official admitted that in the case of a general strike, a great deal of preparation was needed to ensure the participation of migrants:

Our main problem in getting through to the migrant is that there is often a comprehen-
sion gap . . . . The immigrant is often ignorant, so things must be made clear to him.
The general strike on 19 November 1974, for instance, was not sufficiently explained.
As a result, participation by migrants was low (Interview with union delegate, CGT,
Renault-Billancourt, November 28, 1974).

Migrants' comprehension had not been too low to lead a series of wildcat
strikes on the shop floor one year earlier.

Clearly, migrants are more quickly integrated into the work-place environment than into the broader social environment. The political attitudes
which migrants bring with them are not the only factor limiting the quick
integration of migrants into the industrial and social environment. Certainly as important are the ethnic and cultural differences between migrants and indigenous workers and among migrants themselves that serve
as a barrier to communication and create mutual hostilities. Language is
the most obvious division. Surveys of migrants in France point to the
latters' poor command of the French language (Morin, 1969, p. 7). The
inability of migrants to communicate is felt acutely during the early stages
of a migration flow when there are few other migrants of the same ethnic
group with whom they can communicate. A Portuguese construction
worker in France noted:

. . . ten years ago when I arrived there was no one here to explain things . . . . Now it
is different! There are lots of people; when the young Portuguese arrive and don't
know how to express themselves, the others do it for them (Interview quoted in
Federation Syndicale Mondiale, 1974, pp. 39–40).

In Milan, southern workers who had migrated during the late 1950s and
early 1960s also described the isolation they felt from speaking dialects
that could not be properly understood in the north.

Other cultural differences that isolate migrants from the indigenous
population include many seemingly trivial and everyday habits. These
factors, well described by Allal et al. (1974), give the migrant a sense of
being different, and with the intolerance that it reveals in the indigenous
population make him feel inferior. Thus, a migrant family in Milan felt
"mortified" when other tenants castigated them for preparing jars of
tomatoes near the communal entrance of the building. In the village they
came from, it was the custom for villagers to bottle the annual tomato
crop in the street. During the 1960s, there is little doubt that the southern
Italian in Milan felt as ill at ease as the foreign migrant in France. A
Sicilian construction worker in Switzerland explained why he had not
migrated to Milan:

> . . . if I went to Milan it would be the same. I would always be a migrant; I would still miss the warmth of the family . . . in the north they're also racist, perhaps a bit less so than the Swiss, but they're still racist (Interview quoted in CRESME, 1974).

The isolation of migrants from indigenous workers as a result of ethnic differences initially discourages migrants from initiating industrial conflict. More important, it prevents the development of class consciousness. Where conflicts have been led by migrants, they have tended to be based on ethnic solidarity. In Paris, because of the wide variety of ethnic groups, solidarity among migrant workers has been limited. At Renault-Billancourt, for instance, language and cultural differences within the groups of migrants prevents communication. Even among North Africans, the Arabic spoken by Moroccans differs from that spoken by Algerians. Religious differences also prevent communication. In the Renault canteen, Muslims will not sit next to workers who eat pork. Interestingly, the major conflict involving migrant workers at Renault-Billancourt took place in the press department. Many of the migrants in this department had worked there for several years. Participants in the strike noted its class nature:

> . . . some of the old Spanish workers in the department . . . had been at Renault many years, and their families had grown up in France. For them it was unthinkable to return to Spain. Even though they still spoke French with a strong accent, and had difficulty expressing themselves, they nevertheless thought of themselves as part of the French working class (Interview with delegate, CFDT, Renault-Billancourt, October 7, 1974).

In Milan, the development of class consciousness among migrants is far more evident. Migrants participated actively in the union struggles for social reforms of the early 1970s. They ceased to be concerned merely with work-place grievances. Further, the great increase in union membership in Milan after 1969 relied almost entirely on migrant workers. Finally, migrants were also increasingly attracted toward established working-class organization, such as the Communist Party. In Alfa Romeo, southern migrants now account for 60 percent of the Communist Party's membership. Clearly, the lack of ethnic divisions among Italian migrants, combined with their easier integration into the host society, compared to foreign migrants in Paris, allowed the development of a high level of industrial conflict and class consciousness.

Class consciousness among migrants in Milan, it must be stressed, has been limited mainly to those in the large-scale factories. Most migrants have remained politically passive, though perhaps not to the extent of migrants in France. What has largely determined the degree and certainly the pattern of migrants' involvement in workers' conflicts has been the work environment.

THE WORK ENVIRONMENT OF MIGRANTS AND ITS EFFECT ON INDUSTRIAL MILITANCY

Employed mainly as low-skilled workers in the secondary sector, migrants in both Milan and Paris predominate in those jobs vacated by indigenous workers. Most rural migrants lack the formal training to hold skilled positions in a modern industrial society. Today, skilled positions in the factory are invariably acquired by theoretical training, not by apprenticeship. (For a discussion of changing work organization, see Bright, 1958.) Modern industry, however, has increasingly needed unskilled workers who are strong, ready, and willing to carry out a series of undesirable jobs. Migrants have met these needs precisely. A French Ministry of Labor survey carried out in 1971 reported that 93.6 percent of salaried foreigners in France were manual workers, and 66.8 percent were low- or semiskilled (Ministère d'Etat Chargé des Affaires Sociales, 1973). In the case of Paris, the most recent reliable figures are those of the 1968 census. They show that 68 percent of active migrants were manual workers, compared to 35.2 percent of the total active population. Only 5.8 percent of foreign migrants were white-collar workers, as opposed to 36.2 percent of the total population (INSEE, 1972). In Milan, there are many more migrants in the higher occupational echelons than in Paris. Because there are no restrictions on internal migration, professionally qualified people from the southern cities have been free to migrate. Nevertheless, if one looks only at rural migrants in Milan, the figures bear comparison to those of Paris. Rural migrants, in a survey by Paci in the early 1960s, made up 53.4 percent of unskilled and domestic workers, but only 11.2 percent of clerical employees. Corresponding figures for those born in Milan are 24.5 percent and 30.7 percent (Paci, 1974, p. 60).

As low-skilled manual workers, the majority of migrants are employed in the secondary sector of the economy. The 1968 census of the Paris region showed that 61.9 percent of active foreign migrants were employed in the secondary sector, compared to a figure of 41.0 percent for the total active Paris population (INSEE, 1972, Tables D7 and D15). In the 1971 Ministry of Labor survey, 88.2 percent of foreign migrants in France were employed in the secondary sector (Ministère d' État Chargé des Affaires Sociales, 1973). In Milan, rural migrants again tend to predominate in the secondary sector. They are also, however, to be found in the tertiary sector in greater numbers than foreign migrants in Paris. In France, special statutes dating from 1937 forbid the employment of foreigners in a wide range of public service jobs. In Milan, on the other hand, the Neapolitan policeman was a familiar sight of the 1960s.

Within the secondary sector, the construction and metal and mechanical engineering industries have made the most extensive use of migrant labor. In the *comune* of Milan, according to the 1971 census, southern migrants made up 24.8 percent of all workers in the secondary sector, but 36.3 percent of construction workers. In the Paris region, in 1973, 46.5 percent of construction workers were foreign migrants [FNB (Federation Nationale du Bâtiment) figures at 15 March 1973]. For the secondary sector as a whole, probably no more than 26 percent are foreign migrants.[2] In the metal and mechanical engineering industries, automobile plants and foundries are the heaviest employers of migrants. A recent survey on migrants' employment in the Paris region reported that 64 percent of manual workers in the automobile industry and 62 percent of foundry workers were foreign migrants (Rerat *et al.*, 1975). In Milan, management interviews revealed that 60–70 percent of automoble workers are southern migrants.

How does the work environment of migrants affect the general level of militancy? There are two major points. First, variations in militancy among migrants in the automobile and construction industries suggest that migrants, like other workers, respond to their particular work environment. Second, the high visibility of migrants in recent conflicts can be explained by the fact that they are overwhelmingly employed in firms where the work environment is most conducive to the development of conflict.

Many low-skilled workers doing unpleasant jobs probably feel they have legitimate grievances against their employers. Research revealed, however, that the size of the work force, its relative stability, and management policies were major factors determining the militancy of all workers, including migrants.

By several major criteria, workers in the automobile plants of Renault and Alfa Romeo are more militant than construction workers. Automobile workers in these plants have been at the forefront of strike activity.[3] The major union confederations are each represented in the factory, and have thriving memberships (65 percent of workers at Alfa Romeo and 30 percent at Renault were union members in 1974–1975). The Communist Party factory sections, with 1,500 members at Renault and 1,000 at Alfa Romeo, are the largest in their respective countries. In addition, other political parties, including a myriad of small radical groups are also active in each factory.

The construction industry boasts no such level of activity. There is a below-average level of strike activity. Political groups are not represented. Neither are unions on many work sites. Only recently, in the case of Milan, has union membership climbed to respectable levels. By 1975, approximately one-third of construction workers were unionized. In Paris, it remains abysmally low. In 1974, French construction unions claimed a unionization rate of only 10 percent.

The size of the work force is the first reason for the lack of militancy among construction workers. In Milan, in 1973–1974, there were only twelve construction firms with more than 200 employees (none had more than 1,000 employees). In contrast, there were 2,122 firms with less than ten employees, excluding the even smaller artisan firms.[4] In France, there are over 250,000 construction firms, and 90 percent of these have less than twenty employees (Herblay, 1970). The primary obstacle to organizing collective action in the construction industry is legal. In Italy, union officials cannot enter firms with less than fifteen workers. In France, professional elections can be held and union sections formed only in firms with more than fifty employees. Limited organizational resources also affect union activity. They go less far in a myriad of small firms than in a few large ones. Another feature of the construction industry is that workers of the same firm are often scattered around different construction sites. Union organizers find it difficult to coordinate industrial action. Finally, smaller work forces mean a lesser likelihood of finding workers to take on organizational responsibilities.

In the construction industry, the unions claim their greatest success in the organization of large sites, regardless of their location or the origin of the workers:

> . . . it is easier to organize a large site whichever region of the country it is in, and whatever the nationality of the workers . . . (Interview with federal secretary of CGT construction union, Paris, September 4, 1974).

In both Milan and Paris, the success of regional and national strikes also depends on the support of large construction sites. It is considered a bonus if workers on the smaller sites stop work on the day of the strike. Plant-level conflicts are almost entirely limited to large-scale sites. Admittedly, conflicts in small firms rarely come to public attention, sometimes not even to the attention of unionists. But visits to a variety of construction sites in both Paris and Milan showed the prevalence of strike activity on large construction sites. In small firms, workers' grievances were often settled on an individual basis.

A large work force is not a sufficient condition for a high level of industrial conflict. The meager contractual gains won by construction workers, even on the large sites, compared to automobile workers, show the limits of their militancy. Preventing a high level of industrial conflict in the construction industry is the instability of the work force. Militant movements rarely spring up overnight, and for them to be successful a certain degree of work-force stability is needed. The work force in the construction industry suffers from three forms of instability. First, the work site is of limited duration. Even large construction sites are generally limited to a life of two to three years. It may take several months to build up representative organizations among the work force. Then, once the site closes, all the gains achieved by the workers are likely to be lost. This process has been particularly evident in Paris and Milan, especially since workers' contracts are generally limited to the life of the site. Thus groups of militant workers rarely remain within the same firm to continue their industrial action. When a site closes, all the workers are laid off.

A second form of instability arises from the business cycle of the construction industry. In Milan, the most stable sector of the construction industry is the traditional sector.[5] The situation appears similar in France. A report by Pohl, Laule, and Merlet (1974) noted that compared to large firms, small specialized construction firms "are much more easily able to switch to maintenance work when orders for other work begin to fall off." The modern large-scale firms respond abruptly to the business cycle, closing or opening major sites, and even ceasing active trading. Few construction firms have heavy investment in fixed plant. Thus, doors can be closed quicker than in firms in other sectors. Likewise, a militant work force can disappear extremely quickly. A third form of instability in the industry arises from the high turnover of workers, most of whom are employed on a site only so long as their particular skills are needed.

The effect of high work-force instability is to make collective action by workers a rarity. Within the construction industry, prefabrication workshops tend to be highly organized with militant work forces. In the Paris region, at Gennevilliers, a prefabrication workshop manufacturing concrete blocks experienced a six-week strike during 1973 (Interview with CGT zonal official, Gennevilliers, November 18, 1974). There, a permanently employed work force of migrant workers had been in a position to organize strike activity. In a general construction firm in Milan, the owner prided himself on having had workers in his employ for "twenty years or more." In this same firm, an active union movement existed, and a major plant-level dispute had taken place in 1973. The organization of activities lay in the hands of workers' delegates, many of whom had worked in the firm for as long as fifteen years. Despite the delegates' being scattered around several work sites, they knew each other well enough to keep in regular contact by telephone. During the weeks of the strike, they were in a position to coordinate demonstrations and picket lines (Interview with work-site delegate, Sesto San Giovanni, June 10, 1975).

In contrast to the above examples, there are cases of large construction firms where high labor mobility has made strike organization and union development a difficult process. Thus, a major construction firm in Paris with over 5,000 employees had a weak union movement. The explanation lay, at least partly, in the fact that the vast majority of workers, mainly foreign migrants, were employed on the basis of six-month nonrenewable contracts. Skilled workers and technicians, with greater employment stability, were eventually able to form a union section, despite the pressures of a paternalistic and authoritarian management (Interview with secretary of CGT construction union, Nanterre, October 19, 1974; see also Doret, 1972, pp. 9–14).

To some extent, high labor-force mobility also accounted for low levels of worker militancy in the automobile industry during the early and middle 1960s. At Renault and the other major French automobile manufacturers, it was common to employ migrants on six-month terminal contracts. As low-skilled workers employed on the production lines, migrants could be easily hired and fired according to production needs. Certainly, during much of the 1960s, there was considerable fluctuation in these needs at both Renault and Alfa Romeo. Fluctuations were both seasonal and cyclical. Low-skilled production workers, with no need of costly training programs, were infinitely more expendable than skilled workers and technicians. The instability of the low-skilled worker decreased with the economic expansion of the late 1960s. A tightening of the labor market thus was a crucial factor in the outbreak of the major labor disputes among low-skilled automobile workers (mainly migrants) of the late 1960s. Certainly, the strikes by low-skilled migrants at Renault in 1973 seem to have been made possible by the stability of the workers. Migrant strikers in the press shop had an average length of service of over seven years.

Discussing the conditions for the development of industrial militancy, one is in danger of losing sight of the role of migrants. What evidence is there that they respond to their work environment in the same way as indigenous workers? Evidence comes from a comparison of Renault Le Mans and Renault-Billancourt. In October 1974, the former plant, of a total manual work force of 8,028 persons, had a mere 55 foreign migrants. Billancourt with a manual work force of 20,349, had 10,409 foreign migrants.[6] The levels of militancy in both factories, however, have remained similar. Most remarkably, both factories were affected by intense industrial conflict by low-skilled workers in the early 1970s. At Le Mans, French peasants from the Sarthe led a radical egalitarian conflict in 1971. In 1973, a similar conflict took place, but now led by low-skilled workers from North Africa, Spain, and Portugal. Another comparison is between Renault-Billancourt and Chrysler-Simca. In the latter factory, owing partly to the instability of the work force (migrants until recently were given six-month contracts) and management repression, migrants have remained politically docile, not participating in or leading any major strike activity. Remarkably, they even failed to participate in the strikes of May 1968.

The case of Chrysler-Simca raises the issue of management policies toward the work force and its effect on militancy. Certainly, with migrants, management has been in a position to pursue strategies aimed at preventing the development of conflict. Management policies have been aimed principally at breaking up ethnic solidarity among migrants and preventing the formation of stable units of workers. With migrants monopolizing low-skilled jobs, ethnic solidarity among migrants in the Italian automobile industry provided a basis for conflicts involving low-skilled workers. In Paris, however, management policy at the major automobile plants has been directed toward dividing up individual ethnic groups. When, for instance, 300 Yugoslavs arrived at Renault-Billancourt in 1973, they were immediately split up into groups of eight to ten workers and put to work in separate shops. In Milan, such splitting-up of ethnic groups has not been possible. What has been possible in both Milan and Paris was to prevent the formation of a large stable core of workers in the work place. One Milanese constructor who had resorted to subcontracting put his views frankly:

> The problem in the construction industry is that labor unions are so powerful, especially in the larger firms, that it becomes virtually impossible to lay workers off. For this reason, constructors are terrified to take on new labor . . . instead of taking on new labor, one subcontracts. . . . I reckon that a site with more than one hundred workers is ungovernable (Interview with construction worker, Trezzano-sul-Naviglio, June 5, 1975).

Such forms of subcontracting have been largely limited to the constuction industry. Thus in the case of the Milanese automobile industry, management has had little effect on the development of migrants' conflicts. In the Paris automobile industry, its effect has been greater.

Migrants, then, have responded to the work environment in a way similar to indigenous workers. Certain conditions, such as the ethnic division of migrants in France, have hampered the development of collective organization. But migrants have nevertheless become highly visible in industrial conflict. This fact is not too surprising when one considers their predominance in industries such as the automobile industry which has provided one of the major bastions of working-class industrial militancy. Interestingly, even in the construction industry, migrants have been employed in firms which are most conducive to the development of militancy among workers. Migrants, with their low skill levels, have tended to find employment in large-scale, general construction firms where there is the greatest division of labor. They have less easily found employment in the small, traditional firms that require high skill levels of their workers. Thus, in 1973, 51.1 percent of construction workers in France in firms with more than 500 employees were foreign migrants, as opposed to 21.8 percent for firms with 10–49 employees (Ministère d' Etat Chargé des Affaires Sociales, 1973, Table III). In the case of Milan, a small survey by Paci (1974, p. 31) in the early 1960s shows similar findings. Thus, in the large construction firms, where workers' militancy and levels of unionization are greatest, migrants are prevalent. Indeed, as one construction union leader in Milan noted:

> . . . 90 percent of our members are southerners . . . without them there would not be a union. Some of our best activists are southerners [Interview with CISL (Conferenziere Italiena dei Syndicati di Lavorati) construction unionist, May 15, 1975].

As the work environment has affected the levels of militancy among migrants, so too has it affected the form that conflict has taken. The radical egalitarianism which many observers took to be a manifestation of migrant consciousness was now more than a reflection of the grievances of low-skilled workers in the automobile industry. A comparison with the construction industry is instructive.

In the automobile industry, the increased employment of migrants went hand in hand with increased mechanization and division of labor. The parcelization of production meant that low-skilled migrants could be employed directly on the assembly lines with the minimum of training. At the same time, the traditional skilled worker all but disappeared. In his place came the worker-technician, employed mainly to service and repair machinery. The skills of this new breed of skilled worker are learned at technical schools, with an emphasis on theory not practice. Thus there is no longer an apprenticeship system whereby a low-skilled worker can gain promotion on the job. In the construction industry, the situation is different. Many migrants, for instance, having had prior experience of construction even in their home villages, enter the industry with some semblance of skill. For those who have no prior experience, it is still possible to enter the industry at the lowest levels and learn skills on the job. In many firms, therefore, there is career mobility for the low-skilled worker. There is least mobility in the modern prefabrication firms where, as in the automobile industry, an extreme division of labor has taken place.

The different status of low-skilled workers in each industry goes a long way toward explaining differing patterns of industrial conflict. To observers, the grievances of low-skilled migrants in the automobile industry appeared radical and egalitarian. In reality, they had no wider implications than reflecting frustration with the lack of career mobility. Thus low-skilled workers called for an end to the traditional skill hierarchy of the factory and immediate promotion for themselves to a higher professional status, regardless of their formal skills. They also demanded flat-rate pay increases to replace percentage increases. The latter form of increases were considered discriminatory against the lowest-paid workers—the low-skilled. In making these demands, there could be no mutual interest with skilled workers in the factory. The conflicts had, therefore, a corporatist character. In the early stages, they also had an anti-union character. The unions at both Renault and Alfa Romeo were too closely identified with the interests of skilled workers.

In the construction industry, with the possibility of career mobility, there has been little discord between low-skilled and skilled workers. The traditional skill hierarchy continues to be accepted, demands for flat-rate pay increases have not risen spontaneously, and there has been no challenge to the social basis of the unions. In conclusion, therefore, the notion of inherent migrant radicalism and egalitarianism can be discounted.

THE SOCIO-LEGAL ENVIRONMENT AND ITS EFFECT ON MIGRANTS' MILITANCY

Apart from the work environment, the world outside work also intrudes on the migrant and affects his behavior in the work place. In the comparison between Milan and Paris, it is the legal restrictions on foreign migrants in France that partially explain the limitations on migrants involvement in conflict relative to Milan.

Foreign migrants in France have to obtain residence and work permits. These documents are of limited duration. If, therefore, a migrant is fired from a factory, he will not be able to obtain an extension of his residence permit unless he has a valid work permit. This may not be possible if he was fired at the termination of his contract. The foreign migrant, then, is in a continuously precarious position regarding employment, a situation which is hardly conducive to his participation in collective action. Illegal migrants, who in the past have been extremely numerous in France, are in the most precarious position.[7] They have no legal recourse if fired. There are, of course, no illegal migrants at Renault-Billancourt, but they are reportedly present in relatively large numbers in the construction industry. No such difficulties exist for the southern migrant in Milan.

In France, migrants suffer the additional disadvantage of not being permitted to join political organizations, under pain of expulsion from the country. On May 10, 1968, for instance, the French Minister of the Interior announced; "Foreigners who do not observe political neutrality have been, are, and will be expelled from the national territory" (Quoted in Granotier, 1973). Expulsion has not been an idle threat, as witnessed by the large numbers of migrants expelled by the Interior Ministry in 1968. Migrants have also been limited by law from holding certain union positions. This law was rescinded only in 1974. Previously, migrants could be elected personnel delegates but not appointed to union positions. Among migrants, the latter positions were open only to Algerians, who enjoyed a special statute. Algerians were also advantaged in speaking better French than most other migrant groups. In France, it remains illegal for anyone to assume an elected role within the union or factory who cannot read and write French. Large numbers of migrants, many illiterate even in their own languages, are automatically excluded from leadership roles within the organized workers' movement. It is not surprising, then, that Algerians have often been regarded as the most militant migrant group by many unionists.

For some groups of migrants in Paris, the repressive laws of the host society have been less of an obstacle than repression by their own governments. The Portuguese government, prior to the April 1974 *coup d'état,* had an active secret police, the PIDE, spying upon the political activities of Portuguese migrants. The Moroccan government continues to be similarly organized, checking, in particular, on those workers having links to Communist-backed organizations. A number of workers act as paid informers, and sanctions are available for use against recalcitrants. Loans for returning migrants wishing to buy parcels of land may be withheld. Moroccans, then, are especially wary of associating with unionists:

At a café near here (Gennevilliers), when the CGT (Communist union) delegate comes in, many Moroccans will go out so as not to be seen talking to him (Interview with CGT zonal official, Gennevilliers, November 18, 1974).

CONCLUSION

The behavior of migrants in the work place reflects both the form and degree of their integration into the host society. Much of the previous research on migrants' political behavior has suffered from treating migrants as a discrete social group with few internal divisions. The ethnic distinctiveness of migrants shifts attention away from the very real impact that socialization agents, such as the work place, have on migrants' behavior. For the public at large, the docile migrants of the 1960s were described in terms of the illiterate and individualistic peasant. The militant migrant of the 1970s is in turn viewed as the impetuous and uncivilized peasant. Neither of these caricatures take into account the impact of socializing agents within the host society. Nor do they consider the evolution of migrants' behavior in their changing relationship to the host society.

Where attention has focused on the integration of migrants within the host society, generalizations are still made too readily. There are indeed important similarities in the social and economic conditions of most migrants. It is also true that they are overwhelmingly employed in society's undersirable jobs, those rejected by the indigenous population. But what our research has shown, we hope, is that these jobs are far from alike, and that the different work environments which migrants experience have a major impact on their political behavior in the work place. Thus the radical and egalitarian struggles led by the low-skilled migrants in the automobile industry are not typical of the majority of migrants, and particularly of those employed in the more traditionally organized construction industry. There were instead broad similarities in the work-place behavior of both indigenous and migrant workers who shared the same work environment. Thus the French peasants at Renault's Le Mans factory showed little divergence in their grievances to the foreign migrants at the firm's Billancourt factory. Looked at from this point of view, the militant migrant is revealed as a myth. It is not the migrant who is militant but the low-skilled production worker in the automobile factory.

The socializing influence of the work place on the migrant is only one part of the puzzle. The degree of integration of migrants into the host society has a far-reaching impact on migrants' behavior and on the politics of the host society. The migrant in the automobile industry is only a would-be militant. To participate in and to instigate industrial action, migrants must be conscious of group solidarity among their fellow workers. Stability in the work place and the breaking-down of socio-cultural barriers among workers help create solidarity. For many migrants, in both Paris and Milan, the absence of a stable work environment has precluded the development of militancy. Sometimes this lack of stability is inherent in the work conditions of a particular industry, of which the construction industry is one example. Alternatively, it arises because of the particular socio-legal environment. Thus, foreign migrants in France had few defenses against the short-term contracts under which they were employed during the 1960s. There was quite literally not enough time for group solidarity to develop. Migrants remained politically apathetic. In Paris, the eventual militancy of migrants was even further away because of the communication barriers both among migrants of different ethnic groups and between migrants and indigenous workers.

As our research has shown, the fact of workers being migrants does not always mean that they are less militant than other workers. Ethnicity did provide an important basis for group solidarity, particularly in Milan where migrants were drawn from a single ethnic group. Ethnic solidarity could develop because whole departments of factories had been "taken over" by migrants. Ethnic solidarity, incidentally, meant the primacy for a time of work-place issues. The grievances of migrants reflected not their particular ethnic characteristics, but their particular work-place problems. An interest in broader working class issues came only with the development of class solidarity.

It is in the development of ethnic and class solidarity that some of the major differences between the impact of migrants in Milan and Paris emerge. By 1968–1969, ethnic solidarity in Milan had built up among migrants in the more stable automobile industry. It reached the point where migrants began making the instrumental demands which reflected the frustration of their work environment. When, in 1969 and 1970, the national unions embraced these demands (which previously had been expressed only in wildcat strikes) the low-skilled migrants were further integrated into the mainstream of working-class radicalism. The new class solidarity of which migrants were now an integral part provided the basis for the national struggles in the 1970s for the promotion of social reforms. It also led workers at Alfa Romeo, for instance, to insist on new investments by their firm in southern Italy, a demand which certainly expressed class interests rather than the interests of a particular group of factory workers. With this integration of the southern migrant into the northern industrial working class, union membership increased considerably. So too did membership in political organizations such as the Communist Party. Thus, to a large extent, the integration of migrants increased the political strength of the Milanese working class.

In Paris, the foreignness of migrants had precluded such rapid development of class consciousness, and there are even barriers to the development of ethnic solidarity as a result of the legal status of migrants. In the Renault factories, migrants have been sufficiently stable to resort to collective action over shop-floor issues. But there has been little interest in broader class-based issues, indicating a lack of integration into the indigenous working class. Only the long-term settlement of migrants in their adopted country might point to greater involvement in class-based issues. As things stand, the working class in Paris seems destined to remain fragmented along ethnic lines. The influence of the working class as a coherent group in national politics is likely to remain at a lower level than in the Italian case. One would expect to see the continuation of spasmodic conflicts based on ethnic groupings.

FOOTNOTES

This paper was submitted for the Workshop on Comparative Labor Movements, Center for European Studies, Harvard University, 5 Bryant Street, Cambridge, Massachusetts, October 14–16, 1977, co-sponsored by the Council for European Studies. The author would like to express his appreciation to the Social Science Research Council for support for this project through the Foreign Area Fellowship Program.

1. For instance, the Andreotti government in Italy in 1972 and the Heath government in Britain in 1974.

2 Estimate based on Ministry of Labor Survey (*Ministère d' Etat Chargés des Affaires Sociales,* 1973) and ACT Survey of migrants in the Paris area (ACT, 1973, Tome 2).

3. Workers at Renault were at the forefront of major national strikes in 1936, 1947, and 1948; Alfa Romeo workers were active in the wartime movement, and were prominent in industrial conflict in the Milan area during the 1960s.

4. Figures provided by the *Cassa Edile di Mutualita ed Assistenza della Provincia di Milano.*

5. The volume of buildings built by traditional methods is relatively stable from year to year; in contrast, the volume of those built by modern methods (reinforced concrete and prefabrication) is subject to wild fluctuation. See *ISTST* (1966–1973).

6. Figures provided by Regie Nationale des Usines Renault, Direction Centrale.

7. In 1968, over 80 percent of new migrants to France entered clandestinely.

REFERENCES

ACT (1973) *Emploi et Logement des Travailleurs Immigrés.* Tome 2, Rapport Final. Paris: Ministère de l'Amenagement du Territoire, de l'Equipement, du Logement et du Tourisme, Service des Affaires Economiques et Internationales.

Alberoni, Francesco and Guido Baglioni (1965) *L'Integrazione dell'Immigrato nella Societa Industriale.* Bologna: Il Mulino.

Allal, Tewfik *et al.* (1974) *La Fonction Miroir.* Paris.

Bianchi, G. *et al.* (1970) *Grande Impresa e Conflitto Industriale.* Roma: Coines.

Bohning, W.R. (1973) *The Economic Effects of the Employment of Foreign Workers.* Working Paper. Paris: OECD.

Bright, James R. (1958) *Automation and Management.* Boston: Harvard University.

Castles, Stephen and Godula Kosack (1973) *Immigrant Workers and Class Structure in Western Europe.* London: Oxford University Press.

Cesareo, V. (1966) "Immigrati e Associazionisme Volontarie." *Studi Emigrazione.* Anno III (October).

CRESME (1974) *Indagine su Alcuni Problemi dell'Occupazione nel Settore Edilizio.* Documento di Lavoro. Roma:

Doret, Laurent (1972) "Les Relations Humaines selon François Bouyges." *L'Action Politique* 3 (March–April).

Federation Syndicale Mondiale (1974) *Enquete sur les Jeunes Travilleurs Immigres.* Paris: Confederation Generale du Travail.

Fofi, Goffredo (1964) *L'Immigrazione Meridionale a Torino.* Milano: Feltrinelli.

Giunta Regionale Lombarda, Assessorato al Lavoro e Movimenti Demografici (1974) *Conferenza Regionale sui Movimenti Migratori* (Villa Ponti, Varese, 29–30 March).

Granotier, Bernard (1973) *Les Travailleurs Immigres en France.* Paris: Maspero.

Herblay, Michel (1970) "L'Industrie aux 270,000 Entreprises." *L'Expansion* 33 (September).

INSEE (1972) *Recensement General de la Population de 1968, Resultats Sondage au 1/4, Region Parisienne*. Paris: Imprimerie Nationale.

ISTAT (1966–1973) *Annuario Statistico dell'Attivita Edilizia e delle Opere Pubbliche*. Roma:

Minces, Juliette (1973) *Les Travailleurs Etrangers en France*. Paris: Editions du Seuil.

Ministère du Travail, de l'Emploi et de la Population (1973) *Le Dossier de l'Immigration*. (September) Paris:

Morin, Joseph (1969) "Sur 2,358 travailleurs, 67.9% *ne savent ni lire, ni ecrire.*" *Hommes et Migrations* 111.

Paci, Massimo (1974) *Mercato del Lavoro e Classi Sociali in Italia*. Bologna: Il Mulino.

Pizzorno, Alessandro (ed.) (1974–1976) *Lotte Operaie e Sindacato in Italia (1969–1972)*. Vols. 1–6. Bologna: Il Mulino.

Pohl, R., P. Laulhe, and A. Merlet, Les Collection de l'INSEE (1974) *Enquete sur l'Emploi de 1972, Resultats Detailles*. Serie D, Nos. 33–34 (June) Paris: Imprimerie Nationale.

Rerat, F., G. Petit, and M. Bauman (1975) "Les Emplois Tenus par la Main d'Oeuvre Etrangere." In Cahiers du Centre d'Etudes de l'Emploi, *Trois Approches des Problemes d'Emploi*. Paris: Presses Universitaires de France.

LABOR PARTIES, ECONOMIC GROWTH, AND THE REDISTRIBUTION OF INCOME IN FIVE CAPITALIST DEMOCRACIES*

Lars Björn

INTRODUCTION

One of the core areas in the study of social stratification is the process of distribution. The relative importance of the economic market vs. the commands of political decision makers is one of the main criteria by which capitalist and socialist systems of stratification can be distinguished (Lenski, 1970, p. 392). Similarly, comparisons can be made among capitalist systems as to the relative influence of political decisions on the distributive process. The latter is the subject of this chapter, which examines the relative importance of labor cabinet influence and the rate of economic growth as determinants of the redistribution of income in Sweden, Denmark, the United Kingdom, Australia, and the United States from 1920 to 1970.

Comparative Social Research, Vol. 2, pp. 93–128.
Volume 1 published as Comparative Studies in Sociology
Copyright © 1979 by JAI Press, Inc.
All rights of reproduction in any form reserved.
ISBN 0-89232-112-1

The distributive process is indeed complex in the capitalist market systems of the industrialized world, and any study of the process can only deal with a delimited aspect of it. The focus here is the vertical redistribution of income that occurs as a result of government taxing and spending. This excludes above all the dynamics of redistributive conflicts in the labor market which have recently come to the attention of students of the political economy of modern captialism (Martin, 1975; Rein and Marris, 1975; Crouch, 1975).

The complexity of the redistributive process is one of the reasons we find few empirically grounded propositions about its determinants. A review of the literature indicates that it is difficult a priori to rule out almost any variable as a possible cause of variations in government redistributive efforts (Björn, 1976, ch. 6; Carrier and Kendall, 1976). One illustrative example of the state of theoretical development is the role of the *level of economic development*[1] as a cause of redistribution. When we take a cross-sectional view of the world, this variable can account for some of the variation in social security development (Wilensky, 1975, pp. 15–17; Jackman, 1974, pp. 31–32). Among developed democratic nations, it seems to have no explanatory power; political factors better account for cross-sectional variations in social security (Taira and Kilby, 1969, pp. 152–153; Wilensky, 1975, p. 52, 1976, pp. 24–25; Hewitt, 1977, p. 460). When we finally turn to longitudinal studies of these nations, both economic historians (e.g., Rimlinger, 1966) and quantitative analysts (e.g., Klingman, 1973) tell us that economic development seems to be one of the preconditions for development of social welfare programs. Thus, a *general* theory of the relative importance of the level of economic development for redistribution does not seem to be at hand. Given this lack of theory about redistributive processes (also noted by Jackman, 1972, p. 4), an alternative approach to theory construction would seem to be to first develop "models" of redistribution that are applicable within well-defined *historical* boundaries (Bendix, 1969, p. 12; Moul, 1974, make a similar point for other areas of research).

HISTORICAL SCOPE

As already noted we are interested in examining the redistributive process through government action in industrialized capitalist societies. A further limitation of the five societies under study is that we limit ourselves to the

*Lars Björn is an Assistant Professor of Sociology at the University of Michigan, Dearborn. He is a native of Sweden and recently finished his dissertation work at the University of North Carolina, Chapel Hill. A comparative study of working-class politics in Sweden and England as well as a social history of jazz in Detroit are two of his present research efforts.

half century 1920—1970. This is justified on two grounds, one related to the development of the "welfare state," the other to the political institutions of capitalist societies.

As our concern is with differences in redistribution through the public sector, meaning mainly social welfare policies, an appropriate starting point would be when the welfare state has become a commonly accepted "technique" of redistribution. Even though some countries were lagging in their development of social policies to protect the population from the risks of illness, old age, and failures of the market, knowledge about the techniques was widely diffused by the end of World War I.[2] Given our interest in testing hypotheses about the influence of labor parties on redistributive policies, we would like to hold constant some important features of the political institutions of capitalist societies. We limit ourselves to the dynamics of the redistribution in *democratic* societies,[3] where suffrage has long been extended to the adult population and the political party system is well developed. Lipset and Rokkan (1967) in their study of party systems and voter alignments come to the conclusion that since 1920 the pattern of party systems in Western democracies has remained virtually unchanged. Using these limitations only thirteen [4] societies have been continuously democratic since 1920 [5]: Australia, Belgium, Canada, Denmark, Finland, France, Ireland, the Netherlands, New Zealand, Norway, Sweden, the United Kingdom, and the United States.

HYPOTHESES

The major actors in redistributive conflicts in democratic political institutions are *political parties* competing for control of executive and legislative power. These parties have different degrees of social power, partly depending upon their relative success in mobilizing class-specific political support. In most of these societies we find labor (or social democratic) parties which can be defined not only by their electoral and organizational links to the industrial working class, but also by their relatively egalitarian political ideologies. This is contrasted with the political parties receiving support from the "propertied classes" in these industrialized societies (Lenski, 1966, pp. 322–323). Under rationalistic assumptions about political behavior (Korpi, 1971), both of these characteristics of labor parties would lead to the hypothesis that *labor parties are more likely than nonlabor parties to redistribute income in favor of the disadvantaged*. In the present study we test this hypothesis by comparing the redistributive intent (as evidenced by government expenditures) of labor and nonlabor parties in executive power (cabinet positions). There are variations in the degree to which labor parties have formal control of positions of executive power, most easily illustrated by coalitions with other parties. We thus conceive of this characteristic of political actors as a variable called "the relative influence of labor in the cabinet," or in abbreviated form—*labor cabinet influence*.

Students of various orientations have seen purposive class action as an important factor in the shaping of social policy. This includes policy analysts like Lowi (1964), Groth (1971, p. 175), and Piven and Cloward (1971), stratification theorists like Goldthorpe (1970) and Lenski (1966), and a wide range of welfare-state critics, the most prominent being Titmuss (1966, p. 383). More systematic cross-national tests of the relative importance of labor parties for redistributive policies have had inconclusive results. After controlling for economic development, both Jackman (1972, p. 169) and Wilensky (1976, p. 30) find various measures of the political power of the working class unrelated to cross-sectional variations in social security expenditures. Similar results are found in the existing longitudinal studies of Sweden, Norway, and the United Kingdom (Peters, 1972, p. 283; Klingman, 1973, p. 167). On the other hand, with an improved measure of redistribution Hewitt (1977) finds socialist party strength consistently related to the dependent variable, even after controlling for economic development or economic growth. The lack of longitudinal data supporting the labor party hypothesis is one of the factors that makes Hewitt's conclusions tentative, something he is quite aware of (see also Heclo, 1970, p. 415; Parkin, 1971, p. 106).

Political parties gain access to positions of power in democratic societies with different degrees of support in electoral and legislative bodies. We see the *strength of the winning coalition* as a form of potential power built into the political structure of our population (Vanhanen, 1972, p. 389), and this variable is explicitly brought into our empirical analysis of the redistributive intents of cabinets. How this power will be used vis-a-vis vertical redistribution of income can only be predicted from knowledge about *who* has access to it. We can thus formulate an hypothesis about *interaction* effects: *stronger winning coalitions are more likely to redistribute income in favor of the disadvantaged than weaker coalitions, to the degree that they are influenced by labor parties*.

One of the most commonly mentioned constraints on policy makers is *policy itself*, which, in the form of a preceding policy tradition (expressed and acted upon by administrators and politicians), would limit the scope of policy change to *marginal* adjustments from year to year (Heclo and Wildavsky, 1974, pp. 25–26). One of the most commonly observed correlates of social security expenditures, ever since the pioneering efforts of Aaron (1967), has been an index of social insurance program experience.[6] Wilensky recently (1975, p. 25) found that the age of the social security system (logged) and a demographic variable (population over 65) mediated the effects of economic development on social security expenditures. He also offers what seems to be the most plausible interpretation to date[7] of the predictive power of the age of the social security system: it is seen as the result of the politics of bureaucracy (incremental budgeting) (Wilensky, 1975, pp. 10–16). The incrementalist hypothesis is taken into consideration in our longitudinal study by *limiting ourselves to an explanation of variations in the rate of redistributive change*. This decision is also justified on the basis of an examination of changes in income distribution and redistribution (1920-1970). In the countries under study the *level* of redistribution has been relatively stable over time, in comparison with relatively frequent year-to-year changes in the rate of redistributive change (Björn, 1976, ch. 2).

The major competing hypotheses concerning the causes of policy development refer to the relative importance of political and economic variables (see Jackman, 1974, for a review of the literature). Having specified the political variables to be included, we now have to consider *what* economic variables could arguably be related to income redistribution in our population. Since our concern will be with yearly changes in rates of redistribution over a 45-year period, we would be interested in the possible impact of an economic variable on *short-run* fluctuations in our dependent variable. For our time period, changes in the *level* of economic development are minor and more long-run than those in the rate of economic growth. Some writers have also suggested that the rate of economic growth is an intervening variable between the level of economic development and redistribution e.g., Cutright's (1967) elaboration of some of Lenski's hypotheses. By explicitly bringing in economic growth as an explanatory variable, we would consequently capture both the long- and short-run dynamics of the economic environment.

RESEARCH DESIGN

To examine the relative importance of labor cabinet influence and economic growth as determinants of redistribution in capitalist democracies, we chose a longitudinal research design. We have already indicated the lack of such designs; furthermore, a cross-sectional approach to our stated theoretical problem is inherently problematic. Given the small number of societies in our population (13) and the lack of propositional theory, we are likely to have a large number of theoretically relevant variables relative to the number of cases. This presents obvious statistical problems which are compounded by the difficulty of quantifying many of the variables (Taira and Kilby, 1969).

In sampling cases for our longitudinal design, one major constraint was *the number of observations* we could make of labor cabinets. Only in four of the 13 societies in our population have labor parties been in executive power for at least half the time period (1920–1970): Sweden, Norway, Denmark, and the United Kingdom. Among these four, Denmark has experienced the largest and Norway the smallest number of shifts from labor to nonlabor cabinets. This chapter will present data for three of these countries: Sweden, Denmark, and the United Kingdom.

Even though we do not strictly test any hypotheses about the influence of societal characteristics on the politics of redistribution in this chapter, we also present data for two societies which differ in many respects from the other three. The United States has within its party system developed a labor party only in one sense of the concept as used here, that is, by being electorally and organizationally linked to the working class. Particularly since these links are weaker in the United States than in other democracies (except Canada) (see Alford, 1963), we would *ceteris paribus* expect the relative influence of labor parties vs. economic growth to be smaller in the United States. The large number of variables at the societal level that could account for any differences between the United States and the other three societies makes any direct comparison less valuable, however. A better case for comparison with the United States is Australia, another Anglo-American democracy with a similar historical experience (Alford, 1963). Australia differs from the United States in one critical aspect: the existence of a labor party on the European model. Unfortunately, the Australian case presents us with a lack of labor cabinets within our period of investigation.

For each of the five societies data analysis is carried out separately for the time periods before and after World War II. There are strong reasons for assuming that the war had an impact on our dependent and independent variables, including in the latter case unmeasured societal characteristics.[8]

MEASUREMENT OF VARIABLES

Redistribution

Until recently (Hewitt, 1977, p. 453) cross-national studies of income redistribution have used social security expenditures as a proportion of Gross National Product (GNP) as an indicator of the dependent variable (Cutright, 1967; Wilensky, 1975, 1976; Björn, 1976, ch. 7).[9] This operationalization of redistribution can be criticized on several grounds. Most importantly, it is based on the questionable assumption that social security programs constitute a unidimensional empirical phenomenon (Rys, 1966, p. 243). At a minimum, it is necessary to distinguish between two kinds of redistributive effects from social security expenditures: *horizontal* and *vertical* (see Paukert, 1968, p. 426, for a similar critique). The former refers to the transfer of income between individuals, or collectivities, with differing "needs," such as those based on age or family size. Level of income is not considered. In contrast, vertical redistribution of income refers to transfers between income categories (or other hierarchically arranged social categories, such as social classes). It would seem that this distinction is particularly important in a political perspective, since one can roughly characterize the goal achieved by horizontal redistribution as "security," and that by vertical redistribution as "equality."

The distinction between *public assistance* and *social insurance* programs (Marshall, 1970, pp. 99–100; Merriam, 1969, pp. 55–57) captures many of the differences between vertical and horizontal redistribution. The former includes those programs financed from general revenues and distributed[10] through means or/needs tests. The latter programs have, to some degree, preserved the link between contributions and benefits found in private insurance.[11] Our measure of vertical redistribution of income is *the proportion of GNP spent on public assistance programs.*[12] To control for changes in the *horizontal* and *initial* distributions of income we statistically controlled (see next section) for two variables: *the proportion of the population over 65* and *the proportion of unemployed in the nonagricultural labor force.* Furthermore, we controlled for major changes in the distribution of initial (factor) incomes by excluding from our analysis the years of World War II (1940–1945).[13]

Data for our dependent variable were collected yearly (1920-1939 and 1946-1970) from numerous sources, typically the statistical yearbooks of the country in question. A short introduction to these sources is found in Appendix 1.

Labor Cabinet Influence

The influence of labor in cabinets was generally operationalized as the *presence/absence of a labor party in executive power.* In Sweden and Denmark where we find instances of coalition governments between labor and nonlabor parties, a continuous measure of labor influence was also used: *the proportion of the cabinet from labor.* Given the difficulties of weighting the relative influence of different ministers within the cabinet, the relative size of the labor (Social Democratic) parties was assigned on the basis of the make-up of the legislature. (See Appendix 1 for data sources.)

In the United States the Democratic Party cannot be considered a labor

party in terms of its ideology; yet its constituency is predominantly working class. As the Presidency is the locus of executive power in the United
States we characterized each presidential administration as either Democratic or Republican, depending on the party affiliation of the President.
Our units of analysis are not presidential administrations, however, since
the power relationship between the President and Congress changes with
each new Congress. We decided to use *Congresses* as units of analysis in
the U.S. case, as they seem to provide the closest equivalent to cabinets
in parliamentary systems. We measured labor cabinet influence over the
period of cabinet tenure, which varies in length across and within countries. In coding a particular cabinet in a given year (X), the general rule
was followed to assign year X + 1 to cabinets that were in power only
after the first of July of year X. In this way, we allow for a *half-year lag* in
the impact of the acquisition of executive power on redistributive policies.

Strength of Winning Coalition

In parliamentary systems the relative strength of the winning coalition
is defined by the *support given the cabinet in the legislature*. This was
operationalized as the proportion of the lower chamber in parliament
made up of members of cabinet parties. This operationalization need not
correspond to the *actual* support given the cabinet in parliament, since
informal coalitions across party lines do occur. Only for Denmark have
we been able to find data on such informal coalitions (see Appendix 1). On
the other hand, we do know that party discipline in the Swedish case has
been sufficiently strong to make our formal measure of cabinet support a
good approximation of actual support (Nyman, 1966).

For the United States we used a measure of cabinet support (presidential support) which for each Congress indicates the *percentage of legislators from the President's party*. Other measures of presidential support
have been developed by the *Congressional Quarterly* for part of the postwar period, but our chosen measure had substantially the same predictive
power for these years (Björn, 1976, pp. 203–204).

Rate of Economic Growth

The most suitable GNP concept for the assignment of economic growth
rates is GNP at *constant prices*. The lack of data does not allow us to use
the same base year for all countries, or even subperiods within some
countries (for data sources, see Appendix 1). This is regrettable since the
earlier the base year, the more inflated the growth rate (Maddison, 1964,
pp. 194–195). Differences in rates of population growth were controlled
for by the use of a per capita measure of GNP at constant prices.

DATA ANALYSIS TECHNIQUES

Our data analysis can be divided into two stages: first, the application of the two control variables to our dependent variable; and second, the analysis of the determinants of the rate of redistributive change. Whereas in the first stage we relied soley upon *statistical* forms of data analysis, in the second we included a modified contingency table analysis as well.

Using separate unstandardized regression equations before and after World War II we removed the influence of the proportion of the population over age 65 and the proportion of unemployed in the labor force on the level of redistribution (public assistance expenditures/GNP). The rate of redistributive change for year *i* was then operationalized as the *percent change* in the residual from year *i—1* to year *i*. To decrease the sensitivity of measures of percent change to low "initial" (i—1) values (Van Meter, 1974, p. 128), the constant from each regression equation was added to the residual value.

Standardized regressions were one of the techniques used to determine the relative importance of our independent variables for the rate of redistributive change within our six subpopulations (three societies before and after the war). Two unusual features of our regression analysis need to be pointed out. The small number of cases (as low as six) relative to the number of independent variables artifically inflates the multiple correlation coefficient (R^2), and we therefore have chosen to present this coefficient before and after (R^2), a *correction for shrinkage* (McNemar, 1969, p. 206). A second less common feature of our regression analysis is our use of significance tests. Since we are not interested in making a statistical generalization to a population larger than those studied (our six subpopulations), we make use of the level of significance as an indicator of *measurement error* (Galtung, 1967, pp. 358–389). Rather than using an arbitrary level of significance, we indicate in our regression tables the *exact probability that our regression coefficients are different from zero.*

The small number of cases in our subpopulations prevents us from using available techniques for the detection (or correction) of autocorrelation.[14] On the other hand, we have reason to believe that autocorrelation problems of the time-trend type are minimized by our use of change scores for our dependent (and economic growth) variable.

We will also present data analysis below using a modified contingency table analysis, which we chose to call "tabular" analysis. It is similar to contingency tables in that it literally holds variables constant in an examination of the actual values on included variables. Modifications of the contingency table technique were necessary due to the simple fact that we usually did not have enough cases to fill all the cells of a table. Consequently, we could not use conventional statistics to summarize the relationships involved. What our tabular analysis tries to achieve is an analysis closer to the logic of qualitative historical-comparative research. We will present the actual values for each cabinet on the dependent and independent variables, and try to assess to what degree "historical accident" has given our cabinets values which allow us to use the logic of experimental design. Being a case-by-case analysis our tabular analysis suffers from all problems associated with such unaggregated (nonstatistical) estimates. Nevertheless, the nature of our data is such that no one data analysis technique could fully explicate the interrelationships involved. Consequently, a two-pronged form of data analysis, using different assumptions about the comparability of societal phenomena, would seem to be one solution. (For a similar approach, see Wilensky, 1976, p. 27).

RESULTS

The tabular and regression analyses for each country are presented together. This will allow the reader to make a closer comparison of the two types of data analysis. To further facilitate this comparison we will use the first country (Sweden) to exhibit the more unusual features of tabular analysis.

Sweden

In Tables 1 and 2 we present the pre- and postwar Swedish cabinets,[15] giving for each cabinet the rate of redistributive change and (within parentheses) the rate of economic growth. Each cabinet is numbered consecutively within the three categories of our labor cabinet influence variable: Social Democratic cabinet (SD), Social Democratic coalition (SD +), and bourgeois cabinet (B). The interested reader will find a further identification of all cabinets for all countries by year, prime minister, party composition, and cabinet support in the legislature in Appendix 2. On the horizontal axis of the table we have dichotomized our cabinet support in the legislature variable, whereas a dichotomization of our economic growth variable is presented in a more unusual fashion. Our rule of presentation was to place, within each cell, cabinets with a *high* rate of economic growth at the *upper* end of the cell, and those with a low rate of growth at the lower end. When applicable, we have also ranked the cabinets within the two categories using the same rule of presentation.

In terms of the particular table design in Tables 1 and 2 we can now test our labor cabinet hypothesis by comparing rates of redistributive change of cabinets going down by columns, and at the same time holding the rate

Table 1. Rate of change in redistribution for Swedish prewar cabinets,
by labor influence and support in legislature
(rate of economic growth within parentheses).[a]

Labor Influence	High Cabinet Support				Low Cabinet Support		
Social Democratic (SD) Cabinet[b]					3:	1.0%	(2.6%)
Social Democratic (SD+) Coalition	1:	-2.3%	(5.9%)				
	2:	4.3%	(5.0%)				
	mean:	1.0%					
Bourgeois Cabinet[c] (B)					4:	-4.0%	(8.1%)
					2:	-5.0%	(2.9%)
					3:	1.3%	(2.8%)
					5:	.7%	(-3.8%)
					mean:	-1.0%[d]	

[a]Dichotomization on this variable indicated by placement in cell, where an upper position indicates a higher growth rate.

[b]SD_1 and SD_2 are excluded due to lack of data on redistributive change and economic growth.

[c]B_1 was excluded due to lack of data on its rate of economic growth.

[d]B_2, B_3, and B_5.

of economic growth constant by only comparing cabinets found at the same end of the cells in our table. Such a columnar comparison can thus mean a comparison of labor cabinets (Social Democratic cabinets and Social Democratic coalitions) with nonlabor (bourgeois) cabinets *or* a comparison between "pure" Social Democratic cabinets and Social Democratic coalitions. If the latter is carried out, we are also interested in the degree of Social Democratic influence in the coalition, as measured by our continuous measure of labor influence.

A test of our interaction hypothesis concerning the relationship between redistribution and the multiplicative effects of labor cabinet influence and cabinet support in the legislature was carried out differently. Ideally we would first like to compare the redistributive records of cabinets horizontally, thus holding labor cabinet influence and economic

Table 2. Rate of change in redistribution for Swedish postwar cabinets,
. by labor influence and support in legislature
(rate of economic growth within parentheses).[a]

Labor Influence		High Cabinet Support			Low Cabinet Support	
Social		4:	-13.5%	(6.6%)	7:	-4.0%	(4.7%)
Democratic	(SD)	9:	15.0%	(4.0%)			
			———				
Cabinet		mean:	.8%				
					5:	8.0%	(2.8%)
					6:	-1.7%	(2.8%)
					8:	.3%	(2.7%)
						———	
					mean:	2.2%[b]	

Social						
Democratic	(SD+)	3:	3.4%	(3.2%)
Coalition		4:	10.0%	(3.2%)
			———	
		mean:	6.7%	

[a]Dichotomization on this variable indicated by placement in cell, where an upper position indicates a higher growth rate.

[b]SD_5, SD_6, and SD_8.

growth constant while varying cabinet support. Second, we would move on to a test of the interaction hypothesis by comparing the relationships determined in the first step across categories of the labor cabinet influence variable. In practice, the lack of data allowed us to make a full test of this hypothesis in only one case as we shall soon discover. Tests of our economic growth hypothesis were quite straightforward as they simply involved columnar comparisons between cabinets at upper and lower ends of cells.

To summarize the comparisons made between cabinets to test our three hypotheses about the determinants of redistribution, we have for each country constructed a table like the one found below for Sweden (Table 3). One discovers easily that a large number of logically possible comparisons could not be carried out. For our first (labor cabinet influence) hypothesis, for example, we found no comparisons between Social Democratic coalitions and bourgeois cabinets for the prewar period, and more critically, no comparisons between "pure" Social Democratic cabinets and Social Democratic coalitions for the post-war period.

In our regression analysis for Sweden (Table 4), we relied solely on our continuous measure of labor cabinet influence in the postwar years as we

Table 3. Cabinets compared to determine the relationship between three independent variables and the rate of redistributive change: Sweden, 1920-1939 and 1946-1970.

Time Period	Independent Variable	Cabinets Compared[a]	Relationship
Prewar	Labor Cabinet Influence	*Labour vs. Nonlabor:* SD_3 vs. B_2, B_3, B_5	+
		Among Soc. Dem. Coalitions:[b] $SD+_2$ vs. $SD+_1$	+
	Labor Cabinet Influence X Cabinet Support in Leg.	none	no test
	Rate of Economic Growth	B_4 vs. B_2, B_3, B_5	–
Postwar	Labor Cabinet Influence	*Among Soc. Dem. Coalitions:*[c] $SD+_4$ vs. $SD+_3$	+
	Labor Cabinet Influence X Cabinet Support in Leg.	*Among Labor Cabinets:* SD_4, SD_9 vs. SD_7	+
	Rate of Economic Growth	SD_7 vs. SD_5, SD_6, SD_8	–

[a]An identification of all Swedish cabinets by year, prime minister, party composition and cabinet support in legislature is found in Appendix 2.

[b]The coalitions differ in their degree of cabinet support in legislature with $SD+_2$ at 80 percent and $SD+_3$ 70 percent.

[c]The coalitions differ in their degree of cabinet support in legislature with $SD+_4$ at 90 percent and $SD+_3$ at 80 percent.

had no cases of bourgeois cabinets for this time period. If we compare the results of the two types of analysis, we find only one candidate for a contradictory finding: the labor cabinet influence hypothesis in the post-war years. However, this need not be a necessary contradiction, since we have already pointed out the incomplete test of the hypothesis in the tabular form of analysis. We therefore put more faith in our regression analysis for this variable.

Our substantive conclusions with regard to the relative importance of labor cabinet influence and economic growth for the Swedish case clearly favor the importance of the political variable. In prewar years labor cabinet influence is the only variable predicting redistributive change in the hypothesized direction. After the war only the interactive effects of labor cabinet influence and cabinet support produce positive rates of redistributive change.

Table 4. Standardized regression coefficients for
selected independent variables with rates of redistributive
change as dependent variable:
Sweden, 1920-1939 and 1946-1970.[a]

Equation Number	Time Period	Presence/ Absence of Soc. Dem. Cab.	Rate of Economic Growth	Percent Soc. Dem. Cab. X Cab. Support in Leg.	R^2	$\hat{R}^{2b}$	n
1.	Prewar	.57 (.23)	-.46 (.32)		.39	.27	7
2.	Prewar	.74 (.77)	-.47 (.41)	-.17 (.94)	.39	.08	7
		% Soc. Dem. Cab.					
3.	Postwar	-.08 (.83)	-.60 (.16)		.39	.29	8
4.	Postwar	-.43 (.10)	-.78 (.01)	.82 (.02)	.88	.83	8

[a]Figures within parentheses refer to the exact levels of significance, in this case the probabilities of observing the regression coefficients under the null-hypothesis that the true regression coefficients are zero.

[b]R^2 corrected for shrinkage.

Denmark

As Denmark has had a history of coalition governments very similar to that of Sweden, the tabular analysis presents similar problems. Tables 5, 6, and 7 present our tabular analyses for pre- and postwar Denmark,[16] and the lack of data for the earlier period should be as clear as its relative wealth for the postwar years. In the earlier period our tabular analysis can only yield one hypothesis test, and a weak one at that, for the labor cabinet influence hypothesis.

In summing up the results of the three different types of comparisons made to test our labor cabinet influence hypothesis, we conclude that the results vary considerably across types of comparisons. Our hypothesis received *moderate* support in a comparison between labor and nonlabor cabinets, and *no support* in a comparison among labor coalitions. A comparison between "pure" labor cabinets and labor coalitions gave intermediary or *mixed* levels of support to our hypothesis.

Our best tabular analysis test of the interaction hypothesis is found for postwar Denmark. The negative relationship for Social Democratic coalitions and the opposite sign for bourgeois cabinets refutes the interaction hypothesis, even though the positive sign for "pure" labor cabinets could indicate an overall zero rather than a negative relationship between our interaction term and redistribution.

Table 5. Rate of change in redistribution for Danish prewar cabinets,
by labor influence and support in legislature
(rate of economic growth within parentheses).[a]

Labor Influence	High Cabinet Support			Low Cabinet Support		
Social Democratic (SD) Cabinet				1:	-5.3%	(-.3%)
Social Democratic (SD+) Coalition[b]	3:	- 4.3%	(1.8%)			
	2:	10.3%	(1.7%)			
	1:	.5%	(1.1%)			
	mean:	2.3%				
Bourgeois Cabinet (B)				1:	5.5%	(7.9%)
				2:	-2.0%	(3.0%)
				mean:	1.8%	

[a]Dichotomization on this variable indicated by placement in cell, where an upper position indicates a higher growth rate.

[b]SD+$_4$ is excluded due to unavailable data on redistributive change.

Table 6. Rate of change in redistribution for Danish postwar cabinets,
by labor influence and support in legislature
(rate of economic growth within parentheses).[a]

Labor Influence	High Cabinet Support			Low Cabinet Support		
Social Democratic (SD) Cabinet	4:	18.5%	(3.8%)	2:	- 3%	(4.5%)
				5:	14.0%	(3.3%)
				mean:	6.9%	
	3:	- 3.0%	(1.1%)			
Social Democratic (SD+) Coalition	6:	9.2%	(4.4%)	5:	37.3%	(3.9%)
Bourgeois Cabinet (B)	5:	5.3%	(4.5%)	3:	- 4.0%	(3.5%)
	4:	13.0%	(1.7%)			

[a]Dichotomization on this variable indicated by placement in cell, where an upper position indicates a higher growth rate.

Table 7. Cabinets compared to determine the relationship between
three independent variables and the rate of redistributive change:
Denmark, 1920-1929 and 1946-1970.

Time Period	Independent Variable	Cabinets Compared[a]	Relationship
Prewar	Labor Cabinet Influence	*Among Soc. Dem. Coalitions:*[b] $SD+_2$, $SD+_3$ vs. $SD+_1$	+
	Labor Cabinet Influence X		
	Cabinet Support in Leg.	None	no test
	Rate of Economic Growth	None	no test
Postwar	Labor Cabinet Influence	*Labor vs. Non-Labor:*	
		SD_4 vs. B_5	+
		SD_3 vs. B_4	−
		$SD+_6$ vs. B_5	+
		SD_2, SD_5 vs. B_3	+
		$SD+_5$ vs. B_3	+
		Soc. Dem. Cabinets vs. Soc. Dem. Coalitions:	
		SD_4 vs. $SD+_6$	+
		SD_2, SD_5 vs. $SD+_5$	−
		Among Soc. Dem. Coalitions:[c]	
		$SD+_6$ vs. $SD+_5$	−
	Labor Cabinet Influence X Cabinet Support in Leg.	*Among Labor Cabinets:*	
		SD_4 vs. SD_2, SD_5	+
		Among Soc. Dem. Coalitions:	
		$SD+_6$ vs. $SD+_5$	−
		Among Non-Labor Cabinets:	
		B_5 vs. B_3	+
	Rate of Economic Growth	SD_4 vs. SD_3	+
		B_5 vs. B_4	−

[a] An identification of all Danish cabinets by year, prime minister, party composition, and cabinet support in legislature is found in Appendix 2.

[b] The coalitions differ in their degree of cabinet support in legislature with $SD+_2$ at 82 percent, $SD+_3$ at 83 percent, and $SD+_1$ at 70 percent.

[c] The coalitions differ in their degree of cabinet support in legislature with $SD+_6$ at 88 percent and $SD+_5$ at 75 percent.

Table 8. Standardized regression coefficients for
selected independent variables with rates of redistributive
change as dependent variable:
Denmark, 1920-1939 and 1946-1970.[a]

Equation Number	Time Period	Presence/ Absence of Soc. Dem. Cab.	Rate of Economic Growth	Percent Soc. Dem. Cab. X Cab. Support in Leg.	R^2	$\hat{R}^{2b}$	n
5	Prewar	.61 (.51)	.91 (.34)		.31	.14	6
6		3.97 (.32)	.66 (.50)	-3.61 (.37)	.58	.30	6
7	Postwar	.30 (.47)	.10 (.81)		.10	.00	9
8	Postwar	2.55 (.39)	-.15 (.78)	-2.27 (.44)	.21	.00	9

[a] Figures within parentheses refer to the exact levels of significance, in this case the probabilities of observing the regression coefficients under the null-hypothesis that the true regression coefficients are zero.

[b] R^2 corrected for shrinkage.

In our regression analysis for Denmark (Table 8), we relied solely on the dichotomous measure of labor cabinet influence, something which makes only the labor vs. nonlabor cabinet comparisons relevant when juxtaposing our two methodologies. We find no contradictions in the findings for this or any other included variable. It should be pointed out that this conclusion is based on an evaluation of the relationship between the rate of economic growth and redistribution as indistinguishable from zero, given the high levels of significance as well as low coefficients.

Substantively we conclude that in Denmark the rate of economic growth seems to be the variable with the largest effect on redistribution before the war, even though the labor cabinet influence variable also has a positive relationship to our dependent variable. After World War II only labor cabinet influence has a (weak) positive relationship to redistributive change, while the economic growth variable is unrelated to the dependent variable. Interaction effects in the opposite direction to that hypothesized are observed for both time periods.

The United Kingdom

Tables 9, 10, and 11 present our tabular analysis for the British case, and an analysis which is simplified by the lack of coalition governments including the Labour party. In the period before World War II the number of possible comparisons to test our hypotheses are few relative to the later period. For example, our interaction hypothesis can only be given a partial test before the war (with negative results), whereas a full test can be

Table 9. Rate of change in redistribution for British prewar cabinets, by Labour influence and support in legislature (rate of economic growth within parentheses).[a]

Labour Influence	High Cabinet Support			Low Cabinet Support		
Labour (L) Cabinet				1:	-22.8%	(2.2%)
				2:	3.2%	(-1.0%)
Conservative (C) Cabinet	4:	1.2%	(3.7%)	2:	-21.2%	(7.2%)
	5:	39.2%	(2.0%)			
	1:	283.0%	(1.9%)			
	3:	-4.4%	(1.6%)			
	mean:	105.9%				

[a]Dichotomization on this variable indicated by placement in cell, where an upper position indicates a higher growth rate.

Table 10. Rate of change in redistribution for British postwar cabinets, by Labour influence and support in legislature (rate of economic growth within parentheses).[a]

Labour Influence	High Cabinet Support			Low Cabinet Support		
Labour (L) Cabinet	5:	14.2%	(2.1%)	4:	8.8%	(2.0%)
	3:	43.1%	(1.0%)			
Conservative (C) Cabinet	9:	2.9%	(2.8%)	7:	-3.3%	(3.7%)
	8:	-9.6%	(1.4%)	6:	2.4%	(1.3%)
				10:	3.9%	(1.0%)
				mean:	3.2%	

[a]Dichotomization on this variable indicated by placement in cell, where an upper position indicates a higher growth rate.

Table 11. Cabinets compared to determine the relationship between three independent variables and the rate of redistributive change: the United Kingdom, 1920-1939 and 1946-1970.

Time Period	Independent Variable	Cabinets Compared[a]	Relationship
Prewar	Labour Cabinet Influence	L_1 vs. C_2	0
	Labour Cabinet Influence X		
	Cabinet Support in Leg.	*Among Non-Labour Cabinets:*	
		C_4 vs. C_2	+
	Rate of Economic Growth	L_1 vs. L_2	−
		C_4 vs. C_1, C_3, C_5	−
Postwar	Labour Cabinet Influence	L_5 vs. C_9	+
		L_3 vs. C_8	+
		L_4 vs. C_7	+
	Labour Cabinet Influence X		
	Cabinet Support in Leg.	*Among Labour Cabinets:*	
		L_5 vs. L_4	+
		Among Non-Labour Cabinets:	
		C_9 vs. C_7	+
		C_8 vs. C_6, C_{10}	−
	Rate of Economic Growth	L_5 vs. L_3	−
		C_9 vs. C_8	+
		C_7 vs. C_6, C_{10}	−

[a]An identification of all British cabinets by year, prime minister, party composition and cabinet support in legislature is found in Appendix 2.

had in the postwar years (with weak positive results). When comparing our tabular analysis to our regression analysis (Table 12), only one possible contradiction is at hand before the war: labor cabinet influence, with a negative beta-weight and a zero relationship in our tabular analysis. Since the latter is only based on one comparison and the exact level of significance for the Labour cabinet influence variable is moderately high, this seeming contradiction can be easily reconciled.

After the war one possible contradiction can be observed for the economic growth variable, which has a zero relationship in regression analysis and a weak negative one in tabular analysis. There seems to be no easy methodological explanation for this contradiction, but fortunately this has no major impact on our substantive conclusions concerning the relative importance of the variables.

Our prewar data analysis of the British case indicates that none of the

Table 12. Standardized regression coefficients for
selected independent variables with rates of redistributive
change as dependent variable:
the United Kingdom, 1920-1939 and 1946-1970.[a]

Equation Number	Time Period	Presence/ Absence of Labour Cab.	Rate of Economic Growth	Presence/Absence of Labour Cabinet X Cabinet Support in Leg.	R^2	R^{2b}	n
9	Prewar	-.55 (.34)	-.47 (.41)		.25	.10	7
10	Prewar	-.06 (.98)	-.53 (.47)	-.55 (.83)	.27	.00	7
11	Postwar	.57 (.19)	-.16 (.69)		.41	.31	8
12	Postwar	-4.70 (.05)	-.07 (.77)	5.34 (.04)	.83	.76	8

[a]Figures within parentheses refer to the exact level of significance, in this case the probabilities of observing the regression coefficients under the null-hypothesis that the true regression coefficients are zero.

[b]R^2 corrected for shrinkage.

three included variables is related to redistributive change in the hypothesized direction. After World War II political variables can better predict changes in the rate of redistribution than can economic variables. Labour cabinets have been more successful than Conservative cabinets in changing government expenditures in favor of the disadvantaged, irrespective of the rate of economic growth. Labour cabinets have also, better than the Conservatives, taken advantage of stronger cabinet support in Parliament, regardless of the rate of economic growth.

Australia

When we turn to the Australian case we are faced with a serious shortage of labor cabinets falling within our period of investigation. As can be seen in Appendix 2, there is only one labor cabinet before the war, and after the war one of the two A.L.P. (Australian Labor Party) cabinets (Chifley's in 1946) has to be excluded from our analysis because of our use of change-scores for the dependent variable. This lack of cases severely affects the value of our tabular analysis with its case-by-case approach; consequently we have chosen only to present the results of our regression analysis (Table 13). In neither the pre- nor the postwar period do we find extreme values of redistributive change which could hamper the regression analysis.

In pre-war years the labor cabinet influence variable has a larger positive relationship to redistribution than the rate of economic growth. The addition of our interaction term does not add predictive power in the expected direction. After World War II our regression analysis indicates

Table 13. Standardized regression coefficients for
selected independent variables with rates of redistributive
change as dependent variable:
Australia, 1920-1939 and 1946-1970.[a]

Equation Number	Time Period	Presence/ Absence of Labor Cab.	Rate of Economic Growth	Presence/Absence of Labour Cab. X Cab. Support in Leg.	R^2	$\hat{R}^{2}$[b]	n
13	Prewar	.99 (.09)	.77 (.14)		.69	.61	6
14	Prewar	3.92 (.05)	.72 (.07)	-3.01 (.09)	.95	.92	6
15	Postwar	-.05 (.89)	-.35 (.38)		.14	.03	10
16	Postwar	-.14 (.93)	-.35 (.41)	.83 (.96)	.14	.00	10

[a]Figures within parentheses refer to the exact levels of significance, in this case the probabilities of observing the regression coefficients under the null-hypothesis that the true regression coefficients are zero.

[b]R^2 corrected for shrinkage.

Table 14. Rate of change in redistribution for U.S. prewar Congresses,
by party of President and presidential support
(rate of economic growth within parentheses).[a]

Party of President		High Presidential Support			Low Presidential Support	
Democrat	Roosevelt	(4):	41.7%	(.4%)		
	Roosevelt	(3):	4.6%	(.2%)		
		mean:	-18.6%			
	Roosevelt	(2):	-10.4%	(-.3%)		
	Roosevelt	(1):	885.9%	(-1.5%)		
		mean:	437.8%			

Republican				Coolidge	(1):	1.8% (1.0%)
				Coolidge	(2):	-10.1% (.8%)
				Hoover	(1):	20.0% (.7%)
				Harding	(2):	- 1% (-.1%)
					mean:	- 7.1%
	Harding	(1):	-11.0%(-4.7%)	Hoover	(2):	-4.7%(-1.2%)

[a]Dichotomization on this variable indicated by placement in cell, where an upper position indicates a higher growth rate.

that none of the independent variables has predictive power in the expected direction. The accuracy with which we can estimate the size of the beta weights for our labor cabinet influence variable and interaction term is low, and we cannot reject the null-hypothesis that these coefficients are zero. By comparison, the exact level of significance is lower, though moderate for the rate of economic growth, and this variable is possibly negatively related to redistribution.

The United States

An inspection of the redistributive record of the United States cabinets (Congresses) before the war in Table 14 shows that Roosevelt's first Congress has by far the highest rate of growth in our dependent variable. This value can to a large extent be considered a "wild" one, since it "benefits" greatly from the problems of measuring change from a low-base value. Public expenditures in the United States experienced a veritable revolution in the first year of Roosevelt's Presidency. The remaining Democratic Congresses in the period have an average rate of redistributive change lower than that for the Republican Congresses of the 1920s. Nevertheless,

Table 15. Rate of change in redistribution for U.S. postwar congresses,
by party of President and presidential support
(rate of economic growth within parentheses).[a]

Party of President		High Presidential Support			Low Presidential Support		
Democrat	Johnson	(3): 8.7%	(1.8%)	Truman	(4): - 9.2%	(1.6%)
	Johnson	(2): 1.7%	(1.7%)			
		mean: 5.2%				
	Johnson	(1): .5%	(1.6%)			
	Kennedy	: .1%	(1.5%)			
	Truman	(3): 3.3%	(1.4%)	Truman	(2): .0%	(1.4%)
		mean: 1.3%				
Republican				Nixon	: 10.8%	(1.8%)
				Eisenhower	(2): -5.0%	(1.6%)
					mean: 2.9%	
				Eisenhower	(1): 3.1%	(1.5%)
				Eisenhower	(4): -4.6%	(1.5%)
				Eisenhower	(3): 6.3%	(1.5%)
					mean: 1.6%	

[a]Dichotomization on this variable indicated by placement in cell, where an upper position indicates a higher growth rate.

even with considerable allowance for measurement error for Roosevelt (1) there is little doubt that the labor cabinet influence is positively related to the dependent variable in the prewar year.

A comparison of our tabular (Table 16) and regression (Table 17) analyses indicates no contradictory findings in the pre-war period. After the war the lack of accuracy in estimating the beta weights leaves some room for varying judgments as to the direction of the relationships. Given

Table 16. Congresses compared to determine the relationship between three independent variables and the rate of redistributive change: the United States, 1920-1939 and 1946-1970.

Time Period	Independent Variable	Congresses Compared[a]	Relationship
Prewar	Labor Cabinet Influence	Roosevelt (1), (2) vs. Harding (1)	+
	Labor Cabinet Influence X Cabinet Support in Leg.	*Among Rep. Congresses.* Harding (1) vs. Hoover (2)	–
	Rate of Economic Growth	Roosevelt (3), (4) vs. Roosevelt (1), (2)	–
		Coolidge (1), (2), Hoover (1) and Harding (2) vs. Hoover (2)	–
Postwar	Labor Cabinet Influence	Truman (4) vs. Nixon and Eisenhower (2)	–
		Truman (2) vs. Eisenhower (1), (3), (4)	–
	Labor Cabinet Influence X Cabinet Support in Leg.	*Among Dem. Congresses:* Johnson (2), (3) vs. Truman (4)	+
		Johnson (1), Kennedy, Truman (3) vs. Truman (2)	+
	Rate of Economic Growth	Johnson (2), (3) vs. Johnson (1), Kennedy, Truman (3)	+
		Truman (4) vs. Truman (2)	–
		Nixon and Eisenhower (2) vs. Eisenhower (1), (3), (4)	+

[a]An identification of all U.S. Congresses by year, President, party affiliation, and cabinet support in legislature (presidential support) is found in Appendix 2.

Table 17. Standardized regression coefficients for
selected independent variables with rates of redistributive
change as dependent variable:
the United States, 1920-1939 and 1946-1970.[a]

Equation Number	Time Period	Presence/ Absence of Dem. Cab.	Rate of Economic Growth	Presence/Absence of Dem. Cab. X Cab. Support in Leg.	$\hat{R}^2$	R^{2b}	n
17	Prewar	.43 (.24)	-.25 (.48)		.23	.13	10
18	Prewar	2.69 (.21)	-.32 (.37)	-2.29 (.28)	.37	.19	10
19	Postwar	-.08 (.80)	.27 (.41)		.09	.00	12
20	Postwar	-.96 (.50)	.16 (.67)	.90 (.52)	.13	.00	12

[a]Figures within parentheses refer to the exact levels of significance, in this case the probabilities of observing the regression coefficients under the null-hypothesis that the true regression coefficients are zero.

[b]R^2 corrected for shrinkage.

the very minor variation in rates of economic growth (a low of 1.4 and a high of 1.8 percent), it would seem reasonable to completely exclude this variable as a possible predictor of the rate of redistributive change in the postwar United States. The zero or weak negative regression coefficient for labor cabinet influence can both without much difficulty be reconciled with the negative relationship found in our tabular analysis. The latter excludes all Democratic Congresses with strong legislative support, and their redistributive record is better than that of any of the weaker Congresses, Republican or Democratic. The lack of variation in legislative support for the Republican Congresses after the war allows only a partial test of the interaction hypothesis, and the true beta weight could be either zero or weakly positive. Substantively, we conclude that our labor cabinet influence variable is the only variable which is positively related to redistribution in the prewar United States. For this period the economic growth variable and our interaction term (more strongly) are both negatively related to the dependent variable. After World War II none of our predictors have any success in accounting for variations in the rate of redistribution.

Summary
An examination of the relative importance of labor cabinet influence, singly or interacting with cabinet support in the legislature, vs. the rate of economic growth for redistributive change in five nations indicates that the political variables generally had more predictive power than the

economic one. Only in one (prewar Denmark) of the ten cases (pre- and postwar Sweden, Denmark, the United Kingdom, Australia, and the United States) was economic growth a better predictor of rates of redistributive change, and in three other cases (prewar United Kingdom, postwar Australia, and postwar United States), none of the included predictors had an effect on the dependent variable. The additive effects of labor cabinet influence predominate in four cases (prewar Sweden, postwar Denmark, prewar Australia, and prewar United States), whereas its joint effects with cabinet support in the legislature are most important in Sweden and the United Kingdom after the war. These conclusions are unaffected by whether one chooses a regression or modified contingency table analysis of the data.

DISCUSSION

Our longitudinal study of income redistribution in five democratic capitalist societies adds needed empirical weight to the argument that the purposive action of political parties is a more important predictor than the growth of the economy. The lack of quantitative studies of the politics of redistribution over time has commonly been explained by problems of data availability (Hewitt, 1977, p. 462), but it is our hope that this study has demonstrated the possibility of using existing data from a number of sources to better grasp the nature of an important historical process.

Whereas our political variables in general seem to be better predictors of the rate of redistributive change than the rate of economic growth, we face larger difficulties in trying to account for the pattern of findings across societies. There is nothing in the existing historical literature to indicate why prewar Denmark should differ in its redistributive politics from its best case for comparison, prewar Sweden. Similarly, we find it difficult to account for the failure of all predictors in Australia and the United States after the war, as compared with the relative success of our labor cabinet influence variable in the prewar years. One hypothesis worth further testing is one that would see the relationship between labor cabinet influence and redistribution as a *spurious* one in both prewar United States and Australia. The cabinets that account for the observed effects of labor cabinet influence on redistribution both coincide with the Great Depression. The link between this historical event and relief expansion has been described in detail for the United States, but no similar accounts are available for Australia. Piven and Cloward (1971) argue that *collective violence* is the political mechanism that accounts for expansion of relief, as seen in the rapid contraction of welfare after violence has subsided. For Australia we only know that the Great Depression was as severe as in the United States (Schedvin, 1970, p. 340), whereas the other countries studied here experienced less severe dislocations (Lewis, 1969, p. 61). In Australia, as in the United States, the Depression was a time for the rise of a large number of social movements, and there are indications of associated mass violence in urban centers (Jupp, 1968, p.14).

The changing relationship between our political variables and redistribution in the United Kingdom can be interpreted as the result of a major realignment in British politics affecting the strength of the Labour Party. World War II marks the disappearance of the Liberal Party as a contender for executive power, and a rise in the allegiance of the working class to the Labour Party (Butler and Stokes, 1971, p. 14). The existence of a weak labor party in a three-party system can thus be offered as a plausible explanation for the lack of predictive power of our labor cabinet influence variable before the war. A systematic cross-national test of the relationship between realignments, labor cabinet influence, and redistribution is, of course, beyond the scope of the present study. Nevertheless, we have indicated with our study that the feasibility of such an empirical test should no longer be an issue.

APPENDIX 1

MAJOR DATA SOURCES FOR DEPENDENT AND INDEPENDENT VARIABLES

While a complete listing of all data sources employed is given elsewhere (Björn, 1976, Appendices 4-6, 10-12), the following is a summary by country and variable of the most important sources used.

Sweden

Dependent Variable: data on poor relief, unemployment programs, pensions, and family housing supplements were mainly from the *Statistical Yearbook* (Sweden, various years). Important supplements were: Elmér (1960), Sweden (*Socialdepartementet,* 1969), and Welinder (1945).
Labor Cabinet Influence and Cabinet Support in Legislature: Nyman (1966), Rudebeck (1968), and Council on Foreign Relations (various years).
Rate of Economic Growth: Maddison (1964), Bentzel (1952), and OECD (1972).

Denmark

Dependent Variable: data on poor relief, unemployment programs, and pensions were mainly from the *Statistical Yearbooks* (Denmark, various years). Other sources include: Germany (1938), ILO's *Cost of Social Security* (various years), and France (1937).

Labor Cabinet Influence: Council of Foreign Relations (various years), and Westergard-Andersen (1966).

Cabinet Support in Legislature: Damgaard (1969).

Rate of Economic Growth: Maddison (1964), and the *Statistical Yearbooks* (Denmark, various years).

The United Kingdom

Dependent Variable: Data on poor relief, pensions, and unemployment programs were from: Peacock and Wiseman (1961), *Annual Abstract* (Great Britain, various years) and Mitchell (1962).

Labor Cabinet Support and Cabinet Support in Legislature: Butler and Freeman (1963), Thomson (1965), and Mackie and Rose (1974).

Rate of Economic Growth: Peacock and Wiseman (1961), Mitchell and Jones (1971), and *Annual Abstract* (Great Britain, various years).

Australia

Dependent Variable: Data on State poor relief (Commonwealth) pensions, Commonwealth maternity allowances, unemployment benefits (Commonwealth and State) and (Commonwealth) sickness benefits were from various annual editions of the *Yearbook* (Australia, various years). Schedvin (1970) was also used for estimates of unemployment relief for the 1930s.

Labor Cabinet Influence and Cabinet Support in Parliament: Australia (1972), Council on Foreign Relations (various years) and Jupp (1964, p. 9).

Rate of Economic Growth: Australia (1972).

United States

Dependent Variable: Merriam and Skolnick (1968, p. 189) have collected an expenditure series ("Public Aid") which corresponds to our definition of public assistance programs. This series consists of two broad categories: public assistance programs (Federal Categorical Assistance and General Assistance by state and local governments) and "other Public Aid" (includes: emergency relief and work relief, work training programs, etc.).

Labor Cabinet Influence and Presidential Support: Congressional Quarterly (1971).

Rate of Economic Growth: U.S. Bureau of Economic Analysis (1973, p. 107).

APPENDIX 2

SWEDISH, DANISH, BRITISH, U.S., AND AUSTRALIAN CABINETS, 1920 – 1939 and 1946 – 1970

Table 18. Swedish cabinets (1920-1939, 1946-1970) by year, Prime Minister, party composition,[a] and cabinet support in legislature.

Year	Prime Minister	Party Composition	Cabinet Support in Legislature[b] (Percentage)
1920	Branting	Social Democratic (SD_1)	36
1921	DeGeer/von Sydow	Nonpartisan (B_1)	n.a. [c]
1922	Branting	Social Democratic (SD_2)	43
1923-1924	Trygger	Conservative (Right) (B_2)	27
1925	Branting	Social Democratic (SD_3)	45
1926-1928	Ekman	Liberal (B_3)	14
1929	Lindman	Conservative (B_4)	32
1930-1932	Ekman	Liberal (B_5)	30
1933-1935	Hansson	Social Democratic and Center (Agrarian) ($SDD+_1$)	61
1936-1939	Hansson	Same ($SD+_2$)	64
1946-1948	Erlander	Social Democratic (SD_4)	50
1949-1951	Erlander	Same (SD_5)	49
1952-1956	Erlander	Social Democratic and Center (Agrarian) ($SD+_3$)	58
1957	Erlander	Same ($SD+_4$)	54
1958-1960	Erlander	Social Democratic (SD_6)	48
1961-1964	Erlander	Same (SD_7)	49
1965-1968	Erlander	Same (SD_8)	49
1969-1970	Palme	Same (SD_9)	54

Sources: Nyman (1966); Council on Foreign Relations (various years).

[a]In the case of coalitions, the party of the Prime Minister is mentioned first.

[b]The proportion of the lower chamber made up of members of cabinet parties.

[c]Not applicable.

Table 19. Danish cabinets (1920-1939, 1946-1970) by year,
Prime Minister, party composition,[a] and cabinet support in legislature.

Year	Prime Minister	Party Composition	Cabinet Support in Legislature[b] (Percentage)
1920-1923	Nergaard	Liberal (and Conservative) (B_1)	35
1924-1926	Stauning	Social Democratic (and Radical) (SD_1)	37
1927-1928	Madsen-Mygdal	Liberal (and Conservative) (B_2)	32
1929-1932	Stauning	Social Democratic and Radical ($SD+_1$)	52
1933-1935	Stauning	Same ($SD+_2$)	51
1936-1938	Stauning	Same ($SD+_3$)	55
1939	Stauning	Same ($SD+_4$)	52
1946-1947	Kristensen	Liberal (Conservative and Radical) (B_3)	26
1948-1950	Hedtoft	Social Democratic (SD_2)	39
1951-1953	Eriksen	Liberal and Conservative (B_4)	50
1954-1956	Hedtoft/Hansen	Social Democratic (and Radical) (SD_3)	43
1957-1959	Hansen/Kampmann	Social Democratic, Radical, and Justice Parties ($SD+_5$)	40
1960-1964	Kampmann/Krag	Social Democratic and Radical ($SD+_6$)	44
1965-1966	Krag	Social Democratic (SD_4)	44
1967	Krag	Social Democratic (and Socialist) (SD_5)	40
1968-1970	Baunsgaard	Radical, Liberal, and Conservative (B_5)	56

Source: Damgaard (1969, pp. 30-59).

[a]In the case of coalitions, the party of the Prime Minister is mentioned first. Parties included within parentheses are not members of the cabinet, but support the cabinet in Parliament.

[b]The proportion of the lower chamber supporting the cabinet.

Table 20. British cabinets (1920-1939, 1946-1970) by year,
Prime Minister, party composition, and cabinet support in legislature.

Year	Prime Minister	Party Composition	Cabinet Support in Legislature[a] (Percentage)
1920-1922	Lloyd George	Liberal and Conservative (C_1)	66
1923	Baldwin	Conservative (C_2)	56
1924	MacDonald	Labor (L_1)	31
1925-1928	Baldwin	Conservative (C_3)	68
1929-1931	MacDonald	Labour (L_2)	47
1932-1935	MacDonald	Conservative and Liberal (C_4)[b]	90
1936-1939	Baldwin/Chamberlain	Conservative (C_5)	70
1946-1949	Attlee	Labour (L_3)	61
1950-1951	Attlee	Labour (L_4)	50
1952-1954	Churchill	Conservative (C_6)	51
1955-1959	Eden/Macmillan	Conservative (C_7)	55
1960-1964	Macmillan	Conservative (C_8)	58
1965	Douglas-Home	Conservative (C_9)	50
1966-1969	Wilson	Labour (L_5)	58
1970	Heath	Conservative (C_{10})	52

Sources: Thomson (1965); Mackie and Rose (1974); Butler and Freeman (1963).

[a]Proportion of Lower House from cabinet parties.

[b]This was formally a National Government under the Prime Ministership of Labour Leader MacDonald. In fact, MacDonald's acquisition of cabinet leadership was followed by his party going into the opposition. There are strong reasons to regard MacDonald as a figurehead for a Conservative cabinet (Thomson, 1965).

Table 21. U.S. Congresses (1920-1939, 1946-1970) by year, President,
party affiliation, and presidential support.

Year	President	Party Affiliation	Presidential Support (Percentage) [a]
1920	Wilson	Democrat	47
1921-1922	Harding (1)	Republican	65
1923-1924	Harding (2)		54
1925-1926	Coolidge (1)	Republican	58
1927-1928	Coolidge (2)		53
1929-1930	Hoover (1)	Republican	61
1931-1932	Hoover (2)		51
1933-1934	Roosevelt (1)	Democrat	67
1935-1936	Roosevelt (2)		73
1937-1938	Roosevelt (3)		78
1939	Roosevelt (4)		66
1946	Truman (1)	Democrat	56
1947-1948	Truman (2)		48
1949-1950	Truman (3)		58
1951-1952	Truman (4)		53
1953-1954	Eisenhower (1)	Republican	51
1955-1956	Eisenhower (2)		49
1957-1958	Eisenhower (3)		47
1959-1960	Eisenhower (4)		35
1961-1962	Kennedy	Democrat	63
1963-1964	Johnson (1)	Democrat	62
1965-1966	Johnson (2)		68
1967-1968	Johnson (3)		61
1969-1970	Nixon	Republican	43

Source: Congressional Quarterly (1971).

[a]The percent of legislators (both houses) from the President's party.

Table 22. Australian cabinets (1920-1939, 1946-1970) by year,
Prime Minister, party composition, and cabinet support in legislature.

Year	Prime Minister	Party Composition	Cabinet Support in Legislature[a] (Percentage)
1920-1922	Hughes	Nationalist	56
1923-1929	Bruce-Page	Nationalist and Country Parties	56
1930-1931	Scullin	Australian Labor Party	61
1932-1934	Lyons	United Australia Party	51
1935-1937	Lyons	same	64
1938-1939	Lyons	same	61
1939	Page	same	61
1946	Chifley	Australian Labor Party	66
1947-1949	Chifley	same	61
1950	Menzies	Liberal and Country Parties	61
1951-1955	Menzies	same	57
1956-1958	Menzies	same	60
1959-1961	Menzies	same	62
1962-1963	Menzies	same	50
1964-1965	Menzies	same	58
1966	Holt	same	66
1967-1969	McEwen/Gorton	same	65
1970	Gorton	same	53

Sources: For years: Australia, Commonwealth Bureau of Census and Statistics (various years). For Prime Ministers: Australia, Commonwealth Bureau of Census and Statistics (various years). For party composition: Council on Foreign Relations (various years).

[a]Proportion of legislators in lower house from cabinet parties.

FOOTNOTES

*I would like to thank the members of my dissertation committee for help in clarifying many of the ideas presented in this paper, with special thanks to Professor Duncan MacRae, Jr. I am, of course, solely responsible for any errors or misinterpretations. In addition I would like to thank the Campus Grants Committee at the University of Michigan-Dearborn for computer funds.

1. This is the most commonly used predictor of social security expenditures. A review of existing studies also shows that one of the most commonly used political variables, democratization, does not have a uniform relationship to the dependent variable.

2. Other students of social policy have concerned themselves with the different paths in the early development of policy, most successfully Rimlinger (1966).

3. In so doing we control for the impact of the timing of democratization, a variable used by many researchers.

4. Excluded nations are: (West) Germany, Italy, Japan, Austria, and Switzerland (which excluded women from suffrage in national elections until 1971).

5. The period of World War II (1940—1945) is not included.

6. This index is based on a categorization of social insurance programs into five types, and the types conform to a Guttman scale pattern.

7. Taira and Kilby (1969) have given a similar, but vaguer, interpretation in referring to the variable as an "historical-institutional" factor. Otto Eckstein gives the popular empirical index a different light by suggesting that it "in part represents permanent philosophical differences in attitudes toward state intervention in economic affairs; the more interventionist countries began social welfare programs early" (quoted in Taira and Kilby, 1966, pp. 152–153). It thus seems that Eckstein sees the index of social insurance program experience mainly as a reflection of different economic policies, a usage which is akin to Jackman's (1972) use of the index as an indicator of "policy efforts at greater equality."

8. Our dependent variable is affected by major changes in the distribution of factor incomes (see footnote 13, below) during the war years, which makes a comparison of pre- and postwar levels of vertical redistribution difficult. Furthermore, an analysis of the relationship between public assistance expenditures and the two control variables indicate substantial differences even in the direction of the relationships when comparisons were made across the two time periods (Björn, 1976, ch. 7). Preliminary data analysis also indicated substantial differences in the interrelationships among independent variables as between the pre- and postwar years. The impact of World War II on the development of social policy and its politics is a well-known theme in the literature (Marshall, 1970, ch. 6).

9. Hewitt (1977) uses as a measure of redistribution the proportion of social "service" (security) expenditures raised from direct taxes. This operationalization is a decided improvement over previously used measures, but is nevertheless open to the criticisms below.

10. Hewitt's (1977) proposed measure of redistribution does not take the expenditure side into account. That is, he includes in his measure those expenditures that, while disproportionately taken from the rich, are administered as universal (proportional) or pre-rich benefits.

11. The redistributive flows typically associated with social insurance programs equalize incomes between generations. A large proportion of U.S. social security recipients with low incomes are old people receiving pension benefits after themselves having contributed to the system in previous years. To capture this complex process it would be necessary to use a *lifetime* income concept as, among others, Castellino (1971) has pointed out.

12. Their means of finance and administration make public assistance programs more redistributive than any other used grouping of policies. (For evidence, see Nicholson, 1971, p. 82.) Nevertheless, it could be argued that the chosen measure is a better indicator of *partial* (in favor of a specific income group, the poor) than *global* redistribution (reduction of overall income inequality).

13. A review of the literature on changes in income distribution (factor incomes) in four countries (Sweden, Denmark, the U.K., and the U.S.) from 1920 to 1970 indicated that the largest changes occurred during the war years (Björn, 1976, p. 94).

14. The most commonly used test statistic is that developed by Durbin-Watson, and their tables for this statistic do not go below a sample size of fifteen. Our "sample" size varies from six to nine cabinets.

15. The first three cabinets in the 1920s (two Social Democratic and one civil service cabinet) are excluded due to insufficient data on one or more variables.

16. No data on public assistance expenditures were available for the last Social Democratic coalition designated SD $+_4$ in Appendix 2 listing all Danish cabinets.

REFERENCES

Aaron, Henry J. (1967) "Social Security: International Comparisons." Pages 13–48 in Otto Eckstein (ed.), *Studies in the Economics of Income Maintenance*. Washington, DC: Brookings Institution.

Alford, Robert R. (1963) *Party and Society*. Chicago: Rand McNally.

Australia. Commonwealth Bureau of Census and Statistics (various years) *Official Yearbook of the Commonwealth of Australia*. Canberra: Government Printer.

Bendix, Reinhard (1969) *Nationbuilding and Citizenship*. Garden City, NY: Doubleday-Anchor.

Bentzel, Ragnar (1952) *Inkomst*fördelningen i Sverige (The Distribution of Income in Sweden). Stockholm: Industrins Utredningsinstitut.

Björn, Lars (1976) *Labor Parties and the Redistribution of Income in Capitalist Democracies*. Unpublished Ph.D. dissertation. Chapel Hill: University of North Carolina.

Butler, David and Jerome Freeman (1963) *British Political Facts*. New York: St. Martin's Press.

––––– and Donald Stokes (1971) *Political Change in Britain*. New York: St. Martin's Press.

Carrier, John and Ian Kendall (1973) "Social Policy and Social Change-Explanations of the Developement of Social Policy." *Journal of Social Policy* 2 (July): 209–224.

Castellino, Onorato (1971) "Income Redistribution Through Old-Age Pensions: Problems of Its Definition and Measurement." *Public Finance* 3: 457–471.

Congressional Quarterly (1971) *Almanac*. Washington, DC: Congressional Quarterly Service.

Council on Foreign Relations (various years) *Political Handbook of the World*. New Haven: Yale University Press.

Crouch, Colin (1975) "The Drive for Equality: Experience of Incomes Policy in Britain." Pages 215–242 in Leon N. Lindberg *et al.* (eds.), *Stress and Contradiction in Modern Capitalism*. Lexington, MA.: D.C. Heath.

Cutright, Phillips (1967) "Income Redistribution: A Cross-National Analysis." *Social Forces* 46 (December): 180–190.

Damgaard, Erik (1969) "The Parliamentary Basis of Danish Governments: The Patterns of Coalition Formation." *Scandinavian Political Studies* 4: 30–57.

Denmark. Statistiske Departement (various years) *Statistisk Aarbog (annuaire Statistique)*. Copenhagen: Statistiske Departement.

Elmér, Åke (1960) *Folkpensioneringen i Sverige* (Old Age Pensions in Sweden). Lund: Gleerup. (With an English summary.)

France. Bureau de la Statistique (1937) *Annuaire Statistique 1936*. Paris: Bureau de la Statistique.

Galtung, Johan (1967) *Theory and Methods of Social Research*. London: Allen and Unwin.

Germany. Statistisches Amt (1938) *Statistisches Jahrbuch für das Deutsche Reich*. Berlin: Statistiches Amt.

Goldthorpe, John (1970) "Social Stratification in Industrial Society." Pages 452–464 in Celia S. Heller (ed.), *Structured Social Inequality*. New York: Macmillan.

Great Britain. Central Statistical Office (various years) *Annual Abstract of Statistics*. London: Her Majesty's Stationery Office.

Groth, Alexander J. (1971) *Comparative Politics, A Distributive Approach*. New York: Macmillan.

Heclo, H. Hugh (1970) *Politics and Social Policy*. Unpublished Ph.D. dissertation. New Haven: Yale University.

––––– and Aaron Wildavsky (1974) *The Private Government of Public Money*. Berkeley: University of California Press.

Hewitt, Christopher (1977) "The Effect of Political Democracy and Social Democracy on Equality in Industrial Societies: A Cross-National Comparison." *American Sociological Review* 42 (June): 450–464.

International Labour Organization (various years). *The Cost of Social Security*. Geneva. ILO.

Jackman, Robert W. (1972) *Politics and Social Equality: A Cross-National Analysis*. Unpublished Ph.D. dissertation. Madison: University of Wisconsin.

———— (1974) "Political Democracy and Social Equality: A Comparative Analysis." *American Sociological Review* 39 (February): 29–45.

Jupp, James (1964) *Australian Party Politics*. Melbourne: Melbourne University Press.

———— (1968) *Australian Party Politics*, 2nd ed. Melbourne: Melbourne University Press.

Klingman, Charles D. (1973) *The Development of Social Policy: A Longitudinal Analysis of Social Expenditures and Their Impacts in the U.K., France, and Sweden*. Unpublished Ph.D. dissertation. East Lansing: Michigan State University.

Korpi, Walter (1971) "Working Class Communism in Western Europe: Rational or Nonrational." *American Sociological Review* 36 (December): 971–984.

Lenski, Gerhard (1966) *Power and Privilege*. New York: McGraw-Hill.

———— (1970) *Human Societies*. New York: McGraw-Hill.

Lewis, W. Arthur (1969) *Economic Survey, 1919—1939*. New York: Harper and Row.

Lipset, Seymour M. and Stein Rokkan (1967) "Introduction." Pages 1–64 in S.M. Lipset and S. Rokkan (eds.), *Party Systems and Voter Alignments*. New York: Free Press.

Lowi, Theodore J. (1964) "American Business, Public Policy, Case Studies, and Political Theory." *World Politics* 16 (July): 677–715.

Mackie, Thomas T. and Richard Rose (1974) *The International Almanac of Electoral History*. London: Macmillan.

Maddison, Angus (1964) *Economic Growth in the West*. New York: The Twentieth Century Fund.

Marshall, T.H. (1970) *Social Policy*, 3rd ed. London: Hutchinson University Library.

Martin, Andrew (1975) "Is Democratic Control of Capitalist Economies Possible?" Pages 13–56 in Leon N. Lindberg *et al.* (ed.), *Stress and Contradiction in Modern Capitalism*. Lexington, MA: D.C. Heath.

McNemar, Quinn (1969) *Psychological Statistics*, 4th ed. New York: Wiley.

Merriam, Ida C. (1969) "Income Maintenance: Social Insurance and Public Assistance." Pages 55–82 in Shirley Jenkins (ed.), *Social Security in International Perspective*. New York: Columbia University Press.

———— and Alfred M. Skolnik (1968) *Social Welfare Expenditures Under Public Programs in the United States, 1929–1966*. U.S. Department of Health, Education, and Welfare, Social Security Administration. Office of Research and Statistics, Research Report No. 25, Washington, DC: Government Printing Office.

Mitchell, Brian R. and H. G. Jones (1971) *Second Abstract of British Historical Statistics*. Cambridge, MA: Cambridge University Press.

Moul, William B. (1974) "On Getting Nothing for Something." *Comparative Political Studies* 7 (July): 139–164.

Nicholson, J.L. (1974) "The Distribution and Redistribution of Income in the U.K." Pages 71–92 in Dorothy Wedderburn (ed.), *Poverty, Inequality, and Class Structure*. Cambridge, Eng.: Cambridge University Press.

Nyman, Olle (1966) *Parlamentarismen i Sverige* (Swedish Parliamentarism). Stockhom: Medborgarskolan.

OECD (1972) *Economic Survey:* Sweden. Paris: OECD

Parkin, Frank (1971) *Class, Inequality, and Political Order*. New York: Praeger.

Paukert, Felix (1968) "Social Security and Income Redistribution: A Comparative Study." *International Labour Review* 98 (November): 425–450.

Peacock, Alan T. and Jack Wiseman (1961) *The Growth of Public Expenditure in the U.K.* Princeton, NJ: Princeton University Press.

Peters, B. Guy (1972) "Public Policy, Socioeconomic Conditions, and the Political System." *Polity* 5 (Winter): 277–284.

Piven, Frances Fox and Richard A. Cloward (1971) *Regulating the Poor: The Functions of Public Welfare*. New York: Pantheon.

Rein, Martin and Peter Marris (1975) "Equality, Inflation, and Wage Control." Pages 199–214 in Leon N. Lindberg *et al.* (eds.), *Stress and Contradiction in Modern Capitalism*. Lexington, MA: D.C. Heath.

Rimlinger, Gaston V. (1966), "Welfare Policy and Economic Development: A Comparative Historical Perspective." *Journal of Economic History* 26 (December): 556–571.

Rudebeck, Lars (1968) "Det politiska systemet i Sverige" (The Swedish Political System). Pages 445–506 in Edmund Dahlström (ed.), *Svensk samhällsstruktur i sociologisk belysning*. Stockholm: Scandinavian University Books.

Rys, Vladimir (1966) "Comparative Studies of Social Security: Problems and Perspectives." *Bulletin of the International Social Security Association* (July-August): 242–268.

Schedvin, C.B. (1970) *Australia and the Great Depression*. Sydney: Sydney University Press.

Sweden. Statistiska Centralbyrån (various years) *Statistisk Årsbok för Sverige* (Annuaire Statistique). Stockholm: Statistiska Centralbyrån.

—— Socialdepartementet (1969) *Socialhjälpen i Län och Kommuner, 1967* Social Assistance in Counties and Communes, 1967). Stockholm: Socialdepartementet.

Taira, Koji and Peter Kilby (1969) "Differences in Social Security Development in Selected Countries," *Bulletin of the International Social Security Association* 22: 139–153.

Thomson, David (1965) *England in the Twentieth Century*. Baltimore: Penguin.

Titmuss, Richard M. (1966) "Social Welfare and the Act of Giving." Pages 377–392 in Erich Fromm (ed.), *Socialist Humanism*. Garden City, NY: Anchor Books.

U.S. Bureau of Economic Analysis (1973) *Long Term Economic Growth, 1860–1970*. Washington, DC: Government Printing Office.

Vanhanen, Tatu (1972) "Distribution of Power in the 1960s." *Comparative Political Studies* 4 (January): 387–405.

Van Meter, Donald S. (1974) "Alternative Methods of Measuring Change: What Difference Does It Make?" *Political Methodology* 1 (Fall): 125–140.

Welinder, Carsten (1945) *Socialpolitikens Ekonomiska Verkningar* (The Economic Effects of Social Policy) Stockholm: Statens Offentliga Utredningar (14).

Westergård Andersen, Harald (1966) *Dansk politik-i går og i dag 1920–66* (Danish Politics—Today and Yesterday 1920–1966). Aalborg: Fremads Kursbøger.

Wilensky, Harold L. (1975) *The Welfare State and Equality*. Berkeley: University of California Press.

—— (1976) *The New Corporatism, Centralization, and the Welfare State*. Beverly Hills, CA: Sage.

RELIGION AND POLITICS IN THREE NORTHWEST EUROPEAN DEMOCRACIES*

John D. Stephens

INTRODUCTION

Religion has not been the divisive political issue in northwestern Europe that it has been and still is in southern Europe. This is particularly true of the period after the mobilization of the working class into politics which occurred in the latter part of the nineteenth century and the beginning of the twentieth century in all these countries. Today, the party systems of Scandinavia and Britain are class-based systems; both voter preference and issue struggles tend to be socioeconomically rooted. While the similarities of political life in these countries are striking, there are a few important differences which have attracted the attention of sociologists

Comparative Social Research, Vol. 2, pp. 129–157.
Volume 1 published as Comparative Studies in Sociology
Copyright © 1979 by JAI Press, Inc.
All rights of reproduction in any form reserved.
ISBN 0-89232-112-1

and political scientists. The role of religion in politics is one such difference. In this chapter, we will examine the role of religion in the political
life of three of these countries: Sweden, Norway, and Britain. Religion (or
the absence of it) has been identified as an exceptional aspect of the
politics of each of these countries. Sweden has been called "prototypi-
cal" of modernity partly because of the high degree of secularism in
Swedish social and political life (Tomasson, 1970). The relatively high
level of conservative voting in the British working class has been linked in
part to church attendance (Butler and Stokes, 1971). Finally, Norway is
an exception to the rule that homogeneous Protestant countries do not
develop explicitly religious parties of any significance. Using Sweden as a
baseline for comparison, these phenomena will be examined.

The logic of comparing these three countries is based on their similarity
in the Lipset/Rokkan "model for the generation of the European party
system" (Lipset and Rokkan, 1967, p. 33). All three of these countries
established national churches under state control at the time of the Reformation, are overwhelmingly Protestant, and had relatively smooth
transitions to democratic politics. Under these conditions, one would
expect minimal entry of religion into politics and predominance of class
divisions in political life. As Lipset (1960; 1970) points out, this combination of factors should lead to greater strength of the left and an absence of
religious parties. Only for Sweden, however, are all these expectations
completely borne out. The party systems of both Norway and Britain are
class-based (Rose and Urwin, 1969), but as noted Norway does have a
religious party and Britain's Labour Party has not had the electoral success in the working class of the other northern European Social Democratic parties. To elucidate such deviant cases, Rokkan suggests that one
compare two countries which are similar in the Lipset/Rokkan model but
differ in the phenomenon in question.

The model predicts that Sweden and Norway would have equivalent
party systems. According to Lipset and Rokkan, the critical difference
between Scandinavia and Britain is that in Britain the nation-building elite
(N) allied with "a cooperating body of established landowners controlling
a substantial share of the total primary production of the national territory" (L) whereas in Scandinavia the nation-builders "allied with a
cooperating body of urban commercial and industrial entrepreneurs controlling the advancing sectors of the national economy" (U) (Lipset and
Rokkan, 1967, p. 37). In both cases, N is allied with a nationally defined

*John D. Stephens is Assistant Professor of Sociology at Brown University. His research
has been on labor movements and political behavior in the industrial societies and he is the
author of the 1979 Macmillan book *The Transition from Capitalism to Socialism*. He is
currently working on a comparative study of class formation and class consciousness in
Britain and Sweden.

state church (C). They go on to explain that in Scandinavia and other "N-U" cases freeholding peasants rather than large landlords dominate the rural economy making an "N-L" alliance too weak. So in Scandinavia the opposition previous to the emergence of the industrial working class was composed of peasants (L), dissenting sects (D), and the periphery (P) while in Britain it was composed of urban commercial and industrial interests, dissenters, and the periphery (PDU). The labor movement emerged to form the third pole of the party system in both situations. In these Protestant countries, the dominant moderate Social Democratic parties adopted a secular religious position, but not a militant secularism characteristic of Catholic countries. Rather it was an apathetic secularism. In any case, the religious posture of the three political forces was (and is) quite similar in Britain and Scandinavia:

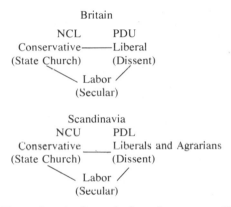

Britain
```
        NCL        PDU
  Conservative——————Liberal
  (State Church)      (Dissent)
              \  Labor  /
              (Secular)
```

Scandinavia
```
        NCU        PDL
  Conservative____Liberals and Agrarians
  (State Church)      (Dissent)
              \  Labor  /
              (Secular)
```

Thus one would predict quite similar relations between religion and politics making the differences that do exist all the more interesting. As Sweden is the ideal typical case, we will examine this case in detail, bringing in Norway and Britain where differences relevant to the religious differences noted exist.

SECULAR SWEDEN

All three countries are highly secularized but Sweden is clearly the most secular (see Table 1). Sweden is probably the most secular society in the world, with the possible exception of Denmark, whose religious history is similar to Sweden's. Only 4 or 5 percent of Swedes go to church on an average Sunday and only 2 percent in Stockholm (Tomasson, 1970, p. 61). And Sweden is the only country in northern Europe that has instituted "objective" teaching *about* (not in) religion in the public schools. However, most Swedes, even atheists, show little or no open hostility to the

Table 1. Belief in God in various countries.
(Percentages)

United States	98
Greece	96
Uruguay (cities)	89
Austria	85
Switzerland	84
Finland	83
West Germany	81
Netherlands	79
Great Britain	77
France	73
Norway	73
Sweden	60

(Figures are percentages who said they believed in God when queried by the Gallup organization in their respective countries.)

Source: New York Times, December 26, 1968.

Church and religion, in contrast to secularists in Catholic countries. Most are indifferent. Few even bother to withdraw from the State Church, an action which would save them the small Church tax they must otherwise pay.

Religion has ceased to be the primary source of moral conviction. A 1964 survey shows the following results to a question on religion and morality (Westerståhl, 1964, p. 287):

	Percent agreeing
There is no other basis for morality other than religion	16
For me, personally, religion is the only basis for morality, but I still believe that men can find another basis for morality	27
Morality does not need to be based on religion	41
None of the above	16

And religion now apparently has little connection to politics. Tomasson (1970, p. 98) points out that "religious beliefs or affiliations are irrelevant in politics. . . . Gunnar Hecksher, the leader of the Conservative Party (1961–1964) even conceded to being an atheist during a television interview in the early 1960s, though he claimed to be sympathetic to the Christian tradition."

At this point we are faced with two questions: (1) why is Sweden so secular?, and (2) why does religion enter politics so little in Sweden?

These are related but separate questions. For instance, on any measure of religiosity the United States appears as one of the most religious of industrial societies. Yet religion does not play the great role in American politics it does in the Netherlands, which has a larger proportion of nonbelievers. Some factors contribute to both variables, others have explanatory power for only one. An explanation of both factors, religiosity and religion in politics, will be attempted. Note that the arguments apply almost equally well to Norway and Britain.

Sweden is a homogeneous society in terms of religion. Some 95 percent of the population belong to the State Lutheran Church. Fourteen percent attend the free churches (dissenting or nonconformist sects), most of whom maintain their membership in the State Church and many of whom also attend the State Church. Homogeneity may tend to depress religiosity and certainly affects the entry of religion into political life. With the exception of Norway, explicitly religious parties do not appear in religiously homogeneous Protestant countries because there is no cleavage on which to mobilize support. The dissenting groups are too small to form the basis of a party. The Pentacostals did set up a Christian confessional party in the early sixties but have never elected a deputy to the riksdag (parliament). As in England and Norway, the dissenting sects have always been an important base of support for the Liberals, but have always been a minority element. Rose and Urwin (1969) classify the Liberals as a class-based party.

THE HISTORICAL BACKGROUND: REFORMATION, POLITICAL MOBILIZATION, AND SECULARIZATION

One element which unifies Sweden, Norway, and Britain in the Lipset/Rokkan model is the similar outcomes to the religious question at the time of the Reformation (pp. 36–37). They all developed "an ecclesiastical body [an Anglican or Lutheran State Church] established within the national territory and given a large measure of control over education." In the three cases, Roman Catholic elements have never been strong enough to create a political party as they did in Germany and the Netherlands.

Weber's Church-Sect distinction and hierocracy-Caesaro-papistic continuum are helpful here (1968, pp. 56, 456, 1158–1212). Both the Anglican and Lutheran Church are *churches,* with strong Caesaro-papistic tendencies. They are churches rather than sects in that membership is based on ritualized rites of passage (baptism, confirmation, etc.) rather than a community of believers ("no fellowship with the wicked"). In addition, churches claim to be universal, have formalized means of grace, and institutionalized charisma of office. On the other hand, unlike the supranational Catholic Church, the Lutheran and Anglican Churches have been subservient to political authority (the Casesaro-papistic tendency). This subservience keeps the church from playing an independent political role (Lipset, 1970, p. 119). However, as Weber noted, the exact political role of religion depends on historical circumstances. It turns out that different social and historical circumstances in the three countries are what explain the different roles of religion in political life. Before returning to a comparison of the countries, let us pin down the exact role of religion in Sweden through a look at Lutheran doctrine with regard to political authority and its development in Sweden.

Lutheran Doctrine and Politics

It will be shown here that the basic Lutheran doctrines support and legitimate existing regimes and that the Swedish Lutheran Church totally supported the monarchy and conservative forces, which helped to discredit it among the rising liberal middle class and socialist industrial working class. For Luther all phenomena were the work of God, including government:

> All who are not Christians belong to the kingdom of the world and are under law, since few believe and still fewer live a Christian life, do not resist the evil, and themselves do no evil, God has provided for non-Christians a different government outside the Christian estate and God's kingdom, and has subjected them to the sword, so that, even though they would do so, they cannot practice their wickedness, and that, if they do, they may not do it without fear nor in peace and prosperity (quoted in Sanders, 1964, p. 27).

Thus, government is a product of sin. God has established in both the worldly and spiritual kingdoms instruments of government, the church for Christian believers, and the state for nonbelievers. The rulers are ordained by God to do their calling: "For He gives to rulers so much property, honor, and power, to be possessed by them above others, in order that they may serve Him by administering this righteousness" (quoted in Sanders, 1964, p. 27). For Luther, the church is primary in the spiritual kingdom and the political order is the foremost controlling agency over man's temporal enterprises. The political ruler should not interfere with religion and ecclesiastical officials should not undertake political activity. So Luther himself was opposed to any caesaro-papism or papal caesarism. But his doctrines do have a Caesaro-papist *tendency* in that they legitimate any existing political order unless, of course, it actually interferes with religion. In addition, he believed that rebellions, such as the peasant rebellion in Germany, were the work of the devil.

Sanders (1964, p. 30) points out that "[c]onsequently, when a Christian supports political stability by rendering to the governing authorities, he strengthens the hand of God against his cosmic opponent."

Though Protestant sects do not participate in political life as institutions, their members may be motivated by their own moral religious beliefs to participate in politics. This is the case with the dissenting sects in both Scandinavia and Britain. The Lutheran, on the other hand, is not allowed this freedom because he is not allowed moral autonomy. Unlike the Catholic, the Lutheran was allowed to read the Bible, but unlike the Protestant sectarians he was not allowed to interpret it. Only a minister of the church could interpret the Bible and any relationship of the layman to God was mediated by him, since men are "blinded by the cunning of the devil" (Sanders, 1964).

Swedish Lutheranism and the Development of Democracy

Swedish Lutheranism corresponded more closely to Luther's own conceptions than did German Lutheranism, as the clergy in Sweden did maintain some limited autonomy. Catholicism never did gain a secure position in Sweden, and the first king of Sweden, Gustav Vasa, had little difficulty in convincing the *riksdag* to declare Sweden an Evangelical Lutheran State in 1544. He, like Henry VIII, was motivated, not by religious belief, but rather by his desire to create a strong centralized state. As Rokkan points out, the Reformation advanced the nation-building process not only by breaking up the supranational authority of Rome but also by standardizing language as a result of translation of the Bible into the vernacular.

Swedish Lutheranism developed in a highly scholastic, almost secular direction: "Becoming a bishop was considered a natural outcome for leading cultural figures. Until mid-century (nineteenth), in fact, appointments to high ecclesiastical office in Sweden were determined by scholarly and cultural attainment; piety and orthodoxy were not of major importance" (Tomasson, 1970, p. 71).

Under these conditions, pietism made considerable headway in Sweden in the eighteenth and nineteenth centuries. At first it was repressed by the state but then tolerated after 1858.

After 1870, Sweden entered a period of rapid economic development along with which came two political movements, first, liberalism supported by craftsmen, the urban radical middle class, and the dissenting groups and, then, socialism supported by the emerging industrial working class. The State Church, which had become increasingly orthodox after 1840, stood solidly behind the old order against these new movements. Not only did the Church support the Conservatives in accordance with

Lutheran doctrine: that doctrine and the Conservatives' Burkean conception of society have similar contents. Hessler summarizes the Church position:

> It is not the case . . . as the liberals sought to delude themselves and others into believing, that one's religious convictions were only a concern between his conscience and God. . . . The conscience is not divine, it is by nature egoistic and it is for this reason corrupted by sin. The individual person does not have the capacity to comprehend the divine revelation. The power was given to the Church. It is not the case as people sometimes make it out to be that the Church is an association of individual members. The Church is an organism with Christ himself at the head. All life in this organism came from Christ through the Word and the sacraments. Because of this the Church has its tremendous authority. And the task which the Church was entrusted is now to be the teacher of the people. . . . The divine will was made apparent through the Church, and one is to take this will into his own conscience (quoted in Tomasson, 1970, p. 71).

The State Church stood in irrevocable opposition to all of the popular movements; labor, liberalism, temperance, and the free churches until the first democratic breakthroughs. The force that the Church was aligned with, the Conservative Party, now only gets some 15 percent of the vote. Tomasson (1970, p. 72) argues that "(t)he fact that the Church committed itself so completely to the values of the old order during the early period of modernization is a crucial factor in the development of the far-reaching secularization that has occurred in . . . Sweden."

Norway

The difference between Norway and Sweden is linked to the timing of national-cultural unification and the first waves of political mobilization among the freeholding peasantry. As mentioned earlier, the Swedish monarchy consolidated itself and established the Lutheran Church in the sixteenth century. Norway, on the other hand, was under Danish domination from 1536 to 1814 and then under Swedish control until 1905. Danish rule was not harsh and the Norwegians gained domestic autonomy in the union with Sweden. However, this long period of foreign domination prevented Norway from developing a unified national culture. Rokkan (1967) argues that the Reformation aided nation building and cultural standardization (1) by allowing the nation-building elite to subordinate the church to the national interest by breaking off the transnational loyalty to Rome, (2) by establishing state control of education, and (3) by standardizing a language in a national territory. In the Swedish case, this was particularly important in eliminating the possibility that Skåne, that section of Sweden directly across the Öresund from Denmark, would develop into a culturally distinct periphery. Sweden took Skåne from Denmark in the seventeenth century. By the time of the first peasant mobilizations in the nineteenth century, Sweden long had been a unified and culturally and linguistically homogeneous nation-state. According to Rustow (1955, p. 26) the first modern Swedish party, the Ruralists, organized in 1867 around a program they kept "for decades to come: Reorganization of the country's defense, equalization of the tax burden, and strict economy with public funds." There was no theme of cultural protest.

Though Norway also became Lutheran in the sixteenth century, Danish domination prevented the Reformation from having some of its important effects on national cultural standardization. The urban patriciate, which was partly of Danish origin, inherited a state apparatus consolidated during the long period of bureaucratic rule and internal order under the Danish reign (Rokkan, 1967; Rokkan and Valen, 1974). But no language or cultural standardization had occurred. Danish had been the official language of the Church and State. Given the similarities of Danish and Norwegian, it was natural that the spoken language of the elite would evolve toward Danish. In the countryside, the peasant dialects, which not only differed from the elite dialect but also from each other, were more resistant to change. Consequently, when the Norwegian peasantry mobilized soon after the formation of the new Norwegian state (1814), their protests were cultural as well as economic. Like the Swedes, they wanted to shift taxation from the countryside to the urban areas. But they came to see the new national center as a general threat to their traditional way of life. According to Rokkan (1967, p. 371), "[t]he Norwegian peasantry was deeply divided by region and locality . . . they showed no concern for the survival of the nation as an integrated unit of action."

With mobilization occurring on the heels of the first attempts at nation-building such cultural differences were bound to become involved in politics. In Norway, this took its expression in the construction of a new language, a blend of the rural dialects, *landsmål* which was adopted by the movement of peripheral protest and contrasted from the evolved form of Dano-Norwegian spoken and written in the cities, *riksmål*. In addition, this peripheral countercultural movement was fed by not only the dissenting groups but also by a fundamentalist movement within the Lutheran Church that has little parallel in England or Sweden. Thus, the religious struggles in Norway were not only between the nonconformists and the State Church, but also between the revival movements and the government-appointed clergy within the State Church. This fundamentalist movement within the Lutheran Church is the key to the development of the Norwegian Christian confessional party *(Kristelig folkepartiet)*. Both this movement and nonconformism are strongest in the south and west of Norway, which are also the strongholds of the Christian party. And, indeed, today nonconformists and Lutheran fundamentalists vote disproportionately for the Christian party. Rokkan (1967, p. 437) argues that the political difference between the south/west and the north in Norway is due to the timing of political mobilization. In the south and west, the breakthrough came in the second half of the nineteenth century and found expression in cultural protest against the national center. In the north, the breakthrough came much later, with the introduction of universal suffrage, and was expressed in socioeconomic protest against local property owners and employers.

Precisely the same argument can be made for the Norwegian/Swedish differences. Sweden was a culturally unified nation long before the first waves of political mobilization. This difference also helps explain the greater secularism in Sweden as compared with Norway. We will elaborate on this point in our discussion of England.

As it turns out, the origin of the Norwegian Christian party does show some similarities to the continental Christian parties. In all cases the parties arise in countries which had some difficulties in nation-building. The claims to supranational authority on the part of the Catholic Church made the nation-building process more difficult in the continental countries, all of which are Catholic or have a substantial Catholic population.

What should be made clear here is that this Norwegian Lutheran fundamentalism is much more doctrinally similar to Protestant sectarianism than it is to the Lutheranism which we described in our historical discussion of Sweden. The fundamentalists fought for greater lay control of the church. This contradicted the authority of the church on questions of dogma interpretation and thus eliminated one crucial aspect of Lutheranism. Essentially, the Lutheran fundamentalist was asserting his right to moral autonomy, a direct personal relationship to God. This, in turn, undermined lay obedience to political as well as religious authorities.

Britain

Like the Swedish monarch, Henry VIII established a national church largely out of political motivations. As we emphasized earlier, the doctrinal similarities of the Lutheran and Anglican churches are striking, particularly with regard to their political implications. The historical relationship between religion and politics in the two situations differ in two important respects. First in Britain religious conflict in politics previous to the mobilization of the working class was much sharper and began much earlier. This is in part due to economic divisions in the politically mobilized sections of the English population. The nation-building elite allied with the landed aristocracy in England faced a mobilized opposition of urban and commercial interests allied with dissent. In Sweden, the nation-builders allied with the urban elite faced a mass of politically apathetic small farmers until the mid-nineteenth century. This difference is partly a consequence of the earlier industrialization of England and partly of the fact that the English economic opposition found it easier to mobilize since they were an urban, educated, well-to-do class as compared to the rural, uneducated Swedish farmers. Religious conflict in British politics was also fed by the overlay of ethnic/national differences among England, Scotland, Wales, and Ireland with religious differences. Religious struggle was particularly acute in England proper during the English Civil War. In the second half of the last century the religious conflict between the Liberals and the Conservatives over the role of the State Church among other matters cannot be said to be much more severe than similar conflicts in Sweden, but the Irish Home Rule issue introduced religious issues into English politics unknown in Swedish politics. As we shall see, the Irish issue affects the voting behavior of the small Catholic minority in Great Britain today.

The second historical difference between Britain and Sweden is central to some of the main hypotheses to be examined in this chapter. The English Conservatives, unlike their Swedish counterparts, took the initiative in extending the suffrage to substantial portions of the working class in the nineteenth century. They organized Conservative workingmen's associations and mobilized workers to support their party at the polls. Given the alliance of religious groups at that time, the Conservatives were most successful among Anglican workers. In Sweden, on the other hand, the Lutheran workers were mobilized almost entirely by the Social Democrats. This difference leads to several hypotheses concerning present-day religious and political behavior. First, following Tomasson's argument, the greater secularization of Sweden compared to Britain should be due to the greater openness of the Conservative Party toward the working class. In both countries, the Conservatives were allied with the State Church. In Sweden, the worker who merely aspired to incorporation in the national community found this aspiration opposed by the church's political ally. Thus the differences in religiosity between the two countries should be particularly sharp among State Church members, especially those who do not support the Conservatives. Second, the differences in the Conservatives' actions vis-à-vis the working class suggest that Butler and Stokes's (1971) two hypotheses about the sources of working class conservatism will be confirmed by comparison of data on Britain and Sweden. The greater conservatism of British workers should be partly explained by their greater religiosity. In addition, the greater conservatism of the present generation of British workers should also be due to the inheritance of Conservative preferences from the last generation of workers. Butler and Stokes show that these factors do explain differences within Britain. What remains to be seen is whether they explain the cross-national differences in political behavior.

Before proceeding to the data analysis, we should try to explain just why the British Conservatives reacted so differently from their Swedish counterparts. The key may be in the differences in the alliance structure laid out by Lipset and Rokkan. The Conservative coalition in England was an alliance of the nation-builders and the State Church with the old landholding class (an "NCL" case). In Sweden, the Conservative coalition consisted of the nation-builders, the State Church, and the urban commercial and industrial entrepreneurs (an "NCU" case). The presence of the urban bourgeoisie in the Swedish coalition may have been an important factor in explaining why the Swedish Conservatives opposed any attempt to incorporate the urban working class into the system. At first glance, the German case, like Britain an "NCL" case, seems to argue against this hypothesis since the German Conservatives were so opposed to the introduction of democratic government. On closer inspection, however, one does find similarities between the two cases.

Both Disraeli and Bismarck did promote the incorporation of the working class but in different ways. Bismarck tried to preempt the growing socialist movement by incorporating the working class economically through the development of welfare state policies. Disraeli aimed at the political incorporation of the working class through suffrage extension. Their alternatives were partly determined by the stage of development of the political movement within the working class. In Germany and in Sweden, the trade union movement and the Social Democratic Party developed very soon after industrialization, mobilizing the working class both in the unions and the party, leaving the Conservatives no chance to penetrate the working class. The German movement was sufficiently successful that Bismarck began to rely progressively more on repression rather than cooptation to control the working class movement. In England, trade union organization lagged somewhat behind industrialization and the development of the Labour Party came substantially later than in either Germany or Sweden, despite the fact that these two countries industrialized much later than Britain.

Thus until the Labour Party began to mobilize workers after the turn of the century, there was a political vacuum within the English working class. The Conservative party stepped in to fill this vacuum. This opportunity was not open to the German or Swedish conservatives. The Germans attempted to coopt the working class economically. The Swedes did nothing. A further factor influencing the differences is political competition in the economic elite. In Britain where the parliamentary government was already established and the landholders and bourgeoisie formed autonomous groups in political competition with one another, both parties attempted to strengthen their position vis-à-vis their opponent by mobilizing the middle class and the better-off sections of the working class to support them. In Germany, the state bureaucratic and landholding elite were in firm control of the government and were faced with, but not opposed by, a politically dependent industrial bourgeoisie. Because the Swedish countryside was dominated by small farming, the Swedish bureaucratic and urban commercial elite faced no strong economic opponents and could only lose their grip on the state through the extension of suffrage.

RELIGION AND POLITICS IN MODERN SWEDEN AND BRITAIN

Since further analysis of survey data can contribute no more to the explanation of the Norwegian phenomenon than Rokkan has already established, we now narrow our focus to a comparison of Britain and Sweden. One of the questions to be examined here, the sources of working class conservatism in England, the so-called Tory worker problem, has been the topic of considerable research. A brief review of this question might be in order here.

In British elections approximately one third of the working class votes for the Conservative Party. This phenomenon has attracted considerable academic and political attention for several reasons. It perplexed academics because this cross-voting was apparently unexplainable by important nonclass cleavages in the British electorate. Politically, it was important because the Conservative Party could only get into office with considerable working-class support. The British class structure is unusual in that around two thirds of the work force is engaged in nonagricultural manual work, compared to one half or less in other advanced industrial societies. In fact, the Conservative Party must get at least half of its voters from the working class in order to win an election. If the Labour Party did as well as the Swedish socialists in terms of working-class support, it would have won every election since the introduction of universal suffrage in 1918.

One explanation of the Tory worker problem is that the British working class is heavily influenced by the "deferential civic culture" of Britain (Almond and Verba, 1963; McKenzie and Silver, 1968; and especially Nordlinger, 1967). In addition to modern democratic norms, this political culture includes traditional norms of acquiescence to political authority and the legitimacy of the traditional ruling class. Certain sectors of the British working class are said to be exceptionally deferential and this is the source of working class conservatism. The errors in this line of thinking are numerous (Westergaard and Resler, 1975; Hill, 1978), but one weakness alone is sufficient to cast serious doubt on the argument. Deference is not very strongly associated with party preference. Hill (1978, p. 19) points out that ". . . only 23 percent of male working class voters could be characterized as 'deferentials' by McKenzie and Silver. . . . Just as damaging to any assumption of a close relationship between deferential attitudes and voting behavior is Nordlinger's finding that while 28 percent of working class Conservatives in his sample exhibited deferential attitudes, 13 percent of Labour voters exhibited these same attitudes." Considering the near tautological nature of the argument in the first place, this is weak evidence indeed.

Parkin (1967) and Butler and Stokes (1971) are on much stronger ground as they move away from psychological variables to social structural ones in their search for an explanation of the Tory worker problem. Butler and Stokes's theses were covered earlier. Parkin argues that all capitalist societies are characterized by a multiplicity of value systems though one value system, the dominant value system, which supports the status quo and traditional social values, is ordinarily by far the strongest. The most important counter, or subcultural, value system is the one centered in working-class institutions, such as trade unions and the Labour Party, and propagated by them. He hypothesizes that "Conservative support will be strongest where involvement in industrial subcultures is weakest—that is, among workers who are comparatively isolated from the normative system created under conditions of large-scale production, who are as a consequence correspondingly more exposed in their occupations to the dominant value system in capitalism" (1967, p. 285). He identifies the strongholds of the working class value system as larger factories and homogeneous working class residential communities. He also points out that housewives are more isolated from working class culture and thus vote more conservatively.

While the factors cited by both Butler and Stokes and Parkin do explain variations in voting behavior within the British working class, neither Butler and Stokes nor Parkin have solved the Tory worker problem. This problem can only be solved through comparative analysis. The statement that the working class in Britain is unusually conservative begs the question: Unusually conservative compared with whom? Obviously not compared with the British middle class. The point of comparison that is implied is the working class in other capitalist democracies in which politics are predominantly class-linked. The Tory worker problem can only be explained by comparison of voting patterns in Britain with those of another society where workers vote more leftist, such as in Sweden.

The Data

To examine this question as well as the question of Swedish secularism, we performed secondary analysis on two nationwide sample surveys. The British data are from Butler and Stokes's 1963 survey of the electorate of England, Scotland, and Wales (N = 2009). The Swedish data are from the Göteborg 1964 election study conducted under the direction of Bo Särlvik (N = 2849).[1] The only drawback the data have for the purposes of this study is that they underestimate the average difference in leftist voting in the two countries because the British survey overestimates Labour strength somewhat. The difference is 3 percent in the data compared to 5 percent for the entire postwar period and 6 percent for the sixties.

For most of this analysis, the party systems will be dichotomized along socialist/nonsocialist lines. The term Socialist will be used to indicate a Social Democratic or Communist preference among Swedes, and Labour will be used to indicate a Labour preference among the British. Bourgeois will be used to indicate a Conservative (now Moderate), Center (formerly Agrarian), Liberal, or other rightist preference among Swedes. Right will be used to denote a Conservative or Liberal preference among British voters. At some points in the analysis it will be necessary to trichotomize the parties along the lines suggested in our discussion of the Lipset/ Rokkan model. The party preferences of the respondents' parents when they were young will be classified in the same way. A simple dichotomy of social class along the manual/nonmanual lines will be used in the analysis.[2] Religious affiliation was the only variable which the surveys did not measure in precisely comparable ways, partly because there are differences between the two countries. Some Swedes attend both the state and free churches. These individuals will be classified as nonconformists in our analysis. The Swedish questionnaires did not ask the religious affiliation of those who reported that they never attended church (14 percent of the sample). Since more than 95 percent of the Swedes belong to the State Church and most of those who do not are nonconformist, it is fairly safe to assume the huge majority of those who do not attend are members of the State Church. The whole group is classified as State Church. To be consistent, we will classify as Anglicans the 64 British respondents who answered "None" to the question "What is your religion?" Thus the small number of atheists in both countries will be classified in the same way.

Denomination and Party Preference

In the samples as a whole, the Swedish Socialists polled a higher proportion than British Labour in both social classes as expected. Seventy-eight percent of Swedish manuals and 31 percent of Swedish nonmanuals registered a leftist preference compared to 68 percent of British manuals and 24 percent of British nonmanuals. According to the hypotheses derived from Butler and Stokes (1971) and Tomasson (1970) the difference should be greater among Lutherans and Anglicans. Table 2 confirms that the lead of the Swedish left is greater among those who attend the State Church. In fact, Labour actually does better than its Swedish counterpart among nonconformists. On the surface, this difference is perplexing. Both labor movements have roots in dissent. Nonconformism was important for the development of organizational skills. But, in both cases, the labor movement, particularly in its political manifestation, came to compete with dissent. Those who continued to adhere to dissent tended to support the Liberals and to some extent in the Swedish case, the Agrarian Party. To explore this question further, we examined the connection between religious affiliation and party preference among the fathers of the respondents.[3] This analysis can present some idea of the differences a generation ago.[3] The results, shown in Table 3, reveal a quite different pattern from that shown in Table 2. The tendency for English nonconformists to vote Liberal is much greater among the fathers of the respondents than among the respondents themselves. As a result, the Swedish and English patterns are more similar in the older generation.[4] Why do the patterns diverge now? The difference is probably a result of the differences in the electoral systems of the two countries. The British system of single-member districts penalizes minor parties and creates a pressure for citizens to vote for one of the two major parties (e.g., see Lipset, 1963, ch. 9). When the Labour Party replaced the Liberals as the second largest party,

Table 2. Party preference by religious preference and class.
(Percentages)

	Manuals		Nonmanuals	
Sweden				
	Lutheran	Nonconformist	Lutheran	Nonconformist
Socialist	81	62	32	28
Middle[a]	16	34	45	66
Conservative	3	4	23	6
N	(995)	(198)	(1,063)	(146)
Britain				
	Anglican	Nonconformist	Anglican	Nonconformist
Labour	66	75	21	25
Liberal	11	11	17	37
Conservative	24	14	62	38
N	(754)	(119)	(420)	(108)

[a]Center and Liberals

Table 3. Fathers' party preference by fathers' class
and religious preference.
(Percentages)

	Manuals		Nonmanuals	
Sweden				
	Lutheran	Nonconformist	Lutheran	Nonconformist
Socialist	86	76	29	27
Middle	9	21	44	61
Conservative	5	3	28	12
N	(706)	(99)	(986)	(178)
Britain				
	Anglican	Nonconformist	Anglican	Nonconformist
Labour	52	50	14	17
Liberal	15	38	17	44
Conservative	34	12	69	39
N	(665)	(132)	(223)	(59)

Liberal voters, many of whom were nonconformists, were faced with either voting for one of the major parties or "wasting" their votes on the Liberals. Most of them switched (Butler and Stokes, 1971, pp. 106–110). Comparing Tables 2 and 3, one can see which parties the nonconformists switched to. The workers moved to the dominant party in their class, the Labour Party, while the nonmanuals resisted change. In the Swedish case, since the proportional representation (PR) system created no such pressure to switch parties, the voting patterns of the younger and older generation are more similar.

It should be pointed out here that research has shown that the decline of the Liberals is in part due to the electoral system. Butler, Stevens, and Stokes (1968) estimate that the Liberals would have garnered between 18 and 31 percent of the vote in 1964 instead of 11 percent if the British system were based on proportional representation. Under PR, the Liberals would have retained not only many of Labour's nonconformist voters but also many Anglican voters from both parties. Thus the difference in electoral support between the Swedish Socialists and British Labour would be even greater were their electoral systems similar. Indeed, under a PR system it is likely that the Labour Party would never have attained a parliamentary majority.

Before we attempt to examine why the Labour Party does so poorly among Anglicans, some differences in the distribution of denominational affiliations between Sweden and Britain should be mentioned. In both countries, 14 percent of the electorate is nonconformist. In Sweden, almost all of the remainder of the population adheres to the State Church, whereas in Britain it is divided between the Church of England, 65 percent, the Church of Scotland, 10 percent, and the Roman Catholic Church, 9 percent. Adherents of the Church of Scotland are just slightly less Labour than nonconformists in their political loyalties. Catholics are much more pro-Labour than any other denomination. The difference is explained by the historical animosities between the Conservative Party, which was allied with the Anglican Church, and the Catholics. The Home Rule issue is one of the more important examples of the struggles which pitted the Conservative Party and the Catholics, many of whom were of Irish origin, against each other.

Political Mobilization and Party Preference

The key to our hypotheses concerning the Tory worker problem and Swedish secularism is the action of the Conservative and Socialist or Labour parties at the time of political mobilization of the working class, roughly 1865–1920 in Britain and 1880–1920 in Sweden. Table 3 does show that there were big differences in the politics of the fathers of the respondents in the two surveys and that the differences are greater among the State Church members. Many of these people came into the electorate well after the initial mobilization period. To get a better idea of the relative success of the parties in that period, one can examine the politics of the fathers of those respondents who are aged 49 and over. Given a generational age difference of 20 to 40 years, this group of fathers should correspond to the first fully mobilized generations. The differences between State Church members in the two countries in this generation is dramatic. The Socialists succeeded in mobilizing 81 percent of Swedish manuals compared to Labour's 37 percent among British manuals. The British Conservatives outdistance their Swedish counterparts 37 percent to 8 percent among manuals. Labour also does poorer in the nonmanual ranks than the Swedish Socialists, 5 percent and 23 percent respectively. Conversely, the British Conservatives were substantially more successful than the Swedes among the nonmanuals, garnering 72 percent of their preferences compared to 35 percent for the Swedes. Part of this difference in Conservative support among nonmanuals can be attributed to social structural differences. The small landholding pattern in Sweden and the subsequent development of the Agrarian Party put the Swedish Conservatives at a disadvantage compared with the British. But the differences in the working class are almost entirely the product of the differences in mobilization efforts of the parties. The Tories' activity and the late arrival of Labour is clearly demonstrated in these figures.

Butler and Stokes (1971) argue that the Tory worker phenomenon is partly the result of the political inheritance from this first generation of mobilized British electors. Table 4 supports their argument.

Table 4. Party preference by class and fathers' party
among Anglicans and Lutherans.
(Percentages)

	Manual	Nonmanual	N
Sweden			
Fathers Socialist	93	63	(800)
Fathers Bourgeois	55	12	(715)
Britain			
Fathers Labour	85	52	(374)
Fathers Right	42	10	(484)

Cell entries are percent with Labour or Socialist Preferences

Among those with leftist fathers, the difference between Swedish and British workers in leftist voting is 8 percent compared to 15 percent for all manual State Church members. The difference among manuals with rightist fathers is only slightly less than for the group as a whole. Overall, more than one third of the difference in voting patterns in the working class is accounted for by this variable alone. Among nonmanuals a similar pattern can be seen. After the controls for fathers' party preference are made, there is almost no difference between Swedish and British nonmanuals with rightist fathers whereas the control does not affect the differences between nonmanuals with leftist fathers. After fathers' party preference is accounted for, the difference between British and Swedish voting patterns is primarily in the cross-pressured groups, manuals with rightist fathers and nonmanuals with leftist fathers.

If the differences due to fathers' party preference are primarily attributable to the action of the parties at the time of political mobilization, then the difference explained by fathers' preference should be the greatest among the respondents over 49 years of age and then decline with youth. Table 5 shows that this is the case particularly in the working classes. Among older manuals, 81 percent of the Swedes support the Socialists while only 61 percent of the British support Labour. Almost two-thirds of this difference is explained by the differences in fathers' party preference. Among the younger manuals the difference in fathers' preference does little to account for the aggregate differences between the two countries in the age/class group. The control reduces the differences among respondents with leftist fathers but increases it among those with rightist fathers. Nonmanuals show a pattern similar to manuals. About half of the cross-national difference in the older cohort is explained by the variation in fathers' preferences. In the younger generation, the control reveals differences between those with rightist and leftist fathers rather than reducing overall variation. Thus, Butler and Stokes (1971, p. 124) are correct in

Table 5. Party preference by fathers' party, class,
and age among Anglicans and Lutherans.
(Percentages)

| | Manuals | | | Nonmanuals | | |
	Fathers Left	Fathers Right	All	Fathers Left	Fathers Right	All
Sweden						
Under 50	93	54	81	64	11	35
Over 49	93	57	81	62	13	27
N	(482)	(217)	(995)	(318)	(498)	(1063)
Britain						
Under 50	84	36	69	50	13	25
Over 49	86	46	61	56[a]	8	14
N	(295)	(238)	(754)	(80)	(247)	(418)

Cell entries are precent with Labour or Socialist preferences

[a]Based on 18 respondents

asserting that the effect of Labour's late entry on the political scene is negligible among the younger cohorts of British voters and that Labour is now "much closer to a full seizure of its 'natural' class base." However, this "natural class base" is still substantially less than the Swedes have achieved.

Religion and Party Preference

To explain the remaining difference between Britain and Sweden, we now turn to the question of religious attendance. The first thing that must be established is the extent to which the two countries differ on this variable and the sources of the differences. The surveys reveal that the percentage of the population who attend church once a month or more is higher in Britain (26 percent) than in Sweden (16 percent). If Tomasson is correct in linking the role of the Conservative Party at the point of the democratic breakthrough to secularism, the differences between the countries should be due to the difference in attendance among State Church members. Controls for party preference should reduce the difference. And one might suspect, given our findings on fathers' preference and the respondents' politics that the differences between the countries would be greatest among the oldest respondents. Surprisingly, none of these hypotheses are supported by the data (Table 6). In fact, the difference in church attendance between Anglicans and Lutherans is small. The cross-national differences are almost entirely due to the differences in denominational distribution mentioned earlier. All other denominations in

Table 6. State Church attendance by sex and party preference.
(Percentages)

	Under 30	30-39	40-49	50-59	Over 59	All	N
Sweden							
Socialist Males	1	2	5	5	9	5	(625)
Socialist Females	2	3	7	9	19	8	(515)
Bourgeois Males	7	7	12	20	29	16	(456)
Bourgeois Females	7	12	19	28	44	24	(462)
All	4	5	10	15	24	12	(2434)
Britain							
Labour Males	4	6	5	6	12	7	(321)
Labour Females	8	2	17	20	15	13	(291)
Right Males	17	6	15	17	15	14	(257)
Right Females	17	25	17	31	36	27	(369)
All	11	10	13	19	21	15	(1342)

Cell entries are percent who attend the Lutheran or Anglican Church once a month or more

both countries have substantially higher rates of attendance than the state churches. Forty-four percent of Swedish nonconformists and 45 percent of British nonconformists attend services once a month or more. In Britain, the monthly attendance figure is 73 percent for Catholics and 39 percent for members of the Church of Scotland. Thus the cross-national differences are primarily due to the presence of the latter two groups in Britain but not in Sweden.

The question of Swedish secularism appears to be a question of State Church secularism. This similarity of the attendance figures for British and Swedish nonconformists and for Anglicans and Lutherans clearly points to some character of doctrine or institutional structure. We would suggest the following interpretation. The question that should be asked is what allowed Protestant sects and the Catholic Church to partly resist the general pressure toward secularization which inevitably accompanies the rise of scientific and rational thought (Weber's *Entzauberung*). They did this in quite different ways. The mobilization of resistance among sectarians came from the bottom in the form of revival movements and the like. The mobilization in the Catholic Church came from the top, beginning with the Counter-Reformation. This difference is clearly linked to doctrinal differences. The moral autonomy of the sectarian allows independent action from the base. Catholics must wait for direction from the Church. This is also the case for Lutherans and Anglicans. The difference is that these state churches never carried out counter mobilizations against growing secularism precisely because they were closely allied with the national elites. For one thing, such a mobilization was unnecessary to secure the institutional interests of the State Church because it was not threatened by the nation-building process as was the Catholic Church. Rather, it was a product of the process and an instrument in it. And unlike the sects, it could depend on state support rather than only on membership support to ensure its survival. Furthermore, at least in Britain and Sweden, political control of the church meant that, historically, elite origins and political reliability were more important than devotion as criteria for appointment as a bishop. Correspondingly, scholasticism rather than devotion tended to dominate religious education.

Norway is deviant in that the Lutheran fundamentalist movement did mobilize to resist secularism. But as we pointed out earlier, this fundamentalism is doctrinally more similar to Protestant sectarianism than to Lutheranism. Norway's resistance to secularism also shows a strange similarity in that respect to Catholic countries: the fundamentalist movement, like the Counter-Reformation, was part of a general resistance to efforts at nation-building.

Then, if religious attendance is similar among State Church members in Britain and Sweden it would appear that it could not explain differences in voting patterns between the two countries. The same logic seems to apply to Parkin's (1967) arguments. Sex distribution hardly differs. The average Swedish factory is smaller than the average English factory (Pryor, 1973) and Swedish residence patterns are less class-segregated than English residence patterns (Janson, 1959). However, a comparison of our earlier findings (Stephens, 1976) with research done on Britain suggested that some of these variables might be useful in explaining the cross-national differences resulting from their differential effect in the two countries. What we found was that in Sweden the size of the work unit explained little variation in voting, and sex explained almost no variation. In Britain, on the other hand, research has shown that size of work unit is strongly associated with how individuals vote (Nordlinger, 1967). Workers in large units are more likely to vote Labour than those in small units. Sex has also been found to be associated with voting in Britain, with women being more conservative than men (Butler and Stokes, 1969).[5]

We suspected that religion would follow a similar pattern. Table 7 confirms that this is the case among manuals. With fathers' party preference controlled, church attendance makes a difference among British manuals but not among Swedish manuals. One can see the same pattern that we saw earlier: the British/Swedish differences are greatest in cross-pressured groups. Among secular (i.e., those attending church less than twice a year) manuals with leftist fathers, the difference between Britain and Sweden is very small, only 4 percent. Among religious (i.e., those that attend church twice a year or more) manuals with leftist fathers there is a 13 percent difference. And the differences between Sweden and Brit-

Table 7. Party preference by class, fathers' party,
and church attendance among Anglicans and Lutherans.
(Percentages)

	Manual		Nonmanual	
	Fathers Left	Fathers Right	Fathers Left	Fathers Right
Sweden				
Attend Twice a Year or More	92	53	56	9
Attend Less Often	93	57	69	17
N	(482)	(217)	(318)	(498)
Britain				
Attend Twice a Year or More	79	34	45	8
Attend Less Often	89	47	56	14
N	(295)	(238)	(79)	(246)

Cell entries are percent with Labour or Socialist preferences

ain among religious manuals with rightist fathers are yet greater, 19 percent. Thus, the British workers are much more likely to respond to cross-pressures against class voting than are Swedish workers. An analysis of sex and voting shows the same pattern (Table 8). Male workers with leftist fathers are similar in the two countries in terms of political preferences. But Swedish female manuals with bourgeois fathers were more likely to have leftist preferences than their British counterparts. Again one can see that after controls for fathers' preference are made, the

Table 8. Party preference by class, fathers' party,
and sex among Anglicans and Lutherans.
(Percentages)

	Manual		Nonmanual	
	Fathers Left	Fathers Right	Fathers Left	Fathers Right
Sweden				
Males	94	54	67	12
Females	92	57	60	12
N	(482)	(217)	(318)	(498)
Britain				
Males	89	48	46	16
Females	81	35	60[a]	6
N	(295)	(238)	(79)	(246)

Cell entries are percent with Labour or Socialist preferences

[a]Based on 35 respondents

cross-national differences are almost entirely due to the greater resistance of Swedish manuals to cross-pressures against class-consistent voting. Table 9 shows this even more dramatically. The more cross-pressures experienced by British workers the less likely they are to vote Labour. Only fathers' party preference makes a difference among Swedes. The pattern is clear enough: the question is how can the pattern be interpreted and explained.

Parkin's (1967) hypothesis is helpful here. He argues that the radical value system will be strongest, and thus Labour voting greatest, where the "industrial subculture" is the strongest. To understand the cross-national differences found here, we have to distinguish the dimensions underlying the variations in the strength of the "industrial subculture." One essential element is the degree of isolation of the networks of interaction of the working class individual from middle- and upper-class individuals. A second element is lack of contact with traditional or dominant institutions, and a third is contact with working class institutions. All these can vary independently, though they will be correlated. For instance, the working class housewife may be thoroughly embedded in a working class social network, but because contact with unions is greater in work life than at home, she is less likely to be influenced by the radical value system than someone who is working. Likewise, a similar housewife who is a member of a religious organization is more likely to be influenced by the dominant value system. What we would like to suggest is that for purposes of cross-national voting research the purely structural aspect of the proximity to the radical value system should be extracted

Table 9. Party preference by fathers' party, sex,
and church attendance among manual Anglicans and Lutherans.
(Percentages)

	Fathers Left		Fathers Right	
	Attend Twice a year or More	Attend Less Often	Attend Twice a Year or More	Attend Less Often
Sweden				
Males	93	94	54	54
Females	90	93	53	63[a]
N	(148)	(334)	(116)	(101)
Britain				
Males	94[a]	87	41[a]	51
Females	73	91	30	41
N	(119)	(176)	(93)	(145)

Cell entries are percent with Labour or Socialist preferences

[a]Based on less than 40 respondents

from the more attitudinal or even behavioral ones because the latter are more likely to have common antecedents with voting than to be causal agents (e.g., Labour voters read Labour papers). Thus, we would suggest that structural location in the working class be measured on a scale of how close one is to the "center" of the working class. For instance, workers in large factories are more central than those in small ones. Workers in homogeneous working class neighborhoods are more central than those in heterogeneous or middle-class ones. Industrial workers are more central than service workers, and so on. With such a scale, we can summarize our finding and the other findings cited earlier as follows: Once fathers' preference is controlled, the support for the British left is almost as great as that for the Swedish left in the working class center; the differences are concentrated in the periphery.

How can this difference be explained? In his study of two small matched samples of industrial workers in Britain and Sweden, Scase (1974) finds that the Swedish workers are more leftist in their voting patterns and moreover that the Swedish Social Democratic workers were more radical than the British Labour workers. Building on Parkin's work, he attributes this to the differential strength of the radical value system. Similarly, our findings could be interpreted as due to the greater penetration of the radical value system into the working class periphery in Sweden. This obviously begs the question of why the radical value system is stronger in Sweden. The "explanation" seems to be a tautology. Scase argues that the difference lies primarily in the Swedish leadership's greater radicalism and interest in grass roots mobilization and political socialization. He admits that there is a feedback effect from the rank and file, but argues that the leaders are more important given the highly centralized nature of the Swedish movement.

While Scase's description of the differences in the leadership's attitudes and behaviors is correct, it is a mistake to attribute this great difference and thus the differences in rank-and-file behavior and attitudes to apparently purely voluntary decisions on the part of the leadership. The fundamental reason why the radical value system has penetrated much further into the structural periphery of the Swedish working class is that labor organization in Sweden is at a high level. In 1965, 61 percent of the Swedish labor force was organized compared to 42 percent of the British labor force. This difference is not primarily a consequence of Swedes being more leftist and thus more likely to join unions, a tautological argument. The primary source of cross-national difference in the level of labor organization is a structural feature of the economy, the degree of industry-level concentration, not subjective states of the population (Stephens, 1979).

While the structural center of the working class in the two countries is by definition the same size, direct contact with the ideological center of the Swedish labor movement is much greater because many more workers are union members. But the differences are not accounted for entirely by direct contact. As we saw, women in Sweden, many of whom are house-wives and thus by definition not union members, do not cross-vote nearly to the extent of British women. The Swedish labor movement manages to pull these peripheral elements into its sphere of influence to a much great-er degree than its British counterpart. The difference in the strength of the daily press in the two countries is only the most telling aspect of this. About 20 percent of the circulation of the Swedish daily press is Social Democratic, whereas there is no real party press in Britain, though a few papers, such as *The Mirror* and *The Daily Herald* (now defunct) do (or did) support the Labour Party at election time. But the daily press is hardly all of the story. The Swedish trade unions and the Social Demo-cratic Party influence opinion through trade union journals, well-attended movement-linked study groups, youth and women's organizations, and rank-and-file propaganda campaigns, just to name a few phenomena. In short, the Swedish labor movement has established a much greater hegemonic presence, to use Gramsci's term (1971, also see Anderson, 1964, for an application of the idea of hegemony to Britain), in Swedish society than the British movement has in British society.

This hegemony affects not only peripheral elements of the working class but also the center, as well as having some influence among non-manuals, particularly lower nonmanuals. Scase did find differences among his sample, all of whom were unionized. Scase's error was attribut-ing these differences only to the leaders' ideology. Probably more impor-tant are the greater resources available to the Swedish leadership com-pared with those of the British leadership. Not only do the Swedes have a larger membership which they can draw on for money and manpower, but the labor movement's control of these resources is more centralized. Both in terms of finances and staff the Swedish trade union central, *Landsor-ganisationen (LO)*, is much better endowed than the British central, the Trade Union Congress (TUC) (Headey, 1970). And Ingham (1974) has shown that the centralized structure of *LO* is also the result of industrial concentration. Thus the labor market situation in Sweden created an ap-paratus which the leadership could use. The lack of resources and central control makes it more difficult for the British leadership to support news-papers, run grass-roots issue campaigns, etc.

Before closing, we would like to make a final comment on the "deferen-tial political culture" school of thought which we criticized earlier. While granting our points on importance of fathers' party preference and the peripheral location of the Tory worker, they might argue that the cross-national differences are explained by the differences in historical inherited political culture. We would answer this argument in the following ways. First, as we just pointed out, the greater strength of the radical value system in Sweden as compared with that in Britain is the result of greater organizational strength and greater centralization of the trade unions, which in turn is due to economic structure not historical cultural factors. In fact, at the turn of the century Swedish society was certainly as hierarchical and deferential as British society. Here, a comparison with Germany is instructive. In the nineteenth century Sweden fell under the cultural dominance of Germany and by the turn of the century their cultures were similar. Yet today the Protestant German worker votes 70 percent Social Democratic, which is more like the British worker than the Swedish worker (Urwin, 1974). Again, the key is in the capacity for action in the German trade unions. Though the trade unions are more centralized than in Britain (but less than Sweden), the strength of their ideological influence is more similar to the British movement since less than one third of the German labor force is organized.

SUMMARY

Homogeneous Protestant societies are usually expected to have party systems and voting patterns based entirely on class. Norway and Britain appear to be partial exceptions to this rule. In this chapter, the social roots of the Norwegian Christian party and the effect of religious attendance and affiliation and other factors on cross-voting in the British working class have been examined through a comparative analysis with Sweden. Building on Rokkan's work, the development of the Norwegian Christian Party was explained by the mobilization of the peasantry which occurred before a strong national cultural center had developed. Events occurring at the time of political mobilization also proved important in explaining the Tory worker problem. The late development of the Labour Party and the Conservative efforts at mobilization of the working class helped explain why the British working class is less leftist than the Swedish working class. We also found that the high degree of secularism in Sweden was not as hypothesized, due to the role of the Swedish Conservative party at the time of mobilization since Anglicans were found to be as secular as Lutherans. Rather, it appears to be the result of elements of Lutheran and Anglican doctrine and their roles as state churches. However, religious attendance did help to elucidate the Tory worker problem. It was found that religion and sex cause cross-voting among British workers but not among Swedish workers. The cross-national difference in leftist voting was almost entirely concentrated in the cross-pressured groups. Previous research suggests that this is part of a general tendency for the differences to be concentrated in the peripheral elements of the working class. We argued that the difference in the periphery was due to the great hegemonic presence of the Swedish labor movement in Swedish society. The key factor creating this hegemony is the high level of labor organization and high degree of trade union centralization in Sweden. The level of organization and degree of centralization have been shown to be due primarily to industrial concentration.

FOOTNOTES

*The author would like to thank Juan Linz and Richard F. Tomasson for their comments on earlier drafts of this work. The author is deeply indebted to Evelyne Huber Stephens for her insights and comments on every draft of the work. The responsibility for the arguments and opinions expressed herein is solely that of the author.

1. These data were made available by the Inter-University Consortium for Political Research. Neither the original collectors of the data nor the Consortium bear any responsibility for the analyses or interpretations presented here. Technical descriptions of the data can be found in publications by the principal investigators.

2. The dividing line used here is consistent with Rose (1974) but not Butler and Stokes (1971). Rose comes closer to the traditional distinction between manual and nonmanual work (e.g., see Mills, 1951).

3. In the Swedish case we had to use respondents' religious affiliation as a substitute for fathers' affiliation. We checked the differences between respondents' and fathers' affiliation for Britain. They were slight.

4. Unfortunately, we could not break the analysis down to examine separately the fathers of the oldest respondents, who were all mobilized when the Liberals were the main opposition force in Britain. The number of nonconformists in this age group alone was too small to obtain reliable results.

5. We consider the British research on residence patterns and politics, including Butler and Stokes (1971), to be inconclusive because of methodological errors (Stephens, 1976). We were unable to analyze the effects of both housing patterns and factory size here because of lack of comparable data.

REFERENCES

Almond, Gabriel and Sidney Verba (1963) *The Civic Culture*. Boston: Little, Brown.
Anderson, Perry (1964) "Problems of Socialist Strategy." Pages 221–289 in Perry Anderson and Robin Blackburn (eds.), *Towards Socialism*. London: Fontana Library.
Butler, David, A. Stevens, and Donald Stokes (1968) "The Strength of the Liberals under Different Electoral Systems." *Parliamentary Affairs* 22:10–15.
—— and Donald Stokes (1971) *Political Change in Britain*. New York: St. Martin's Press.
Gramsci, Antonio (1971) *Prison Notebooks*. New York: International Publishers.
Heady, Bruce (1970) "Trade Unions and National Wages Policy." *Journal of Politics* 32:407–439.
Hessler, Carl Arvid (1964) *Statskyrkodebatten*. Stockholm. Almqvist and Wiksell.
Hill, Robert (1978) *Sources of Variation in the Class Consciousness of the British Working Class*. Unpublished Ph.D. dissertation, Providence, RI: Brown University.

Janson, Carl-Gunnar (1959) "Stadens Struktur." Pages 209–236 in Edmund Dahlström (ed.), *Svensk samhällsstruktur i sociologisk belysning*, Stockholm: Svenska Bokförlaget.

Ingham, Geoffrey (1974) *Strikes and Industrial Conflict*. London: Macmillan.

Lipset, Seymour M. (1960) *Political Man*. Garden City, NY: Doubleday.

———— (1963) *First New Nation*. New York: Basic Books.

———— (1970) *Revolution and Counter-Revolution*. Garden City, NY: Anchor Books.

———— and Stein Rokkan (1967) "Cleavage Structures, Party Systems, and Voter Alignments: An Introduction." Pages 1–64 in Seymour M. Lipset and Stein Rokkan (eds.), *Party Systems and Voter Alignments*. New York: Free Press.

McKenzie, Robert and Allan Silver (1968) *Angels in Marble*. Chicago: University of Chicago Press.

Mills, C. Wright (1951) *White Collar*. New York: Oxford University Press.

Nordlinger, Eric A. (1967) *The Working Class Tories*. London: MacGibbon and Kee.

Parkin, Frank (1967) "Working Class Conservatives: A Theory of Political Deviance." *British Journal of Sociology* 18:278–290.

Pryor, Frederic (1973) *Property and Industrial Organization in Communist and Capitalist Countries*. Bloomington: Indiana University Press.

Rokkan, Stein (1967) "Geography, Religion, and Social Class: Cross-cutting Cleavages in Norwegian Politics." Pages 367–444 in Seymour M. Lipset and Stein Rokkan (eds.), *Party Systems and Voter Alignments*. New York: Free Press.

———— and Henry Valen (1974) "Norway: Conflict Structure and Mass Politics in a European Periphery." Pages 315–370 in Richard Rose (ed.), *Electoral Behavior*. New York: Free Press.

Rose, Richard (1974) "Britain: Simple Abstractions and Complex Realities." Pages 481–542 in Richard Rose (ed.), *Electoral Behavior*. New York: Free Press.

———— and D. W. Urwin (1969) "Social Cohesion, Political Parties, and Strains in Regimes." *Comparative Political Studies* 2:7–67.

Rustow, Dankwart A. (1955) *The Politics of Compromise*. Princeton, NJ: Princeton University Press.

Sanders, Thomas G. (1964) *Protestant Conceptions of Church and State*. Garden City, NY: Anchor Books.

Scase, Richard (1974) "Relative Deprivation: a Comparison of English and Swedish Manual Workers." Pages 197–216 in Dorothy Wedderburn (ed.), *Poverty, Inequality, and Class Structure*. Cambridge: Cambridge University Press.

Stephens, John D. (1976) *The Consequences of Social Structural Change for the Development of Socialism in Sweden*. Unpublished Ph.D. dissertation. New Haven: Yale University.

———— (1979) *The Transition from Capitalism to Socialism*. London: Macmillan.

Tomasson, Richard F. (1970) *Sweden: Prototype of Modern Society*. New York: Random House.

Urwin, D. W. (1974) "Germany: Continuity and Change in Electoral Politics." Pages 109–170 in Richard Rose (ed.), *Electoral Behavior*. New York: Free Press.

Weber, Max (1968) *Economy and Society*. New York: Bedminster Press.

Westergaard, John and Henrietta Resler (1975) *Class in a Capitalist Society*. New York: Basic Books.

Westerståhl, Jörgen (1964) "Samkristna Skolnamdens naminsamlingsaktion." *Statsvetenskaplig Tidskrift* 67:277–290.

IDEOLOGICAL PROFILES OF WEST GERMAN AND ITALIAN SOCIALISTS AND CHRISTIAN DEMOCRATS: A FACTOR ANALYSIS*

Peter H. Merkl

Political ideology in advanced industrial societies is far more subject to drastic changes than is the case in pre-industrial or industrializing societies (Inglehart, 1976; Sjoberg, Hancock, and White, 1972; Putnam, 1972; Mayer and Burnett, 1977). While mass ideological changes may tend to follow social and political change, however, the ideological attitudes of the active membership of certain political parties are relatively stable during the lifetime of the membership career as the mind of the activist strives for logical cohesion and consistency in the face of discordant facts. To be sure, the views of the party activists are changing too but more slowly than political mass opinion in contemporary societies. At any rate, the old partisan ideologies of the 1920s and 1930s, and even of the 1950s,

Comparative Social Research, Vol. 2, pp. 159—178.
Volume 1 published as Comparative Studies in Sociology

no longer tell us much about what goes on in the minds of active Socialists or Christian Democrats in major European countries today. (See, for example, Alberoni *et al.*, 1967; Barnes, 1967; Galli and Prandi, 1970; Galli, 1968; Rokkan, 1970, pp. 367–368; Lawson, 1970, pp. 92–111; Dittberner and Ebbighausen, 1973; Kaack, 1971, pp. 470–497; Flechtheim, 1973, pp. 385–416.) How does a rank-and-file Italian Socialist feel about the Church today, or about the promise which economic growth holds for the poor? What are the attitudes of West German Christian or Social Democrats toward the remaining class barriers of German society? How do the views held relate to broader, underlying attitudes or to the topical opinions? This is the complex of questions addressed by this inquiry into the ideology and attitudes of West German (SPD) and Italian Socialists (PSU) and Christian Democrats (German: CDU; Italian: DC) at the end of the 1960s.

THE NATURE OF THE SAMPLE

This is a part of a larger study of the ideological attitudes of 415 West German and Italian Socialists and Christian Democrats gathered in 1968 and 1969 by Doxa and Infas. The timing had to do with the Italian and German election campaigns of those years and also with the presence of controversial grand coalition governments in both countries. Those were also the days of the Vietnam agony, although its reception in Italy and West Germany was quite different and even more ideological than in the United States itself (Doxa, 1968, pp. 22–29). The ensuing upheaval, particularly among German and Italian university youth, at first seemed to make this timing seem unfortunate since there are evidently no obvious young rebels in the sample.[1] With the benefit of hindsight, however, the timing now appears to enhance the historical perspective on that point in party history which preceded the era of *Ostpolitik* in West Germany and the dramatic surge of the Italian Communists (PCI) to the gates of power.

The Italian sample of 213 was drawn in a geographically representative manner in August 1968 from a list of known party members previously interviewed by Doxa, as follows: From the three provinces of the industrial northwest 30 DC and 32 PSU; from the agrarian northeast, 9 DC and 8 PSU; from central Italy, 21 DC and 36 PSU; from the South, 25 DC and 24 PSU; and from the islands, Sicily and Sardinia, 17 DC and 13 PSU, altogether 102 DC and 113 PSU respondents. The most obvious weakness

*Peter H. Merkl is a Professor of Political Science at the University of California, Santa Barbara. He is an authority in the theory of comparative politics, and on German and Italian politics. His most recent book is *Political Violence Under the Swastika: 581 Early Nazis* (1975). He is also the author of *Modern Comparative Politics* (2nd ed., 1977).

of the sample drawn is that it is considerably higher in the level of education than both parties are thought to be. The German sample of 200 was based on a random sample drawn from a large party member study conducted by Nils Diederich in Hesse, North Rhine Westphalia, and Lower Saxony: 53 CDU and 34 SPD from Lower Saxony, 17 CDU and 21 SPD from North Rhine Westphalia, and 30 CDU and 45 SPD from Hesse. Although this appears to be a well-balanced cross section, the lack of geographical coverage does constitute a weakness.

To describe some of the basic dimensions of the two samples, we have set them side by side by size of commune, Table 1, by occupation, Table 2, and by age, Table 3.

Table 1. Party members by size of commune.
(Percentages)

	DC	PSU	Italians	CDU	SPD	Germans
Below 2,000	5.9	5.3	5.6	17	34	25.5
2,000-5,000	19.6	15.0	17.2	14	15	14.5
5-10,000	5.9	5.3	5.6	23	6	14.5
10-20,000	15.7	13.3	14.4	8	4	6.0
20-100,000	29.4	25.7	27.4	28	13	20.5
Italy: 100-200,000 (Germany: 100-250,000)	2.9	15.9	9.8	1	5	3.0
Italy: 200,000 and over (Germany: 250,000 and over)	20.6	19.5	20.0	9	23	16.0
Total	100	100	100	100	100	100
	(102)	(113)	(215)	(100)	(100)	(200)

Table 2. Party members by occupation.
(Percentages)

	DC	PSU	Italians	CDU	SPD	Germans
Independents & family helpers	10.8	12.4	11.6	27	3	15.0
Professions	4.9	5.3	5.1	2	–	1.0
NGE, students	12.7	15.9	14.4	–	–	–
Managers, high civil servants, teachers	20.6	21.3	20.9	14	3	8.5
Public service	19.6	11.5	15.4	9	8	8.5
White collar (priv.)	13.7	12.4	13	22	26	24.0
Blue collar	11.8	17.7	14.9	10	34	22.0
Retired, on pension	–	–	–	15	25	20.0
Framers	5.9	3.5	4.7	–	–	–
NA	–	–	–	1	1	1.0
Total	100	100	100	100	100	100
	(102)	(113)	(215)	(100)	(100)	(200)

*Table 3.*Party members by age.
(Percentages)

	16-24	25-34	35-44	45-54	55 and over	Totals	
DC	9.8	29.5	25.5	17.6	17.6	100	(102)
PSU	9.9	27.9	26.2	18.9	17.1	100	(111)
Italians	9.9	28.6	25.8	18.3	17.4	100	(213)

	16-24	25-34	35-49	50-64	65 and over	Totals	
CDU	6.0	17.0	38.0	24.0	15.0	100	(100)
SPD	–	17.0	34.0	26.0	23.0	100	(100)
West Germans	3.0	17.0	36.0	25.0	19.0	100	(200)

THE IDEOLOGICAL PARAMETERS

The study focuses on the political socialization and views of the respondents (Merkl, 1971, 1976). Among many other questions, they were asked ten dichotomous attitude questions which attempted to fathom their ideological attitudes at several levels:

1. Dedication to Party—Private orientation
    Underlying Attitudes:
2. Social Trust—Distrust
3. Democracy—Authoritarianism
4. Pro-Bureaucracy—Bureaucratophobia
    Ideological Issues:
5. Class Barriers (Class Order)—Free Social Mobility
6. Capitalistic Development—Interventionism (Revolution)
7. Clericalism (Tolerance)—Anticlericalism (Secularism)
    Topical Issues:
8. Grand Coalition (Centro-Sinistra)—Anti-coalition
9. European Integration—Gaullism
10. United States in Vietnam—Anti-Vietnam

The questions were presented in dichotomous pairs (see Appendix) to maintain their dialectical nature and to facilitate processing of the data. A few extra parameters were added for the German respondents which obviously had no Italian equivalent and are included here only as a tangential perspective. They were also of a topical nature:

11. Outlawing the NPD—Toleration
12. Recognizing the DDR—Nonrecognition

We expected that the questions of suppressing either the neo-Nazi NPD or the New Left, and of course the recognition of the East German Republic, would divide the SPD and CDU and relate in interesting ways to the other dichotomies. The cross tabulations carried out among them indeed showed some surprising linkages. In both parties, for example, members exhibiting social trust were significantly more tolerant toward the NPD but also more inclined not to want to recognize the East German DDR than were the distrustful ones. Those who showed less dedication to their party and those who were more democratically inclined, and exhibited pro-bureaucratic attitudes (especially in the CDU), also were more often tolerant toward the NPD but not the DDR than their opposites. The upshot appeared to be a kind of establishment consensus on the NPD and on nonrecognition of the DDR, among the *bien-pensants* of both parties and especially in the CDU which was still in power then. The more traditional attitudes among the more distrustful Social and Christian Democrats tilted more toward banning the NPD and recognizing the DDR.[2]

The ten questions were grouped on three levels in order to test hypotheses deriving the topical positions from broad ideological attitudes, and the latter from deeper dimensions of social adjustment and personal integration. Our choice of underlying issues turned out to be quite revealing, especially the social trust-distrust and the authoritarian-democratic dimensions. Hatred of bureaucracy appears to be too unevenly distributed today to facilitate comparisons, although it appeared in many pivotal relationships. Dedication to party turned out to be unexpectedly ambiguous, although the pronounced difference between the organization-happy Germans and the private-oriented Italians alone was a feature worth noting (see Appendix).

The nature of the ideological issues made it necessary to have different versions for the Socialists and the Christian Democrats. On the question of class barriers, for example, the Socialists[3] were asked whether they perceived their society as a rigid class society or as one open to upward mobility. The Christian Democrats were asked to choose between a preference for a class order and free mobility. Next, the Socialists were asked whether they took a rosy view of capitalistic development or insisted on the necessity of political or revolutionary intervention in the economy. The Christian Democratic choice was between a free market economy and *dirigisme*. On church influence the Socialists chose between religious tolerance and anticlericalism, the Christian Democrats between pro-clericalism and insistence on the secular autonomy of their party.[4] The measurement intended to ascertain ideological cohesion or dissensus on traditional positions within each party, not to hold up all party members to an absolute standard. The results (Appendix) show in most cases a good deal of dissensus which was desirable for further statistical manipulation. The breakdown on the ideological issues, at least, also shows the extent to which rank-and-file party members have broken away from the orthodox positions of yesteryear, a differential we cross-tabulated elsewhere with age, date of joining the party, and other variables in order to show when and how far the "end of ideology" has progressed in these parties. Evidently, the days of the traditional, proclerical Italian Christian Democrats and the Socialist *mangiapreti* (anticlericalism) are over.

The choice of topical issues, other than the extra questions for the Germans, proved predictably short-lived in topicality. The question of continuing the grand coalition in Germany and the *centro-sinistra* government in Italy at the time produced enough dissension to bring out the wings of opposition in each party. We have used it elsewhere to relate to specific policy issues, to party factions, and to satisfaction with the party's record. Gaullism, and the Vietnam issue, on the other hand, only brought out an isolationist faction of the Italian PSU. The other three parties were so united on one position that there was little leeway for further statistical manipulations.

RELATING ATTITUDES TO ONE ANOTHER

To relate the different attitudes to one another and to test the relationships between levels of attitudes, we cross-tabulated all ten ideological parameters for each party and presented each cross-tabulation in the form of a two-by-two table. Our first such table, for example, crossed social trust-distrust with dedication to party—private orientation, listing all the positive against all the negative responses (neutral responses omitted) of the 100 SPD members.

	Distrust	Trust	Original Marginals
Dedicated	12	16	31%
Private	10	26	49%

Twelve of the distrustful German Social Democrats turned out to be dedicated to their party, 10 private-oriented. Sixteen of the trusting Socialists were dedicated and 26 private-oriented. There appears to be at first glance a tendency for social distrust and dedication to go together—with the distrust perhaps motivating a person to become dedicated to party work—as well as for trust and private-orientation to be paired.

There are many ways of interpreting the rows of two-by-two tables on each issue. We can brood over a particular two-by-two table and examine its vertical, horizontal, or diagonal relationships in the light of the substantive issues involved. We can also relate a two-by-two table to other variables or compare it to its equivalent for the other parties or the other country. One of the early findings of this study was that the differences between the two countries rather outweighed the expected similarities among all Socialists or all Christian Democrats. We can also look down the entire SPD column of cross-tabulations between distrust-trust and other parameters, for example, using distrust-trust as the independent variable, and reflect on how this variable relates to all the others, Thus we find that distrustful SPD members tended to be more dedicated, more authoritarian, less pro-bureaucratic, less optimistic about social mobility, more pro-capitalistic, more anticlerical, less in favor of the grand coalition, of the American presence in Vietnam, and of European integration, more hostile to the NPD, and friendlier to the DDR than trusting Social Democrats. The relationships add up to a kind of party profile against the background of a socially distrustful or trusting attitude.

We can also compare this SPD profile to that of the CDU, and further to those of the PSU and DC. The two German parties differed from each other only in a few salient points to which, of course, we have to add the differences in the ideological issues which we programmed into the questionnaire. The patterns of all the Germans, on the other hand, differed substantially from both Italian parties which again differed from each other only in minor ways.

This manner of examining the *prima facie* relationships in the two-by-two tables may be more meaningful to the researcher, but it is not satisfactory to statistical method which calls for a more exacting test of significance. We used Kendall's Q as an index of the strength of the relationship between each pair of variables and added a chi-square test (x^2) for proof of significance of the relationship.[5] Whenever a two-by-two table had a Q of $\pm .450$ or more, we marked it with an asterisk (*) and also calculated its x^2. A Q of $\pm .5$ (**) was considered as indicating a strong relationship. A x^2 value of 2.706 (*) indicates a 90 percent probability that the relationships are "true" or nonrandom. A x^2 of 3.841 (**) raises this probability to 95 percent and above 6.635 (***) it is 99 percent. The large number of two-by-two cross-tabulations of the ideological parameters becomes much smaller when we consider only the statistically significant tables,[6] and also because every two-by-two table appears twice, the second time rotated by 90°.

For the SPD, for example, we noticed at once the strong interrelationship of all three underlying attitudes, with particular emphasis on the combination of trust, democracy, and a pro-bureaucratic attitude which evidently form a kind of syndrome. As for the ideological and topical

levels, religious tolerance relates closely to this syndrome of the underlying attitudes and it also seemed to increase the respondent's support for
the grand coalition and for the American presence in Vietnam. The belief
in the absence of class barriers correlates significantly with pro-
bureaucratic sentiment and with loyalty to the coalition. Attitudes for or
against capitalistic development are strangely absent from the list of significant cross-tabulations of both German parties, which is perhaps a sign
of their contemporary political irrelevance in the Federal Republic.
Capitalism was not an issue until the neo-Marxists of the 1970s revived it
from a decade or more of slumber. Dedication to party shows no significant relationship to any other attitude in the SPD. Among the topical
issues, finally, the SPD has only one set of significant relationships,
namely, between the supporters of the United States in Vietnam and
those who wanted to deny recognition to the DDR, which is certainly a
plausible connection.

The CDU, by comparison, had far fewer significant relationships in our
cross-tabulation tables. There are none among the underlying attitudes
although authoritarianism relates to pro-clerical and democracy to secular
attitudes, thus demarcating two strains of Christian Democratic thinking.
The CDU also has the same link between pro-bureaucratic attitudes and
the belief in social mobility as the SPD. There are two more foci among
the CDU cross-tabulations. One is around the loyalty to the grand coalition which relates highly to social trust and to pro-bureaucratic attitudes,
as well as to nonrecognition of the DDR. Nonrecognition in turn relates to
social trust and also to the issue of authoritarianism. To understand this
linkage, one has to recall how much CDU power used to be based on
ignoring the East. Finally, the CDU is the only party to have any significant relationships between dedication to party and other variables, namely,
with Europeanism and with tolerating the NPD. Dedicated Christian
Democrats tended to wanting to get rid of the NPD while the private-
oriented were prepared to tolerate it.

The Italian PSU, like the SPD, had many significant tables linking what
appears to be a hard core of beliefs. Socially distrustful Socialists, for
instance, tend to be antibureaucratic, while the trusting are sympathetic
to the bureaucrats. By the same token, the distrustful are more often
anticlerical and complain about class barriers, and vice versa. The
heaviest concentration of significant relationships is here among the
ideological issues. Those who regard Italy as a class society not only tend
to be distrustful and antibureaucratic. They are also more often interventionist and anticlerical, while those who believe in social mobility tend to
be pro-capitalistic and religiously tolerant. The linkage between anticlericalism and the belief in class barriers and between the latter and interventionism is particularly strong. We are evidently dealing here with the

remaining core of traditional Socialist beliefs. Their support for the *centro-sinistra* government, moreover, closely relates not only to pro-capitalism and a nondichotomous view of society, but also to support for the Americans in Vietnam and for a United Europe. Those unhappy with the coalition, naturally, perceive class barriers, advocate drastic intervention in the economy, and oppose both Vietnam and a United Europe. We are evidently dealing with a fault line between right- and left-wing factions of the PSU. The chief difference between our SPD and PSU samples appears to lie in the stress of the SPD on a set of interrelated underlying attitudes while the PSU seems to have its center of gravity clearly at the ideological level from where the positions on the topical issues are determined. The PSU, it would appear, had a more political membership than the SPD whose views are evidently based more on common feelings.

The Italian DC, finally, had almost as strongly interlinked a set of underlying attitudes as the SPD. In particular, social trust here relates to pro-bureaucratic feelings which in turn correlate with the democratic strain in the DC. The underlying attitudes each relate to an ideological issue, trust-distrust to economic interventionism, authoritarianism-democracy to the church issue, and from bureaucracy to social mobility. But from the topical issues, there is only one isolated link, namely, that from the economic interventionists to support for the coalition with the Socialists which obviously describes the common ground between these coalition parties. It should be emphasized that both Italian parties are much higher than the Germans in their social distrust and in their inclination to intervene in the economic processes.

FACTOR ANALYSIS AND CONCLUSION

With so many different variables confusing the picture, a way of summarizing the principal relationships had to be found. Which of our ideological parameters share a common underlying factor? What kind of factor? To answer these questions, we factor-analyzed the correlations among the ten parameters for each of the four parties. The factors emerge from the Rotated Factor matrix tables below and, in each case, require that we label them according to their highest loadings.[7] Since the parameters are all dichotomous and dialectical in nature, we have to conceive of the factors as ways of defining the issues within each party rather than as a high degree of consensus on issues, as a shared concern rather than an agreed direction. The outstanding factors in each case will help us to understand the ideological substance behind each of these parties.

Table 4 for the DC shows the high loadings of each factor. Factor 1 can be characterized as *political authoritarianism* as it seems to control both

Table 4. Rotated factor matrix for the DC.

	Factor 1	Factor 2	Factor 3	Factor 4	Commonalities
Distrust	0.23	-0.11	0.04	| 0.72 |	0.58
Authority	| 0.82 |	0.19	-0.02	0.08	0.72
Bureaucracy	| 0.67 |	-0.31	0.12	0.08	0.57
Class barriers	-0.01	0.04	| 0.64 |	| 0.34 |	0.53
Capitalism	-0.07	| 0.30 |	0.10	| 0.76 |	0.69
Church influence	0.26	0.01	| 0.45 |	| 0.36 |	0.40
Dedication	| 0.46 |	| 0.60 |	-0.01	0.10	0.58
Coalition	0.13	| -0.80 |	0.01	0.08	0.67
Europeanism	0.01	-0.09	| 0.78 |	-0.06	0.61
Vietnam	-0.03	| 0.43 |	| 0.53 |	-0.34	0.58

democratic-authoritarian and pro-bureaucratic sentiments, as well as dedication to the party. Factor 2 links dedication to party with support for the *centro-sinistra* and, at a lesser level, support for Vietnam and belief in economic interventionism. We can call it *party loyalty*. Factor 3 is probably the most important factor and governs a combination of Europeanism, belief in social mobility, support for the American presence in Vietnam, and enlightened political Catholicism. In the light of the quarter century of DC governments, it could be called the *establishment consensus* or pride in the achievements of the party. Factor 4, finally, ties together faith in capitalistic development and social trust in a kind of "faith in people," the opposite of individual and organized exploitation. It is noteworthy that only factors 1 and 4 tie underlying attitudes to the other levels. The link between social trust and the ideological attitudes is as revealing as the linkage in factor 1 if we recall the peculiar DC emphasis on *dirigisme*. Trusting Christian Democrats went heavily for state intervention in the economy, even though they are equally convinced that there are no class barriers holding back social mobility in Italy. Taken together these four factors account for the Italian Christian Democratic stand on all ten issues.

Table 5 on the PSU also has four factors. Factor 1 is the most important[8] and appears to be a *basic ideological dimension* of Italian socialism, expressing distrust toward the upper classes, the bureaucracy, the capitalists, the Church, and toward exploitative individuals. It forms a striking contrast to the DC's factor 1 with its stress on leadership, the state, and party solidarity. Factor 2 reflects a preoccupation with some of the most divisive issues of the day, namely, the coalition, Vietnam, and the choice between Gaullism and Europeanism. It should perhaps be called the *party unity factor,* since it mirrors the Socialist preoccupation

Table 5. Rotated factor matrix for the PSU.

	Factor 1	Factor 2	Factor 3	Factor 4	Commonalities
Distrust	0.04	0.02	0.12	0.58	0.50
Authority	-0.08	-0.18	-0.11	0.88	0.83
Bureaucracy	0.75	-0.02	0.16	0.10	0.60
Class barriers	0.76	-0.04	-0.21	0.03	0.63
Capitalism	-0.65	0.21	0.12	-0.05	0.49
Church influence	0.55	0.14	0.10	0.49	0.57
Dedication	0.11	-0.05	-0.88	0.02	0.79
Coalition	-0.24	0.79	0.01	-0.16	0.70
Europeanism	-0.10	0.54	-0.50	-0.05	0.55
Vietnam	0.07	0.75	0.04	0.04	0.57

with recurrent schisms in the Italian Socialist camp. Factor 3 stresses the private orientation of party members along with Gaullism, a kind of individual and continental declaration of *truculent independence*. Factor 4, finally, is dominated by the concern for democracy (versus authoritarianism) and for tolerating religious loyalties, as well as a suspicion of exploitative individuals. We can call it the *democratic utopian strain*.

If we compare the factors that seem to underlie the concerns of both Italian parties, it is hardly surprising to find basic ideological dimensions uppermost, especially among the Socialists. The ideological strain among the DC, after two decades of governing the country, naturally became so suffused with establishment loyalties and vested interests as to lose the ideological purity to be expected for an opposition. The party loyalty factor among the DC and the party unity factor in the PSU (which broke up into two components within a year of our measurement) also complement each other. There is, furthermore, the political authoritarianism of the DC and the democratic-utopian strain in the PSU, states of mind that may well be typical of the more active elements in the two parties. Finally, there are the more incongruous leftovers, the "faith in people" of the DC, with overtones of the clerical issue and of supportive attitudes toward Vietnam, and the PSU's strange combination of Gaullism and private orientation. Since the PSU scored far higher on Gaullism than the other three parties, we may well be dealing with a deeply rooted isolationist dimension which resists manipulation from the outside both on a personal and a continental level.

Table 6 for the German CDU presents rather different factors. Factor 1 combines support for the grand coalition, and trust in people and in the bureaucracy, with support for the American ally in Vietnam. It appears to be a factor of *trusting cooperation* at all levels and was already one of the

Table 6. Rotated factor matrix for the CDU.

	Factor 1	Factor 2	Factor 3	Factor 4	Commonalities
Distrust	0.51	-0.16	0.28	-0.48	0.59
Authority	-0.15	0.11	0.87	0.06	0.79
Bureaucracy	0.66	-0.39	0.04	0.16	0.62
Class Barriers	0.09	-0.80	-0.06	0.09	0.66
Capitalism	0.14	-0.05	0.42	-0.16	0.23
Church influence	0.35	-0.06	0.55	0.33	0.53
Dedication	0.02	0.06	0.04	0.86	0.74
Coalition	0.71	0.02	0.24	-0.08	0.58
Europeanism	0.11	0.61	-0.04	0.25	0.44
Vietnam	0.66	0.30	-0.15	-0.01	0.55

clusters noted earlier. The second factor loads highly on the traditional conception of a "natural order of classes" (or free mobility), on bureaucracy, and on Europeanism. This may well reflect a *Christian conservatism*. Factor 3, by stressing authority (democracy), capitalistic development, and secularism appears to indicate a strain of industrial authoritarianism, sometimes referred to euphemistically as *"democratic capitalism,"* in the CDU. We are reminded of the CDU election poster of several years ago which showed Ludwig Erhard and two "bosses" striding confidently across a factory yard *(Erfolg und Erfahrung)* under the respectful glances of the workers. This factor also had modest loadings on social trust and on the coalition which may indeed reflect such an industrial authoritarianism. The last factor, finally, can be called the *sectarian* one in that it links clericalism and social distrust with dedication to the party. The reader may be reminded of the "tower" of Catholic isolation in which the forerunner of the CDU, the old Center Party, was long said to be. Cooperation and trust, Christian conservatism, "democratic capitalism," and the sectarian strain evidently made up the ideological substance of the CDU in 1969.

Table 7 for the SPD again raises different dimensions. Factor 1 is here a grand combination of trust in people and in the bureaucrats with a strong commitment to democracy, equality, and religious toleration. We can call it *a cooperative, democratic faith* based especially on high loadings at the underlying level. Factor 2 mixes support for the American ally with Europeanism and getting along with the churches, a combination of historically bitter pills for the SPD, but also a kind of *internationally cooperative attitude*. The third factor links faith in capitalistic development with support for the grand coalition and can be called *reformism*. Finally, the last factor stresses dedication to the party along with an

Table 7. Rotated factor matrix for the SPD.

	Factor 1	Factor 2	Factor 3	Factor 4	Commonalities
Distrust	0.72	0.07	0.20	-0.06	0.56
Authority	0.68	0.12	-0.10	-0.19	0.53
Bureaucracy	0.77	-0.06	-0.15	0.17	0.64
Class barriers	0.60	0.01	0.28	0.44	0.63
Capitalism	0.17	0.17	0.76	-0.13	0.66
Church influence	0.42	0.60	0.18	0.10	0.58
Dedication	-0.05	0.05	0.09	0.83	0.70
Coalition	0.31	0.28	0.69	0.00	0.66
Europeanism	-0.14	0.65	0.09	-0.33	0.56
Vietnam	0.04	-0.75	0.20	0.32	0.72

awareness of class barriers and of the European and Vietnam issues. it can be referred to as the *solidarity* factor as it links party loyalty to issues that were once highly controversial in the party.

The CDU and SPD factors are not identical but they have a few features in common that deserve comment. There is the combination of social trust and pro-bureaucratic sentiment which plays a role in factor 1 of both parties. It is more difficult than in Italy to find factors that link underlying, ideological, and topical attitudes. The reader may recall that the existence of such links was one of our initial premises. With the CDU, the underlying trust and pro-bureaucratic attitudes are indeed linked to the topical attitudes toward the coalition and toward Vietnam by a common factor. Similar links tie authoritarianism in factor 3 to ideological issues, namely, clericalism and capitalism. In fact, all four factors tend to load on two levels, if in varying degrees. As for the SPD, the three underlying attitudes of factor 1 clearly relate to the Socialist view of class barriers and of church influence (especially since 1959). But the attitude toward capitalistic development, interestingly, is no longer controlled by the same factor as it probably was in the 1920s.

Comparing the German to the Italian varimax tables, the question of linkage between the levels is particularly revealing. It shows that only the CDU factors all load on the underlying issues as well as on the other two levels. The DC factors, by comparison, vary in the degree of linkage they provide. Factor 1 links only two underlying issues with a topical one. Factor 2 has all its heavy loadings among the topical issues and only a light one among the ideological issues. Such concentration among the topical issues is also true of the second and third factors of the PSU. Factor 3 of the DC links only the ideological and the topical levels and the same is true of the second, third, and fourth factors of the SPD.

There is also the question of how clear and autonomous the factors are in each case. It would appear that the CDU is ideologically the most heterogeneous party of the four. It has four encompassing factors, and the loadings are more often divided among several factors than with any of the other parties. The Italian DC seems next in heterogeneity on our ten issues. The difference between the SPD and the PSU is harder to assess. The PSU which earlier emerged as the most ideology-minded, in the sense of orthodox Socialist concerns, may well seem unexpectedly heterogeneous because it harbored two fairly distinct party traditions in 1968, that of the old Nenni Socialists (PSI) and that of the Saragat Social Democrats (PSDI). Their differences cropped up again and again in our cross-tabulations. The SPD, on the other hand, seems to exhibit not only a single, dominant underlying factor, but also a certain regularity with which it links each of the ideological factors to different topical issues. But the SPD also has many of its more prominent loadings split among several factors, while the PSU exhibits a clearer, more economical structure of linkages.

The time has come to look back upon the road we have traveled and to raise the question of what all these measurements amount to in the end. Our basic quest was for an understanding of the nature of ideological attitudes among party activists in the late sixties. Our measurement deliberately undertook to de-intellectualize the concept of ideology and to concentrate on the cohesion and interplay of political attitudes of various levels: underlying, ideological, and topical. As we took our party samples through the different steps of our methodology, certain clusters of attitudes clearly began to appear. The SPD emerged with a strong cluster of underlying attitudes, trust-democracy–pro-bureaucratic sentiment, and its obverse. The Italian PSU, by way of contrast, had a strong cluster of ideological attitudes such as anticlericalism—economic intervention—class barriers (often linked to social distrust and antibureaucratic sentiment) and its obverse. The ideological cluster here also dominated the attitudes toward the center-left coalition, the United States in Vietnam, and a United Europe. The CDU has less prominent features, and the DC again seems to stress underlying issues more than issues at the other levels.

The factor analysis, finally, sharpened our perception of the underlying factors and how they tie together the various issues and levels. Thus it was hardly surprising that the Italian DC should have an "establishment consensus" and "political authoritarianism" as its most influential factors, and that the "basic ideological dimension" of Italian socialism supplies that role in the PSU. The "cooperative, democratic faith" of the SPD and the heterogeneity of the concerns of the CDU round out a picture that is not unexpected. The "end of ideology," or de-ideologization of West German politics asserted by the late Otto Kirchheimer is a fact even among the party activists. The survival of political ideology in Italy, particularly on the left (LaPalombara, 1964) by the same token is no less real.[9]

FOOTNOTES

1. Evidently the young Italian rebels never joined the PSU or its successors, while their German counterparts joined the SPD and became its *Jusos* only after the survey.

2. The relationship between the ideological questions proper and these extra questions was not particularly revealing except for the religiously more tolerant SPD and the more secular CDU members who both favored tolerating the NPD and not recognizing the DDR. Among the topical issue groups, the opponents of the grand coalition (presumably the extremes in both parties) were for suppressing the NPD and DDR recognition. The cross-tabulation tables on all the ideological parameters are available on request.

3. The Italian respondents were selected from the PSU of 1968, a (as it turned out) short-lived merger of the old PSI and the PSDI minus the secessionist PSIUP. This is not a perfect equivalent of the German SPD, considering the presence of the PCI and PSIUP, but represented a reasonably homogeneous political subculture at the time.

4. These adjustments were meant to bring the known views of party members as much as possible into a meaningful, dichotomous framework. See, for example, Cicchitto *et al.* (1968); La Palombara (1964).

5. Kendall's Q will show a strong relationship in an $\dfrac{a \mid b}{c \mid d}$ table if 1) $a > c$ but $d > b$ and/or 2) the vertical ratios are greatly dissimilar. X^2 compares the actual to the expected frequencies in each of the four boxes of a two-by-two table in order to control against the weaknesses of Q, which tends to indicate chiefly the vertical and diagonal relationships.

6. The original cross-tabulation tables with these markings are available on request.

7. For a brief explanation of the method, see Garson (1971, pp. 201–211). The factor analysis program used was the BIOMED program of the Health Sciences facility at UCLA. On a different factor analysis program (SPSS), we obtained substantially the same varimax factors for the DC except that there were five, the fifth factor being support for the American presence in Vietnam. This second analysis singled out factor 3 as accounting for 38.9 percent of the variances (and factor 5 for another 12.7 percent) and factor 1 as accounting for 20.1 percent.

8. The SPSS analysis gave 61.9 percent as the percentage of variances explained by this factor and 24.9 percent as the percentage accounted for by factor 2. The BIOMED program did not supply this information.

9. On the role of social distrust ideology in Italy, see especially Zariski, 1972, pp. 93–96, 109–116.

REFERENCES

Alberoni, Francesco *et al.* (1967) *L'attivista di partito*. Bologna: Il Mulino.

Barnes, Samuel H. (1967) *Party Democracy: Politics in an Italian Socialist Federation*. New Haven: Yale University Press.

Cicchitto, Fabrizio *et al.* (1968) *La DC dopo il primo ventennio*. Padua: Marsilio.

Dittberner, Juergen and Rolf Ebbighausen (1973) *Parteiensystem in der Legitimationskrise*. Opladen: Westdeutscher Verlag.

Doxa (1968) *Opinioni politiche degli Italiani alla vigilia delle elezioni.*

Flechtheim, Ossip K. (ed.) (1973) *Die Parteien der BRD.* Hamburg: Hoffman & Campe.

Galli, Giorgio (1968) *Il bipartitismo imperfetto.* Bologna: Il mulino.

—— and Alfonso Prandi (1970) *Patterns of Political Participation in Italy.* New Haven: Yale University Press.

Garson David G. (1971) *Handbook of Political Science Methods.* Boston: Holbrook Press.

Inglehart, Ronald (1976) "The Nature of Value Change in Post-industrial Societies." Pages 57–99 in Leon N. Lindberg (ed.), Politics and the Future of Industrial Society. New York: McKay.

Kaack, Heino, (1971) *Geschichte und Struktur des deutschen Parteiensystems.* Opladen: Westdeutscher Verlag.

La Palombara, Joseph (1964) *Interest Groups in Italian Politics.* Princeton, NJ: Princeton University Press.

Mayer, Lawrence C. and John H. Burnett (1977) *Politics in Industrial Societies: A Comparative Perspective.* New York: Wiley.

Merkl, Peter (1971) "Partecipazione ai sindacati e ai partiti in Germania Occidentale e in Italia." *Rivista Italiana di Scienza Politica* 1: 326–329.

—— (1976) "Party Members and Society in West Germany and Italy." Pages 153–172 in Rudolf Wildenmann (ed.), *Form und Erfahrung, ein Leben für die Demokratie, Festschrift für F.A. Hermens.* Berlin: Duncker & Humblot.

Putnam, Robert D. (1972) "Studying Elite Political Culture: The Case of Ideology." Pages 334–393 in Ginseppe Di Palma (ed.), *Mass Politics in Industrial Societies.* Chicago: Markham.

Rokkan, Stein (1970) *Citizens, Elections, Parties.* New York: McKay.

Sjoberg, Gideon, M. Donald Hancock, and Orion White, Jr. (eds.), (1967) *Politics in the Post-Welfare State: A Comparison of the United States and Sweden.* Bloomington, IN: Carnegie Seminar.

Zariski, Raphael (1972) *Italy: The Politics of Uneven Development,* Hinsdale, IL: Dryden.

APPENDIX: THE PARAMETERS

Table 8. Dedication to own party.
(Percentages)

	SPD	CDU	West Germany	Italy	PSU	DC	All Social-ists	All Christian Democrats
Very dedicated	20	24	22	5	6	4	13	14
Rather dedicated	11	9	10	3	4	2	7	5
In the middle	17	12	15	5	5	5	..	8
Rather private-oriented	16	21	18	17	15	20	15	20
Very private-oriented	33	31	32	68	66	70	51	50
DK, neither	3	3	3	2	4	–	3	1
	100	100	100	100	100	101	100	98
N	(100)	(100)	(200)	(215)	(113)	(102)	(213)	(202)

Table 9. People take advantage of you (social distrust)
(Percentages)

	SPD	CDU	West Germany	Italy	PSU	DC	Social-ists	Christian Democrats
They sure do	11	8	10	29	35	22	24	15
They rather do	15	13	14	24	27	22	21	17
In the middle	18	18	18	16	13	20	15	19
Not really	31	32	31	14	8	22	19	27
Definitely not	21	23	22	12	12	13	16	18
DK, neither	4	6	5	4	5	3	5	4
	100	100	100	99	100	101	100	100
N	(100)	(100)	(200)	(215)	(113)	(102)	(213)	(202)

Table 10. Are authority, leadership needed
for democracy? (Authoritarianism)
(Percentages)

	SPD	CDU	West Germany	Italy	PSU	DC	Social-ists	Christian Democrats
Indeed they are	9	17	13	8	5	11	7	14
They rather are	17	16	17	8	4	13	10	14
In the middle	20	17	18	9	10	8	15	12
You need coopera-tion more than authority	28	25	27	23	23	23	25	24
Definitely no strong man needed	22	19	20	41	42	40	33	30
Dk, neither	4	6	5	11	15	6	10	6
	100	100	100	100	99	101	100	99
N	(100)	(100)	(200)	(215)	(113)	(102)	(213)	(202)

Table 11. Bureaucrats are petty, lazy.
(Percentages)

	SPD	CDU	West Germany	Italy	PSU	DC	Social-ists	Christian Democrats
They sure are	4	4	4	15	21	9	13	6
They rather are	6	5	6	14	20	7	13	5
In the middle	10	3	6	15	15	16	13	9
They are really not	23	24	24	19	14	25	18	24
Definitely not	53	60	56	31	23	39	37	50
Dk, neither	4	4	4	6	6	5	5	4
	100	100	100	100	99	101	99	98
N	(100)	(100)	(200)	(213)	(111)	(102)	(211)	(202)

Table 12. Our society still has class barriers.
(Percentages)

	SPD	CDU	West Germany	Italy	PSU	DC	Social-ists	Christian Democrats
It sure does (should)	7	9	8	16	20	11	14	10
It rather does	11	9	10	11	14	8	13	8
In the middle	10	18	14	16	17	15	14	16
It hardly does	27	19	23	19	15	24	21	21
Definitely not	45	41	43	32	26	39	35	40
Dk, neither	–	4	2	6	8	4	4	4
	100	100	100	100	100	101	101	99
N	(100)	(100)	(200)	(215)	(113)	(102)	(213)	(202)

Table 13. Does capitalistic development free the people?
(Percentages)

	SPD	CDU	West Germany	Italy	PSU	DC	Social-ists	Christian Democrats
It sure does	22	35	29	11	16	5	19	20
It rather does	29	14	21	17	23	10	26	12
In the middle	17	13	15	9	8	11	12	12
Drastic political change is rather needed	16	15	16	22	12	33	14	24
Definitely need drastic change	14	16	15	37	38	35	26	26
DK, neither	2	7	4	4	4	5	3	6
	100	100	100	100	101	99	100	100
N	(100)	(100)	(200)	(213)	(112)	(101)	(212)	(201)

Table 14. Church influence should be tolerated.
(Percentages)

	SPD	CDU	West Germany	Italy	PSU	DC	Social-ists	Christian Democrats
It should indeed	42	24	33	24	40	6	41	15
It rather should	22	9	16	8	14	2	18	5
In the middle	13	12	12	13	19	8	16	10
Rather not	6	13	10	14	10	19	8	16
Definitely not	16	39	27	35	11	63	13	51
DK, neither	1	3	2	5	7	3	4	3
	100	100	100	99	101	101	100	100
N	(100)	(100)	(200)	(215)	(113)	(102)	(213)	(202)

Table 15. Was entering the grand coalition an unwise step?
(Percentages)

	SPD	CDU	West Germany	Italy	PSU	DC	Socialists	Christian Democrats
It sure was	10	7	9	12	14	9	12	8
It rather was	8	9	9	4	2	6	5	8
In the middle	11	11	11	11	12	10	11	10
Not really	19	27	23	19	18	20	18	24
Definitely was not	50	42	46	48	46	50	48	46
Dk, neither	2	4	3	7	9	6	6	5
	100	100	101	101	101	101	100	101
N	(100)	(100)	(200)	(215)	(113)	(102)	(213)	(202)

Table 16. Support for the U.S. in Vietnam
(Percentages)

	SPD	CDU	West Germany	Italy	PSU	DC	Socialists	Christian Democrats
Strongly supports U.S.	29	43	36	34	19	50	24	47
Rather supports U.S.	37	37	37	16	13	19	24	26
In the middle	16	4	10	7	8	7	12	5
Rather supports V.C.	4	3	4	8	12	4	8	3
Strongly supports V.C.	4	3	4	21	33	9	19	6
DK, neither	10	10	10	13	14	12	12	11
	100	100	101	99	99	101	99	98
N	(100)	(100)	(200)	(215)	(113)	(202)	(213)	(202)

Table 17. A European Federation or a Europe of Fatherlands?
(Percentages)

	SPD	CDU	West Germany	Italy	PSU	DC	Social-ists	Christian Democrats
Definitely for European federation	56	60	58	33	27	39	41	40
Rather European	20	28	24	16	12	21	16	24
In the middle	8	3	6	11	8	15	8	9
Rather Gaullist	5	3	4	9	12	5	9	4
Strongly Gaullist	5	3	4	19	25	13	15	8
DK, neither	6	3	5	12	15	8	11	5
	100	100	101	100	99	101	100	100
N	(100)	(100)	(200)	(215)	(113)	(102)	(213)	(202)

Table 18. Recognition of DDR (W. Germany only).
(Percentages)

	SPD	CDU	Total
Definitely in favor of recognition	21	9	15
Rather in favor	14	8	11
In the middle, neither	13	19	16
Rather against recognition	19	15	17
Definitely against recognition	30	47	39
DK	3	2	2
	100	100	100
N	(100)	(100)	(200)

Table 19. Toleration of the NPD.
(Percentages)

	SPD	CDU	Total
Should be tolerated	25	35	30
It rather should	25	14	20
In the middle	13	10	11
Rather against toleration	7	9	8
Definitely against toleration	27	27	27
DK, neither	3	5	4
	100	100	100
N	(100)	(100)	(200)

PART II

STUDIES IN UNDERDEVELOPMENT

COMPARATIVE ADVANTAGE, THE WORLD DIVISION OF LABOR, AND UNDERDEVELOPMENT*

Charles Ragin and Jacques Delacroix

INTRODUCTION

The principle of comparative advantage of classical economics implies that all trade partners benefit from the specialization induced by international exchange. A fortiori, such specialization should have beneficial effects on economic growth when it is reinforced by the differential endowment of trading partners in the factors of production. Without overtly denying the overall validity of this principle, a growing body of Marxist-inspired theories of underdevelopment argues that the modes of poor countries' participation in international trade impede their economic progress. These theories variously cite: (a) the vulnerability of poor countries to the vagaries of international markets ("market vulnerability" arguments), (b) the distortion of class development and the rerouting of

Comparative Social Research, Vol. , pp. 181—214.
Volume 1 published as Comparative Studies in Sociology
Copyright © 1979 by JAI Press, Inc.
All rights of reproduction in any form reserved.
ISBN 0-89232-112-1

class conflict into noncreative avenues associated with certain positions in the world division of labor ("class-centered" arguments), (c) the subjection of poor countries to mechanisms of unequal exchange ("unequal exchange" arguments); (d) the retardation or abortion of the process of internal structural differentiation associated with certain forms of participation in world trade ("structural differentiation" arguments).

In the first part of this paper we contrast some of the broadest implications of the comparative advantage argument with predictions derived from Marxist-inspired theories. This first test is performed over all cases for which data are available. This "sample" therefore includes cases (countries) at very different levels of development. The analysis of this larger sample is necessary since some of the arguments in question posit uniform consequences of certain economic behaviors *across* levels of development. The first test is not meant as an exhaustive examination of either classical or Marxist-inspired theories. It serves, rather, to establish, despite a paucity of previous empirical confirmation, the credibility of the Marxist perspectives against the more general and more widely supported comparative advantage argument.

In the second part of this paper, we present a more detailed analysis based on a theoretical conceptualization of the variable effects of participation in international trade for countries at different levels of development. Specifically, we contrast the effects of *intensity* and *forms* of participation in international trade on the economic performance of three groups of countries. The first group is composed of rich countries; the second, of intermediate countries, some of which are rapidly developing, and the third, of poor countries, most of which are characterized by no growth or very slow growth. By splitting our sample into three groups we are able to comment on the relative plausibility of each of the relevant Marxist-inspired arguments.

WORLD TRADE AND DEVELOPMENT: AN OVERVIEW

The Principle of Comparative Advantage
According to the principle of comparative advantage formulated by Ricardo (1971, pp. 147–167), all countries maximize their growth by trad-

*Charles Ragin and Jacques Delacroix are both members of the Department of Sociology, Indiana University, Bloomington. Jointly, they are now writing a monograph on economic development tentatively entitled *Imperialism and Development: A Dispassionate Empirical Analysis*. In this work they systematically test the major sociological perspectives on economic development with post-1950 data on Third World countries. The perspectives they consider include world systems theory, dependency theory, modernization theory, and their own synthetic theory which allows for both exogenetic and ontogenetic factors.

ing with one another, whether or not they differ in their respective endowments in the factors of production. Samuelson [1939; 1962 (in response to Kemp, 1962); 1970, pp. 645–664] remarks that the economic advantages procured by trade are multiplied when the national specialization it fosters is also based on a differential distribution of natural and other resources. These arguments apply to countries at all levels of development and to trade between countries at all such levels. (See also Kindleberger, 1958, pp. 238–239; 1964; Pincus, 1967.)

In the absence of any detailed study (for a brilliant but opaque exception see Linder, 1961; also Brewster, 1971), it is possible to offer some reasonable speculations about the comparative advantage less developed countries enjoy in their commercial relations with more developed countries.

Underdeveloped countries are poor in the sense that large segments of their populations subsist at low wage levels which correspond to an excess or underemployment of labor. Less developed countries should therefore enjoy a relative advantage in the production of commodities that require inexpensive, abundant, and moderately skilled labor. In addition, the bulk of the underdeveloped part of the world enjoys an advantage verging on the absolute with respect to the availability of certain resources which nature has distributed capriciously. Coffee, cocoa, and bananas, for example, do not grow in the temperate zone where most developed countries are located. Most of the tin, copper, and aluminum ores and most of the petroleum reserves required for continued world industrial expansion are likewise found outside the temperate zone.

If the less developed countries' economic behavior conformed to the principle of comparative advantage, they should tend to export more or less labor-intensive commodities processed from the raw materials favored by their natural circumstances (Cairncross, 1962). Such countries' exports, accordingly, should consist largely of plantation and mine products (Mandel, 1975, p. 59) and, more generally, of primary products, rather than of manufactures and other processed goods. They should import from developed countries those primary products the latter are better able to produce and all kinds of processed goods. (See Pincus, 1967, pp. 48–49 for an elaboration of this argument.) These include, in particular, industrial equipment and durable consumer goods. The more developed countries should export *only* those primary products that their natural conditions favor and that do *not* require intensive labor (see also Haberler, 1936).

Hence, if all countries adhered to the principle of comparative advantage, a worldwide division of labor would emerge characterized, in part, by the specialization of poor countries in the production of primary products for export.

But this division of labor is not the only predictable consequence for the structure of world trade of generalized conformity to the principle of comparative advantage. Considering each country individually, the combination of a general advantage relative to labor costs with specific natural endowments should result in the *narrow* specialization of poor countries. Each should export only a few primary commodities in order to maximize

Table 1. Descriptive data.

Variable			Category[a]	
		Poor	Intermediate	Rich
1. GNP/capita 1950[b]	m	87.9	291.0	1203.9
	sd	30.8	127.1	399.6
	min	37.0	152.0	703.0
	max	144.0	623.0	2358.0
2. GNP/capita 1969[b]	m	128.7	539.3	2016.1
	sd	70.1	330.5	501.1
	min	48.0	192.0	1495.0
	max	324.0	1354.0	3603.0
3. Change in GNP/capita[b]	m	45.7	289.4	811.1
	sd	57.2	282.7	243.7
	min	-19.0	-72.0	425.0
	max	220.0	1021.0	1245.0
4. Trade/GNP[c]	m	.372	.482	.342
	sd	.261	.496	.155
	min	.046	.098	.067
	max	1.39	3.111	.645
5. Community Concentration[d]	m	.835	.745	.501
	sd	.117	.206	.229
	min	.559	.358	.267
	max	.990	.994	.965
6. Primary Products Specialization[e]	m	.940	.804	.478
	sd	.134	.239	.301
	min	.310	.180	.090
	max	.990	.990	.990

[a]Poor = countries with GNP/capita 1950 less than $150; Intermediate = countries with GNP/capita 1950 greater than $150 and less than $650; Rich = countries with GNP/capita 1950 greater than $650.

[b]In constant dollars at factor costs.

[c]Total value of imports plus exports/GNP (1955).

[d]Value of 5 largest exports/value of all exports (1955).

[e]Value of exports in SITC categories 0-4 (or equivalent)/value of all exports (1955).

the benefits derived from specific natural endowments. Note that a concomitantly narrow specialization in processed exports need not be the rule for rich countries. Such countries are freer to diversify their production in all spheres that are not labor intensive because of the lesser importance of natural endowments relative to labor costs in these countries' economies (Kindleberger, 1964, pp. 48–49; Pincus, 1967, pp. 48–50). Thus, a second feature of the structure of world trade as determined by conformity to the principle of comparative advantage would be *high commodity concentration* in the exports of poor but not of rich countries.

In fact, at a crude level, the observable structure of world trade as indicated by measures of *forms* of participation in trade looks pretty much as it would if most countries adhered to the principle of comparative advantage: the poorer the country, the greater its propensity to export primary products and the higher the concentration of its export mix (see Table 1: Descriptive Data).

The Neo-Marxist Critique

According to most classical economists (Haberler, 1959; Cairncross, 1962), conformity with comparative advantage only maximizes the growth benefits participants in trade derive from their unequal resources; trading does not guarantee evenly paced growth to all participants (see also Samuelson, 1962). Nevertheless, the idea that trade may be responsible for the *underdevelopment* of some participants in trade is foreign to the comparative advantage perspective. Since the 1950s, however, a growing body of neo-Marxist theory has pinned the blame for the apparently persistent underdevelopment of much of the world on the global division of labor and on the corresponding international trade structure. Since the latter seems to result from a high degree of actual conformity with the dictates of comparative advantage, neo-Marxist theory raises a series of crucial questions regarding the desirability of this conformity for the poor countries.

It is often difficult to discern statements that can be put to a systematic quantitative test in this ever-growing mass of complex and overlapping arguments frequently tainted with ideological emotionalism. Nevertheless, two answerable questions appear again and again and constitute the central themes of this literature:

1. Does the developed capitalist segment of the world (the "core") profit from the continued underdevelopment of the remainder (the "periphery"), and does it take deliberate action to perpetuate an exploitative relationship?

2. Does the existing structure of the world capitalist economy and the place of poor countries within it interfere with the economic progress of the latter?

In this study we will address primarily the second question, but some of our findings trace the outline of an answer to the first. We begin with a delineation of four distinct trains of neo-Marxist thought which seek to answer these questions. We document our examination of these arguments with the better-known names associated with each.

(a) *The Market vulnerability argument*. Furtado (1965), Gomez (1966), Maizel (1958), Magdoff (1969), and Galeano (1971), among others, postulate that the world demand for primary products must undergo relative decline, forcing many poor countries into even more direct and more fruitless competition. The negative effect of this trend is thought to be aggravated by the price fluctuations that characterize primary products. The adverse effects of such fluctuations are compounded when exports are concentrated, as is usually the case (Stallings, 1972, p. 31). The resulting instabilities in the foreign exchange earnings of poor countries ought to impair their capacity for public and private planning in proportion to their reliance on international trade.

Mandel (1975, p. 58) refutes the historical necessity of a secular decline in the demand for primary products. Furthermore, the decline in the terms of trade, cited by Prebisch in 1950 as evidence of a secular decline, is less than apparent for the post-World War II period, even if we arbitrarily exclude petroleum prices from consideration. Finally, the weight of the available empirical evidence (Coppock, 1962; MacBean, 1966; Erb and Schiavo-Campo, 1969; Naya, 1973; Glezakos, 1973[1]; Askari and Weil, 1974) does not support the price fluctuations argument.

(b) *Class-centered arguments*. This body of literature links underdevelopment both to the structure of the global division of labor and to the predatory activities of core capitalist interests. It is bound together by its assignment of a central role to class variables in the relationship between patterns of specialization in international trade and differential development. Dependency theorists in this tradition, such as Frank (1967; 1972)—prompted by Dos Santos (1969)—and Berman (1974) propose a sociological version of Baran's (1957) economic theory of transnational exploitation. To summarize (perhaps crudely) this perspective: core capitalists appropriate the surplus generated by the cheap labor of periphery countries applied to indigenous natural resources. This appropriation is made possible by the complicity (Borricaud, 1966; Galtung, 1971) or, at least, the historically induced ineptitude (Frank, 1972; Berman, 1974) of the elites of peripheral areas who fail in the performance of their national entrepreneurial and managerial task.

The incapacity of the indigenous elites to perform their historical role as midwives to industrial capitalism is variously linked by these authors to the unfavorable position of poor countries in the world division of labor. Paige (1975) and more recently Mamdani (1976) have documented the objective complicity of resident elites in the foreign led exploitation of local resources.[2] However intellectually compelling this line of reasoning, almost no systematic empirical evidence has been presented linking economic dependency, class phenomena, and inferior economic performance.[3] On the other hand, strong, implicitly negative evidence has been offered by Tugwell (1974), and theoretical counterarguments by Leff (1968) and Lim (1968). [See Hill (1975) for a complete review of this literature.]

The class-centeredness of this body of theory gives it some kinship to Wallerstein's (1974) long-term historical reconstruction of a similar relationship. Wallerstein argues that different class structures have an unequal potential for generating creative class tensions (1974, pp. 346–357). He traces the different contemporary national class structures back to different modes of labor control developed in the core, semi-periphery, and periphery. In turn, the different modes of labor control are associated with the specific functional roles assigned to different regions in a world division of labor in expansion since the sixteenth century. According to this scheme,[4] the historically determined assignment of some regions to the production of bullion, plantation products (e.g., sugar), and other primary commodities ultimately led to the dominance of these regions by nonentrepreneurial and parasitic elites (e.g., Peru, Brazil, and the Caribbean area). In Europe, the production of commodities that require some active cooperation on the part of workers (e.g., manufactures) led to several uniquely European developments. Among these were the evolution in that region of politically able lower strata and the leadership of an industrializing bourgeoisie. In this perspective, the continued dominance of the area is well served by the creative flight forward of a bourgeoisie whose antagonistic working class supplies a realistic leadership alternative.

Wallerstein's formation does not require that deliberately predatory core activities persist in underlying the development gap.[5] Underdevelopment has become a structural condition of the world capitalist economy. The core continues to benefit from the poverty of the periphery as an automatic consequence of past historical developments which must soon be succeeded by a dialectical upturning of the world system (Wallerstein, 1974b).

(c) *The unequal exchange argument.* Of major interest to us in this study is the matter of unequal exchange. There are important differences between the two main representatives of this school of thought, Mandel (1975) and Emmanuel (1972; 1974); nevertheless, it is possible to specify the main features of the unequal exchange perspective without betraying the subtleties of its several versions. At a minimum, it is possible to sketch the main mechanisms that would account for the *measurable* underdevelopment of the periphery through unequal exchange and to relate these mechanisms to the *observable* modes of poor countries' participation in trade.

For a variety of reasons relating to the imperfectly capitalistic mode of production prevailing in poor regions, periphery labor is *less* productive than core labor (see Mandel, 1975, pp. 45–53, 352–361). According to Mandel (1975, p. 53), "The exchange of commodities produced in conditions of a higher productivity of labour against commodities produced in conditions of a lower productivity of labour [is] an unequal one; it [is] an exchange of less against more labour, which inevitably led to the *drain,* an outward flow of value and capital from [peripheral] countries to the advantage of Western Europe," Under conditions of "freely competitive capitalism" (roughly, until the turn of the century) trade between core and periphery interferes with primitive accumulation in the latter. In the subsequent age of "classical capitalism," the export of surplus capital from the core to the periphery (an unavoidable consequence of normal capitalist competition in the core) intensifies the drain of surplus value. Furthermore, the export of capital during "classical capitalism" distorts the periphery's remaining potential for development away from industrialism, making periphery economies "complementary" to those of the core (Mandel, 1975, p. 57). "[T]his meant especially that they had to concentrate on the production of . . . raw materials" (Mandel, 1975, p. 57). This suffocation of economic development in the periphery was accompanied by a "long term social and political alliance between imperialism and local oligarchies [which] froze pre-capitalist relations of production in the village [sic]" (Mandel, 1975, p. 56). (Note that a consequence of this freeze has to be the perpetuation of the pre-existing relative advantage of the periphery: the availability of cheap labor.)[6]

Thus, while Mandel, and unequal exchange theorists in general, do not necessarily consider the concentration of the exports of periphery countries into primary products a direct cause of underdevelopment, they view such forms of trade participation as a sign that value is being lost through unequal exchange.[7] On the contemporary scene: "International movements of capital constantly reproduce and extend the international productivity differential . . . and are themselves, in turn, further determined by this differential" (Mandel, 1975, p. 343). These mechanisms of unequal exchange, according to Mandel, insure the perpetuation of underdevelopment in the periphery. Note that since the actual vehicle of unequal exchange is trade, the magnitude of the drain from the periphery to the core and the ensuing de-development of the latter should be proportional to the intensity of the involvement of periphery countries in trade.

(d) *The internal structural differentiation argument.* Some scholars (Singer, 1950; Hirschman, 1958; Young, 1970; Galtung, 1971; Amin, 1974, and in a peculiar fashion Bettleheim, 1972) emphasize the influence of participation in world trade on the evolution of the internal social structures of poor countries, considered in their nonpolitical aspects. Often such scholars (e.g., Galtung) do not distinguish clearly between the particular class dynamics (or shortage thereof, e.g., Mamdani) prevailing in dependent countries and equally important features of these countries' social structure that are largely unrelated to class phenomena. The equation of class structure with the larger societal framework is regrettable, because the distinction, well established by Marx himself in *Capital,* suggests yet another approach to the study of the effects of involvement in trade on underdevelopment. While this approach is well delineated by Hirshman (1958) and others (see Young, 1970), it is advisable to go back to Marx's formulation because it provides a convenient starting point for the specification of the *interaction* between class dynamics and the process of structural differentiation.

Marx and Engels vividly describe in *The Communist Manifesto* (1848) the titanic performance of the European bourgeoisie bringing forth the new industrial epoch. This historical process is described in terms of an imperfectly diachronic process:

1. The destruction of pre-capitalist relations of productions, and

2. the unprecedented development of the forces of production by the emergent bourgeoisie.

Following Adam Smith, Marx credited the second phenomenon very largely to the specifically capitalist innovation of the factory system (1967, p. 359). The characteristic "division of labor in the workshop" (Marx, 1967; Rueschemeyer, 1977, pp. 3–4), which constitutes its core, accelerates the generation of surplus and establishes conditions favorable to the appropriation of surplus by capitalists. Ensuing capital accumulation and concentration, in turn, stimulate exponentially further industrial development.

This unique process of class formation is not the only distinguishing feature of capitalist development in Europe. It is possible to argue (based on sections of *Capital,* Vol. I) that this process took place within the framework of a uniquely favorable pre-existing societal structure. In the few pages he devotes to the non-European world, Marx contrasts (the unfortunately named) "Asiatic Societies" with European societies from the standpoint of their respective "division of labor in society." There is a crucial difference between the "division of labor in the workshop" and the "division of labor in society" that is often obscured by Marx's own terminological inconsistency. Marx (1967, p. 356) defines the "division of labor in the workshop" as the (mostly) sequential fragmentation of production *in one work site and under one authority* (which was originally that of the capitalist). The steps in the workshop division of labor are work-stations (Marx, 1967, pp. 342–345). "Division of labor in society," on the other hand, refers to the movement of *commodities* (i.e., merchandise which changes hands commercially) from one workshop (farm, mine, factory) to another. Note that this transfer of products across the steps of the societal division of labor normally implies spatial as well as ownership (and consequently authority) discontinuities. Marx illustrates this process with the movement of goods from the cattle farm to the tannery, to the shoe factory, etc. (1967, p. 354). The societal division of labor more than the workshop division of labor involves both sequential (example above) and lateral linkages (as when a locomotive is assembled, Marx, 1967, p. 342) in the production network. Whereas a high degree of division of labor in the workshop is a specific contribution of capitalism, the societal division of labor is "common to all economic formations" (Marx, 1967, p. 359).

The mechanisms by which a high degree of societal division of labor promotes economic development, independent of class effects, are intricate and numerous. Nevertheless, they can be summarily described in contemporary sociological terms;

1. With each increase, the societal division of labor reacts back upon itself by creating the conditions for further expansion (Marx, 1967, p. 383). The separation of the tannery from the cattle farm paves the way for the separation of the shoe factory from the tannery.

2. Each increase in the societal division of labor leads to the multiplication of intermediary social roles, especially occupations such as clerks and merchants. Likewise it stimulates the creation or expansion of institutions charged with adjudicating commercial disputes, in particular within the judiciary sphere of government (see Galtung, 1971, pp. 85–90).

3. Each increase in the societal division of labor incites the growth of "connective tissues" in the form of transportation and communication networks. The growth of the latter, in turn, facilitates the expansion of general service institutions such as universities (Galtung, 1971) by enlarging the scope of economic activity. (Ten thousand unconnected Indian villages cannot support a university even though they may possess plurally the resources to do so.)

4. Each increase in the societal division of labor creates new discontinuities in the ownership of commodities (i.e., merchandise changes hands) which constitute so many taxation opportunities. These combine with the increased adjudicating functions imparted to the government by the growing complexity of commerce to enlarge the scope of realized (actual) competence of the state apparatus. The first manifestation of this change is often the state's assumption of leadership in the creation and expansion of transportation and communication networks. To the extent

that the state's intervention in economic affairs, in the formative period, is conducive to growth, increases in the societal division of labor accelerate economic development via the strengthening of the state.

Thus, increases in societal division of labor tend to be self-multiplying, and, most significantly, they make possible a fuller exploitation of existing resources by stimulating the general "internal structural differentiation of society" (as used recently by Ruschemeyer, 1977) *outside* the sphere of production proper.[8] All three effects discussed above ought to have overall beneficial consequences for economic development *whether or not they operate within and about capitalist relations of production.*[9]

On the eve of the capitalist revolution, different regions were characterized by different primeval degrees of societal divisions of labor with perceptible economic consequences. Marx (1967, p. 358) attributes the economic stagnation of Mogul India to the endless replication of an initially low societal division of labor. In Europe, however, endogenetic development combined the specific capitalist innovation of the workshop division of labor with a *high* pre-existing degree of division of labor in *society*. Furthermore, the increased production of surplus value and its concentration, initiated by the workshop division of labor, supplied the requisite resources for a new and unprecedented expansion of the societal division of labor in accord with the interests of the bourgeoisie (as suggested by Ruschemeyer, 1977, pp. 6–9, at a more abstract level of discourse).

Since the action of the division of labor in the workshop on the division of labor in society and its converse take place concurrently, it is easy to confuse the one with the other. Nevertheless, they can be distinguished in principle and empirically. In particular, it is important to keep in mind that changes in the division of labor in society may have an independent influence on economic development. Consequently, anything that interferes with the expansion of the *societal* division of labor should form an obstacle to economic development (above and beyond any accompanying deficiency in the class structure).

In this perspective *primary product specialization* and *commodity concentration* should be associated with slow economic development irrespective of their influence on class dynamics.[10] This is because *both* forms of participation in world trade *impede* internal structural differentiation, the former by minimizing *sequential* linkages in the production sphere and elsewhere, the latter by limiting *lateral* linkages in the economy and in other institutional spheres. These obstacles to development may be combined with the deleterious consequences of class distortions, as suggested by Galtung (1971) and Baumgartner, Buckley, and Burns (1976), but the two effects are separable.

PARTICIPATION IN TRADE AND LEVEL OF DEVELOPMENT

Neo-Marxist (i.e., Leninist) perspectives on underdevelopment rest on distinctions between categories of countries that are syntactic rather than directly observable. Typically, the existence of core and periphery countries is considered axiomatic, and no formal or empirical criteria for the assignment of countries to these categories are established. The (usually) post hoc addition of a "semi-periphery" or "sub-imperialist" category increases the flexibility of these theories without increasing their formalization. This lack of formalization is unfortunate since indicators of development and underdevelopment, particularly GNP/capita, reveal relatively uniform gradations of countries in levels of development rather than discrete categories. The "development gap" is thus a useful but fluid abstraction rather than a palpable reality (Finsterbusch, 1973).

Empirical examination of neo-Marxist theories, however, requires that we group countries according to level of development for two distinct reasons. First, *all* Marxist-inspired theories posit variable effects of trade participation, depending on level of development. By contrast, the principle of comparative advantage posits uniform effects across all levels of development for certain kinds of economic behavior. The doctrine of comparative advantage, for example, argues that trade fosters the national specialization of both developed and underdeveloped countries and that such specialization is likely to enhance overall economic growth since economies of scale normally result. Marxist-inspired theories, on the other hand, argue that trade is likely to harm the periphery (via the mechanisms discussed above) and to further the economic growth of the core. To examine all countries without distinguishing between countries at very different levels of development, therefore, might needlessly favor the comparative advantage argument over the Marxist-inspired theories.

Second, in the absence of direct measures of the inequality of trade-borne exchanges or of the distortion of class development, the examination of countries grouped according to level of development may be the only way to judge the relative merit of the various Marxist-inspired theories. This task requires that we distinguish between developed (or core) countries and underdeveloped (or peripheral) countries *and between* poorer underdeveloped countries ("poor" countries) and the richer underdeveloped countries ("intermediate" countries). We show the necessity of these distinctions below in a discussion of the predictions of the various Marxist-inspired theories. We begin the unraveling of these arguments with an examination of the predictions of the structural differentiation perspective.

The forms of periphery countries' participation in world trade (which conform largely to the principle of comparative advantage) ought to impede their structural differentiation and consequently lower their economic growth below their theoretical potential. This view is entirely compatible with one that predicts that initial incorporation into the world capitalist economy should trigger growth responses.[11] Two growth-*inducing* mechanisms may be hypothesized:

(1) The beginning of a process of degeneration of "traditional," precapitalist relations of production (Laclau, 1971; Terray, 1972; Stavenhagen, 1968; 1975). This does not imply the instantaneous or even the long-term establishment of capitalist *relations* of production on the classical European model (Meillassoux, 1972). The generalization of cash transaction, for example, may destroy politically and kinship-based constraints on productivity without effecting the separation of ownership from labor, which is a prerequisite for the emergence of capitalist relations of production.

(2) The partial alignment of the production technologies (i.e., "forces of production") of the export sector on the more efficient ones developed by more advanced trade partners. (Mandel, 1975, pp. 54–62 describes with apparent ambivalence such a process.) This alignment may be forced by cross-boundary technological linkages in the case of industrial raw materials (e.g., Zaire's copper must satisfy Belgian metallurgical requirements) or by the dictates of foreign consumer markets in the case of food products (e.g., Brazilian coffee and Central America's bananas are produced according to the specifications of the North American market).

Both the erosion of pre-capitalist relations of production and the partial development of the forces of production along capitalist *technological* lines (however imperfect) attendant upon incorporation into the world capitalist economy should improve productivity. Furthermore, these events should be propitious for economic development on the Euro-American model. There is no logical contradiction between this argument and the idea that some forms of participation in trade slow economic development by impeding structural differentiation. Both arguments are derivable from the structural differentiation perspective. These superficially contradictory effects must occur as *sequentially ordered* phases of development: Initial incorporation into the world capitalist economy is likely to stimulate growth, while the specialization that follows incorporation becomes a fetter to continued development.

This formulation can be tested by studying the effects of trade on the economic performance of the two categories of underdeveloped countries discussed above, the poor countries and the intermediate countries. If trade has a positive effect on the economic growth of the most underdeveloped countries and a negative effect on the growth of the less underdeveloped countries, then the sequential effect model outlined above is supported. If uniformly negative effects are obtained, however, then this evidence may be taken as support for either the class-centered argument or the unequal exchange argument.

Unequal exchange theorists (e.g., Mandel, 1975, pp. 55, 345–346) do not deny the positive economic effects of initial incorporation into the world capitalist economy. Indeed, Mandel (1975, pp. 151–152) argues that Japan's incorporation into the world capitalist economy resulted in economic growth because the relative *inefficiency* of nineteenth-century transportation gave Japan a respite from foreign investment sufficient to allow domestic capital to develop. However, according to Mandel (1975, pp. 51–55), in the twentieth century incorporation is soon followed by the appearance in the newly incorporated area of foreign (core) capital which preempts the possibility of indigenous capital accumulation and intensifies the process of unequal exchange. Thus, any current evidence that the most underdeveloped countries benefit from trade contradicts the logic of the unequal exchange perspective. Ultimately, whether the advantages resulting from incorporation into the world capitalist economy are nullified by the phenomenon of unequal exchange is an empirical question. However, it would be difficult to reconcile the unequal exchange perspective with any evidence that the overall effects of trade on growth are positive for either category of underdeveloped countries.

Class-centered theories, on the other hand, present the observable dependency of underdeveloped countries as the contemporary consequence of a long historical process which extends over several centuries. According to these theories (ignoring the many divergences among them), the incorporation of outlying areas into the world capitalist economy took place gradually, but a long time ago. Except for a very few, minuscule areas (e.g., New Guinea), this incorporation was virtually completed at the turn of the century (see Chirot, 1977, pp. 18–23). While these theories allow for changes in the mode of exploitation of the periphery by the core, they have little room for the survival into the twentieth century of socioeconomic formations untouched by the transformative forces of world capitalism

Consequently, *current* evidence of a beneficial effect of international trade on the most underdeveloped countries must be interpreted as the result of random fluctuations in the functioning of the world capitalist economy. The alternative is to view such evidence as supportive of the thesis of the erosion of pre-capitalist relations of production. If participation in world trade has been recently eroding pre-capitalist relations in poor countries, however, the reliance on long-term processes inherent in the class-centered dependency argument appears superfluous. This is all the more true if this recent reshaping has *beneficial* consequences on economic performance rather than deleterious ones. Thus, since the underdevelopment of the periphery began several centuries ago, the effects of participation in the world capitalist economy must be negative for both the poor countries and the intermediate countries. The class-centered theories are best supported when the growth-stunting effects of the distorted class develoments that accompany trade are similar for these two categories of countries.

In the next section, devoted to design and measures, we examine the problem of grouping countries according to level of development.

DESIGN AND MEASURES

Measuring Level of Development
We argue above that the internal structural differentiation perspective is best supported if trade is shown to enhance the development of the very poor countries but not that of the intermediate countries. This diachronic influence of trade on growth can be discerned only in an analysis of countries categorized according to levels of initial development. The resulting categories must exhibit sufficient inter- and intra-group variance in the relevant explanatory variables to allow the assessment of the magnitude of the diachronic influence of trade hypothesized. Hence, we must operationalize the concept of level of development before we arrange cases into categories on the basis of this measure.

For the short period considered (1950–1969), simple economic growth and the more diffuse process of development would be difficult to distinguish. Thus we use the same measure to assess the economic *performance* of countries (i.e., their developmental progress) and to group them into categories according to initial level of development. In accord with Emmanuel (1974) and Kuznets (1964; 1968), we use GNP/capita as an indicator of level of development. Finsterbusch (1973) has shown that, despite frequently expressed misgivings, GNP/capita correlates highly with a large number of diverse, conventional indicators of development. [12]

Grouping Countries According to Level of Development
Most theorizing within the Marxist-inspired tradition is directed toward a specification of the mechanisms that maintain underdevelopment. Accordingly, these theories explicitly distinguish the "developed countries" (or the "core") from the "underdeveloped" countries that form the major object of their analyses. The first task, therefore, in our effort to distinguish categories of development is to group those countries that were already developed in 1950, the beginning of the period of observation. This set should correspond roughly to what theorists in the neo-Marxist

tradition would identify as the "core." Thus, countries in this set should include all countries that were rich in 1950 and remained rich throughout the 1950–1969 period.

An examination of the available GNP/capita data over this period allows the identification of just such a set. Every country that had a GNP/capita in 1950 of at least $650 experienced substantial growth during the 1950-1969 period. Indeed, for the 15 countries in this category, the average absolute increase in GNP/capita was over $800; the minimum increase was about $425 (see Table 1). The poorest member of this group of rich countries in 1969 had a GNP/capita of $1,495, more than double that of the

Table 2. Countries.

Poor
Angola
Afghanistan
Burundi
Bolivia
Brazil
Burma
Chad
Cambodia
Cameroun
Dahomey
Ethiopia
Ghana
Haiti
India
Indonesia
Iran
Iraq
Jordan
Kenya
Malagasy Republic
Malawi
Mali
Mozambique
Niger
Niberia
Pakistan
Philippines
Rwanda
Saudi Arabia
Senegal
South Korea
South Vietnam
Sri Lanka
Sudan
Syria

Poor (continued)
Thailand
Taiwan
Tanzania
Tunisia
Uganda
UAR (Egypt)
Upper Volta
Yemen
Zaire
Zambia

Intermediate
Algeria
Argentina
Austria
Costa Rica
Cuba
Chile
Colombia
Cyprus
Dominican Republic
El Salvador
Ecuador
Guatemala
Guyana
Greece
Honduras
Hong Kong
Ireland
Italy
Israel
Japan
Jamaica
Libya
Lebanon

Intermediate
(continued)
Mauritius
Morocco
Mexico
Malaysia
Malta
Nicaragua
Panama
Paraguay
Peru
Portugal
Spain
South Africa
Surinam
Trinidad and Tobago
Turkey
Uruguay
Venezuela
Yugoslavia

Rich
Australia
Belgium
Canada
Denmark
Finland
France
West Germany
Iceland
Netherlands
Norway
New Zealand
Sweden
Switzerland
United Kingdom
United States

poorest member in 1950. Below $650 GNP/capita in 1950, the next richest country is Argentina at $623. Argentina, however, experienced a meager increase of $153 in GNP/capita over this same period. The 15 countries in the "developed" category correspond closely to the intuitive idea of a capitalist core (see Table 2) as it would have been used in 1950.

Among the remaining countries (those clearly underdeveloped in 1950), two groups can be distinguished according to the pattern of growth each experienced in the 1950-1969 period. Countries toward the very bottom of the distribution of GNP/capita in 1950 on the whole experienced little growth. Indeed, there is not a single country with a 1950 GNP/capita below $150 that experienced an absolute increase greater than $225 between 1950 and 1969. The average increase in GNP/capita from 1950 was only $46; several countries in this group experienced an apparent absolute decline in GNP/capita (see Table 1).

For countries with a GNP/capita greater than $150 but less than $650 in 1950, however, we get a different picture. Some countries experienced absolute increments to their GNP/capita as great as those experienced by the 15 developed countries. Japan, for example, increased from $251 GNP/capita in 1950 to $1,218 in 1969. The *average* increase in GNP/capita for the richer of the underdeveloped countries (i.e., those with GNP/capita in 1950 greater than $150) was $289, greater than the *largest* increase experienced by any of the poor countries (GNP/capita in 1950 less than $150). (See Table 1.)

This division of the world into core (N = 15) and periphery (N = 86) and the division of the latter into intermediate (N = 41) and poor (N = 45) allows a more rigorous examination of the various Marxist-inspired arguments concerning the relationship between trade participation and the differential distribution of GNP/capita gains.

Measuring the Intensity of Trade Participation

In previous analyses of trade participation several measures of the intensity of participation have been used. These include the ratio of exports to GNP, the ratio of imports to GNP, the ratio of exports plus imports ("trade") to GNP, as well as modifications of these ratios using only *merchandise* exports or imports and *exportable* GNP. Since the value of exports and the value of imports for most countries are roughly equivalent, the three basic measures of intensity of trade (exports/GNP, imports/GNP, and trade/GNP) are virtually perfectly correlated in any cross-sectional analyisis of countries. Furthermore, Kuznets (1964) has shown that minor modifications of the basic ratios (e.g., using exportable GNP as the denominator) have slight effects, if any, on the international distribution of trade intensity.

Though sociological studies (e.g., Rubinson, 1976; Boli-Bennet, 1977) of trade intensity have favored the use of exports/GNP, we prefer the practice of most economists (e.g., Kuznets, 1964), which is to use trade/ GNP (see also Stallings, 1972; Lotz and Morss, 1970). The use of the latter measure has two advantages: (1) Exclusive use of exports/GNP obscures the fact that the beneficial or harmful effects of trade may be due to importing as well as exporting. (2) Trade/GNP is probably more reliable than exports/GNP or imports/GNP since in any one year a country may import less to correct for trade deficits of previous years or it may import more in expectation of a future trade surplus. This measure directly expresses the influence of a country's participation in the world economy relative to its total national economy. Those countries that are most dependent on external markets score high on this measure, while those countries with well-developed internal markets obtain low scores.[13]

Measuring the Forms of Trade Participation

Primary products specialization. According to the principle of comparative advantage, specialization in primary product exports is economically progressive when it accompanies certain natural and structural conditions. Such specialization is treated as an impediment to developmental progress by several versions of neo-Marxist theory. To measure such specialization is somewhat problematic since production is a continuous process, and no commodity is truly "unprocessed" (Delacroix, 1977).

During the early 1950s, however, the *finer* distinctions that might be made between the level of processing of most of the commodities traded on international markets are relatively inconsequential. Most commodities traded required either very little or a great deal of processing. Thus, while in the abstract processing can be viewed as continuous, in the realities of international trade in the 1950s, the commodities traded fell into one of two fairly discernible categories, primary products and finished products.

To measure specialization in the export of primary products, we compute the percentage of exports classified in SITC (Standard International Trade Classification) categories 0 to 4. The types of commodities contained within these five categories include raw materials of a diverse nature, from live animals to all kinds of food and fibers to unprocessed ores. In SITC categories 5 to 9 are highly processed commodities or sets of commodities requiring very different levels of processing. Some substances in category 5, for example, occur naturally, while others require extensive refining. Fortunately, the more heterogeneous categories (5 and 9) account for a very small portion of the export of any country. Our analysis would not have been altered significantly by reassignment.

Commodity concentration. Another indication that specialization has been induced by international trade is the specialization of a country in a small number of commodities. As discussed earlier, natural conditions can increase the benefits reaped from such specialization according to the principle of comparative advantage. According to Marxist theorists, however, specialization in the export of a small number of the relatively few products for which there is a large international demand (e.g., coffee, sugar, cotton, textiles, copper, aluminum) is seen as an impediment to the developmental progress of underdeveloped countries.

To measure commodity concentration we sum for each country the total value of its five most important exports and compute the percentage of total exports these commodities form. Thus, those countries that export a very small number of commodities score very close to 100 percent on this measure, while those countries that export a large number of commodities, *regardless of the amount of processing required,* score close to zero. Thus, some countries may be specialized in the export of primary products but obtain a low score on commodity concentration by exporting a great variety of commodities. (The correlation of our measure of commodity concentration with a measure using only the *three* largest commodities used by Lotz and Morss (1970) and by Stallings (1972) is .93; the correlation between our measures of commodity concentration and primary products specialization is .71.)

Model

An examination of indicators of development over time suggests the remarkable stability of cross-national inequality. This is true no matter which indicator of development is examined. To study change in the level of development, it is necessary therefore to select a time lag that is sufficiently long to allow meaningful differences between countries to be discerned. The time period selected must also be historically homogeneous in order to allow the observation of normal transnational exchanges, and it must be one in which consistent data are available for a large number of countries.

With these limitations in mind we use the 1950–1969 period. By 1950 most combatant nations had recovered from the instabilities introduced by World War II; after 1969 GNP/capita data are reported by the World Bank at market prices instead of factor costs, introducing a discontinuity in the data.[14] Furthermore, a temporal discontinuity is introduced in the 1970s by the Arab oil embargo and the subsequent activation of OPEC. (Note that the 1950–1969 period thus favors, perhaps needlessly, Marxist theories since in the 1970s a subset of underdeveloped countries experienced rapid economic growth via the nearly exclusive export of a primary product.)

Since rich countries generally experience larger absolute increases in GNP/capita over time than poor countries, the simple difference measure (GNP/capita 1969–GNP/capita 1950) cannot be used as a measure of *change* in level of development. Instead, it is necessary to model change in level of development via panel regression analysis (Chase-Dunn, 1975). GNP/capita 1969 thus serves as a dependent variable, and GNP/capita 1950, an independent variable (or lagged dependent variable). This model controls at once for the stability of countries' levels of development over time and the tendency for rich countries to experience greater absolute increases in GNP/capita. Thus, in our analysis of the effects of the intensity of trade participation (trade/GNP) and the forms of trade participation (primary products specialization and commodity concentration), GNP/capita 1969 serves as the dependent variable, and GNP/capita 1950 and our measures of intensity of trade (1950) and forms of trade participation (measured around 1955 to maximize the number of cases in the analysis) serve as the independent variables.

Cases
Our analysis covers 101 countries. This set includes (a) the quasi-totality of countries that were independent in 1950, and (b) colonial administrative entities that were to become independent or at least semi-autonomous (e.g., Hong Kong) during the 1950-1969 period. This set includes virtually the universe of noncommunist countries in 1970 minus the few cases for which data are unobtainable. We show in Table 2 a list of these countries grouped by level of development.

ANALYSIS

Findings for the Full Sample
Table 3 shows the estimates of the effects of trade/GNP (trade intensity), and primary products specialization and commodity concentration (forms of trade participation) on GNP/capita 1969 in a panel regression that includes GNP/capita 1950 as a lagged dependent variable. The equation covers all 101 cases for which data are available.

The purpose of this equation is to establish the credibility of the Marxist-inspired theories against the more widely accepted comparative advantage perspective. The latter perspective argues that trade-induced specialization should yield economies of scale for specializing countries.

Table 3. Regression of GNP/capita 1969 on GNP/capita 1950
and measures of trade participation (full sample).

Dependent Variable		Independent Variables			
		Initial Wealth	Trade Intensity	Forms of Trade Participation	
		GNP/capita 1950	Trade/ GNP	Primary Products Specialization	Commodity Concentration
GNP/capita 1969	beta	.836	-.004	-.158	-.063
R² = .941	B	1.402	-7.44	-428.4	-212.7
N = 101	P	.000	NS	.000	.089

Measures of the intensity and forms of trade participation are *not* expected to have a *detrimental* impact on economic progress.

In fact, as we show in Table 3, the Marxist argument does have some support. Primary products specialization has a strong, significant, negative effect on economic growth for the whole sample (beta $= -.16$, p $=$ .001), and commodity concentration has a weaker, nearly significant negative effect (beta $= -.06$, p $= .09$). Since these two measures share about half of their variance (r $= .71$), it is likely that the exclusion of either variable from the equation would enlarge the effect of the other on economic growth. The negative effects of these two measures on economic growth seem to violate expectations based on the comparative advantage perspective.

The nonsignificant effect of trade/GNP, while not directly contradicting the comparative advantage perspective, would not surprise theorists in the Marxist-inspired tradition. According to these theorists, the effect of trade on economic growth should vary with level of development: trade is thought to harm the underdeveloped countries, while it is believed that developed countries benefit from trade. We address this and other questions in the following section in which we examine the effects of trade on countries at different levels of development.[15]

Findings for the Poor Countries

Table 4 shows the estimates of the effects of trade/GNP, commodity concentration, and primary products specialization on economic growth for our set of 45 poor countries (those with GNP/capita 1950 less than $150). In this group of poor countries the average value of trade/GNP is only slightly lower than the average for the full sample (.37 versus .41); commodity concentration is higher (average $= .83$ versus .75 for the full sample), and primary product specialization is also higher (average $= .94$ versus .82). Nevertheless, there is a great deal of variation in the extent to

Table 4. Regression of GNP/capita 1969 on GNP/capita 1950
and measures of trade participation (poor countries).

Dependent Variable		*Independent Variables*			
		Initial Wealth	Trade Intensity	Forms of Trade Participation	
		GNP/capita 1950	Trade/ GNP	Primary Products Specialization	Commodity Concentration
GNP/capita 1969	beta	.566	.346	.016	-.033
R² = .634	B	.1289	92.68	8.48	-19.595
N = 45	P	.000	.007	NS	NS

which these countries conform to this pattern. Poor countries' scores on trade/GNP range from .05 to 1.39. On commodity concentration they range from .56 to .99. On primary products specialization they range from .31 to .99. (See Table 1.) This unevenness in the conformity of poor countries to any fixed position in the international division of labor allows us to examine the effects of different degrees of participation in the world capitalist economy and of different forms of such participation on the economic progress of the most underdeveloped countries.

The results of this examination are presented in Table 4. The only significant betas in the equation are for the estimates associated with initial GNP/capita and the estimates of the effect of trade/GNP which is large (beta = .35) and significant (p = .007).

The failure of primary products specialization and commodity concentration to affect economic growth among poor countries suggests that the processes described by the class-centered and unequal exchange arguments are not relevant to the fate of the poor countries. While one might argue that the deleterious effects of commodity concentration and primary products specialization are offset by the beneficial impacts of trade, this does not appear to be the case. If trade/GNP is removed from the equation the estimates for the effects of these two measures remain nonsignificant. Instead, the benefits of trade, which (we hypothesize) include the erosion of pre-capitalist relations of production and the acceleration of surplus value extraction due to technological improvements, are not diluted by any structural impediments linked to commodity concentration and primary products specialization.

Findings for the Intermediate Countries

Table 5 shows the same equation for the group of 41 intermediate countries (GNP/capita in 1950 between $150 and $650). Countries in this group, on the average, trade more than the poor (average trade/GNP equals .48 versus .37), and their exports tend to be slightly more diversified (average

Table 5. Regression of GNP/capita 1969 on GNP/capita 1950
and measures of trade participation (intermediate countries).

Dependent Variable		*Independent Variables*			
		Initial Wealth	Trade Intensity	Forms of Trade Participation	
		GNP/capita 1950	Trade/ GNP	Primary Products Specialization	Commodity Concentration
GNP/capita 1969	beta	.516	-.014	-.325	-.178
$R^2 = .600$	B	1.342	-27.078	-444.59	-286.69
N = 41	P	.00	NS	.028	NS

commodity concentration equals .75 versus .83) and slightly more processed (average primary products specializations equals .80 versus .94)
than the exports of the poor. (See Table 1.) Note that in this group are
most, if not all, of the truly *developing* countries. As discussed in the
Design and Measures section, some countries in this group experienced
absolute increases in GNP/capita as great as those experienced by fully
developed countries. Not all countries in this group, however, experienced rapid growth. Many experienced only moderate increases, and a
few experienced an absolute decline in GNP/capita.

The substantial variation in growth that characterizes these countries
indicates that in this group initial GNP/capita must have less of an impact
on subsequent increases in GNP/capita. Wide variation in growth experiences is coupled with wide variation in these countries' scores of the
measures of intensity and forms of trade participation. These conditions
provide fertile ground for testing of the Marxist-inspired arguments re-
viewed above.

The estimate of the effect of trade/GNP on subsequent growth for this
group of poor countries is weak, negative, and not significant (Table 5).
Thus, the hypothesis that the indigenous resources of underdeveloped
countries are drained off via unequal exchange fails to receive confirmation for this group. On the other hand, the estimate of the effect of primary
products specialization is negative (beta = −.33) and significant (p = .03).
The estimate of the effect of commodity concentration is also negative
(−.18), but not significant at the .05 level (p = .20).

The finding that one form of poor countries' trade participation (primary products specialization) is negatively associated with economic
growth by itself could be taken as evidence for either the class-centered
arguments or the internal structural differentiation perspective. One might
argue that the apparent effect of primary products specialization constitutes an indirect expression of an unmeasured class variable. The measure
might indicate, for example, the maintenance of a parasitic and nonen-

trepreneurial landlord-comprador upper class—e.g., see Paige (1975) on Vietnam. Though this parasitic class may have been created in the distant past, its harmful impact could continue into the present. If this were true, however, a similar pattern should be observed for the poor countries since the stunting effects of distorted class development should also afflict the poor. As we show above, however, poor countries benefit from their participation in trade.

The pattern observed for the poor countries and for the intermediate countries supports instead the structural differentiation perspective: Once a certain level of development is attained (marked by the erosion of pre-capitalist relations of production and the improvement of technology along capitalist lines) the forms of a country's participation in the world economy may become impediments to the future progress of the societal division of labor and to structural differentiation in general.

The findings in Table 5 likewise do not support the unequal exchange perspective. Unequal exchange occurs when countries exchange commodities embodying different quantities of labor. If one country, for example, trades 1,000 tons of bananas (a primary product) incorporating 100 days of its inhabitants' labor for one refrigerator incorporating only 25 days of its trading partner's labor, a drain occurs to the banana exporter's detriment. Conceivably, poor countries could minimize this loss by refraining from the export of the labor-intensive commodity. This argument, which is supported by the negative effect of primary commodity specialization in Table 5, is consistent with the unequal exchange perspective. For this perspective to be *confirmed*, however, the effect of trade/GNP in Table 5 should also be negative and significant since this measure indicates the *extent* of the purported unequal exchange and of the resulting drain. Instead, the estimate of this effect is close to zero and not significant. It is unlikely, therefore, that the economic improvement of many countries in this middle group is the result of an escape from unequal exchange.

Further analysis of the data for intermediate countries provides even greater support for the internal structural differentiation perspective. If trade has an adverse effect on the economic progress of poor countries because of the impediment to structural differentiation posed by the *forms* of poor countries' participation in trade, then *both* measures of the forms of trade participation should have a negative effect on economic growth. These measures should have *convergent* negative effects on economic growth since, within a classical Marxist perspective, the economic performance of countries with high scores on either of these measures should resemble that of the "Asiatic Society." (That is, these countries should stagnate.)

To ascertain the degree to which these two measures of the forms of trade participation do in fact have convergent, negative effects on economic growth, we allow commodity concentration a greater chance to explain variation in economic growth by removing primary products specialization from the equation. We report the results of the analysis in Table 6, equation 1. For comparative purposes we also present in Table 6 an equation with commodity concentration excluded and primary products specialization retained (equation 2). Note first that in equation 1 the estimate of the effect of commodity concentration on subsequent growth is negative (beta = −.38) and significant (p = .002). This finding conforms to the expectation that the effect of commodity concentration on growth is convergent with the effect of primary products specialization. Indeed, equation 2 shows that the estimate of the effect of primary products specialization (with commodity concentration excluded) is similar in magnitude (beta = −.44) and level of significance (= .001). Furthermore, the proportion of the variance explained in each of these equations is very similar (.542 for equation 1 versus .581 for equation 2); this slight difference in explained variance is not significant at the .05 level. Perhaps more important, the estimates for the B's associated with these similarly constructed measures (they both refer to proportions of total exports) are virtually identical (−603.28 for commodity concentration versus −608.39 for primary products specialization). Thus, the impact on economic growth of a percentage point decrease in commodity concentration is equivalent to the economic impact of a percentage point decrease in primary products specialization.

The near-perfect substitutability of these two measures, in spite of an only moderate correlation between them (.63), suggests that the two aspects of the form of trade participation they represent have very similar

Table 6. Regression of GNP/capita 1969 on GNP capita 1950 and measures of trade participation showing separate effects of commodity concentration and primary products specialization (intermediate countries).

Dependent Variable		Independent Variables			
		Initial Wealth	Trade Intensity	Forms of Trade Participation	
		GNP/capita 1950	Trade/ GNP	Primary Products Specialization	Commodity Concentration
GNP/capita 1969	beta	.560	.017	–	-.375
$R^2 = .542$	B	1.456	11.637	–	-603.288
N = 41	P	.000	NS	–	.002
GNP/capita 1969	beta	.523	-.061	-.439	–
$R^2 = .581$	B	1.361	-40.700	-608.084	--
N = 41	P	.000	NS	.001	--

consequences for economic growth. The pattern of findings we show supports the argument that the forms of trade participation represented by commodity concentration and primary products specialization become obstacles to structural differentiation once development along capitalist lines has already taken place. The fact that these measures of the forms of participation do not register any effect on growth for the very poor countries provides further support for this argument.

Findings for the Rich Countries

We hesitate to generalize about the effects of trade involvement on the economic performance of the 15 rich countries because of the small size of this group. Yet some tentative explanations can be given to the counter-intuitive findings reported in Table 7.

The countries in this group are of unquestionably developed status at the beginning of the period of observation. They are characterized by high GNP/capita, large internal economies, well-diversified exports, and little propensity to specialize in primary exports. Contrary to popular belief, however, there is significant variation *within* this category in forms of participation in trade. Their scores on primary products specialization range from .09 to .99, while their scores on commodity concentration range from .27 to .96 (see Table 1).

These countries' initial levels of development, denoted by GNP/capita 1950, explain much of their subsequent growth (beta = .79). The forms of these countries' participation in world trade appear to have no effect on their growth; the estimates attached to commodity concentration and primary products specialization are close to zero and not significant. Since all these countries are unquestionably developed in 1950, this finding is consistent with the explanation we gave for the findings relative to the intermediate countries: the rich are past the point where their structural differentiation may be thwarted by any particular form of participation in trade.

Table 7. Regression of GNP/capita 1969 on GNP/capita 1950
and measures of trade participation (rich countries).

Dependent Variable		*Independent Variables*			
		Initial Wealth	Trade Intensity	Forms of Trade Participation	
		GNP/capita 1950	Trade/ GNP	Primary Products Specialization	Commodity Concentration
GNP/capita 1969	beta	.794	-.277	-.123	.005
R^2 = .904	B	.995	-927.69	-210.59	10.166
N = 15	P	.000	.056	NS	NS

The intensity of these countries' involvement in trade is greater than is usually recognized. It is less than that of the intermediate countries but close to that of the poor (.34 versus .48 and .37, respectively). The intensity of their involvement in trade is negatively associated with their economic growth. The estimate of the effect of trade/GNP is large and negative (beta $= -.28$) and significant at the .05 level.

This tentative finding is in apparent contradiction with neo-Marxist theories *and* with the principle of comparative advantage. The first perspective argues that rich countries are the prime beneficiaries of trade via the exploitation of their trade partners. Thus, it would seem that those rich countries more active in international trade should receive more of the benefits of presumed exploitation. This is the exact opposite of what we find.

Furthermore, the relatively processed and well-diversified exports of the rich countries should allow them to reap the benefits promised by the principle of comparative advantage; their place in the world division of labor, as denoted by their scores on these variables, appears to be in conformity with this principle (Table 1). In the presence of a high industrial capactiy and high wage levels, the influence of natural resources should be slight in the determination of kinds and range of exports (Michaely, 1962, p. 15). However, apparent adherence to the principle of comparative advantage seems to be accompanied by deleterious consequences.

One explanation of the counter-intuitive effect of trade/GNP on growth points to these countries' trade patterns. On the average, over 70 percent of the rich countries' foreign trade in the 1950–1969 period involved transactions among one another. Rich countries' trade with intermediate and very poor countries made up a fairly small portion of their total trade (Pincus, 1967, p. 49). Consequently, the findings in Table 7 are compatible with a situation in which the trade of each rich country with the underdeveloped worlds affords it the benefits promised by comparative advantage, while its trade with developed partners does not. This account of the negative effect of trade/GNP still contradicts a very *strict* interpretation of the principle of comparative advantage. The latter would argue that even though differential factor endowments maximize the benefits of trade (Pincus, 1967), countries should benefit from trade even in the absence of differential endowments (Samuelson, 1962).[16]

DISCUSSION: EXPLOITATION AND CLOSURE

The findings of this study raise more questions than they answer. Nevertheless, they narrow the range of plausible connections between participation in trade and development. The main finding is that, contrary to popular perception but in line with classical economics *and* classical Marxism, the least-developed countries benefit from their participation in trade. However, as neo-Marxist scholars have suspected for some time, there is a point in the development of poor countries at which participation in trade is likely to have counterproductive results. This is suggested by the findings for the intermediate countries. The specific evidence we adduce in support of this argument, however, supports neither class-centered dependency theories nor unequal exchange theories. Both of these persepctives are compatible with the findings for the intermediate countries. Neither, however, can be reconciled with the findings for the poor countries.

The fact that the developmental progress of intermediate countries is impeded by the form of their participation in international trade has two important theoretical consequences. First, this finding contradicts the broadest implications of the principle of comparative advantage. Second, it supports an explanation of the relationship between trade and development rooted in classical Marxism: Once the initial benefits of trade overcome the fetters of primeval underdevelopment, the position in the international division of labor assigned to latecomers impedes their internal structural differentiation and hence their continued growth.

The policy implications of our findings are not as obvious as they may seem. The interruption of trade relationships with the core is not the obligatory solution to the problem posed by blocked internal structural differentiation. It is true that Soviet bloc countries (not included in this study) experienced dramatic economic growth while practicing nearly complete economic isolation from the capitalist core. However, it is not evident that autarky, rather than the ability of Communist regimes to stymie wage demands and reduce consumption or to stimulate mass social mobilization, accounts for the undebatable economic success of these countries.[17] Furthermore, several of the countries in the intermediate category combined heavy trade participation with equally dramatic economic growth. Japan, Greece, Spain, and Hong Kong are examples. Research suggests that some periphery countries are able to protect themselves from the adverse consequences of trade through deliberate political measures. The expansion of school enrollment, typically a state function, may counteract the negative effects of primary products specialization, for example (see Delacroix, 1977; the political sensitivity of the educational expansion-economic growth relationship is illustrated in Delacroix. and Ragin, 1978). Tugwell (1974) has shown that the managerial capacity of a state under certain conditions may be enhanced by raw material specialization. This increased managerial capacity can be used to counter the deleterious structural concequences of primary products specialization.

The likelihood of such voluntaristic action depends to a large extent on the orientation of elites in the periphery and more specifically on their aptitude for economic nationalism. According to several versions of class-centered dependency theory, elites in the periphery are lured into alliances with core capitalism; these alliances are thought to prohibit the emergence of economic nationalism in the periphery.[18] In the absence of evidence supporting the thesis of exploitation, however, the active complicity of elites in the periphery is very much in question. Our findings do not exclude the possibility of exploitation,[19] but they do undermine the popular picture of an international system in which core nations drain surplus value from the periphery. In fact, the only category of countries which appears to suffer from the intensity of participation in trade is the core itself. The thesis of exploitation is further undermined by our findings which show that (1) the poor countries benefit from the intensity of their participation in trade and (2) the intermediate countries do not suffer from the intesity of their participation in trade.

In general, the results of this study strongly suggest that (1) it is wise to separate the question of imperialism from that of underdevelopment (particularly with respect to arguments based on trade), and (2) any link between imperialism and underdevelopment must be established on empirical grounds.

FOOTNOTES

*We wish to express our gratitude to our students Tanner Akman and Peter Oberto for their intelligent collaboration at various stages in the preparation of this paper and to Professors Michael Armer and Paul Kuznets for their comments on an earlier draft.

1. Glezakos' study, often cited in support of this hypothesis, presents evidence based on only twenty cases. It is easily superseded by the more powerful contrary evidence in Askari and Weil (1974), which rests on 70 cases.

2. Mamdani's analysis, in particular, can be usefully linked to Schultheis' (1975) study of the economic regression of Uganda under Amin.

3. Chase-Dunn (1975) and Rubinson (1976) only demonstrate a positive relationship between some forms of dependency and internal income inequality. The latter is, of course, not an appropriate substitute for the qualitative properties of class structure (Stavenhagen, 1975, pp. 19–39).

4. This scheme might not be acknowledged by Wallerstein, though it seems to us to constitute the organizing principle of his work.

5. See Chirot (1976) for a very elaborate discussion of the geopolitical implications of this perspective.

6. This is also a necessary corollary of Mandel's next statement ("This decisively limited the extension of the 'internal market' . . . .") since such limitation places a ceiling on wages.

7. "The hunt for raw materials went hand in hand with imperialist capital export and was to a considerable extent a causal determinant of it" (Mandel, 1975, p. 57).

8. Unfortunately, after distinguishing carefully between "the older 'division of labor' " and the "more inclusive . . . structural differentiation" (1977, p. 2), Rueschemeyer (1977, pp. 3–4) seems to use the two terms interchangeably. We wish to keep the two terms completely separate. The term "division of labor" whether it be "world," "societal," or "workshop" refers strictly to organizational principles governing the production of material products. For lack of a more rigorous definition (Reuschemeyer, 1977, p. 1), we use the expression "internal structural differentiation" to refer to the functional division of structures in all the nonmaterial-producing spheres of society. This distinction between "division of labor and "structural differentiation" is consistent with the classical Marxist distinction between "infrastructure" and "superstructure."

9. This point is made—in the negative—even more forcefully by Bettelheim (1972). Following Marx (1967, p. 356), he argues that the blockage of the development of the *forces of production* in pre-capitalist societies is enough in and of itself to prevent the establishment of capitalist *relations of production,* thus reversing the sequence favored by Frank (1972).

10. We do not disagree with Rueschemeyer's (1977, p. 23) suggestion that "power constellations and power interests" are likely to be "of eminent importance as proximate causes in actual processes of differentiation, . . ." In our terms, to say that class dynamics influence internal differentiation is not the same as confusing the two. Each particular case of suspected influence of the one upon the other must be treated as a separate empirical question.

11. Dommen and Monaldi (1976) report with apparent reluctance that the export activities of the poorest countries seem to be associated with their economic growth, even after suspected measurement biases have been taken into account. (This finding is superficially in line with Warren, 1973).

12. Two important criticisms have been made of the use of GNP/capita as an indicator of development. The first, that this measure overestimates the development gap (Jenkins, 1970, p. 36) does not concern us much here because we are interested in changes in levels of development. The second criticism, however, is relevant to the first and suggests that even in the study of economic change the use of GNP/capita is hazardous. It has been argued that apparent economic growth among poor countries might simply reflect improvements in national accounting procedures. Furthermore, such improvements are likely to be stimulated by the expansion of the export sector (Dommen and Monaldi, 1976) irrespective of the genuine influence of the latter upon growth. We note, however, that such improvements in national accounting practice are less likely to occur in the absence of growth. Secondly, a close examination of the reported growth of those poor countries whose data we trust least reveals no patterned difference between the reputed growth of these poor countries and those whose data we trust most (e.g., Egypt, Pakistan, India). Third, the very poorest countries in our sample, those most likely to be characterized by inadequate accounting improving with time, were mostly colonies in 1950 (the beginning of the period of observation). Our general research experience indicates that the political independence which they gained during the period of observation (circa 1960) is likely to have been followed by a worsening of national accounting practices. Consequently, little of the apparent economic growth experienced by these countries between 1950 and 1969 can be linked to improved national accounting practices.

13. Kuznets (1964) has argued that this measure must correlate negatively with size of national economy since (1) GNP is the denominator, and (2) since international trade involves both large and small economies, international transactions weigh more heavily on the fate of small economies. Our research has shown this to be the case only for the highly developed countries, however. In our statistical analysis of the relationship between the forms and intensity of trade participation we included the log of GNP (since the distribution

of GNP is highly skewed) and found no significant effect of log GNP on growth and no significant alteration of the effects of the other independent variables in any of the equations we computed.

14. The correlations between GNP/capita in 1969 at factor costs with GNP/capita in 1970 and 1972, both at market prices, are over .98. The use of these other measures would probably have no effect on the results we report. We prefer the 1969 data because they are more consistent with 1950 data and thus allow precise *descriptive* statements to be made for individual countries.

15. Splitting our countries into three groups does not reduce the potential impact of trade/GNP, primary products specialization and commodity concentration. These measures vary substantially within each of the three categories of countries. Also, a more sophisticated analysis (not shown here) indicates that no explanatory information is lost when the sample is trichotomized.

16. Another explanation of the negative effect of trade/GNP on growth for rich countries might point to the fact that the propensity to trade among rich countries varies inversely with size (the correlation between trade/GNP is -.84). Thus, it could be argued, small rich countries must trade more since economies of scale cannot be practiced *within* the domestic economy. A related account of the negative effect of trade/GNP might point to the fact that the movement of capital can *replace* the movement of commodities (Kindleberger, 1964, pp. 82–83) and that a high trade/GNP in the case of rich countries may indicate an absence of attractive investment possibilities (which could be a consequence of small size).

17. Note however that the performance of the Soviet block countries can be contrasted with another group of countries that belong to the intermediate category (GNP/capita 1950 greater than $150 and less than $650) but *did* not resort to autarky in this period, the Latin American countries. These countries continued to trade well after they had reached a level of development that would dictate the avoidance of conformity to the principle of comparative advantage. (Note also that a communist country that did not adopt the autarkic route, Yugoslavia, experienced a rate of growth inferior to other communist countries.)

18. The thesis that the forms of trade participation of intermediate countries obstruct their internal structural differentiation also helps to account for the historical impotence of these countries' elites: As compared to nineteenth-century European bourgeoisies, periphery elites face an environment poor in entrepreneurial opportunities and inimical to the development of a strong state apparatus.

19. Our findings are compatible with two interpretations of the world capitalist economy as "imperialistic." (1) The stagnation of intermediate countries may keep potential competitors out of the capitalist arena. (2) The arrested development of intermediate countries may be the *disproportionate* consequence of a global division of labor which may only *marginally* benefit some or all of the core countries.

REFERENCES

Amin, S. (1974a) *Accumulation on a World Scale: A Critique of the Theory of Underdevelopment.* New York: Monthly Review Press.
—— (1974b) "Accumulation and Development: A Theoretical Model." *Review of African Political Economy* 1(1): 9–26.
Askari, H. and G. Weil (1974) "Stability of Export Earnings of Developing Nations." *Journal of Development Studies* 11(1): 86–89.
Baran, P. (1957) *The Political Economy of Growth.* New York: Monthly Review Press.
Baumgartner, T., W. Buckley, and J. Burns (1976) "Unequal Exchange and Uneven De-

velopments: The Structuring of Exchange Patterns." *Studies in Comparative International Development* 11(2): 51–72.

Berman, B.J. (1974) "Clientelism and Neo-Colonialism: Center-Periphery Relations and Political Development in African States" *Studies in Comparative International Development* 9(2): 3–25.

Bettelheim, C. (1972) "Theoretical Comments." Appendix 1 in A. Emmanuel, *Unequal Exchange: A Study in the Imperialism of Trade*. New York: Monthly Review Press.

Boli-Bennet, J. (1977) "Global Integration and the Rise of the Universal Omnivorous State." Unpublished paper, Stanford, CA: Stanford University.

Bourricaud, F. (1966) "Structure and Function of the Peruvian Oligarchy." *Studies in Comparative International Development* 2(2): 17–31.

Brewster, H. (1971) "Economic Dependence: A Quantitative Interpretation." Paper presented at Institute of Commonwealth Studies, University of London.

Cairncross, A.K. (1962) *Factors in Economic Development*. London: Allen and Unwin.

Chase-Dunn, C. (1975) "The Effects of International Economic Dependence on Development and Inequality: A Cross-National Study." *American Sociological Review* 40(6): 720–738.

Chirot, Daniel (1977) *Social Change in the Twentieth Century*. New York: Harcourt Brace Jovanovich.

Coppock, J.D. (1962) *International Economic Instability*. New York: McGraw-Hill.

Delacroix, Jacques (1977) "The Export of Raw Materials and Economic Growth: A Cross-National Study." *American Sociological Review* 42(5): 795–808.

——— and Charles Ragin (1978) "Modernizing Instituions, Mobilization, and Third World Development: A Cross-National Study." *American Journal of Sociology* 84(1): 123–150.

Dommen, E. and V. Monaldi (1976) "L'Exportation: Facteur Dominant de la Croissance Economique des Pays les Moins Dèveloppès ou Illusion Statistique?" *Geneva-Aftrica-Acta Africana* 15(2): 64–72.

Dos Santos, T. (1969) "La Crise de la Thèorie du Dèvelopment et les Relations de Dèpendance en Amèrique Latine." *L'Homme et la Sociéte* 12 (April-June): 43–68.

Emmanuel, A. (1972) *Unequal Exchange: A Study in the Imperialism of Trade*. New York: Monthly Review Press.

——— (1974 "Myths of Development Versus Myths of Underdevelopment." *New Left Review* 85 (May-June): 61–79.

Erb, G. F. and S. Schiavo-Campo (November 1969) "Export Instability, Level of Development and Economic Size of Less Developed Countries." Bulletin of Oxford University Institute of Economics and Statistics.

Finsterbusch, K. (1973) "Recent Rank Orderings of Nations on Level and Rate of Development." *Studies in Comparative International Development* 8(1): 53–70.

Frank, A. G. (1967 *Capitalism and Underdevelopment in Latin America*. New York: Monthly Review Press.

——— (1972) *Lumpenbourgeoisie, Lumpendevelopment: Dependence, Class, and Politics in Latin America*. New York: Monthly Review Press.

Furtado, C. (1965) "Development and Stagnation in Latin America: A Structuralist Approach." *Studies in Comparative International Development* 1(11): 159–175.

Geleano, E. (1971) "Latin America and the Theory of Imperialism." Pages 205–224 in K. T. Fann and D.C. Hodges eds. *Readings in U.S. Imperialism*. Boston: Porter Sargent.

Galtung, J. (1971) "A Structural Theory of Imperialism." *Journal of Peace Research* 8(2): 81–117.

Glezakos, C. (1973) "Export Instability and Economic Growth: A Statistical Verification." *Economic Development and Cultural Change* 21(4): 670–678.

Gòmez, R. R. (1966) "ECLA, Prebisch, and the Problem of Latin American Development." *Studies in Comparative International Development* 2(8): 121–132.

Haberler, G (1936) *The Theory of International Trade*. London: William Hodge.

—— (1959) *International Trade and Economic Development*. Cairo: National Bank of Egypt.

Hill, Helen (1975) " 'Peripheral Capitalism,' Beyond 'Dependency' and 'Modernization'." *Australian and New Zealand Journal of Sociology* 11(1): 30–37.

Hirschman, A. O. (1958) *The Strategy of Economic Development*. New Haven: Yale University Press.

International Bank for Reconstruction and Development (1971) *World Tables*. Washington, DC: IBRD.

Jenkins, Robin (1970) *Exploitation: The World Power Structure and the Inequality of Nations*. London: MacGibbon and Kee.

Kemp, M. C. (1962) "The Gains from International Trade." *Economics Journal* 72: 883–889.

Kindleberger, C. (1958) *Economic Development*. New York: McGraw-Hill.

——*Foreign Trade and the National Economy*. New Haven: Yale University Press.

Kuznets, Simon (1964) "Quantitative Aspects of the Economic Growth of Nations: Part IX. Level and Structure of Foreign Trade: Comparisons for Recent Years" *Economic Development and Cultural Change* 13(1): 1–106.

—— (1968) *Toward a Theory of Economic Growth*. New York: Norton.

Laclau, E. (1971) "Feudalism and Capitalism in Latin America." *New Left Review* 67 (May-June): 19–38.

Leff, N. H. (1968) "The Exportable Surplus Approach to Foreign Trade in Underdeveloped Countries." *Economic Development and Cultural Change* 17(3): 346–355.

Lim, Y. (1968) "Trade and Growth: The Case of Ceylon." *Economic Development and Cultural Change* 16(2): 245–260.

Linder, S. B. (1961) *An Essay on Trade and Transformation*. New York: Wiley.

Lotz, J. and E. Morss (1970) "A Theory of Tax Level Determinants for Developing Countries." *Economic Development and Cultural Change* 18(3): 328–341.

Magdoff, H. (1969) *The Age of Imperialism: The Economics of U.S. Foreign Policy*. New York: Monthly Review Press.

Maizel, A. (1958) *Export and Economic Growth of Developing Countries*. Cambridge, MA: Cambridge University Press.

Mamdani, M. (1976) *Politics and Class Formation in Uganda*. New York: Monthly Review Press.

Mandel, E. (1975) *Late Capitalism*. London: Humanities Press.

Marx, Karl (1967) *Capital: A Critique of Political Economy*. New York: International Publishers.

—— and F. Engels (1969) *The Communist Manifesto*. Chicago: Regnery.

McBean, A. (1966) *Export Instability and Economic Development*. Cambridge, MA: Harvard University Press.

Meillassoux, C. (1972) "From Reproduction to Production: A Marxist Approach to Economic Anthropology." *Economy and Society 1(1): 93–*105

Michaely, M. (1962) *Concentration in International Trade*. Amsterdam: North Holland.

Myrdal, G. (1956) *Development and Underdevelopment*. Cairo: National Bank of Egypt.

Naya, S. (1973) "Fluctuation in Export Earnings and Economic Patterns in Asian Countries." *Economic Development and Cultural Change* 21(4): 629–641

Paige, J. (1975) *Agrarian Revolution*. New York: Free Press.

Pincus, J. (1967) *Trade, Aid, and Development*. New York: McGraw-Hill.

Prebisch, R. (1950) *The Economic Development of Latin America and Its Principal Problems.* New York: United Nations.

Reuschemeyer, D. (1977) "Structural Differentiation, Efficiency, and Power." *American Journal of Sociology* 83 (1): 1–25.

Ricardo, David (1971) *Principles of Political Economy and Taxation.* Baltimore: Penguin.

Rubinson, R. (1976) "The World Economy and the Distribution of Income Within States: A Cross-National Study." *American Sociological Review* 41 (4): 638–659.

Samuelson, Paul (1939) "The Gains from International Trade." *Canadian Journal of Economics and Political Science* 5 (2): 195–205.

—— (1962) "The Gains from International Trade Once Again," *Economic Journal,* 72: 820–829.

—— (1970) *Economics,* 8th edition. New York: McGraw-Hill.

Schultheis, M. J. (1975) "The Ugandan Economy and General Amin." *Studies in Comparative International Development* 10 (3): 3–44.

Singer, H. W. (1950) "The Distribution of Gains Between Investing and Borrowing Countries."*American Economic Review, Papers and Proceedings.*

Stallings, B. (1972) *Economic Dependency in Africa and Latin America.* Beverly Hills, CA: Sage Publications.

Stavenhagen, R. (1968) "Seven Erroneous Theses about Latin America." Pages 13–31 in J. Petras and M. Zeitlin (eds.), *Latin America, Reform or Revolution?* New York: Fawcett Publications.

—— (1975) *Social Classes in Agrarian Societies.* New York: Anchor Doubleday.

Streeten, P. (1971), "How Poor are the Poor Countries?" Pages 141–150 in D. Seers and L. Joy (eds.), *Development in a Divided World.* Baltimore: Penguin.

Terray, C. (1972) *Marxism and Primitive Societies.* New York: Monthly Review Press.

Tugwell, F. (1974) "Petroleum Policy in Venezuela: Lessons in the Politics of Dependence Management." *Studies in Comparative International Development* 9 (1): 84–120.

United Nations (1953–1969) *Yearbook of International Trade Statistics.* New York: United Nations.

Von Eschen, D. (1975) "Three Structural Theories of Economic Development." Paper read at 1975 Annual Meeting of the American Sociological Association, San Francisco.

Wallerstein, I. (1974a) *The Modern World System: Capitalist Agriculture and the Origins of the European World Economy in the Sixteenth Century.* New York: Academic Press.

—— (1974b) "The Rise and Future Demise of the World Capitalist System." *Comparative Studies in Society and History* 16 (4): 387–415.

Warren, B. (1973) "Imperialism and Capitalist Industrialization." *New Left Review* 81 (September–October): 3–44.

Young, R. (1970) "The Plantation Economy and Industrial Development." *Economic Development and Cultural Change* 18 (3): 343–360.

DOES DEMOCRACY HINDER ECONOMIC DEVELOPMENT IN THE LATECOMER DEVELOPING NATIONS?*

Robert M. Marsh

POLITY AND ECONOMIC DEVELOPMENT

Much previous theory and research have dealt with the socioeconomic preconditions or causes of political development (Lipset, 1959; Almond and Coleman, 1960; Cutright, 1963; Cutright and Wiley, 1969; Jackman, 1973). Political scientists have responded with various degrees of criticism of the idea that the polity is but a reflex of society and economy, and Huntington (1965) has made the case for the autonomy of the political vis-à-vis socioeconomic variables.

This study asks: among nations that are latecomers to the development process, how, and to what extent, does the degree of democracy or politi-

Comparative Social Research, Vol. 2, pp. 215—248.
Volume 1 published as Comparative Studies in Sociology
Copyright © 1979 by JAI Press, Inc.
All rights of reproduction in any form reserved.
ISBN 0-89232-112-1

cal competition facilitate or hinder economic development? At least three positions have been taken in earlier analyses of this problem. First, the *Authoritarian* model of economic development holds that democracy hinders economic development. Second, the *Springtime of Freedom* thesis argues that in general the less-developed nations will be more successful in their economic development efforts if they attend to the need for freedom instead of only the need for bread. Third, there is the *Skeptical* orientation, which rejects the view that there is any determinate relationship between democracy and economic development.

Before reviewing these three theoretical orientations, the problem of ideological bias must be met head on. The definitions given below of "democracy" and "political competition" are of the Western, liberal, parliamentary variety. They are quite different from the definitions of "democracy" in communist and some Third World regimes. Many scholars of development have rejected liberal definitions of democracy as inappropriate or irrelevant to the conditions and needs of the less-developed nations. In response to these criticisms, it should be noted that though authoritarian regimes may claim to have "democratic centralism," "participatory democracy," "workers' councils," and so forth, it is a mistake to take these claims at their face value and to base our classification of political systems on them (Linz, 1975). To be sure, a liberal democratic bias has at times impaired comparative political studies. For example, the study of "political institutionalization" may focus only upon liberal, pluralist modes of institutionalization, instead of recognizing that other modes may be more effective in maintaining stability in developing nations. To fail to consider alternatives to liberal democratic arrangements in these nations indeed reflects a serious bias. This is not the case in the present study, however, because we attempt to isolate a *continuous variable,* defined at one extreme as the *absence* of competitive, pluralistic, democratic political institutions and behavior, and at the other extreme, by their presence to a high degree. In this sense, the question of whether democracy hinders or facilitates economic development is to be resolved on empirical grounds, not on the basis of ideology.

Another clarification concerns the "bigness" of government. My approach to the polity in developing nations falls on a different axis than on

*Robert M. Marsh is Professor of Sociology at Brown University. He spent the 1977–1978 academic year at Harvard University with the East Asian Research Center. His interests are in complex organizations and modernization with an area specialization in China and Japan. His most recent book is *Modernization and the Japanese Factory* written with Hiroshi Mannari (1976). Currently he is analyzing data on technology, organizational structure, and performance in 50 Japanese factories, and collecting data for a study of organizational changes in Japanese universities.

the Big Government vs. Laissez Faire Government dimension. I agree with the prevailing view that latecomer nations cannot realize economic development on the basis of arrangements described by the earlier Western doctrine that "that government is best which governs least." Granted that the latecomer nations in the post-World War II era need governmental structures which perform a wide range of functions, and which penetrate many sectors of society, these nations still vary in their forms and degrees of political competition. In other words, the *scope* of political institutions and their *degree of democracy* or *political competition* should be treated as phenomena which vary somewhat independently of each other.

The Authoritarian Model of Economic Development

It is widely asserted in both political theory and political policy that "if economic development is the all-embracing goal, the logic of experience dictates that not too much attention can be paid to the trappings of democracy" (LaPalombara, 1963, p. 57). DeSchweinitz (1964, p. 267) has developed this view: "Because of the deterrents to growth which have prevented autonomous development in [less-developed] nations, the impulse for industrialization must come from the center of political power and spread outward into society, rather than, as was the case in the West during the nineteenth century, coming from society itself."

Moreover, although economic growth, freedom, and democracy are consistent with each other in the advanced Western countries, "the underdeveloped economies confront circumstances which restrict their opportunities to maximize these objectives simultaneously. *If they are to grow economically, they must limit democratic participation in political affairs*" (DeSchweinitz, 1964, p. 277, italics added). Pye (1966, p. 72), Meyer, Hannan, and Rubinson (1973, pp. 27–28), Chirot (1977), and others have clarified the authoritarian model of development by identifying the mechanisms through which nondemocratic polities are said to achieve more rapid economic development than their democratic counterparts. The authoritarian regimes are better able to keep current consumption down, thereby creating needed savings and freeing funds for investment. They exert a firmer control over the reorganization of labor markets. They can be more efficient in the allocation of resources in general. By organizing economic action collectively, avoiding overspecialization in primary production, and controlling foreign investors, they achieve an autarky which prevents their becoming economically dependent on the advanced nations. Their small, tight political elite freezes debate and imposes its will on society; in this way discontent and conflict are suppressed. They unite cultural groups into a strong nation-state by being able more easily to manage conflicts among traditional subgroups and among those new groups formed by the development process.

In summary, the Authoritarian model asserts that "new states cannot 'afford' democracy because they must place a prior value on economic growth" (Pye, 1966, p. 72). "[N]ondemocratic governments tend to fare better than democracies in leading their societies to rapid industrial . . . advances" (Chirot, 1977, p. 85). The choice facing the latecomer nations, says Chirot, "is not, in any case, between Western-style democracy and something else, but between Indian-style stagnation and effective change" (Chirot, 1977, p. 224).

The Springtime of Freedom Thesis

McCord's 1965 book, *The Springtime of Freedom,* was written to persuade Third World leaders that the authoritarian path creates more problems than it cures. Among the dysfunctions of authoritarian rule, according to McCord, is its tendency to restrict the flow of information from the people to the regime, its ability to waste a nation's resources even more extravagantly than in a democracy, and its tendency to transform conflicts normal to the development process into more extreme confrontations. More technical theoretical reasons why democracy makes for more rapid economic development have been presented by Holt and Turner (1966). They suggest, with historical evidence from the contrasting cases of England and Japan (successful development) and France and China (unsuccessful in the early stages), that during the "take-off" phase of economic development, the government's contribution is maximized when it becomes involved in the process of resource mobilization and resource allocation but not in resource management. With regard to resource management, they argue,

> [I]t is *theoretically possible* to establish an institution like the autonomous public corporation, through which the government is able to own the means of production without having political considerations unduly hampering the management. But the *probability* that in a developing area such a sophisticated organization will be able to keep politics out of management is very small. . . . [P]olitical considerations will tend to supersede economic criteria in the decision-making process. This situation is likely to result in levels of efficiency below those predicted by individuals who base their judgment entirely on economic and technological factors [Holt and Turner, 1966, p. 339].

Among the less developed nations, an increasingly common form which those with authoritarian regimes assume is the military junta or dictatorship. Heeger has specified some of the reasons why these military-bureaucratic regimes may not engender successful economic development. Military objectives in war are clear, whereas objectives in politics are always in question. Civil servants cannot administer laws by "advancing in serried ranks of battle formation" (Heeger, 1974, p. 108). The armed forces in most developing societies are divided by ethnic cleavages, hostility between officers and those in the ranks, rifts within the officer corps itself, and cleavages between those military officers who assume governmental positions and the majority of military officers who do not. Even if the political center is cohesive, the weak linkages between center and periphery limit the center's capacity to deal with problems in the periphery (Heeger, 1974, p. 137). Indeed, Heeger (1974, p. 122) goes so far as to say that "military rulers have generally proved to be even less adroit as leaders than were their predecessors."

The "Springtime of Freedom" thesis is probably a minority position among both students of development and Third World leaders. Nevertheless, the fact that it has been articulated reminds us that there is a coher ent body of theory which, in contrast to the Authoritarian model's prediction of a negative relationship between democracy and economic development, predicts that this relationship will be positive, i.e., that democracy aids economic development, while an authoritarian polity retards development.

The Skeptical View

Pye's (1966) reason for doubting that there is any systematic relationship—positive or negative—between democracy and economic development is that historically economic growth has taken place within a variety of political systems with a variety of public policies. La Palombara and Weiner (1966) review the literature on the relationship between political parties and development. The dominant elite may be committed to using the power of the state to speed economic development, but on the basis of the available evidence, they suggest, it is unclear whether the democratic or the authoritarian state is the better means toward this end. On the one hand, "there is little convincing evidence that the best or only road to economic modernity is that of an authoritarian or totalitarian regime dominated by a single party" (LaPalombara and Weiner, 1966, p. 6). At the same time, the evidence for the democratic alternative is no more conclusive.

The purpose of the study reported here is to derive from the above theoretical considerations a causal model. This model, to be tested empirically over time with a world-wide sample of less-developed societies, comes closest to the first of the three positions just outlined, and is therefore called the Authoritarian model of Economic Development. The causal model is framed in these terms not because I believed in advance that the Authoritarian view would necessarily fit the facts better than the Springtime of Freedom or the Skeptical views, but because the Authoritarian position seems to have the widest support by scholars and political leaders. In any case, the analysis should provide empirical answers to the questions raised.

THEORETICAL MODEL

While the main variables one derives from the above discussion are democracy or political competition (independent variable) and economic development (dependent variable), other intervening variables need to be specified if the model is to approximate the complexities of the real world at all. What is distinctive about my version of the Authoritarian model of development is that it focuses on a process by which an economically underdeveloped nation's degree of democracy at time t influences the level of societal conflict at time $t + 1$; the level of conflict and government sanctions at time $t + 1$ in turn influence the degree of democracy at time $t + 2$; and, finally, the latter three variables have causal implications for both the level and the rate of economic development at time $t + 3$. This causal model is outlined in Figure 1. Definitions of the concepts will be given, and then the model will be elaborated.

Definitions

Conflict is conceptualized in terms of three of its more specific social structural manifestations: protest demonstrations, riots, and armed attacks. A *protest demonstration* is defined as "a nonviolent gathering of people organized to protest the policies, ideology, or actions of a regime, a government, or political leaders" (Taylor and Hudson, 1972, p. 88). Protest demonstrations may take the form of meetings, rallies, boycotts, etc. A *riot* is defined as action by a large number of the ruled in which destruction of property or bloodshed is more than marginal (Taylor and Hudson, 1972, p. 67). A riot is thus more violent than a protest demonstration, but more spontaneous than the third form of conflict, armed attacks. An *armed attack* is defined as "an act of violent political conflict carried out by an organized group with the object of weakening or destroying the power exercised by another organized group . . . typically a regime, government, or political leader, or his ideology, policy or actions" (Taylor and Hudson, 1972, pp. 102, 68). Unless otherwise noted, "conflict" refers to these three forms, and only to these three, in this study.

Government sanctions are defined as "an action taken by the authorities to neutralize, suppress, or eliminate a perceived threat to the security of the government" (Taylor and Hudson, 1972, p. 69). Three types of sanctions are censorship; restrictions in the form of martial law, curfews, etc.; and domestic espionage (Taylor and Hudson, 1972, pp. 69–70).

The aspects of a society's political system on which the model focuses is its degree of *political competition* or *democracy*. Competition refers to the nature of the political opposition. A more competitive political system is defined as one in which an opposition is institutionalized and given legitimacy; even extremist political parties are fully admitted into the party system; there is a balance of power in the sense that minority parties receive more than a negligible proportion of the vote. A polity is also defined as competitive to the extent that there is institutionalized opposition to the executive branch of government by a legislature; that is, the national legislature has autonomy and is not a mere "rubber stamp" of the executive. If competition emphasizes the nature of the formal political opposition, the second conceptual dimension—democracy—stresses the degree and nature of political participation by the mass of the society's members. When the elite allows only that form of political participation which they can control, and which does not require them to share political decision-making power, we have a mass mobilizational type of participation (LaPalombara and Weiner, 1966, p. 2). This is defined as less democratic than a system in which there is a diffusion of power and widespread participation *which has an influence on the decisions made by political leaders.* Thus, a polity is defined as democratic to the extent that there is an equal distribution of political power. ("Power" is defined as the extent to which an individual or group can control their own action and the action of others.) Since all societies have a political elite—a small group with a disproportionate amount of political power—the definition can be stated as follows: a polity is democratic to the extent that the political power of the elite is minimized and the political power of the widest part of the non-elite is maximized (Bollen, 1977).

The final conceptual variable in the model, *economic development,* is defined as the degree to which the society transforms inanimate energy resources in the consumption per capita of its goods and services. We shall consider both a society's *level* of economic development as of a given point in time and its *rate* of economic development over time.

Causal Relationships

With the key conceptual variables in the model defined, the causal relationships and mechanisms posited in the Authoritarian model of Economic Development can now be adumbrated. Our concern here is exclusively with the economically less developed nations of the world.

Figure 1. Causal model to be tested.

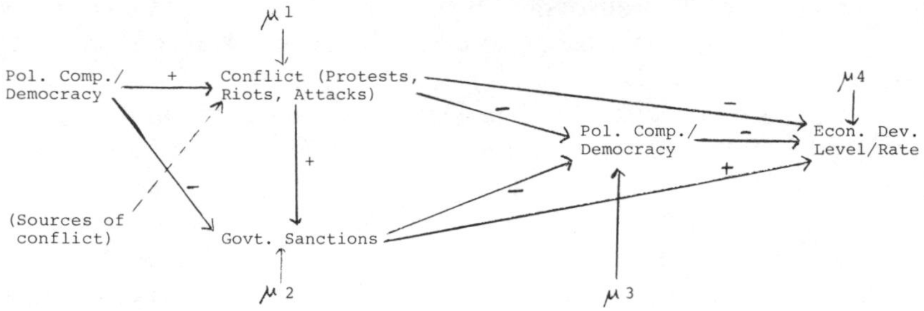

Among these nations, what does the causal diagram in Figure 1 state as the determinants of conflict, of government sanctions, of political competition/democracy, and of economic development?

Determinants of conflict. Less-developed societies have particularly severe conflicts, of which the model specifies two types of causes. The first are unmeasured exogenous sources of conflict: such things as economic and other inequalities, the desire by groups out of power to gain power, and communal or ethnic tensions. These give rise to the three kinds of conflict—protest demonstrations, riots, and armed attacks. The second cause of these conflicts is the degree of competitiveness or democracy of the political system itself. This source of conflict is analytically separated from other sources because it is treated as an endogenous variable in the model, to be measured empirically. The model posits that political competition/democracy is positively related to conflict. This is because democracy institutionalizes conflicting bases of power, and allows their free expression, whereas more authoritarian polities can legitimately *suppress* even the milder expressions of conflict, protest demonstrations. Because the underlying sources of these conflicts may be, at least in the short run, unsolvable, the model leads us to expect more overt conflict in democratic than in authoritarian polities.

Determinants of government sanctions. When conflict is expressed overtly in the form of protests, riots, and attacks, this puts pressure on any kind of regime—democratic or authoritarian—to resort to negative government sanctions. For this reason the model predicts that conflict will have a positive relationship to government sanctions. In other words, faced with protests, riots, or attacks, any government is tempted to resort to such sanctions as censorship, martial law, curfews, mobilizing troops for domestic security, and domestic espionage. However, the model also asserts that politically competitive/democratic regimes, for reasons just noted, are *more constrained* than authoritarian regimes from resorting to government sanctions in order to suppress conflicts. "[I]n otherwise comparable situations, elites are less inclined to resort to repression in nations where political authorities are held accountable for their actions by free and competitive elections" (Hibbs, 1973, p. 186). Feierabend and Feierabend also suggest this relationship in their six-point scale of governmental coerciveness-permissiveness: democracies have high permissiveness scores, while the countries of the communist bloc (1948–1960) tend more toward the coercive end of the scale (Feierabend and Feierabend, 1971, Table 1). Thus, the model posits a *negative* causal influence of political competition/democracy on government sanctions.

According to the model, then, government sanctions are a positive direct result of conflict, a negative direct result of political competition/democracy, and a positive indirect result of political competition/democracy via conflict. Democracy has a negative direct impact on a government's resort to sanctions, but because democracy also allows the expression of *more* conflict—which induces *more* sanctions—it has a positive indirect effect on the resort to sanctions. However, the model posits that, *holding the level of overt conflict constant* across societies, democracies will resort to negative sanctions *less often* than nondemocratic regimes.

Determinants of political competition/democracy. The model states that the level of political competition and democracy is affected by prior levels of conflict and government sanctions. First, the greater the conflict, the greater the pressure on the political system to reduce the expression of conflict (not necessarily its sources) by becoming less democratic. This follows from the earlier point that a nondemocratic regime can legitimately suppress conflict to a greater extent than a competitive, democratic regime. The authoritarian regime can suppress conflict because "the regime knows best what is in the true interests of the people." Thus, the negative causal arrow from conflict to political competition/democracy in Figure 1. Second, the more a regime resorts to negative government sanctions, the less democratic it becomes: outright suppression of conflict is, in principle. *not* "the way it is done" in a politically competitive system.[1] Thus, the negative causal arrow from government sanctions to political competition/democracy.

In addition to these two direct (negative) effects, conflict also has an indirect negative effect on political competition by increasing the resort to government sanctions. That is, the model asserts that conflict impels the regime to resort more to negative sanctions, and this in turn *reduces* the level of democracy in the system.

Table 1. Summary of effects on economic development
posited in Figure 1.

	Direct Effects		Indirect Effects		Sum
Independent Variable	+	−	+	−	
Conflict		1	2		Mixed (±)
Political competition/democracy		1			−
Government sanctions	1		1		+

Determinants of economic development level and rate. At this point in the model, the underlying theoretical reasoning is first that conflict impedes smooth economic development. This has not gone unnoticed in the literature. "The common presumption is that higher levels of political violence dissipate valuable . . . resources—government revenues for unproductive defense and coercion, valuable manpower, limited political trust" (Enloe, 1976, p. 270). Kuznets avers,

> . . . clearly some minimum political stability is necessary if members of the economic society are to plan ahead and be assured of a relatively stable relation between their contribution to economic activity and their rewards. One could hardly expect much economic growth under conditions of political turmoil, riots, and unpredictable changes in regimes [Kuznets, 1966, p. 451].

Hence, the negative causal arrow from conflict to economic development in Figure 1. Second, there is also a negative causal effect of democracy on economic development. As we noted in the beginning of this paper, the Springtime of Freedom thesis holds that democracy aids development, and skeptics argue that there is no systematic relationship between the two. However, in this paper, we are testing neither of these versions of theory, but instead, the Authoritarian model, which argues that when a regime is constrained to accede (at least to some degree) to the demands of its many, diverse publics—as is relatively more true in a democracy— it cannot be as efficient in its drive toward development. The type case of this argument is, of course, Stalinist forced draft industrialization. Third, the model holds that negative government sanctions have a direct positive effect on economic development.

In addition to these three direct effects on economic development, the model also specifies three *indirect* effects. Because conflict reduces democracy, which in turn facilitates economic development, conflict has an indirect *positive* effect on development. Conflict stimulates a regime to resort more to negative sanctions, which in turn reduces "confusion and disorder" and thereby facilitates economic development; this is another mechanism by which conflict has a *positive* indirect effect on economic development. Finally, resort to government sanctions decreases the level of democracy, and this in turn aids economic development; thus, sanctions also have a *positive* indirect effect on development.

It is hoped that the precise causal specification of this Authoritarian model at least begins to come to grips with the real world. Social structures and processes rarely have only a single, consistent train of consequences; they have both direct and indirect effects, and both positive and negative impacts on other structures and processes. In this case, the model specifies a pattern of causal effects whose complexity, while certainly not fully realized, is at least suggested in Table 1.

METHODS

Earlier research (Olsen and Firebaugh, 1974) has suggested that different causal patterns may obtain in the relationships among political, social, and economic development in the relatively more-developed nations as compared with the less developed nations. The aim of this paper is to estimate the above causal model as it applies to the national political units which had in common a relatively low level of economic development as of 1955, and to follow the course of development of this set of nations through the subsequent 15 years,[2] to ascertain the effects of the independent and the intervening variables on the ultimate dependent variable, economic development level in 1970, and rate of economic development from 1960 to 1970. The universe, therefore, consists of those political units whose level of economic development, as measured by energy consumption per capita in 1955 (UN, various years; Taylor and Hudson, 1972; Banks, 1971, Segment 8, Field G) was below 1,000 kgs. of coal equivalents. (For comparison, in 1955 the U.S. energy consumption per capita was 7,768 kgs., the United Kingdom, 5,000 kgs., and the Soviet Union, 2,220 kgs.). Of the world's 158 political units enumerated by Taylor and Hudson (1972), 29 were eliminated because their energy consumption per capita level in 1955 was 1,000 kgs. or over; another 31 had to be dropped from the universe because no data were available on the relevant variables, or because they are protectorates or other kinds of nonnational political units. The remaining 98 political units constitute the universe of this study; however, data were not available for all 98 cases on some of the political and energy variables (see Table 2). Instead of attempting to estimate the missing data, cases with missing observations are simply dropped from a particular regression; consequently, none of the figures estimating the model has an N larger than 95.

The universe of 98 cases provides a good geographic representation of

Table 2. Correlation matrix for all variables (Pearson r).

	N	X̄	S.D.	Range	Pol. 62-66	Dem. 60	Dem. 65	Ln Prot. 57-61	Ln Riots 57-61	Ln Attacks 57-61	Ln Sanctions 57-61	Ln Prot. 60-64	Ln Riots 60-64	Ln Attacks 60-64	Ln Sanctions 60-64	Ln Energy /cap 70	Ln Energy 60-70
Pol. comp. 57-59	50	13.3	11.5	0-33	.92	.89	.90	.23	.33	.09	.01	.24	.27	-.05	.03	.28	-.36
Pol. comp. 62-66	82	19.3	17.0	0-55		.79	.92	.27	.31	.15	.09	.21	.23	.04	.02	.33	-.33
Pol. dem. 60	85	55.7	26.4	11.9-99.8			.85	.17	.29	.18	.00	.19	.27	.10	.04	.22	-.32
Pol. dem. 65	95	48.6	26.4	5.2-99.8				.23	.22	.01	.00	.17	.20	-.10	-.04	.33	-.29
Ln Protests 57-61	98	1.1	1.3	0-4.5					.67	.50	.65	.73	.52	.45	.60	.30	-.25
Ln Riots 57-61	98	1.8	1.6	0-5.0						.62	.64	.63	.74	.58	.59	.16	-.26
Ln Attacks 57-61	98	2.2	2.1	0-7.7							.69	.39	.47	.83	.60	.14	-.12
Ln Sanctions 57-61	98	2.8	1.6	0-6.5								.54	.47	.59	.83	.31	-.16
Ln Protests 60-64	98	1.3	1.4	0-4.6									.70	.51	.64	.32	-.19
Ln Riots 60-64	98	1.7	1.6	0-5.0										.60	.61	.17	-.15
Ln Attacks 60-64	98	2.4	2.0	0-7.3											.67	.02	-.11
Ln Sanctions 60-64	98	2.9	1.4	0-5.9												.19	-.11
Ln Energy/cap 70	98	5.5	1.4	2.1-9.0													-.18
Ln % Energy change 60-70	95	-2.4	1.2	-5.1-0.0													

the world's less developed nations during the 1955–1970 period: Central and South America and the Caribbean, 22 cases; Europe 8; Middle East 10; Africa 38; Asia 20. (See the Appendix for a complete list.)

The primary data sources are Taylor and Hudson's 1972 edition of *World Handbook of Political and Social Indicators,* and Banks's *Cross-Polity Time-Series Data* (1971). Data for the political competition variable for various years are taken directly from Banks's Aggregate Competition Index score (Segment 10, Field P) for each nation. This index sums four items—the effectiveness of the lower house of the national legislature (0 for no legislature to 3 for a legislature which possesses significant governmental autonomy, e.g., ability to override an executive veto); the process by which legislators are nominated (0 for no legislature to 3 for competitive nominating process); legislative coalitions (0 for no coalition, no opposition, to 3 for more than one party, no coalitions); and party legitimacy (0 for no parties, or all but dominant party and satellites excluded, to 3 for no parties excluded). A nation's score each year, then, ranges between 0 and 12; the higher the score, the more competitive the nation's political system.

Data for the second political variable, democracy, are taken from Bollen (1977), who developed an index to measure the extent to which power is equally distributed in a society. The index has six components: Freedom of the press (Nixon, 1960); freedom of group opposition (Banks, 1971, Segment 10, Field 0); effective executive selection (Banks, 1971, Segment 1, Field J); legislative selection (Banks, 1971, Segment 1, Field P); fairness of elections (Taylor and Hudson, 1972, "electoral irregularity" variable); and the reciprocal of the extent of "elite power through government sanctions" (Taylor and Hudson, 1972). Space limitations prevent a fuller description of this index of democracy; see Bollen (1977) and the original sources. Suffice it to say that the six components were scored so that the total score ranges from 0 to 100, with 100 indicating a high level of democracy. A factor analysis of the six indicators yielded a single factor. The Pearson correlation of the Bollen index of democracy with other well-known measures of democracy range from .46 with Neubauer (1967, p. 1007) to .85 with Cutright and Wiley (1969, p. 39).

The Bollen index of democracy has even higher correlations with the Banks political competition variable for given points in time:

	Bollen Democracy		
	1960	1965	N
Banks Political Competition 1957–1959	.89		50
Banks Political Competition 1962–1966		.92	82

This is partly because two components—party legitimacy or freedom of group opposition and effectiveness of the legislature or legislative selection—are common to both Banks and Bollen. Both the political competition and the democracy measures will be retained in the analysis, because, while they generally have the same relationships to other variables in the model, there are exceptions. Another possible source of tautology is that one of the six components of Bollen's index of democracy contains the government sanctions variable in Figure 1. High correlations between democracy and government sanctions in our analysis would thus be tautological. However, the actual correlations are near zero between each of the two government sanctions variables used (aggregated separately for 1957–1961 and 1960–1964) on the one hand and each of Bollen's democracy variables (for 1960 and 1965). Evidently, the other five components of Bollen's index of democracy act to randomize the connection between the government sanctions component and this same component when it is a separate variable. This result again argues in favor of using both the Banks and the Bollen indexes in this analysis.

The number of *protest demonstrations, riots, armed attacks,* and *government sanctions* each year is taken directly from the "Events data" for 1948 to 1967 in Taylor and Hudson (1972). These data were compiled from *The New York Times Index,* and such supplementary sources as the *Africa Diary, Asian Recorder, Middle East Journal,* and the Associated Press card file (for Latin America and Europe). For a discussion of coding, intercoder reliability, etc., as they bear on the conflict and sanctions events data, see Taylor and Hudson (1972, ch. 3, and Appendix 1).

The final variables in the model are *economic development level,* measured by the nation's energy consumption per capita in 1970, and *rate of economic development,* measured by the nation's mean annual percent change in energy consumption per capita from 1960 to 1970.[3]

Of the variables in the analysis, several had highly nonnormal or skewed distributions. Variables with a skewness of 1.5 or more were: protest demonstrations, riots, and armed attacks, both 1957–1961 and 1960–1964; government sanctions, both 1957–1961 and 1960–1964; energy consumption per capita, both 1960 and 1970; and average annual per cent change in energy consumption per capita, 1960–70.[4] All these variables were *positively* skewed, i.e., more cases have low values on the variable than high. In other words, most nations have *low* levels of conflict, *low* frequencies of resort to government sanctions, a *low* level of economic development, and *low* rates of economic development over the 1960–1970 decade. In the analysis, the natural log (Ln) of each of these variables is used. The political competition and democracy variables are relatively normally distributed, and therefore appear in the analysis in their raw form.

A matrix of Pearson correlation coefficients between all the variables in the study is presented in Table 2.

FINDINGS

Trends in Political Competition in Developing Nations
Before we begin to test the causal model, a comment on "the decline in democracy in the developing nations" is in order. Banks (1971) gives political competition scores only for 1946–1966. Since most of the African, and a number of the Asian nations did not gain independence until about 1960, political competition scores are given for only 53 of our universe of less-developed nations in 1955. Prevailing theory (Lipset, 1959; Almond and Coleman, 1960; Cutright, 1963; Cutright and Wiley, 1969; Jackman, 1973) suggests a strong positive relationship between economic development and political competition. What is surprising, therefore, is not so much that the mean political competition score (on the 0–12 scale) of these 53 nations was only 4.3 in 1955 as that several of these nations, despite their low level of economic development, had absolutely high levels of political competition. These "deviant cases" included Japan and India (score of 11), Costa Rica, Uruguay, the Philippines, and Sri Lanka (10), Chile, Greece, Turkey, Burma and Lebanon (9), and Mexico and Brazil (8).

The trend toward a decline in democracy in the developing nations has been documented both on the basis of case studies and cross-national comparisons (Banks, 1972). Embarking upon independence with constitutions and political institutions closely modelled after those of the democratic West, one after another of the new nations has moved away from a competitive political system and toward one or another form of less democratic polity. What the Banks data show clearly is that political competition declined in the nations which gained independence after 1955, while its level remained essentially the same in the 53 poor nations that were already independent in 1955.

Less-Developed Nations: Independence	N	Mean Political Competition 1955	1960	1966
Prior to 1956	53	4.3	4.2	4.4
1956 or later	27		4.6	2.7
	80[5]			

Thus, on the basis of the political competition scores we shall use, the decline of democracy is not a phenomenon that characterizes all economically underdeveloped nations, but rather, those which gained independence only after 1955.

The Effect of Polity on Conflict
As we begin to estimate the coefficients in the causal model in Figure 1, we first regress each of the three conflict variables on the prior level of political competition or democracy.

Proposition 1:   The greater the political competition or democracy, the higher the subsequent levels of protest demonstrations, riots, and armed attacks. This proposition is tested by six bivariate regressions in Figures 2A and 2B. Contrary to the proposition, political competition 1957–1959 has no significant[6] causal effect on protests, riots, or armed attacks during 1960–1964 in the 50 nations for which there are data. Nor does Bollen's democracy 1960 variable have any significant causal effect on protests or attacks in a more inclusive set of 85 nations during 1960–1964; its only significant causal effect is on riots. The more democratic the nation was in 1960, the more riots it had in the subsequent five years; but this relationship is rather weak (beta = .27).

With five out of six disconfirmations, proposition 1 is largely disconfirmed. Among the less developed nations, the amount of overt conflict is not significantly greater in democratic than in authoritarian regimes. This finding parallels that of Hibbs (1973, p. 120, table 7.3, and p. 121, table 7.5). Hibbs shows that when Ln energy consumption/capita 1960 and Ln population size 1960 are controlled, Cutright's Political Development Index (1963 version) has no significant effect on Internal War, Hibbs's measure of the more severe forms of conflict. Nor did Cutright's political index have any significant effect on Collective Protest, Hibbs's factor measuring less severe forms of conflict, even without controlling for energy consumption/capita.

Figure 2.   The effect of democracy on conflict.

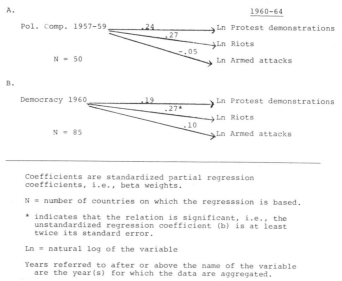

Coefficients are standardized partial regression coefficients, i.e., beta weights.

N = number of countries on which the regresssion is based.

* indicates that the relation is significant, i.e., the unstandardized regression coefficient (b) is at least twice its standard error.

Ln = natural log of the variable

Years referred to after or above the name of the variable are the year(s) for which the data are aggregated.

The Effect of Polity and Conflict on Government Sanctions

Proposition 2: Government sanctions are a positive direct result of the conflict variables and a negative direct result of political competition/ democracy; the effect of each independent variable upon sanctions is significant when the other independent variables are held constant. This proposition is tested in Figures 3A and 3B. Of the variables on which government sanctions 1960–1964 is regressed, it is lagged in relation to political competition (1957–1959) and democracy (1960), but regressed on "simultaneous" conflict variables (1960–1964). The logic of this is that whereas the level of democracy has a more long-term contextual influence on whether governments resort to sanctions, governments are more likely to respond quickly to protests, riots, and armed attacks (Hibbs, 1973, pp. 90–91).

As predicted, protest demonstrations and armed attacks have significant positive effects on government sanctions. This is true when political competition 1957–1959 is controlled, and it is also true when democracy 1960 is controlled. Proposition 2 is not confirmed in the case of the third conflict variable, riots 1960–1964: this has no significant causal effect on

Figure 3. Multiple regression of government sanctions on democracy and conflict.

A.

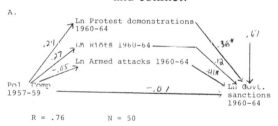

B.

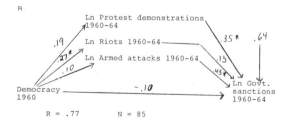

For meaning of symbols, see Figure 2. The coefficient above the vertical arrow is the residual, i.e., the unexplained variance ($\sqrt{1 - R^2}$).

sanctions 1960–1964. However, there is a .70 correlation between protests and riots, and their collinearity spuriously reduces the effect of riots on sanctions, once the effect of protests on sanctions has entered the multiple regression. Thus, when protests 1960–1964 is eliminated from the regressions in Figures 3A and 3B, riots explain much of the variance in sanctions previously explained by protests. (The beta weights are: attacks .47*, riots .33*, political competition −.03; and, in the alternative regression: attacks .48*, riots .35*, and democracy −.09. An asterisk means a significant beta, i.e., the coefficient is at least twice its standard error.)

If proposition 2 is largely confirmed with regard to the effect of the conflict variables on government sanctions, it is disconfirmed in regard to the influence of political competition or democracy on subsequent resort to government sanctions. When the level of conflict across nations is held constant, neither political competition 1957–1959 nor democracy 1960 has any significant lagged effect on sanctions during 1960–1964. (Nor does political competition 1960–1964 have any significant synchronous effect on sanctions 1960–1964, when the conflict variables are held constant.) This is an important negative finding for the Authoritarian Model of economic development. *There is no evidence that, among the less-developed nations, democracies respond any less drastically than more authoritarian regimes to given levels of conflict.* Why does democracy or political competition not have an inhibiting effect on the government's resort to sanctions as a response to conflict? One possibility, which can only be suggested here, is that for this constraining effect to operate, it presupposes a society which is more highly developed economically. In other words, governmental restraint in applying sanctions as a response to conflict may be a luxury that only economically advanced democracies can afford. In this view, the economically less developed democracies of concern here are in such a precarious, potentially or actually unstable, position that their democratic political institutions have no more vitality *in this respect* than those of the more authoritarian regimes. Confronting a given level of conflict, poor democracies appear to react in terms of essentially the same level of negative sanctions as do the poor nondemocratic regimes.

A different argument is that any government—democratic or otherwise—*must* respond to armed attacks against itself with negative sanctions: to fail to do this is to write its own death warrant. This is somewhat less the case in regard to riots, which may not be directly anti-government, but only a "threat to order." By this logic, it is only in its response to the least violent form of conflict—protest demonstrations—that a democracy can be more restrained than an authoritarian regime. This argument and the relevant data are as follows:

| | Beta for: | |
	Political competition 1957–59	Democracy 1960
(1) Controlling for the level of armed attacks, political competition/ democracy has no relationship to sanctions. *Confirmed:*	.07	−.02
(2) Controlling for the level of riots, political competition/democracy has a somewhat stronger (than in 1) negative relationship to sanctions. *Weakly confirmed:*	−.14	−.13
(3) Controlling for the level of protests, political competition/democracy has a still stronger (than in 2) negative relationship to sanctions. *Disconfirmed:*	−.13	−.08

Thus, although democratic and authoritarian regimes respond alike to the most severe form of threat—armed attacks—democratic regimes are not significantly more restrained than authoritarian regimes in their response to the less severe forms of conflict, riots, and protests. The expected *increase* in the magnitude of the betas as one moves from the most severe to the least severe conflicts is not, in fact, observed.

The model in Figure 1 also posited that political competition/democracy has a positive indirect effect on government sanctions via conflict. This would be confirmed if there were significant positive path coefficients *from* political competition (or democracy) *to* each conflict variable, and significant positive coefficients *from* each conflict variable to sanctions. This condition is met in none of the six pairs of paths in Figures 3A and 3B. In five instances, the path from political competition or democracy to a conflict variable is nonsignificant, and in the one instance where it is significant, the path from riots to sanctions is nonsignificant. Therefore, political competition/democracy does not have the hypothesized positive indirect effect on sanctions by generating more conflict which in turn elicits more government sanctions.

In summary, only one of the three postulated causes of government sanctions—conflict—is observed. The other two—the direct effect of political competition/democracy on sanctions, and the indirect effect of political competition/democracy via conflict on sanctions—are not, in fact, operative.

The Effect of Early Polity, Conflict, and Sanctions on Later Democracy

Having started with the influence of political competition/democracy, we now consider how the variables it influences (according to the model) in turn shape the subsequent level of political competition/democracy.

Proposition 3: Conflict and government sanctions each have an independent, direct, negative influence on subsequent political competition/democracy. Figure 1 postulates that the greater the conflict and the more the government resorts to negative sanctions, the lower a nation's later level of political competition/democracy will be. Political competition index scores are available in Banks 1971 only through 1966, and Bollen's democracy index scores only for 1960 and 1965. Since proposition 3 requires that all the independent variables operate at an earlier time, when the dependent variable is political competition 1962–1966, the conflict and sanctions variables are for 1957–1961 (Figure 4A); when democracy 1965 is the dependent variable, conflict and sanctions variables are for 1960–1964 (Figure 4B).

Figure 4. Multiple regression of democracy on conflict and government sanctions.

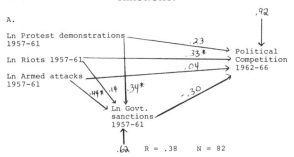

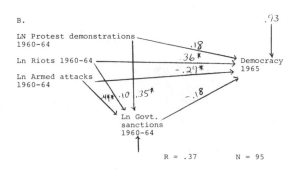

For meaning of symbols, see Figures 2 and 3.

When political competition 1962–1966 is regressed on prior levels of conflict and sanctions, instead of the predicted negative influences we observe one significant positive influence (riots) and three nonsignificant influences. When democracy 1965 is regressed on prior levels of conflict and sanctions, only armed attacks have the predicted significant negative influence. Riots during 1960–1964 have a significant positive influence on democracy 1965. Thus, out of eight lagged relationships, only one—the tendency for earlier armed attacks to reduce later levels of democracy— supports the model. The model did not anticipate that prior levels of riots would have significant *positive* effects on both political competition and democracy. In this sense, proposition 3 is largely disconfirmed. Since 1960–1964 armed attacks have a negative effect on democracy, but 1957–1961 attacks have no effect on political competition 1962–1966, even that relationship cannot be accepted with much confidence as a general pattern. Nor does resort to government sanctions reduce subsequent levels of political competition/democracy.

What our findings do suggest is that if developing countries sometimes become *less* democratic because of conflict (armed attacks), they also become *more* democratic and politically competitive as a result of another form of conflict—riots. Before speculating on why riots might heighten democracy, while protest demonstrations do not, it should be noted that collinearity is again relevant. The correlation between protests and riots during 1957–1961 is .67, and during 1960–1964 is .70. When riots is dropped from the regression, the effects of protests 1957–1961 on subsequent political competition becomes significant (beta = .27). A second way to reduce this collinearity is to combine a country's scores on both protests and riots for a given time period. This new variable, ln protests + riots 1960–1964, had a significant, but positive, effect on subsequent political competition and on democracy.

If we take these findings at their face value, we are again reminded, as Hibbs (1973) and others have noted, that "conflict" is a multidimensional phenomenon which has contrary effects on other variables, in this case, on subsequent political competition and democracy. Regressing each of the latter variables on various combinations of the conflict and sanctions variables (not shown here), we found that whenever riots *or* protests, *or* protests and riots, have a significant effect, it is always to *increase* later political competition or democracy; and whenever armed attacks *or* government sanctions[7] have a significant effect, it is always to *reduce* later levels of democracy.

The robustness of these relationships can be ascertained by seeing which "hold up" when *early* political competition/democracy is held constant. When political competition 1962–1966 is regressed on the independent variables in Figure 4A, controlling for political competition 1957–

1959, even riots ceases to have any significant net effect. However, when democracy 1965 is regressed on the independent variables in Figure 4B, controlling for democracy 1960, armed attacks continues to have a significant negative effect on democracy (beta = $-.28$). The effect of riots is again seen to be spurious—it has no effect on democracy independent of the effect of the earlier level of democracy. Thus, *the one robust relationship in Figure 4A-B is the negative impact of armed attacks 1960–1964 on democracy 1965:* this is independent of the influence of the prior level of democracy.

Figure 1 also posits an indirect negative effect of conflict on political competition/democracy via sanctions. Does the evidence in Figures 4A and 4B support the idea that conflict impels a regime to resort more to negative sanctions which in turn weakens the level of democracy in the system? By the usual criterion that both the path from conflict to sanctions and that from sanctions to political competition/democracy must be significant, we find no evidence whatever for this indirect influence of conflict on political competition or democracy. Even when the path from a conflict variable to sanctions is significant in Figures 4A and 4B, the path from sanctions to political competition or democracy is not significant.

To summarize this stage of the analysis, Figures 4A and 4B largely disconfirm the relevant segment of the Authoritarian model of economic development, diagrammed in Figure 1. It is now time to turn to the model's ultimate dependent variable—economic development.

The Effect of Early Conflict, Sanctions, and Political Competition/Democracy on Economic Development Level

Among the nations that were economically underdeveloped (less than 1,000 kgs. energy consumption/capita) in 1955, by 1970, the range in level of development was from Bulgaria (3,936 kgs.) to Burundi (8 kgs.). The mean for the 98 cases for which there were data was 540 kgs., with a standard deviation of 711 kgs. As noted above, the dependent variable is the natural log of energy/capita 1970. How do the prior variables in the model influence nation's level of economic development in 1970?

Proposition 4: Level of economic development in 1970 is a result of the prior operation of three sets of variables: conflict, government sanctions, and political competition/democracy. Specifically, early conflict and political competition/democracy each has an independent, direct, negative influence on the later level of economic development; and early government sanctions have an independent, direct, positive influence on the later level economic development. This part of the model introduced in Figure 1 is tested in Figures 5A and 5B.

It appears that the model is totally disconfirmed. Political competition

Figure 5. Multiple regression of energy level on democracy, conflict and government sanctions.

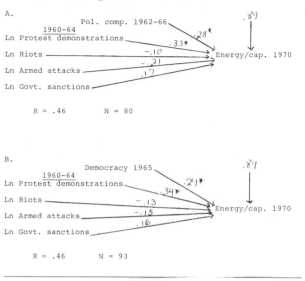

A.

Pol. comp. 1962-66

1960-64

Ln Protest demonstrations

Ln Riots

Ln Armed attacks

Ln Govt. sanctions

.33*

.28*

-.10

-.21

.17

.89

Energy/cap. 1970

R = .46   N = 80

B.

Democracy 1965

1960-64

Ln Protest demonstrations

Ln Riots

Ln Armed attacks

Ln Govt. sanctions

.34*

.21*

-.13

-.15

.16

.89

Energy/cap. 1970

R = .46   N = 93

For meaning of symbols, see Figures 2 and 3.

1962–1966 and democracy 1965 have a positive, rather than the predicted negative, influence on 1970 level of economic development. Only one of the conflict variables—protest demonstrations 1960–1964—has a significant effect on 1970 level of development, but protests increase the level of development, rather than retarding it, as the model postulated. Riots and armed attacks, contrary to theory, appear to have no effect on later development level. Nor do government sanctions aid development: they too have no apparent effect.

Before attempting to make too much of these findings, we must meet a key requirement of panel regression analysis. Do the theoretical variables continue to have the relationships with economic development observed in Figures 5A-B *net of the prior level of economic development?* The temporal autocorrelations of ln energy consumption/capita are .90 for the years 1955 and 1970, and .95 for 1960 and 1970. When energy/capita 1970 is regressed on the five variables in Figure 5A and on energy/capita 1960, only energy/capita 1960 (beta = .78) and attacks 1960–64 (beta = −.19) have any significant effect on 1970 development level. Political competition 1962–1966 has no significant independent influence on 1970 development level, net of 1960 development level. The same findings emerge when 1970 development level is regressed on the five variables in Figure 5B and on energy/capita 1960: democracy 1965 ceases to have a significant effect on 1970 development level when 1960 development level is held constant; and of the other independent variables, only armed attacks has a significant negative effect (beta = $-.18$) on 1970 developmental level. The overwhelming effect is again 1960 energy/capita (beta = $.77$).

When 1970 development level is regressed on only political competition 1962–1966 and energy/capita 1960, or on democracy 1965 and energy/capita 1960, the political variables are again seen to have no effect on 1970 development level, net of prior development level.

What this means is that among our universe of less developed nations, those nations that were somewhat more politically competitive or democratic in the late 1950s or in 1960 were *already* somewhat more highly developed economically than those with more authoritarian polities. The Pearson correlations are:

	Ln energy/capita	
	1955	1960
Political competition 1957–1959	.39	.36
Democracy 1960	.19	.25

This edge in economic development which the more democratic nations had at the beginning of the period we are studying was maintained sufficiently until the end of the period to give the appearance that if and as the level of democracy rose after 1960, it would have the effect of increasing the level of economic development by 1970. This finding is spurious in the sense that what appears to be the influence of prior democracy is in fact due to the common variance shared by early political competition/democracy and early energy/capita level. The political variables are now seen to have no influence on later economic development level *net* of prior level of economic development.

When we turn from direct to indirect effects on 1970 development level, the model fares no better. The indirect effect of conflict on development level via political competition, and that of government sanctions on development level via political competition/democracy are both disconfirmed by virtue of the absence of any significant independent effect of political competition/democracy on 1970 development level. The indirect effect of conflict on development level via sanctions is also disconfirmed by the fact that 1960–1964 sanctions have no significant net effect on 1970 development level.

In summary, the Authoritarian model of economic development is largely *disconfirmed* with regard to the effect of the polity, conflict, and sanctions variables on economic development level at a single point in time, 1970. Not one of the variables had a significant effect on development level *in the direction posited* in the model. Where the model posited negative influences, we observed either positive influences (of protests) or no influence (of political competition/democracy and of riots). Where the model predicted positive influences (of sanctions), we found no influence. The only support for the model is that when 1960 energy/capita is held constant, along with the other independent variables, armed attacks have the predicted *negative* influence on subsequent development level, but even this influence, though significant, is weak.

Since economic development is obviously a process which occurs over time, a more appropriate test of the model in Figure 1 uses the rate of development over time, rather than the level of development at one point in time. It is to this more dynamic variable that we now turn.

The Effect of Early Conflict, Sanctions, and Political Competition/Democracy on Economic Development Rate

As already noted, the rate of economic development is measured by the nation's mean annual percent change in energy consumption/capita between 1960 and 1970. In our universe of less developed nations, the mean energy/capita increased from 284 kgs. in 1960 (range: 4–1,453 kgs., N=95) to 540 kgs. in 1970 (range: 8–3,936 kgs., N=98). This is a 90.1 percent increase over the decade. The range for the annual mean increase was from −3.0 percent to +63.9 percent. At one extreme are nations whose energy consumption per capita was lower in 1970 than in 1960: Haiti −29.7 percent, Burundi −23.0, China −17.7, Indonesia −16.4, Egypt −8.6, and so forth. At the other extreme are the nations which, from a low base line in 1960, had dramatically rapid increases in per capita energy consumption by 1970: Mauritania 638.9 percent, South Vietnam 481.2, Gabon 371.8, Ethiopia 321.3, Laos 314.3, Thailand 312.9 percent, etc. The dependent variable in Figures 6A and 6B is, of course, the natural log of this energy/capita change variable.

We shall now again test proposition 4 (see p. 236), the only difference being that the dependent variable is now rate, rather than level, of economic development. First, the model is disconfirmed in that none of the three conflict variables (1960–1964) has the predicted (significant) negative influence on development rate. This finding supports Hibbs (1973) who argued that mass political violence (what I have called conflict) has no systemic relationship to the rate of economic growth. As Hibbs (1973, pp. 37–40) points out, severe and protracted violence in specific places and times may hinder economic development, but no general relationship exists.

Second, the model is disconfirmed in that government sanctions (1960–1964) have no significant positive influence on development rate. However, with regard to the core independent variable in the Authoritarian model—political competition/democracy—the model is confirmed. When the other variables are controlled, political competition 1962–1966

Figure 6.   Multiple regression of rate of energy change on democracy,
conflict and government sanctions.

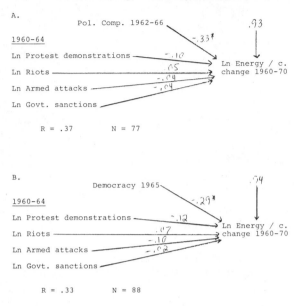

For meaning of symbols, see Figures 2 and 3.

has a significant negative influence on development rate; so, too, does
democracy 1965. In this sense, we may say that while the influence of the
conflict and sanctions variables on development rate is essentially nil, the
higher the level of political competition or democracy during the mid-
1960s, the lower the rate of economic development between 1960 and
1970. The political system, then, does appear to have the effect on development that the Authoritarian model postulates. *An authoritarian polity facilitates development, while a competitive, democratic polity retards
development.*

To discover whether this relationship is robust enough to "survive"
controlling for 1960 development level, we regressed energy/capita
change 1960–1970 on the same five variables as in Figures 6A-B and also
on ln energy/capita 1960. Whereas economic development *level* in 1960 is
highly positively correlated with economic development level in 1970, the
rate of development between 1960 and 1970 is significantly negatively
correlated with 1960 level of development (r = −.28). In other words,
nations already relatively high in energy/capita in 1960 generally achieved
somewhat lower percentage increases in energy/capita between 1960 and
1970. This suggests two points. First, dynamic economic development

rate is a very different variable than static economic development level. Second, the relatively small effect of 1960 energy/capita level on 1960– 1970 development rate (−.28) should mean that controlling for 1960 energy/capita will not alter the findings observed in Figure 6A-B. This is precisely what we find. There continues to be a significant negative effect of early political competition (−.35) and democracy (−.29) on the rate of development when 1960 energy level is held constant, whereas the latter variable has no significant effect on the rate of development, net of the other variables in the model.

Finally, we test for the *indirect* effects on development rate posited in Figure 1. First, the indirect positive effect of the conflict variables via political competition/democracy on development rate is observed in only one of the six pairs of paths: armed attacks 1960–1964 have a significant negative influence on democracy 1965 (beta = −.29), and the latter variable in turn has a significant negative influence on development rate 1960–1970 (beta = −.29). In the other five pairs of paths, although the coefficient from political competition 1962–1966 or democracy 1965 to development rate 1960–1970 is significantly negative, the prior coefficients from a conflict variable to political competition/democracy are either nonsignificant or significantly positive (see Figure 4A-B). The first indirect influence is therefore largely disconfirmed.

The second indirect influence postulated—a positive influence of conflict on development rate via sanctions—calls for two significant positive paths linking the three variables. This is totally disconfirmed since the path from early government sanctions to development rate is nonsignificant (see Figure 6A-B). The third indirect influence involves a negative effect of sanctions on later political competition/democracy, followed by a negative effect of the latter variables on development rate. What we observe is the significant negative effect of political competition or democracy on development rate, but the prior effect of sanctions on political competition/democracy is nonsignificant (see Figure 4A-B). Thus, the indirect effects on development rate postulated in the model are almost completely disconfirmed.

Controlling for Population Size

Hibbs (1973) suggests that the amount of conflict in a society may be partly a function of the society's population size, and, therefore, the log of population size should be introduced as a control variable. This was done in each of the regressions in Figures 3 through 6. Introducing ln population 1960 (Taylor and Hudson 1972, codebook variable 1006) left the betas for the original independent variables essentially unchanged in all the Figures except Figure 4B, where riots cease to have a significant effect on democracy 1965 net of population size. In all the figures except Figure

3A-B, population size itself had no significant effect on the dependent variable net of the effect of the original independent variables. In Figure 3A-B, controlling for the conflict variables, population size had a significant positive independent effect on sanctions 1960–1964. In other words, apart from the tendency for nations with more protests and more attacks to have more negative government sanctions, nations with larger populations also tended to resort more to government sanctions than did those with fewer people. Apart from these exceptions, then, controlling for population size does not alter our earlier conclusions.

CONCLUSIONS

There are at least three theoretical positions concerning the extent to which, and how, a nation's level of democracy or political competition influences its later economic development. There is the Authoritarian model, which asserts that "latecomer" nations must have a nondemocratic polity in order to achieve economic development; the Springtime of Freedom thesis, which claims that even in latecomer nations, as in the early modernizers, a democratic polity facilitates rather than hinders economic development; and the Skeptical view, which insists there is no evidence of any systematic effect of degree of democracy on economic development, either positive or negative. A causal model was derived from the first of these theoretical positions, in which the predicted negative effect of democracy on economic development was elaborated by the introduction of conflict, government sanctions, and democracy as variables which intervene between early level of democracy and later economic development. This Authoritarian model of development was estimated by means of multiple regression analysis, based on data for all nations that were economically underdeveloped (less than 1,000 kgs./capita energy consumption) in 1955 and for which data on the relevant variables were available. The course of development in this set of 98 nations was followed through 1970, and the results of the several stages of the regression analysis are summarized in Figure 7.

Figure 7 eliminates those causal paths in Figure 1 which were found to be statistically non-significant. How has the original Authoritarian model been revised? Proposition 1, which stated that early political competition/democracy causes higher levels of all three kinds of conflict, is largely disconfirmed. Neither political competition nor democracy has any effect on protest demonstrations or armed attacks, and while democracy has a positive effect on riots, political competition has no effect. Thus, among economically less-developed societies, those with democra-

Figure 7.   Results of testing model in Figure 1.*

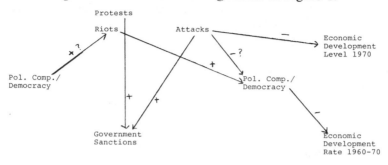

* Paths are drawn only if the unstandardized partial regression coefficient in
Figures 2-6 is at least twice its standard error. Paths to the economic
development dependent variables differ somewhat from those in Figure 5A-B
because this version takes into account the regression which controlled for
1960 energy/capita level, which altered the effects of protests and attacks
on 1970 energy/capita level, i.e., on economic development level 1970.
When the directional sign (+ or -) stands alone, it means the relationship
had the same direction for both political competition and democracy; when
it is followed by ? it means the direction was observed for political
competition, or democracy, but not both.

tic political institutions and behavior have essentially the same level of
conflict as those with more authoritarian polities.

With regard to proposition 2, only one of the three postulated causes of
government sanctions—conflict—is confirmed. The other two—the direct negative effect of political competition/democracy on sanctions, and
the indirect positive effect of political competition/democracy on sanctions via conflict are largely inoperative. The important point here is that
when less developed nations are confronted with a given level of conflict,
democracies respond no less drastically—are no more restrained from
resorting to government sanctions—than the more authoritarian regimes.

Proposition 3 stated that the greater the conflict and the more frequent
the resort to negative government sanctions, the lower the subsequent
level of political competition/democracy would be. Figure 7 shows that
sanctions have no effect on subsequent democracy, and that only one of
the three conflict variables—armed attacks—has the expected negative
influence, and even that is observed only for democracy, not for political
competition. Because of this, and because the indirect negative effect of
conflict on political competition/democracy via sanctions is not observed
empirically, proposition 3 is also largely disconfirmed.

The predicted effects of the earlier variables on the *level* of economic
development in 1970 are also largely absent. When 1960 economic development level is controlled, political competition/democracy has no effect on 1970 development level, nor do government sanctions affect development level. And among the three conflict variables, only armed

attacks has the predicted negative effect on economic development level. The indirect effects of these variables on development level were also not observed. Thus, proposition 4 is also disconfirmed.

It is only with regard to the *rate* of economic development between 1960 and 1970 in the less-developed nations that the Authoritarian model gains some support. Although neither the three conflict variables nor government sanctions have any effect on the rate of development, both political competition and democracy have significant negative influences on the rate of economic development, net of earlier levels of economic development, conflict, and sanctions. In this restricted, but crucial, sense, our analysis provides evidence for the Authoritarian model, and against the Springtime of Freedom thesis and the Skeptical view. Political competition/democracy does have a significant effect on later rates of economic development; its influence is to *retard* the development rate, rather than to facilitate it. In short, among the poor nations, an authoritarian political system increases the rate of economic development, while a democratic political system does appear to be a luxury which hinders development.

Several suggestions can be made for future research. First, although this paper has paid more attention to explicating and estimating a particular causal structure than to maximizing explained variance, it is obvious that with the exception of government sanctions 1960–1964 and energy/capita 1970, we have explained less than twenty per cent of the variance in each of our dependent variables. Measurement error accounts for some of this, but what is clearly called for are better measures of the present independent variables, and additional explanatory variables.

One step in this direction is to explore whether the political competition and democracy variables we have used obscure important variations among types of totalitarian and authoritarian regimes. In this context it is instructive to contrast the quantitative conception of political competition and democracy as continuous variables, found in Banks (1971) and Bollen (1977) with the qualitative, typological approach to political systems of Linz (1975).[8] He distinguishes three major types of political regimes: democratic, totalitarian, and authoritarian. A totalitarian regime is characterized by the simultaneous presence of three elements: an ideology, a single mass party or other mobilizational organizations, and power concentrated in an individual or a small group that is not accountable to any large constituency and cannot be dislodged from power by institutionalized means. An authoritarian regime may have one or two of these characteristics, but by definition never all three at the same time. An authoritarian regime is defined by three other characteristics: limited, not responsible, political pluralism; a lack of extensive and intensive political mobilization; and a "mentality" rather than an overarching ideology. Linz then distinguishes several subtypes of authoritarian regimes: bureaucratic-military, organic statism, post-independence mobilizational, racial and ethnic "democracies," post-totalitarian authoritarian, etc. Research should be done to ascertain whether, among nations with similar scores on Banks's political competition or Bollen's democracy there is more than one of Linz's types or subtypes, and if there are, whether by distinguishing between them a stronger relationship between polity and economic development is found. The shortcoming of this approach is, of course, that one sooner or later may uncover stronger relationships only at the expense of having so few cases per subtype that the proposition is case-historical rather than cross-national comparative.

A second task for future research is to specify further the mechanisms by which different political regimes effect, with varying success, economic development. Linz is again relevant, for he identifies what these mechanisms may be. Of those not noted at the beginning of this paper (see p. 217), Linz (1975, p. 289) quotes Lucena who suggests that the bureaucratic-military type of regime both assists capitalists and also obstructs them by capturing them in its regulatory nets. This type may also admit technocrats into the bureaucratic-military elite, thereby facilitating economic development. The organic statism type of authoritarian regime rejects both the individualistic assumptions of liberal democracy and class conflict. Instead, it organizes society in terms of "organic structures"—one for peasants, another for workers, still another for professionals, etc. Linz suggests that this type of authoritarian polity rejects both free market entrepreneurial capitalism and the public ownership of the means of production-centralized planning complex. The mechanism by which this and other types of regimes influence economic development need to be considered for inclusion in the causal model.

Finally, a somewhat different approach is to construct a causal structure for each of the "models of development" being offered to, or constructed by, the less developed nations. Evans, for example, describes the "Brazilian model" of development in the following terms:

> The classic development paradigm of indigenous private entrepreneurship combined with pluralistic parliamentary rule has been successfully abandoned. In its place there is a new paradigm: repressive military leadership combined with technocratic decision-making in the political sphere; state entrepreneurship and discipline combined with liberal capitalist incentives in the economic sphere; and emphasis on nationalist symbolism combined with openness to international corporations in the sphere of external relations (Evans, 1974, pp. 41–42).[9]

FOOTNOTES

1. The possibility or probability that even a democratic government may have to resort to negative sanctions when faced with the more severe forms of conflict—riots and armed attacks—will be considered below.

2. Some of these nations had, of course, become relatively highly developed economically by 1970: Bulgaria's energy consumption/capita was 3,936 kgs., Japan's 3,215, etc. They remain in our universe because they "began" in 1955 with an energy/capita under 1,000 kgs.

3. For example, Cuba's energy/c. in 1960 was 847 kgs., and in 1970, 1109 kgs. This was a 30.9 percent increase during the decade, or a mean increase of 3.1 percent/year.

4. To smooth out annual fluctuations in these and the political competition variable, each variable is aggregated over a period of from three to ten years. The exceptions are the Bollen democracy variables, which are for the specific years 1960 and 1965, respectively, and the energy per capita *level* variables—1960 and 1970—since this is less subject to short-term fluctuations for given nations.

5. Of our universe of 98 nations, 18 have no political competition scores in Banks (1971).

6. To be significant, a regression coefficient must be at least twice its standard error.

7. Although sanctions has a non-significant effect in both Figures 4A and 4B, it is collinear with armed attacks (.69 during 1957–1961 and .67 during 1960–1964). Consequently, when the attacks variable is dropped, controlling for other independent variables, sanctions has a significant effect (beta = $-.32$) on democracy.

8. For a somewhat different classification of a range of political systems, see Hughes and Kolinsky (1976).

9. Published by permission of Transaction, Inc. from *Studies in Comparative International Development* 9 (3), Copyright (c) 1974 by Transaction, Inc.

REFERENCES

Almond, Gabriel A. and James S. Coleman (1960) *The Politics of Developing Areas*. Princeton, NJ: Princeton University Press.

Banks, Arthur S. (1972), "Correlates of Democratic Performance." *Comparative Politics* 4 (January): 217–230.

———— (1971) *Cross-Polity Time-Series Data*. Cambridge, MA: M.I.T. Press.

Bollen, Kenneth (1977) *Political Democracy: A Macro-Theoretical and Empirical Analysis*. Unpublished Ph.D. dissertation. Providence, RI: Brown University.

Chirot, Daniel (1977) *Social Change in the Twentieth Century*. New York: Harcourt Brace Jovanovich.

Cutright, Phillips (1963) "National Political Development." *American Sociological Review* 28 (April): 253–264.

————, and James A. Wiley (1969) "Modernization and Political Representation: 1927–1966." *Studies in Comparative International Development* 5:23–44.

Enloe, Cynthia (1976) Review of Fred R. von der Mehden, "Comparative Political Violence." *American Political Science Review* 70 (March): 270.

Evans, Peter B. (1974) "The Military, the Multinationals, and the 'Miracle': The Political Economy of the 'Brazilian Model' of Development." *Studies in Comparative International Development* 9 (Fall): 26–45.

Feierabend, I. K., and R. L. Feierabend (1971) "The Relationship of Systemic Frustration, Political Coercion, and Political Instability." Pages 417–440 in John V. Gillespie and

Betty A. Nesrold (eds.), *Macro-Quantitative Analysis: Conflict, Development, and Democratization.* Beverly Hills, CA: Sage.

Heeger, Gerald A. (1974) *The Politics of Underdevelopment.* New York: St. Martin's Press.

Hibbs, Douglas A. (1973) *Mass Political Violence.* New York: Wiley.

Holt, Robert T., and John E. Turner (1966) *The Political Basis of Economic Development.* Princeton, NJ.: Van Nostrand.

Hughes, Arnold, and Martin Kolinsky (1976) "'Paradigmatic Fascism' and Modernization: A Critique." *Political Studies* 24 (December): 371–396.

Huntington, Samuel P. (1965) "Political Development and Political Decay." *World Politics* 17 (April): 386–430.

Jackman, Robert W. (1973) "On the Relation of Economic Development to Democratic Performance." *American Journal of Political Science* 17 (August): 611–621.

Kuznets, Simon (1966) *Modern Economic Growth.* New Haven, CT: Yale University Press.

LaPalombara, Joseph (1963) "Bureaucracy and Political Development: Notes, Queries and Dilemmas." Pages 34–61 in Joseph LaPalombara (ed.), *Bureaucracy and Political Development.* Princeton, NJ: Princeton University Press.

———, and Myron Weiner (1966) "Political Parties and Political Development." *Items* 20 (March): 1–7.

Linz, Juan J. (1975) "Totalitarian and Authoritarian Regimes." Pages 175–411 in Fred I. Greenstein and Nelson W. Polsby (eds.), *Macropolitical Theory.* Reading, MA: Addison-Wesley.

Lipset, Seymour M. (1959) "Some Social Requisites of Democracy." *American Political Science Review* 53 (March): 69–105.

McCord, William (1965) *The Springtime of Freedom.* New York: Oxford University Press.

Meyer, John W., Michael T. Hannan, and Richard Rubinson (1973) "National Economic Growth, 1950–65: Educational and Political Factors." Unpublished manuscript.

Neubauer, Deane F. (1967) "Some Conditions of Democracy." *American Political Science Review* 61 (December): 1002–1009.

Nixon, Raymond B. (1960) "Factors Related to Freedom in National Press Systems." *Journalism Quarterly* 37 (December): 13–28.

Olsen, Marvin E. and Glenn Firebaugh (1974) "Transforming Socioeconomic Modernization into National Political Development." Unpublished manuscript.

Pye, Lucian W. (1966) *Aspects of Political Development.* Boston: Little, Brown.

de Schweinitz, Karl (1964) *Industrialization and Democracy,* Glencoe, IL: The Free Press.

Taylor, Charles L. and Michael C. Hudson (1972) *World Handbook of Political and Social Indicators,* 2nd edition. New Haven: Yale University Press.

United Nations (various years) *Statistical Yearbook.* New York: Statistical Office, United Nations.

APPENDIX

Universe of Cases Studied (N=98).

Latin America and Caribbean
Cuba
Haiti
Dominican Republic
Jamaica
Barbados
Mexico
Guatemala
Honduras
El Salvador
Nicaragua
Costa Rica
Panama
Colombia
Guyana
Ecuador
Peru
Brazil
Boliva
Paraguay
Chile
Argentina
Uruguay

Europe
Spain
Portugal
Italy
Albania
Yugoslavia
Greece
Cyprus
Bulgaria

Middle East
Iran
Turkey
Iraq
United Arab Republic
Syria
Lebanon
Jordan
Saudi Arabia
Yemen
Afghanistan

Asia
China
Mongolia
Taiwan
North Korea
South Korea
Japan
India
Pakistan
Burma
Sri Lanka
Nepal
Thailand
Cambodia
Laos
North Vietnam
South Vietnam
Malaysia
Singapore
Philippines
Indonesia

Africa
Mali
Senegal
Dahomey
Mauritania
Niger
Ivory Coast
Guinea
Upper Volta
Liberia
Sierra Leone
Ghana
Togo
Cameroun
Nigeria
Gabon
Central African Republic
Chad
Congo (Brazzaville)
Congo (Kinshasa) Zaire
Uganda
Kenya
Tanzania
Burundi
Rwanda
Somalia
Ethiopia
Angola
Mozambique
Zambia
Malawi
Lesotho
Malagasy Republic
Mauritius
Morocco
Algeria
Tunisia
Libya
Sudan

ELITES AND THE POPULATION PROBLEM IN FIVE THIRD WORLD NATIONS*

Robert E. Kennedy, Jr. and Pablo Pindas

Political and military elites in many less-developed nations have been pre-eminent in deciding the futures of their countries. Other groups, such as government officials and businessmen, have had considerable influence on the course of economic development (Bottomore, 1964, pp. 92–101). Such elites often decide if there is going to be a population or family planning program in their countries, how it will be organized, what funding it will receive, the information and services it will provide, and the coverage it will have (Hill, 1968; Radel, 1973; Clinton, 1975). They not only have the ability to make such decisions, within limits they also can

Comparative Social Research, Vol. 2, pp. 249—260.
Volume 1 published as Comparative Studies in Sociology

create the appropriate political climate to facilitate the implementation and acceptance of population policies (Demeny, 1975).

Elite failure to face population problems, it is sometimes assumed, is due to an ignorance of the impact of rapid population growth on their society (Ilchman, 1975; Shaw, 1976). As Berelson (1964, p. 100) argued, one of the best ways to persuade government leaders to actively support population programs is to bring to their attention the "true demographic situation and its implications." In spite of the importance of the topic, empirical studies of elites and the population problem are relatively rare. The 69-page subject index to Driver's (1971, pp. 1211–1280) mammoth bibliography on world population policy, for example, contains no entry for elites. The reasons for the scarcity are apparent. Members of elites are often difficult to identify, inaccessible for direct questioning, and even when interviewed, at times uncommonly cautious in their replies. In large countries, furthermore, regional as well as national leaders should be taken into account. Faced with these constraints, field researchers generally have had to be satisfed with the study of one or another segment of a nation's potential elite (Burch and Shea, 1971; Landstreet and Mundigo, 1971). The early work on the topic by Stycos (1965a, 1965b), for example, dealt with such accessible categories as intellectuals in Latin America and village opinion leaders in Turkey.

Younger scholars have shown the greatest interest in the subject, with the result that most of the recent studies are doctoral dissertations. Our report of the Mexican situation is drawn from Pindas' (1978) research which, in turn, was designed to optimize its comparability with similar studies elsewhere, especially Radel's (1973) work in Kenya. The primary source of data in both are personal interviews with elite members which inquire into the respondents' knowledge of population processes and support for population programs. This differs from conventional family planning surveys which ask about the family planning attitudes and practices of individuals.

Following Radel, Pindas excluded "pre-elites" such as students, and took persons who, by their current position and status in the society, were clearly in the upper reaches of their areas. Radel completed interviews with 112 individuals, including 10 government ministers and 28 legislators, with the balance being made up of civil servants, business executives,

*Robert E. Kennedy, Jr. is an Associate Professor of Sociology at the University of Minnesota, Minneapolis. He is the author of *The Irish: Emigration, Marriage, and Fertility* (1973), and of articles dealing with the social demography of Ireland and of Irish immigrants in other nations. Pablo Pindas is Professor of Sociology at the Iberoamerican University, Mexico City, and also Head of the Research Department, Biology of Reproduction, Social Security Institute, Mexico City. His major research interest concerns the social conditions that facilitate effective population policy implementation.

professors, and leaders of mass media. In Mexico, Pindas defined the nation's elite population as the 3,497 high-ranking individuals publicly associated with 457 government departments, private organizations, and economic enterprises. From this list a quota-sampling procedure selected the specific individuals to be interviewed. Recognizing the importance of regionalism in Mexico's political history, about half of the leaders were purposely drawn from the local level, one-third at the regional, and the balance at the national level. Roughly equal numbers were drawn for each of six occupational categories: educational, political, professional, economic, religious, and mass communications. The survey itself was carried out in 1975 by Pindas and others, and resulted in 626 completed interviews.

The largest comparable study to date is Badrudduza's (1967) survey of 2,361 civil servants, professors, physicians, and lawyers in Pakistan. In Honduras, Mundigo (1972) questioned 300 elite members, 100 each from the categories of government official, industrial manager, and lawyer. An earlier survey in Mexico in 1967 (Santos-Pérez, 1972) questioned 268 professors, physicians, mass media professionals, and leaders in politics, religion, and the economy. And in Peru, Clinton's (1971) survey of 81 elite members included professors, civil servants, government officials, physicians, lawyers, religious leaders, and business executives. Where possible, the results of Pindas' 1975 Mexican survey are compared with these earlier studies, and used to provide additional insight into possible differences within the elite by occupational group or by national versus local sphere of influence.

KNOWLEDGE OF DEMOGRAPHIC FACTS

Previous studies have shown that the majority of elite members have reasonably accurate knowledge of their nation's total population size, from about 80 percent in Kenya and Pakistan to 93 percent in Peru (Badrudduza, 1967, p. 84; Clinton, 1971, p. 97; Radel, 1973, p. 186). This awareness is partly a result of the publicity given to population problems in these countries and, in Peru, also to a definition of the elite which included many individuals directly involved in population or family planning activities. In Mexico, 83 percent of Pindas' sample knew that the nation's inhabitants numbered between 50 and 60 million, ranging from 79 percent among local to 92 percent among national leaders. No significant difference was found on this matter among the six occupational categories.

Less well known is the number of years required for the population to double at current rates. Yet even here the proportion knowing the correct answer of 20 to 25 years was notable: 30 percent in Kenya (Radel, 1973, p. 186), 51 percent in Honduras (Mundigo, 1972, p. 166), and 53 percent in Mexico. There were no differences in Mexico either by sphere of influence or among the five secular occupational categories. There was a statistically significant difference between the secular leaders taken as a group (56 percent gave the correct response) and the religious leaders (43 percent). The Mexican leaders also were asked for a more detailed item of demographic knowledge: the intermediate projection of the size of the nation's population in the year 2000. The correct figure of from 130 to 139 million was stated by only 8 percent, with 10 percent answering 140 mil· lion or more, and 64 percent responding with a figure of less than 115 million.

A set of ten such questions was used to construct a "knowledgeability" index. The other items included Mexico's rate of population growth compared with that of Europe, the average family size, the relationship between fertility and social class and rural/urban residence, and whether population growth was more rapid than economic growth. The index was patterned after that developed by Radel (1973, pp. 187–189), though his differed in being based on 12 rather than 10 items (Table 1). The results strengthen the impression of a relatively high level of acquaintance with their country's basis demographic situation. The patterns are strikingly similar even though Radel used a four and Pindas a three category scale. Less than one in five Kenyan or Mexican leaders fell into the "poor" or "low" knowledge category, while the majority in each country could be considered as having "moderate" to "high" demographic awareness.

Table 1. Knowledgeability of demographic facts
among Kenyan and Mexican elites.
(Percentages)

Knowledgeability	Kenya	Mexico
Excellent	7	
High		21
Good	39	
Moderate	38	62
Low		17
Poor	16	
Total	100	100
Number	(112)	(517)

Sources: Radel (1973, p. 188); Pindas (1978, p. 113).

PERCEIVED ADVANTAGES AND DISADVANTAGES OF RAPID POPULATION GROWTH

Adequate demographic knowledge does not necessarily lead to a pessimistic view about rapid population growth. Elites in developing nations, as individuals in industrial societies, hold diverse opinions about the impact of growing populations. Shaw (1976) identified 22 nations in which the government perceived population growth either to be a minor issue or a positive benefit. Pindas asked the Mexican leaders a set of four questions about their perceptions of population growth, and summarized their responses in an index grouping those who perceived only advantages, only disadvantages, or both. Comparing the results with those of similar questions asked of elites in Kenya, Pakistan, and Peru, the Mexican and Kenyan leaders were relatively more optimistic (Table 2). One in five or more of the elites in both countries saw only advantages to a growing population. The most frequently mentioned advantage in Kenya (Radel, 1973, p. 199), in Mexico, and the second most often given in Pakistan (Badrudduza, 1967, p. 179) was "potential," a category that included such answers as greater manpower for production, and population as a stimulant for economic development. Of those indicating an advantage, half of the Pakistanis, one-fourth of the Kenyans, but only one-twentieth of the Mexicans saw a growing population as increasing international prestige (including military strength).

The responses of the elite in Honduras were not included in Table 2 because they were posed a slightly different question: "Does Honduras have a population problem?" (Mundigo, 1972, p. 169). Of the total sample of 300 government officials, managers, and lawyers, one-third said "yes" and of these, 30 individuals stated that the problem was an insufficient

Table 2. Perceptions of elites in four nations of the advantages or disadvantages of a growing population. (Percentages)

Country	Advantages		Disadvantages			
	Only	Both	Only	DK/NA	Total	Number
Mexico	24	30	43	3	100	(626)
Kenya	20	44	32	4	100	(112)
Peru	16	20	57	7	100	(81)
Pakistan	10	12	75	3	100	(200)

Sources: Pindas (1978, p. 144); Radel (1973, p. 197); Clinton (1971, p. 113); Badrudduza (1967, p. 172).

population. Only one-quarter perceived rapid population growth as being disadvantageous. Difficulties were seen in realizing adequate levels of nutrition, housing, and education, and in coping with internal migration. Among those favoring population growth, the reasons most commonly given were that the nation had enough land to accommodate a larger population, that the country "needed" more population generally, and that the problem was not in size but in geographic distribution. Only six of the leaders said that the country's defense requires a larger population.

Leaders with ambivalent attitudes accounted for important segments of the elites of both Kenya and Mexico. Depending on whether they were grouped with persons at either extreme, one could conclude that a majority saw at least some disadvantage to rapid population growth, or that a majority saw at least some advantage. In Mexico there was a significantly greater degree of optimism among the religious leaders, among whom two-thirds saw at least some advantage compared with less than half among the secular.

At this point we can say that in Mexico, as in other developing nations, a reasonably good knowledge of demographic facts can co-exist with optimistic or ambivalent attitudes about the implications of rapid population growth. Two occupational groups within the Mexican elite illustrate the point. The "political" segment was most knowledgeable about the country's population size and growth rate relative to European countries, but they also had the highest proportion perceiving "only advantages" to population growth. The "communications" category, on the other hand, scored lowest on the index of demographic knowledge, especially on such issues as present population size, growth rates, and average family size, yet this group had the highest proportion perceiving "only disadvantages."

We believe this is due in part to situational effects: persons in the best position to learn the abstract facts of the nation's demography are often out of touch with people, who, in their everyday lives, suffer the consequences of rapid population growth. While political leaders may have some contact with ordinary people during periodic political campaigns, the mass media elite have detailed knowledge of the daily problems of greatest concern to their audiences or readerships. If we assume that local leaders are more directly involved in the common problems of their constituencies than are the national leaders, then that also helps explain why the local leaders were more pessimistic about population problems even though they had significantly less demographic knowledge than did the national leaders.

KNOWLEDGE OF POPULATION POLICIES

Mexico is one of the best cases to study elite awareness of population policies because recent changes suddenly reversed that nation's long-standing pronatalist stance. In April 1972 a program was revealed by high government officials aimed at creating the conditions necessary to reduce the rate of population growth. In January 1973 the government's family planning program began field activities. In December 1973 the General Population Law of 1947 was amended to create a National Council on Population and to define the country's position regarding emigration, immigration, registration cards for citizens, internal migration, and issues dealing with population size and growth. The National Council on Population was charged with coordinating population, economic, and social development policies. Its membership included the Secretaries of Government, Education, the Presidency, the Treasury, Health and Public Welfare, Foreign Affairs, Labor, and Agrarian Reform. Most of the Mexican elite had little knowledge of these events at the time of the 1975 survey. Over two-thirds (70 percent) had no information about the specific contents of the 1973 Population Law, and less than two-thirds (62 percent) did not know about the functions of the National Council on Population.

The Mexican elite also was asked what they understood by the term "population policy." A current United Nations definition (1972) includes measures affecting size, growth, and composition of the population, and its internal and international geographic distribution. Berelson's (1971) statement includes three principal features: (1) actions by governments, (2) population events, and (3) intentions and consequences. Only one-fifth (19 percent) gave answers indicating a fairly adequate notion of the elements of either of these two widely used definitions. The remaining four-fifths identified population policy with such concepts as "birth control," "responsible paternity," and "family planning." The great majority of the Mexican elite, thus, had inadequate knowledge of the complexities and range of issues included in the phrase "population policy."

An index of specific knowledge about Mexican population policies was constructed from six questions dealing with past stances of the government, the definition of what population policy is, and information about current policy. Only 12 percent of the sample could be considered to have a "high" level of detailed knowledge about national population policies. The balance was roughly equally divided between those with "moderate" or partial knowledge (46 percent) and those with "low" or little knowledge (42 percent). As might be expected, the political leaders were best informed with 21 percent having a high level of knowledge. The professional elite, which included medical and public health leaders, was among the least well informed with 52 percent in the "low" category. Interestingly, there was no significant difference between the religious and the secular leaders, or among the national, regional, or local elites.

SUPPORT OF POPULATION POLICIES

Other studies have generally found strong elite support for the family planning component of national population policies. In Pakistan 92 percent of the elite favored a government sponsored family planning program (Badrudduza, 1967, p. 204). Over four-fifths of the Peruvian elite believed the government should provide family planning information and services. And in Kenya half of the elite favored a strong government program fully responsible for family planning in the nation, while an additional third said that the government should have a program but be only partially responsible for the entire effort (Radel, 1973, p. 226). The exception was the elite of Honduras. Mundigo (1972, pp. 212, 213) reported that half of the elite was opposed to any national family-planning program, and almost half did not want any government involvement in population control. In fact, 14 percent thought that there should be a government program to increase population growth.

Building on these earlier studies, Pindas was primarily interested in seeing whether there was any connection between knowledgeability of population policies and support for them. He found little association between the two. In spite of the fact that only 12 percent of the sample had a high level of knowledge, 68 percent expressed "strong" support for policies and programs to reduce the population growth rate. Degree of support was measured by an index of six questions asking about agreement with the establishment of national population policies, the use of family planning methods by the population, the advocacy of "responsible parenthood," the use of sterilization, the use of birth control methods by the respondent's own children, and the provision of sex education in public schools.

One reason for the lack of association between policy knowledge and support is that respondents considered each item in the "supportiveness" index in its own right with little regard for abstract demographic processes or current national policy. Virtually all (97 percent), for example, said they favored "responsible parenthood programs." Such a high consensus is the result of different meanings given to the expression by the various groups. As used by the religious leaders, the term refers to the responsibility of parents for their children. The government's use of the expression includes in addition the connotation of developing family-planning activities. Each could read what they chose into the phrase and thus agree with it. Similarly, 96 percent of the sample agreed with the establishment of a national population policy. For some this meant a national family-planning program to reduce the population growth rate. But for others their agreement merely indicated an acceptance of the fact that population had an impact for better or worse, and thus should be taken into account in making national plans.

Another reason for the lack of association was opposition from religious leaders to certain birth control practices—this in spite of their being as well informed on population policies as the secular leaders. While 73 percent of the secular leaders gave "strong" support to population policies and programs, only 37 percent of the religious leaders did so. The item of greatest disagreement was whether one would support programs promoting birth control: 78 percent of the secular leaders said "yes," compared with 33 percent of the religious leaders. One could read this response, of course, as saying as much as one-third of the religious elite was willing to support such programs, clearly revealing the split existing in that group. Another item on which the two categories differed was whether the respondent would "always" approve of the private use of birth control methods by couples: 53 percent of the secular and 31 percent of the religious leaders said they would. Once again, instead of pointing to the difference between the two groups, one could instead emphasize that a large minority of the religious elite expressed clear support for individual birth control.

An analysis of the secular leaders by occupational group also shows the lack of association between policy knowledge and population program support. The political segment was highest on both measures, and, in fact, 82 percent indicated strong support for such policies and programs. The inconsistency lies with the communication and education elites. The former were least knowledgeable (7 percent in the "high" category), yet second only to the political leaders in their strong support of population policies and programs (77 percent). In contrast, the educational leaders were the second most knowledgeable (14 percent ranked as "high"), and yet they were the weakest in their support (65 percent giving "strong" support). Again the situational context of the elites provides at least part of the explanation. By the nature of their work, educational leaders are well placed to learn the specifics of recent government changes in population matters. But unlike political or mass media elites, the members of the educational elite are not expected to take strong stands on any public policy—whether dealing with population or any other matter—and many did not do so.

PERCEIVED RESPONSIBILITY FOR SUPPORT OF FAMILY PLANNING

The educational leaders' weak support was due in part to the belief by some that it was not their responsibility to become involved in family planning matters. In 1967 Santos-Pérez (1972) asked his sample which social groups they thought should favor the use of contraceptive methods by the general population. In 1975 Pindas asked the same question to see how attitudes had changed following the great policy shift by the government during the early 1970s (Table 3). Although there was a marked increase generally in support by the end of the period, the relative ranking of the various groups remained about the same. The elite members thought that physicians and government officials should favor the use of contraceptive methods by the population, while believing that businessmen and newsmen (mass media professionals) should take a neutral, study only, stance. As expected, they thought that religious leaders should be opposed, but by 1975 the proportion holding this view fell to less than one in twelve.

In 1967 the elite's overall perception of the matter was that physicians and government officials were on one side, the religious elite on the other, and the other elite segments were standing on the sidelines. Social and educational leaders in 1967, for example, were expected to be even less involved than the religious elite. By 1975, however, almost all of the elite perceived that all social groups should not oppose the use of contraceptive methods and that social and educational leaders should take an ac-

Table 3. Elite perceptions of the attitude selected social groups should have regarding the use of contraceptive methods by the population, Mexico, 1967 and 1975.
(Percentages)

		Should Study Only			
Should Favor		Or Be Neutral		Should Oppose	
1967	1975	1967	1975	1967	1975
Medicine 52	Medicine 76	Business 59	Business 48	Religion 28	Religion 8
Gov. Off. 41	Gov. Off. 70	Media 52	Media 48	Soc./Ed. 19	Medicine 4
Religion 41	Soc./Ed. 65	Soc./Ed. 47	Religion 34	Medicine 19	Gov. Off. 4
Media 34	Religion 58	Gov. Off. 43	Soc./Ed. 32	Gov. Off. 16	Soc./Ed. 3
Business 34	Media 50	Religion 30	Gov. Off. 26	Business 14	Business 3
Soc./Ed. 33	Business 50	Medicine 29	Medicine 20	Media 14	Media 2

Note: Percentages sum to 100 within each social group, and are based on 245 responses in 1967 and 593 in 1975.

Sources: Santos-Pérez (1972, pp. 129, 133, 135); Pindas (1978, p. 200).

tive, positive role, second only to the physicians and the government officials. We interpret this to mean that the problem no longer is seen as just a medical or moral issue, but also as a matter of public education. Sex education in public schools is probably the single most important issue drawing the educational leaders, some reluctant, into participation in the problem.

CONCLUSION

Radel (1973, pp. 263–273) concluded that in Kenya there is no statistically significant relationship between accuracy of knowledge about population and perceived seriousness of the population problem. Our review of available field research confirmed this interpretation, and suggested at least one reason. The segments of the elite that are best informed, such as the political elite, may also be the most optimistic about the benefits of a growing population. Being under cross-pressures from ambivalent attitudes about population growth, their abstract knowledge of a certain set of demographic facts is not sufficient to change their more deeply held beliefs regarding the advantages of increased manpower for economic or military purposes.

Groups that gave the strongest support often were the least well informed about demographic processes or policies. Such elite categories, as the Mexican mass media professionals and the local secular leaders generally, presumably had greater knowledge of the everyday problems of ordinary people, those most likely to suffer directly from problems caused by rapid population growth. Other segments, as in the instance of Mexico's educational elite, may have been relatively well informed but did not see any active role for themselves in making public policy. And even when drawn into the problem, they still may give only reluctant support. We take this to mean that knowledge of the concrete implications of rapid population growth is more effective in persuading elites to give strong support to population policies and programs than abstract information about the demographic situation. Knowing the nation's total population size or doubling time is less important than realizing the population related difficulties in achieving adequate levels of nutrition, housing, education, or employment.

REFERENCES

Badrudduza, M. D. (1967) "Attitudes of Pakistani Elites Toward Population Problems and Population Policy: A Study of Professors, Lawyers, Doctors and Government Officers in Pakistan." Unpublished Ph.D. Dissertation. Ithaca, NY: Cornell University.

Berelson, Bernard (1964) "On Family Planning Communication." *Demography* 1: 94–105.
———, (1971) "Population Policy: Personal Notes." *Population Studies* 25 (July): 173–182.
Bottomore, T. B. (1964) *Elites and Society.* New York: Basic Books.
Burch, Thomas K. and Gail A. Shea (1971) "Catholic Parish Priests and Birth Control: A Comparative Study of Opinion in Columbia, the United States, and the Netherlands." *Studies in Family Planning* 2:122–136.
Clinton, Richard L. (1971) *Problems of Population Policy Formation in Peru.* Chapel Hill, NC: Carolina Population Center, Population Program and Policy Design Series No. 4.
——— (1975) "The Decisional Environment: Knowledge and Attitudes of Elites as a Determinant of Population Growth Reduction Policies." Pages 143–155 in R. Kenneth Godwin (ed.), *Comparative Policy Analysis.* Lexington, MA: Lexington Books.
Demeny, Paul (1975) "Population Policy: The Role of National Governments." *Population and Development Review* 1 (September):147–161.
Driver, Edwin D. (1971) *World Population Policy: An Annotated Bibliography.* Lexington, MA: Lexington Books.
Godwin, R. Kenneth (1975) *Comparative Policy Analysis: The Study of Population Policy Determinants in Developing Countries.* Lexington, MA: Lexington Books.
Hill, Reuben (1968) "Research on Human Fertility." *International Social Science Journal* 20:226–262.
Ilchman, Warren F. (1975) "Population Knowledge and Population Policies." Pages 217–265 in R. Kenneth Godwin (ed.), *Comparative Policy Analysis.* Lexington, MA: Lexington Books.
Landstreet, Barent, Jr, and Axel I. Mundigo (1971) "University Students." Pages 191–211 in J. Mayone Stycos (ed.), *Ideology, Faith, and Family Planning in Latin America.* New York: McGraw-Hill.
Mundigo, Axel I. (1972) "Elites, Economic Development, and Population in Honduras." Unpublished Ph.D. dissertation, Ithaca, NY: Cornell University.
Pindas, Pablo (1978) "Mexican Leaders' Roles and Perceptions of Population Growth, Policies, and Programs." Unpublished Ph.D dissertation. Minneapolis: University of Minnesota.
Radel, David J. (1973) *Elite Perceptions of Population Problems and Potential Solutions.* Honolulu: The East-West Center.
Santos-Pérez, Guillermo (1972) "Los Lideres mexicanos ante el cambio demográfico." Thesis presented for the Licentiate in Public Administration and Political Science. Mexico City: Universidad Nacional Autónoma de México.
Shaw, R. Paul (1976) "Government Perceptions of Population Growth." *Population Studies* 30 (March):77–86.
Stycos, J. Mayone (1965a) "Opinion of Latin American Intellectuals on Population Problems and Birth Control." *Annals of the American Academy of Political and Social Science* 360:11–23.
——— (1965b) "The Political Role of the Turkish Village Opinion Leaders in a Program of Family Planning." *Public Opinion Quarterly* 29 (Spring):120–130.
——— (ed.), (1971) *Ideology, Faith, and Family Planning in Latin America.* New York: McGraw-Hill.
United Nations (1972) "Report of the Special Consulting Group of Experts on Population Policy." New York: United Nations, Department of Economic and Social Affairs, Population Commission.

PART III

THEORIES IN COMPARATIVE
SOCIOLOGY

ALEXIS DE TOCQUEVILLE AND THE POLITICAL SOCIOLOGY OF LIBERALISM*

Timothy A. Tilton

Unearthing the foundations of a theorist's work tends to be a laborious exercise, but unless this enterprise is successfully carried to a conclusion, the results are likely to be partial and deceptive. At present scholarly spadework on the foundations of Tocqueville's thought is incomplete; the prevalent understandings of his writings offer only fragmentary views. The excellent studies by Drescher (1964, 1968), Herr (1962), Lively (1962), Richter (1963, 1969), and Smelser (1976) provide an abundance of useful insights on specific facets of Tocqueville's work, but the findings of these scholars have not yet merged into a synthetic interpretation of

Comparative Social Research, Vol. 2, pp. 263—287.
Volume 1 published as Comparative Studies in Sociology
Copyright © 1979 by JAI Press, Inc.
All rights of reproduction in any form reserved.
ISBN 0-89232-112-1

Tocqueville's writings. They have failed to disclose the functional theory of liberal society that lies buried in his work.

Tocqueville believed that his task was to develop "a new science of politics . . . for a new world." This new world was the emerging world of political and social democracy, a society characterized by "general equality of condition" (Tocqueville, 1967, Vol. I, pp. lxxi–lxxii). In France the democratic revolution had proceeded without proper guidance; "the most powerful, the most intelligent, the most moral classes of the nation"—in short, the elite as Tocqueville perceived it—had never seized control of the movement in order to instruct and purify it. The democratic revolution in France had been abandoned to its wild instincts and

> . . . [t]he consequence has been that the democratic revolution has taken place in the body of the society, without that concomitant change in the laws, ideas, customs, and manners, which was necessary to render such a revolution beneficial. Thus we have [in the France of the 1830s] a democracy, without anything to lessen its vices and bring out its natural advantages; and although we already perceive the evils it brings, we are ignorant of the benefits it may confer [Tocqueville, 1967, Vol. I, pp. lxxiii–lxxiv].

These benefits Tocqueville saw in America, "the image of democracy," a relatively attractive vision of a possible French future in which the necessary changes in laws, ideas, customs, and manners had been achieved. America represented the most complete and successful development of democratic principles: one might study it not only out of legitimate curiosity, but in order to draw political lessons for France.

The purpose that underlay all of Tocqueville's political writings was to teach Frenchmen how they might preserve liberty in an increasingly democratic age. He hoped to provide the French elite with a new science of politics containing the information necessary for intelligent political conduct. Statesmen required an accurate assessment of the evolutionary tendencies of their era, but sweeping historical generalizations would of themselves provide little help. The politician who would be effective needed a detailed knowledge of the affairs of his own country, its national peculiarities and idiosyncrasies. Such knowledge of general trends and of distinctive national traits could best be obtained, Tocqueville believed, through comparative studies of historical development. Thus the responsible French politician who sought to maximize liberty in his country ought to study not only its history, but ought to compare its development with that of other nations like America and Britain.

*Timothy A. Tilton is an Associate Professor of Political Science at Indiana University, Bloomington. His most recent work centers on the political theory of the welfare state. He has recently co-authored, with Norman Furniss, *The Case for the Welfare State* (1977).

Insofar as Tocqueville operated within a given tradition of inquiry, insofar as a particular paradigm defined his problems, methods, and fundamental assumptions, it was Montesquieu's social science that served as his model. Like Montesquieu, Tocqueville combined the vocations of the political theorist and the political sociologist. His debt to his renowned liberal predecessor was enormous, not only with regard to such relatively minor topics as the effect of geography upon political affairs, but also on such central matters as the use of comparative historical studies, the importance of both the institutional structures and the moral atmosphere (*l'esprit*) in the life of a society, and, above all, the concern with the social determinants of liberal society. Montesquieu, however, had not had to cope with "modernity"—with the new era of "democracy"—and hence Tocqueville had to adapt and develop Montesquieu's work in order to ascertain the conditions for liberal society in the new era.

Tocqueville conceived of his own studies as an effort to elucidate the sources of human freedom, and they can be properly understood only with this conception of his purpose. His work, informed by a keen perception of the historical transition toward more egalitarian societies, and enlightened by a thorough and immediately personal knowledge of politics, represents one of the great examples of comparative historical sociology. This analysis of his treatment of the functional requisites for a liberal society begins where Tocqueville's investigations begin—with the comparative study of the institutions and attitudes required for liberty to flourish in concrete historical circumstances. It proceeds by sketching the theory of liberal society Tocqueville extracted from his empirical work and concludes by noting the functionalist nature of Tocqueville's theory and its implications for any assessment of his own politics.

FREEDOMS IN FOUR HISTORICAL SETTINGS

To Tocqueville freedom was "a *sacred* thing," a primary value, an end in itself, and not merely a means to other goods. To be free was to be uncoerced in matters that affected only oneself:

> According to the modern, the democratic, and, we venture to say, the only just notion of liberty, every man, being presumed to have received from nature the intelligence necessary for his own general guidance, is inherently entitled to be uncontrolled by his fellows in all that concerns himself, and to regulate at his own will his own destiny [cited in Lively, 1962, p. 12].

Tocqueville never gave a thorough account of this notion of freedom; he thought it unnecessary.

His second major focus in his comparative investigations was the degree of equality of condition societies manifested. To understand a modern society correctly one had to know how far the ineluctable trend toward democracy had proceeded within it. These notions of "equality" and "democracy" Tocqueville used with as much imprecision as he did the idea of freedom; he did not trouble to define them carefully and he used them inconsistently to cover a wide range of phenomena. At times "democracy" referred to the political phenomena of popular sovereignty and formal equality of legal rights. On other occasions Tocqueville employed the term to refer to the free and unconstrained social intercourse that arose in societies stripped of aristocratic trappings and courtly etiquette. At still other moments Tocqueville wanted to designate an economic situation characterized by considerable equality of property and income. His use of the term "equality" displayed similar variations, and moreover he used both terms to stand for the totality of these conditions: Democracy, or equality of condition, is ultimately the condition of political, legal, social, and economic equality.

Tocqueville compared societies according to their position on these two scales of freedom and equality of condition. He seldom performed this exercise openly, but it underlay much of his exposition. Schematizing his view, one might derive the picture shown in Figure 1. Given that nations with comparable degrees of equality might exhibit drastically different levels of freedom, the question naturally arises: Why? As Figure 1 demonstrates, the trend toward democracy cannot explain the origins of freedom; what then does determine whether a society becomes liberal or tyrannous? Occasionally Tocqueville suggested that this question defied analysis and that such issues were better reserved to the inscrutable providence of God than to the irreverent investigations of sociologists. Some nations simply "have freedom in the blood" and others do not; the genuine love of freedom, so essential to the existence of political freedom,

Figure 1.

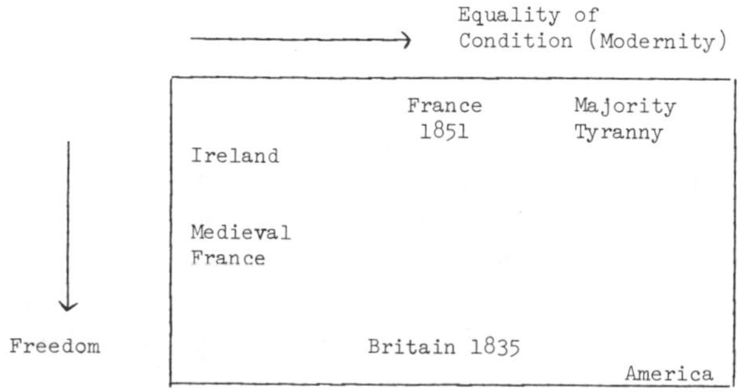

		Equality of Condition (Modernity) →	
	Ireland	France 1851	Majority Tyranny
	Medieval France		
Freedom		Britain 1835	
			America

is a "lofty aspiration . . . which defies analysis" (Tocqueville, 1955, p. 169). More often, however, Tocqueville was bold enough to think that he could trace the origins of liberal society to a combination of general and accidental causes.

In his *Recollections* Tocqueville offered a tempting generalization for the sociology of knowledge. He contended that men of letters analyze great historical events in a way quite different from that of men of politics. The *litterateurs*, separated from the flow of daily events, attribute all to sweeping general causes, whereas politicians, absorbed in the immediate and particular incidents of political life, tend to exaggerate the role of accident and chance. Tocqueville, with a foot in both camps, stressed the need for both sorts of analysis:

> I detest these absolute systems, which represent all the events of history as depending upon great first causes linked by the chain of fatality, and which, as it were, suppress men from the history of the human race. . . . I believe . . . that many important historical facts can only be explained by accidental circumstances and that many others remain totally inexplicable. Moreover, chance, or rather that tangle of secondary causes which we call chance, for want of the knowledge how to unravel it, plays a great part in all that happens on the world's stage, although I firmly believe that chance does nothing that has not been prepared beforehand. *Antecedent facts, the nature of institutions, the cast of minds and the state of morals* are the materials of which are composed those impromptus which astonish and alarm us [Tocqueville's emphasis, 1948, p. 68].

Here Tocqueville offers his general view of social development and the sorts of causes social analysts must take into account.

In the course of his life Tocqueville studied the politics of a vast range of societies; medieval Europe, the *ancien régime*, revolutionary and modern France, Great Britain in the reform era, Jacksonian America, Ireland, Switzerland, Algeria, and the German states at the time of the French Revolution. It is impossible to reproduce here either the broad scope of his studies or the concrete richness of *Democracy in America* and *The Old Regime and the French Revolution*, but in order to ascertain Tocqueville's views on the institutional and attitudinal requisites for freedom it is essential to consider a modest sample of his political analyses. To this end I have selected his discussion of two aristocracies (Ireland and the *ancien régime*), one transitional society (Great Britain), and the great example of modern democracy (the United States). This selection not only includes Tocqueville's major interests; it allows one to assess the degree of liberty and its determinants in a variety of regimes.

Tocqueville's writings on Ireland dispel any notion that Tocqueville was an undiscriminating defender of aristocracy. To Tocqueville Ireland displayed the least attractive qualities of aristocracy and none of its re-deeming benefits. In his travel notes Tocqueville summarized his impressions of Irish misery and observed that "If you want to know what can be done by the spirit of conquest and religious hatred combined with the abuses of aristocracy, but without any of its advantages, go to Ireland" (Tocqueville, 1968an p. 113). His traveling companion and intellectual collaborator, Gustave de Beaumont, was equally blunt: "A bad aristocracy is the first cause of all the evils of Ireland" (Drescher, 1964, p. 109). For both, Ireland provided a vivid and depressing example of an illiberal aristocratic regime.

Tocqueville traced Ireland's deplorable condition to the separation of the aristocracy from the people. English rather than Irish, Protestant rather than Catholic, the aristocracy remained socially aloof and jealously guarded its vast landed holdings and its control of the system of justice. Tocqueville's stay in the village of Newport-Pratt in Connaught exposed him to a microcosm of Irish society; the village displayed all the signs of utter destitution and imminent famine, but the village priest told Tocqueville that "On the nearby meadows the Marquis of Sligo has a thousand sheep and several of his granaries are full" (Tocqueville, 1968a, p. 190). This distance between the aristocracy and the common people stimulated the growth of religious animosity and class hatred.

Under these circumstances it would seem that neither the broad distribution of authority nor the sense of community essential to a liberal society could develop, yet Tocqueville's optimism that humankind could create a decent society did not leave him, even in Ireland. In conquering Ireland, the English had allowed the forms of liberty to persist, even while stripping them of their content. They had left intact the freedom of the press, the right of association, habeas corpus, and the jury, relying upon their wealth and their control of the magistracy to retain their power. By 1835, Tocqueville believed, the Irish were beginning to exploit the possibilities inherent in these liberal institutions:

> The time has at last come when the Catholics, having become more numerous and rich, have begun to claim their place among the magistrates and on the bench of the jury; when the electors are advised to vote against their landlords; when the freedom of the press has served to prove the despotism of the aristocracy; the right to assemble at a meeting has allowed them to become kindled at the sight of their slavery, since then tyranny has been beaten . . . [Tocqueville, 1968a, p. 178].

This passage, Tocqueville's most hopeful reflection while in Ireland, overstated the degree of Catholic emancipation, but it demonstrates both Tocqueville's emphasis upon the importance of liberal institutions and his remarkable prescience about fundamental political developments.

Tocqueville's description of the French *ancien régime* was far more differentiated, both in its historical periodization and in its moral evaluation, than were his notes on Ireland. Tocqueville's treatment of the old regime was historical rather than static; he began by analyzing its beginnings in the Middle Ages. In the fourteenth-century France had had laws and institutions remarkably similar to those of England and Germany. The towns and villages enjoyed a considerable degree of autonomy and self-government. A spirit of local patriotism flourished, fortified by local institutions for the administration of justice, by provincial assemblies, and by a sense of community between nobles and commoners. When necessity demanded, the nobility and the Third Estate could still unite to defend their political privileges against centralizing monarchs:

> A famous example of this cooperation between the classes is the association jointly formed by the nobles and the citizens of many French towns at the beginning of the fourteenth century with a view to defending the liberty of the nation and the ancient rights of the provinces against encroachments of the royal power. Many such incidents took place in this period. . . [Tocqueville, 1955, pp. 85–86].

Tocqueville was incapable of repressing a certain nostalgia for this period, for France in the fourteenth century retained a decentralized structure of authority and a spirit of liberty that it had since lost.

In Part II of *The Old Regime* Tocqueville recorded the gradual decay of these conditions for a free society in France. He described how French kings had suppressed the provincial assemblies and had centralized public administration until

> . . . we find a single central power located at the heart of the kingdom and controlling public administration throughout the country; a single Minister of State in charge of almost all the internal affairs of the country; in each province a single representative of government supervising every detail of the administration; no secondary administrative bodies authorized to take action on their own initiative; and finally, "exceptional" courts for the trial of cases involving the administration or any of its officers [Tocqueville, 1955, p. 57].

This centralization of authority sapped local energy and enterprise to such a degree that "It never occurred to anyone that any large-scale enterprise could be put through successfully without the intervention of the state" (Tocqueville, 1955, p. 69).

These changes in institutional structure reflected the decline of the French spirit. Tocqueville traced the downfall of the *ancien régime* to the imposition of the *taille* in 1439, citing this event as the first example of the loss of a sense of community and a spirit of liberty:

It was on the day when the French people, weary of the chaos into which the kingdom had been plunged for so many years by the captivity of King John and the madness of Charles VI, permitted the King to impose a tax without their consent and the nobles showed so little public spirit as to connive at this, provided their own immunity was guaranteed—it was on that fateful day that the seeds were sown of almost all the vices and abuses which led to the violent downfall of the old regime [Tocqueville, 1955, pp. 98–99].

From this moment the inequality of taxation among classes grew and the rift between them deepened; the French people split into small, isolated, self-regarding groups, incapable of cooperation and devoid of a sense of community. In England the aristocracy and the lower orders continued to operate in a climate of freedom, to preserve mutual contact, and to maintain their liberties, but in France the aristocracy began to degenerate into a caste: "Those who were not of noble blood were automatically excluded from the magic circle . . ." (Tocqueville, 1955, p. 82). It yielded its functions while consolidating its privileges—until at last the blatant injustice of the situation resulted in the total rupture of the sense of community and culminated in violent revolution.

And yet even in the late stages of the *ancien régime* "a peculiar kind of freedom" survived. "Any notion that the old regime was an era of servility and subservience is very wide of the mark," Tocqueville observes. "There was far more freedom in that period than there is today [in the regime of Louis Napoleon], but it was a curiously ill-adjusted, intermittent freedom, always restricted by class distinctions and tied up with immunities and privileges" (Tocqueville, 1955, pp. 82, 108,119). This strange freedom persisted because beneath the centralized surface there remained a few institutions which checked the accretion of centralized power and there still stirred a spirit of individualism and resistance. The sale of offices had created a curious flaw in the machinery of centralized absolutism; by introducing personnel over whom it had little control the central power robbed itself of administrative efficiency and checked its own power. The church had maintained its independence until the end and in 1789 its clergy showed itself "as hostile to despotism, as favorable to civil liberty, as eager for political freedom as the Third Estate or the nobility" (Tocqueville, 19 55, p. 113). The judicial institutions of the *ancien régime* had remained those of a free people indisposed to show servility to the ruling power. Freedom of speech had endured and the debilitating effects of materialism had yet to make themselves felt.

Despite these remnants of liberal society monarchical centralism had virtually extinguished the prospects for a liberal and democratic society in France. "Though this peculiar, ill-assimilated, and, as it were, unwholesome liberty prepared the French for the great task of overthrowing des-

potism," Tocqueville wrote, "it made them by the same token less qualified than perhaps any other nation to replace it by stable government and
a healthy freedom under the sovereignty of law" (Tocqueville, 1955, p.
120). As Richard Herr (1962, p. 55) has persuasively argued, Tocqueville's central thesis in *The Old Regime* is that "the destruction of political
liberty and the barriers erected between classes made France unfit for
freedom under democracy." First, Louis XVI's efforts to reform and
liberalize floundered because of popular inexperience with liberal institutions. Then in 1789 France experienced one of those "sublime moments
which sweep her to heights which no other people will ever reach." The
men of 1789 temporarily overcame all obstacles, fusing the nation into a
single unit bent on liberty. "The spectacle was short, but it was one of
incomparable grandeur" (Tocqueville, 1968b, pp. 86–87). Nonetheless,
this effort and succeeding ones within Tocqueville's lifetime were con-
demned to failure, for it was impossible to graft political liberty onto
institutions and a spirit which were opposed to it. The kings of France
had, in the course of the *ancien régime,* damaged the structural and
spiritual bases of a free society beyond repair.

England, in contrast to France, managed to preserve and to develop the
medieval foundations for liberal society. By the seventeenth century England had become, in Tocqueville's estimate, "a quite modern society":

> . . . classes intermingled, the nobility no longer had the upper hand, the aristocracy
> had ceased to be exclusive, wealth was a steppingstone to power, all men were equal
> before the law and public offices open to all, freedom of speech and of the press was
> the order of the day [Tocqueville, 1955, p. 18]

Because of the freedom prevailing in England, the aristocracy and the
common people were forced to mingle together in the conduct of local
affairs. To ensure their power the English aristocracy was willing to
shoulder a heavy burden of taxation, to execute arduous public duties,
and even to enlist the aid of the common people against the king. In the
process the English aristocracy developed fluid boundaries. Wealth,
rather than birth alone, became its basis, and hence new recruits could
gain access to its ranks; in Tocqueville's terminology, it ceased to be a
caste and became a true aristocracy.

> It was not merely parliamentary government, freedom of speech, and the jury system
> that made England so different from the rest of contemporary Europe. . . . England
> was the only country in which the caste system had been totally abolished, not merely
> modified. Nobility and commoners joined forces in business enterprises, entered the
> same professions and—what is still more significant—intermarried [Tocqueville, 1955,
> pp. 82–83].

This free and open social intercourse not only enabled the aristocracy to preserve its authority into the democratic age; it fortified the sense of community essential to a free society.

Tocqueville greatly admired the institutions the English had employed to preserve their freedom. It was these institutions that had allowed them to survive the Wars of the Roses and Tudor despotism with their liberty intact, despite the fact that the spirit of liberty had been temporarily lost:

> But what was able to raise the English people from that state of degradation? The same thing as had thrown them down. The *spirit* of the constitution had been broken, but the *forms* remained; it was like the corpse of a free government. When spirits stupefied by the disasters of the civil war began little by little to revive, when numbed hearts beat again, when the passage of time had given the Commons the strength they lacked or thought they lacked, in a word, when the nation awoke, it found the tools for its regeneration at hand, and with the *spirit* of its ancestors all the *means* to be like them [Tocqueville, 1968a, p. 21]. (My italics.)

The critical institutions that the English had preserved were above all local government and judicial guarantees—in short, decentralized administration and an independent judiciary. England had a centralized legislature but not a centralized executive. By retaining the execution of the laws in the hands of locally elected officials, by subjecting the central authorities to continued scrutiny, and by controlling the administration through the judiciary the English had discovered the secret of an active but not tyrannical administration, one that avoided the abuses of the French administrative system and one that the Americans would imitate. This administrative technique, the openness of its aristocracy, and the preservation of liberal institutions and a liberal spirit made England an attractive contrast to nineteenth-century Ireland and France.

Unlike France and England, the United States had no medieval tradition, but like them, its origins illuminated its current politics. All nations, Tocqueville thought, continued to bear the marks of their birth, and America was no exception. The Americans began life liberal and democratic. The early laws of New England displayed the features of a liberal constitution more fully than any other contemporary state. The activity of the people in public affairs, the free voting of taxes, the accountability of elected officials, personal liberty, trial by jury, the basis of the township system—all were established as a matter of course, for the Americans were remarkably well educated in the principles of liberal society. The people themselves had "no notion of superiority one over another;" they did not transplant an aristocracy in American soil. They did bring with them and reaffirm intense religious faith, which they regarded as the natural companion of liberty and morality. These favorable beginnings allowed the Americans to create a liberal society without the complications of having to destroy illiberal political institutions, overthrow an aristocratic social order, or disestablish an authoritarian religion.

That America had been born free and had remained so Tocqueville never doubted. His problem was to explain what conditions maintained this liberal democracy. He distinguished three separate kinds of causes; in order of increasing importance they were "providential acts," "laws," and "manners." "Providential acts," the accidental and least important causes, included geographic isolation, the absence of a great capital city, the natural abundance of the American continent, and the equality and republican manners of the original settlers. Tocqueville stressed the importance of America's distance from the major world powers; "consequently," he argued, "they have no great wars, or financial crises, or inroads, or conquest to dread; they have neither great taxes, nor large armies, nor great generals, and they have nothing to fear from a scourge which is more formidable to republics than all these evils combined, namely, military glory" (Tocqueville, 1967, Vol. I, p. 341). The lack of a great capital promoted liberty because a great urban throng, like the London "mob" or the Parisian "crowds," could not intimidate the government. Natural abundance and general prosperity contributed to the stability of all governments, but particularly to democratic ones; since the people ruled, they must be happy, or they would rebel against the state. Finally, the character of the original settlers imparted a liberal, democratic, and republican bias to the nation's development. The Americans did not require a violent revolution and all its vicissitudes to become liberal and democratic; they enjoyed these attributes from their beginnings.

Providential acts alone could hardly explain the American phenomenon. Other areas of the American continents had had similar advantages and had failed to create liberal democracies. Hence, one needed to examine the second most important determinant of American freedom, its laws or institutional structure. Here Tocqueville isolated four elements of great importance: decentralized administration and local government, the practice of judicial review, freedom of the press, and freedom of association.

Tocqueville believed that decentralized administration in the hands of a vigorous public could frequently accomplish what the most energetic centralized administration would be unable to do, but his preference for decentralization rested on political grounds rather than considerations of administrative efficiency. In America decentralized administration and local government contributed to liberal democracy in four ways: they encouraged popular participation in government, instilled a sense of community interest, provided for a sense of order, and served as a check against centralized power. When citizens participated in local government, they came to see it as their creation and consequently to take an interest in its activities and in maintaining it inviolate from external interference. In this way local institutions both promoted the spirit of liberty and maintained a pluralistic structure of authority.

Judicial review afforded American judges immense political power; indeed, Tocqueville contended that "the power vested in the American courts of justice, of pronouncing a statute to be unconstitutional, forms one of the most powerful barriers which has ever been devised against the tyranny of political assemblies" (Tocqueville, 1967, Vol. I, p. 106). American judges were able to punish agents of the executive branch when they violated the law; no separate system of administrative law stood in their way. The Americans had succeeded in tempering this great positive power by refusing to allow the judiciary to initiate legal proceedings. The power of the judiciary was passive; it could act only when called upon to do so.

Tocqueville regarded the liberty of the press with mixed feelings, but considered it indispensable to liberty, for in America it admirably performed its essential functions of scrutiny, criticism, and communication. He harbored no such reservations about freedom of association, for the possibility of people's joining together to oppose concentrated political power was vital to the preservation of their liberty. The Americans possessed a singular gift for this kind of activity: "In no country in the world has the principle of association been more successfully used, or applied to a greater multitude of objects, than in America" (Tocqueville, 1967, Vol. I, p. 216).

The most important cause supporting liberty in America, however, was neither providential grace nor legal institutions, but the manners of the American people and the spirit of liberty these manners generated. Tocqueville used the term "manners" *(moeurs)* to cover a wide range of social phenomena, among them morality, religion, commerce, education, family relations, and sociability. The scope of this paper permits investigation only of the first three.

Morality Tocqueville regarded as the indispensable cement of a free society: "No free communities ever existed without morals" (Tocqueville, 1967, Vol. II, p. 237). He considered morals the work of women. How fortunate it was, then, that American women were uniquely prepared to carry on this work! Armed with religion and reason, the American woman had learned to regard her matrimonial duties as sacrosanct and to sacrifice her pleasures to her duties. Chastity of this sort Tocqueville occasionally seems to equate with morality in the larger sense and thus to suggest that chastity is essential to freedom, but without explaining why.

Religion also served to bridle and to restrain persons from egoistic and antisocial actions. Democratic man could never be weaned entirely from material indulgence, but religion could aid him in properly understanding the limits of self-interest. Equality tended to isolate men from each other, "to concentrate every man's attention upon himself; and it lays open the soul to an inordinate love of material gratification. The greatest advantage of religion is to inspire diametrically contrary principles" (Tocqueville, 1967, Vol. II, p. 25). The American churches were uniquely advantaged in carrying out this function. Independent of state authority, devoted to civil liberty, respected by their members, they bore none of the burden of justifying questionable exercises of political authority, an embarrassing assignment that afflicted the established churches of France, England, and Ireland.

Not only morality and religion, but even commerce, as practiced in America, sustained liberty. The operation of small shops inculcated habits of independence. Tocqueville claimed that

[C]ommerce renders men independent of each other, gives them a lofty notion of their personal importance, leads them to seek to conduct their own affairs and teaches them how to conduct them well; it therefore prepares men for freedom, but preserves them from revolution (Tocqueville, 1967, Vol. II, p. 305).

Thus, even in the practice of their trades, in the mundane detail of everyday life, the Americans schooled themselves in liberal habits.

THE THEORY OF LIBERAL SOCIETY

Tocqueville's comparative inquiry into the political sociology of liberal society persuaded him that a *pluralistic structure of authority* and a *spirit of liberty* were the fundamental requisites for a free community. In treating both as conditions of free society, Tocqueville recalls Montesquieu and the authors of the *Federalist Papers*. Like Montesquieu and "Publius," Tocqueville believed that concentrated state power was a recipe for tyranny and that legal institutions could achieve little without a spirit of liberty and virtue prevalent among the population. The centrality in Tocqueville's comparative political analysis of these two requisites for a free society, a pluralistic structure of authority, and a spirit of liberty, requires that they receive careful investigation here.

For Tocqueville, unlimited sovereign power was in itself a bad and dangerous thing. Only God could be trusted with omnipotent power, for God alone had wisdom and justice proportionate to his power.

Human beings are not competent to exercise it [unlimited power] with discretion. . . .
There is no power on earth so worthy of honor in itself, or clothed with rights so
sacred, that I would admit its uncontrolled and all-predominant authority. When I see
that the right and the means of absolute command are conferred on any power whatever, be it called a people or a king, an aristocracy or a democracy, a monarchy or a
republic, I say there is the germ of tyranny, and I seek to live elsewhere, under other
laws [Tocqueville, 1967, Vol. I, p. 306].

Absolute political authority, in whomever's hands it might be concentrated, necessarily endangered personal liberty; therefore, a wise nation
erected safeguards against the possibility of such tyranny: It created a
pluralistic 'structure of authority.

Tocqueville had little confidence in the traditional Aristotelian solution
to the problem of avoiding despotism; he did not advocate the "chimera
of mixed government." "I do not think," he wrote in *Democracy in
America,* that "it is possible to combine several principles in the same
government so as really to oppose them to one another." "Accurately
speaking," he continued, "there is no such thing as a *mixed* government,
in the sense usually given to that word, because, in all communities some
one principle of action may be discovered which preponderates over the
others." If a society is to be stable, there must be an authority which can
propound binding rules and judgments. There must, in short, be a locus of
legal sovereignty, but this sovereignty should not be absolute: "Social
power superior to all others must be placed somewhere; but I think that
liberty is endangered when this power finds no obstacle which can retard
its course, and give it time to moderate its own vehemence" (Tocqueville,
1967, Vol. I, p. 306).

Tocqueville espoused this principle consistently. In his *Recollections*
he posed the central issue for the French constitution-makers of 1848 as a
choice between unlimited sovereignty or a pluralistic structure of public
authority:

Were we to persevere in the learned and somewhat complicated system of counter-
poises, and place powers held in check, and consequently prudent and moderate, at
the head of the Republic? Or were we to adopt the contrary course and accept the
simpler theory, according to which affairs are placed in the hands of a single power,
homogeneous in all its parts, uncontrolled, and consequently impetuous in its measures, and irresistible? [Tocqueville, 1948, pp. 205–206].

Tocqueville argued for the creation of a pluralistic structure of authority
within the government itself: A bicameral legislature ought to be preferred
to a unicameral, irremovable to removable judges. For Tocqueville as for

Madison, power had to be opposed to power, "ambition must be made to counteract ambition" (Hamilton, Madison, and Jay, 1961, p. 322).

Essential to the maintenance of this pluralistic structure of authority was an *Independent Judiciary*. Again and again Tocqueville returned to the importance of this institution, writing upon the comparative performance of the French, American, English, Irish, and Swiss judiciaries. Here as elsewhere Tocqueville employed American experience and institutions to expose (what he deemed) defects in French practice. The Americans subjected everyone to the rule of law; government officials did not enjoy the privilege of being tried in separate administrative courts. All citizens had the right to indict public functionaries before the ordinary courts and judges could convict state officials. This arrangement Tocqueville found markedly superior to the French system of administrative law with its presumption that the relationship between private citizens and agents of the state was of a peculiar nature. The judiciary's *raison d'être* was to preserve individual liberty; it accomplished this end by restraining the legislative and executive elements of government and subjecting all citizens to the rule of law.

A second critical obstacle to a tyrannical concentration of state power Tocqueville found in decentralized administration. Tocqueville was willing to allow centralized government (the concentrated prosecution of the nation's common interests; e.g., its foreign relations), but not centralized administration (the concentrated direction of merely regional or local affairs; e.g., repairing church roofs). By distributing the executive authority of the government among diverse bodies, a nation reduced the chances of implementation of a concerted despotic design. An abundance of administrative authorities would frustrate the effort to impose a central directive throughout the nation. This principle assumed particular significance in democratic countries. There the union of centralized government and centralized administration would prove disastrous:

> If the directing power of the American communities had both these instruments of government at its disposal, and united the habit of executing its commands to the right of commanding; if, after having established the general principles of government, it descended to the details of their application; and if, having regulated the great interests of the country, it could descend to the circle of individual interests, freedom would soon be banished from the New World [Tocqueville, 1967, Vol. I, p. 319].

Fortunately, in America the central government, like medieval sovereigns, could not always execute its decrees itself. It had to entrust the execution of its will to agencies not under its exclusive control. Local governmental units—townships, municipalities, and counties—stood as potential obstacles to centralized control. The pluralistic structure of administrative authority helped prevent the tyranny of the majority, and hence Tocqueville could conclude that even if an oppressive law were passed, liberty would still be protected by the mode of executing that law (Tocqueville, 1967, Vol. I, p. 320).

The French had never sufficiently comprehended the costs of administrative centralization nor satisfactorily combated its growth. Both absolutist monarchs and revolutionary democrats had contributed to increased centralized power. The staunchest political foes agreed on this one principle—that centralized executive power was indispensable. Even revolution did not touch this dominant fact of French political life, as Tocqueville argued in *The Old Regime and the French Revolution,* and as he observed in his memoirs of the revolution of 1848: "In France there is only one thing we can't set up: that is, a free government; and only one institution we can't destroy: that is, centralization" (Tocqueville, 1948, p. 202).

Tocqueville conceded that France's more exposed international position required a greater degree of administrative centralization than was necessary in America; nonethless, the French had easily exceeded the appropriate stopping point. The effects were severely detrimental to personal freedom. The central executive agency implemented its will without opposition. Gone was the spirit of local independence and initiative which American federalism and local government fostered and which was essential to a free society. In destroying the privileges of the provincial aristocrats, monarchs and revolutionaries had also destroyed a check on centralized power. The only feasible functional equivalent for these aristocratic powers in a new pluralistic structure of authority was an abundance of locally elected authorities. Election assured the independence of the administrator from the central power. This type of local administration might not always display the same effectiveness as a central bureaucracy, but its political advantages were undeniable and far outweighed any loss of efficiency: Decentralized administration promoted liberty.

A pluralistic structure of political authority would be, as Tocqueville recognized, insufficient to maintain a liberal society. Constitutional devices alone could not preserve freedom. Absolute monarchs could and had undermined the independence of judiciary bodies like the *parlements.* Popular democratic movements might similarly conquer all the structures of state power and impose their will upon entire populations. If freedom was to be attained and preserved, additional centers of private authority within the society were essential to supplement and to support the distribution of state power.

Foremost among these additional centers of authority were *voluntary associations* of private individuals. These associations set limits to governmental powers. "A political, commercial, industrial and even scientific or literary association is an enlightened and powerful citizen whom no one can dictate to at will or oppress without publicity, and which in defending its own rights against the exigencies of power, safeguards the common liberties of the country" (Tocqueville, 1967, Vol. II, p. 388). Prior to the democratic revolution aristocracies performed this function; in democratic societies voluntary associations had to assume this role, for there were no longer "natural" antagonists of centralized rule.

> There are no countries in which associations are more needed to prevent the despotism of faction or the arbitrary power of a prince than those which are democratically constituted. In aristocratic nations, the body of the nobles and the wealthy are in themselves natural associations which check the abuses of power. In countries where such private associations do not exist, if private individuals cannot create an artificial and temporary substitute for them, I can see no permanent protection against the most galling tyranny . . . [Tocqueville, 1967, Vol. I, p. 221].

If men did not incline to associate for political purposes, their liberty was in jeopardy. Single-handed, a person could not protect himself against incursions of the public power; he must associate with his fellows to defend his own interests.

Americans formed such associations; the French did not. When Tocqueville wrote of the multitude of private American organizations, he could not conceal his amazement:

> The political associations which exist in the United States are only a single feature in the midst of the immense assemblage of associations in that country. Americans of all ages, all conditions, and all dispositions, constantly form associations. They have not only commercial and manufacturing companies, in which all take part, but associations of a thousand other kinds—religious, moral, serious, futile, general or restricted, enormous or diminutive. . . . Wherever, at the head of some new undertaking, you see the government in France, or a man of rank in England, in the United States you will be sure to find an association [Tocqueville, 1967, Vol. II, pp. 128–129].

These associations helped provide the structural pluralism essential to a free society, but they could flourish only where the freedom to assemble and organize was legally recognized. France had been slow to extend such liberties. The penal code of 1810 had regulated the right of association for groups of twenty or more meeting on a periodic basis; an 1834 statute eliminated mention of regular meetings, effectively removed the limit of twenty members, and otherwise stiffened the restrictions on association (Lively, 1962, p. 128). Under such circumstances even those Frenchmen who still retained initiative, a desire to help themselves, and gregarious impulses had difficulty organizing.

Association, Tocqueville realized, assumed communication among the members of the association. In considerable measure this communication proceeded through direct personal contact, but in large countries potential associates could not always communicate with one another directly. To fill this gap a *free press* was vital. The press circulated political information over vast areas. It propounded party platforms and principles. it afforded a "means of intercourse between those who hear and address each other, without [their] ever coming into immediate contact (Tocqueville, 1967, Vol. I, p. 212). In short, the press rendered an essential contribution to the process of political association.

Not only did the press promote the formation of plural centers of authority, it in itself constituted such a center, or centers, for in America Tocqueville found a multitude of local newspapers propagating a wide variety of political views. So long as this diversity of opinion prevailed, the press could exercise little more than local influence, but "when many organs of the press adopt the same line of conduct, their influence in the long run becomes irresistible . . ." Such unity in the decentralized American press was unlikely, but unity was not required for the press to perform its essential function: to expose political abuses and "to summon the leaders of all parties in turn to the bar of public opinion." The free press allowed the citizen to appeal to his fellows against official abuses. It was the democratic instrument of liberty *par excellence:*

> The more I consider the freedom of the press in terms of its main consequences, the more I am convinced that in the modern world it is the prime and, so to speak, the constitutive element of liberty. A people that wishes to remain free has therefore the right to demand that it should be respected at any price [Tocqueville, 1967, Vol. I, p. 219].

Despite his reservations about the intrinsic value of an uncensored press, Tocqueville deemed a free press an indispensable element in the pluralistic structure of authority, for it not only countered the government on its own, but assisted other private organizations in their endeavors.

Like Montesquieu, Tocqueville believed that one could not satisfactorily understand a society by concentrating on the structure of its institutions, nor that one could prescribe merely institutional remedies for social ills. At least as important as the formal structure of an institution was the spirit that animated it. Institutions which once served the cause of liberty might dessicate into empty shells, as the case of the *parlements* demonstrated. Institutions which promoted liberty in one country might fail miserably in another if the proper climate of opinion were lacking; they could not simply be imported like rounds of cheese or barrels of wine.

Montesquieu had used the terms "nature" and "principle" of government to make this distinction between the "structure" and "spirit" of a society:

> There is this difference between the nature and principle of government, that the former is that by which it is constituted, the latter that by which it is made to act. One is its particular structure, and the other the human passions which set it in motion [Montesquieu, 1966, p. 19].

Tocqueville shared this concern for analyzing the animating passions, attitudes, and opinions of societies. At times, for example when discussing the tyranny of the majority, he suggested that the force of opinion might overwhelm the formal structures of government and infuse them with its content. He told the French Chamber of Deputies that ". . . it is not the mechanism of laws that produces great events, gentlemen, but the inner spirit of the governments" (Tocqueville, 1948, pp. 14–15). Given this intense interest in the "spirit" of society, it would be surprising if Tocqueville did not establish "spiritual" conditions for the existence of a free society, and indeed for him "the spirit of liberty" is an essential requisite of a free society.

What attitudes comprise "the spirit of liberty"? First, there is an element of *raw energy* and *assertiveness*. Freedom is not for the passive; usurpers are always alert for opportunities to seize it from the unwary. Tocqueville's writings abound with references to the vitality and energy of peoples. At times, he thought, nations became so flaccid and decadent that they were incapable of operating a free society. The proper degree of liveliness and vigor were, by their nature, somewhat esoteric and indefinable, somewhat beyond the range of sociological analysis, but they were essential to the spirit of liberty.

The spirit of liberty is characterized, secondly, by a widespread *concern for the public welfare* and a *sense of community*. Like the ancient republics admired by Montesquieu and Rousseau, a modern republic demanded not private men absorbed in business interests but citizens devoted to the good of the community. Modern freedom rested not on apathetic withdrawal of the masses of men from politics—an interpretation favored by many of Tocqueville's admirers in the 1950s—but upon active public involvement in the community's affairs.

Tocqueville discovered this public-spiritedness and participatory activity in the New England townships and praised them as essential to the continuation of a free society. The variety of offices in these townships offered opportunities for public service and esteem to a vast number of individuals. The prosecution of public concerns educated and elevated the common man, attaching him to his community with ties of interest and affection. It instilled in him a respect for law. Tocqueville described the spirit of the New England townships in terms that betray his admiration:

> The native of New England is attached to his township because it is independent and free; this cooperation in its affairs insures his attachment to its interests; the well-being it affords him secures his affection; and its welfare is the aim of his ambition and of his future exertions. He takes part in every occurrence in the place; he practices the art of government in the small spheres within his reach; he acustoms himself to those forms without which liberty can only advance by revolutions; he imbibes their spirit; he acquires a taste for order, comprehends the balance of powers, and collects clear practical notions on the nature of his duties and the extent of his rights [Tocqueville, 1967, Vol. I, p. 64].

This sense of community drew the New Englanders together, not merely by the material links of self-interest, but also by the intangible bonds of fellow-feeling; it formed an integral part of the "spirit of liberty."

Egoism was radically opposed to public spiritedness. Exacerbated everywhere by the progress of democracy, selfish ambition appeared in a particularly virulent form in France. Tocqueville's description of the middle-class regime created by the revolution of 1830 revealed his deep suspicion and distrust of the psychology of the French bourgeoisie:

> The particular spirit of the middle class became the general spirit of the government; it ruled the latter's foreign policy as well as affairs at home: an active, industrious spirit, often dishonorable, generally orderly, occasionally reckless through vanity or egoism, but timid by temperament, moderate in all things except in its love of ease and comfort, and last but not least mediocre. It was a spirit, which mingled with that of the people or of the aristocracy, can do wonders; but which, by itself will never produce more than a government shorn of virtue and greatness. Master of everything in a manner that no aristocracy has ever been or may ever hope to be, the middle class, when called upon to assume the government, took it up as an industrial enterprise; it entrenched itself behind its power, and before long, in their egoism, each of its members thought much more of his private business than of public affairs; of his personal enjoyment than of the greatness of the nation [Tocqueville, 1948, p.3].

This exaggerated love of self stands in sharp contrast to the sense of community that infuses a liberal democratic regime.

Closely related to this sense of community is a third ingredient of the spirit of liberty, what Montesquieu called *political virtue:* i.e., habitual moral behavior directed toward the good of the community (cf. Wood,

1970). A free society did not endorse license; rather it required a high degree of self-control on the part of its members. If citizens did not exercise personal restraint, the state must necessarily intervene to coerce them, with a consequent diminution of freedom. This self-repression did not arise as a matter of course; it had to be instilled into prospective citizens: "It is difficult to make the people participate in government; but it is still more difficult . . . to inspire them with the feelings which they need in order to govern well" (Tocqueville, 1967, Vol. I, p. 391). Education, a proper religious training, and the activity of women in the home all might contribute to the propagation of virtue.

The spirit of liberty demanded energy, a strong sense of community, and political virtue. It may seem tautological to trace freedom to a spirit of liberty, but Tocqueville's assertion is distinctly more than an empty truism. Tocqueville recognized that no amount of institutional engineering can unfailingly generate the attitudes upon which freedom rests; every person bears a moral responsibility for the creation and preservation of the spirit of liberty, for the presence or absence of this spirit (and of a pluralistic structure of authority) determine the degree of freedom a society may enjoy. Together a pluralistic structure of authority and a spirit of liberty reinforce each other; separated, each is weakened and exposed to destruction. If both are absent, freedom must also disappear.

CONCLUSION

Tocqueville's theory of liberal society is a functionalist theory. It holds for both traditional and modern societies. In response to the question of what makes liberal society work and persist, Tocqueville gives a classical liberal answer: resistance to overweening centralized authority. For such resistance to arise, both the proper institutions and the proper attitudes must be present. Liberty requires a pluralistic structure of authority which fosters independent centers of potentially countervailing power, and if these centers are to function as effective obstacles to despotism, the spirit of liberty must remain alive and uncorrupted among the citizenry.

In both traditional and modern societies the spirit of liberty rests on popular assertiveness, a spirit of community, and political virtue. The government, whether monarchical or parliamentary (and Tocqueville puts remarkably little emphasis on this distinction), must be characterized by limited sovereign power, an independent judiciary, and decentralized administration. The society must generate independent "secondary powers" capable of challenging government authority, but the social basis of the pluralistic structure of authority differs sharply in aristocratic and democratic societies:

> The notion of secondary powers, placed between the sovereign and his subjects, occurred naturally to the imagination of aristocratic nations, because those communities contained individuals of families raised above the common level, and apparently destined to command by their birth, their education, and their wealth. The same notion is naturally wanting in the minds of men in democratic ages, for converse reasons; it can only be introduced artificially, it can only be kept there with difficulty; whereas they conceive as it were without thinking upon the subject, the notion of a single and central power, which governs the whole community by its direct influence [Tocqueville, 1967, Vol. II, p. 347].

The task, then, for democratic statesmen is to discover functional equivalents for the aristocracy as secondary powers.

Tocqueville suggested three promising substitutes, voluntary associations, lawyers, and a free press. Tocqueville's enthusiastic approval of voluntary associations is well known, but perhaps less appreciated is his explicit endorsement of them as functional equivalents for aristocrats. In a notable passage Tocqueville stated,

> I firmly believe that an aristocracy cannot again be founded in the world; but I think that private citizens, by combining together, may constitute bodies of great wealth, influence, and strength, corresponding to the persons of an aristocracy. By this means, many of the greatest political advantages of aristocracy would be obtained, without its injustice or its dangers [Tocqueville, 1967, Vol. II, p. 387].

Lawyers displayed an even closer resemblance to an aristocracy: by habit and taste they were aristocrats; they revered forms, and, superior in their wisdom, they felt a certain contempt for the common people. Consequently they were uniquely suited to counterbalance the democratic multitude. Finally, the press could serve both to publicize abuses of authority and to ease communication among the opponents of tyranny.

Tocqueville's effort first to understand the general structural and functional requisites of liberal society and then to show how in varying historical circumstances different, but functionally equivalent mechanisms might fulfill these fundamental requirements manages to avoid the major difficulties that have plagued modern functional analysis. His analysis is not static but dynamic. He gives his highest allegiance not to order but to liberty. He entertains no illusions that the requisite conditions for liberal society must emerge and endure; for him human beings, not social systems or logical schemes, always determine historical outcomes. The most telling criticisms of much modern functional analysis leave Tocqueville untouched.

Tocqueville's theory is vulnerable on a different point. It is intended for, and more applicable to, agricultural or commercial societies, not modern industrial societies. Tocqueville (1967, ch. 20) simply did not expect industrialism to be such a potent instrument of social change. On the contrary, he expected democratic currents to overwhelm the nascent aristocratic tendencies of industrialism. Manufacturing establishments would remain "a monstrous exception" in a generally agricultural and commercial society. The "masters" would be unable to form themselves into a class, for their economic basis was fluid and evanescent industrial wealth rather than the stable aristocratic anchorage of land. Industrial fortunes would disappear and those who held them for relatively brief periods would fail to develop common traditions and purposes. There would be wealthy individuals but not a class of the wealthy. This fact could hardly be very consoling to those who remained permanently poor, but the fact remains that Tocqueville never regarded their plight as the central issue for modern society.

Beyond raising nagging questions about the prospects for liberty in societies with active interventionist governments, vast centralized administrations, and corporatist interest groups, Tocqueville's relevance to modern welfare states might appear slight, but before dismissing him, one should note that Tocqueville could envision liberty under a more active government. Europe's social ills, and particularly the problem of poverty, he conceded, necessitated greater public intervention. In such circumstances societies ought not only to maintain secondary powers, but also devise special expedients to liberalize administration. In the English Poor Law Tocqueville found the appropriate insitutional arrangements: "Find a means: (1) to subject the centralizing power to publicity; (2) to have its *local* decisions carried out by elected authorities, then I see no objection to extending its power as much as you like . . ." (Tocqueville, 1968a, pp. 98–99).

Modern interpreters have seized on parts of Tocqueville's liberal theory of society to enhance their own intellectual positions and to claim Tocqueville as their own. During the 1950s conservatives regularly invoked Tocqueville as the classical proponent of the theory of mass society, the prophet of middle-class mediocrity and boorishness, and the sober student of politics who foresaw the dangers of majority tyranny. The approved conservative reading of Tocqueville simply excluded his celebration of the intense democracy of the New England towns and his recurrent emphasis upon a thriving public life. Liberals have employed Tocqueville to sanction a pluralism that he would have detested, the pluralism of large corporate interests rather than the pluralism of "secondary powers" and voluntary associations. For them Tocqueville's condemnation of egoistic individualism, his stress upon the moral climate of society, and his insistence that the clash of interests occur within an atmosphere of public-spiritedness are so many dead letters.

These positions mistake the thrust of Tocqueville's comparative sociology and his liberal theory of society. Tocqueville's investigations always originated from and returned to questions of French politics, and his general political position remained firm: Die-hard conservatism was utterly irresponsible, doomed not only to fail but to corrupt the future prospects for a free society. He found the choice between aristocratic and democratic societies one with genuinely tragic dimensions: neither could realize all of the attractive possibilities of human life; each, of necessity, prohibited the achievement of important human values. Nonetheless, the task of the conservative was not to attempt to prolong unduly the vanishing aristocratic order, but to make the best possible accommodation to democracy, to discover and promote the functional equivalents of aristocratic power.

FOOTNOTE

*I am grateful to my colleague Whitney Pope for a number of enlightening discussions of Tocqueville's sociology. These talks helped stimulate this essay and have contributed to such merits as it may have.

REFERENCES

Drescher, Seymour (1964) *Tocqueville and England*. Cambridge, MA: Harvard University Press.
—— (1968) *Dilemmas of Democracy: Tocqueville and Modernization*. Pittsburgh: University of Pittsburgh Press.
Hamilton, Alexander, James Madison, and John Jay (1961) *The Federalist Papers*. New York: Mentor.
Herr, Richard (1962) *Tocqueville and the Old Regime*. Princeton, NJ: Princeton University Press.
Lefebvre, Georges (1955) "A propos de Tocqueville." *Annales historiques de la revolution française* 27:313–315.
Lively, Jack (1962) *The Social and Political Thought of Alexis de Tocqueville*. Oxford: Clarendon Press.
Montesquieu (1966) *The Spirit of the Laws*. New York: Hafner.
Richter, Melvin (1963) "Tocqueville on Algeria." *Review of Politics* 25(3):362–398.
——(1969) "Comparative Political Analysis in Montesquieu and Tocqueville." *Comparative Politics* 1(2):129–160.
Smelser, Neil (1976) "Alexis de Tocqueville as Comparative Analyst." Pages 6–37 in *Comparative Methods in the Social Sciences*. Englewood Cliffs, NJ: Prentice Hall.
Tocqueville, Alexis de (1948) *The Recollections of Alexis de Tocqueville*. Trans. by George Lawrence. London: Harvill Press.
—— (1955) *The Old Regime and the French Revolution*. Trans. by Stuart Gilbert. New York: Doubleday Anchor.

———— (1967) *Democracy in America*, 2 vols. Trans. by Henry Reeve. New York: Schocken Books.

———— (1968a) *Journeys to England and Ireland*. Trans. by George Lawrence and K. P. Mayer. Garden City, NY: Anchor Books.

———— (1968b) *"The European Revolution" and Correspondence with Gobineau*. Trans. by John Lukacs. Gloucester, MA: Peter Smith.

Wood, Gordon (1970). *The Creation of the American Republic*. Chapel Hill: University of North Carolina Press.

Zeitlin, Irving (1971) *Liberty, Equality, and Revolution in Alexis de Tocqueville*. Boston: Little, Brown.

EGALITARIAN POLITICAL MOVEMENTS, SOCIAL WELFARE EFFORT AND CONVERGENCE THEORY: A CROSS-NATIONAL ANALYSIS*

John B. Williamson and Joseph W. Weiss

INTRODUCTION

The convergence theory postulates that all industrial nations, regardless of their historical and cultural traditions and regardless of their present political and economic structures are becoming increasingly alike. The ideas which underlie this theory can be directly traced to such nineteenth-century theorists as Maine (1964), Tocqueville (1952), and Toennies (1963). During the first half of this century relatively little was done with the theory, but in recent years it has attracted a great deal of research interest: (Kerr *et al.*, 1964; Pryor, 1964; Weinberg, 1969; Mishra,

Comparative Social Research, Vol. 2, pp. 289—302.
Volume 1 published as Comparative Studies in Sociology
Copyright © 1979 by JAI Press, Inc.
ISBN 0-89232-112-1

1973; Baum, 1974; Jackman, 1974, 1975; Wilensky, 1975; Meyer, Boli-Bennett, and Chase-Dunn, 1975; Williamson and Fleming, 1977). In its simplest form the convergence theory is quite general. As a result several interpretations are possible.

One interpretation of the convergence theory is that the levels of economic and technological development are the dominant factors shaping modern societies. That is, the less-developed nations will become increasingly like the presently developed nations as they approach these nations in level of development. Implicit in this interpretation is the assumption of a linear relationship between level of development and a variety of social structural characteristics, including the proportion of Gross National Product (GNP) which is allocated to social welfare expenditures. Also implicit is the assumption that political factors are of little or no importance in accounting for these social structural characteristics. This first interpretation of the convergence theory will hereafter be referred to as the *linear interpretation*.

This interpretation is well illustrated by the work of Kerr *et al.* (1964). Kerr argues that industrial societies are becoming alike in their social structures through an evolutionary process resulting from the impact of economic and technological growth on the occupational structure. This growth increases the middle levels of the stratification systems, creating a large relatively homogeneous middle class. Kerr has termed this process by which economic and technological factors transform and standardize industrial nations the "logic of industrialization."

In Kerr's specification of the convergence theory political and ideological movements have little or no effect on the degree of social inequality in industrial nations. Social inequality in industrial societies is reduced through the expanding division of labor. A larger proportion of the population enter higher occupational levels and, as a result, are able to obtain a larger share of the society's material wealth.

Several recent studies support the view that economic and industrial development are substantially more important than political structure in determining social equality effort. Wilensky (1975) in a cross-national study of 60 countries finds that political system and ideology have only a weak impact on the social security effort. He argues that GNP per capita, through its impact on age structure of the population, is a stronger deter-

*John Williamson is an Associate Professor of Sociology at Boston College. He is co-author of *Strategies Against Poverty in America* (Wiley, 1975), and of *The Research Craft* (Little, Brown, 1977). He is an authority in the areas of poverty and social gerontology. He is currently writing a book entitled *Exploiting Aging*. Joseph Weiss is a Ph.D. graduate student in sociology at the University of Wisconsin, Madison, He is a fellow with the Center for Evaluation Research, Training and Program Development. He is co-author of "Mandatory Sentences: Recipe for Retribution," *Federal Probation* (December 1977).

minant of social security expenditures than elite ideology or political system. Similarly, Pryor (1968) finds in an analysis of seven market and seven centrally planned economies that economic development is a more powerful determinant of welfare expenditures than is economic system. Cutright (1965) shows that economic development is a stronger predictor of social insurance program coverage than is political representativeness. He concludes that the role of politically relevant secondary groups in influencing government decisions is modest. Jackman (1974) finds that the effect of political democracy on various measures of social equality is spurious when level of economic development is controlled. Lewis (1963) in a study of labor unions and relative wages in the United States finds that the impact of unionism on wage inequality among all workers is minimal.

However, there is also evidence that supports the proposition that political factors can be important determinants of social equality effort. Jackman's (1975, pp. 120–131) analysis of 60 noncommunist countries shows that countries with strong labor union membership are more egalitarian in their social insurance program coverage. Pryor's (1968, pp. 473–475) statistical analysis of 19 countries demonstrates a positive and significant relationship between labor union strength and social welfare effort.

We now turn to a second interpretation of the convergence theory, to be referred to as the *curvilinear interpretation*. This interpretation postulates that all industrial nations, regardless of their current economic and political structure, are asymptotically approaching a common form of the welfare state. Implicit in this interpretation is the assumption of a curvilinear relationship between level of development and the various social structural characteristics associated with the welfare state.[1] That is, the effect of an increase in GNP on other aspects of society is stronger at lower levels of development, and it decreases as the level of development increases. Reasoning along the lines of this second interpretation of convergence theory we would still expect the effect of political factors to be minor relative to the effect of economic development. But we would expect this to be more evident when we use a curvilinear (logarithmic) measure of economic development.

The curvilinear interpretation of convergence theory is illustrated by Wilensky (1975, pp. 18–19), who argues that the richer nations become, the more they slow down and level off in the rate for spending for social welfare programs. He presents an analysis of quartile averages of social security spending for 64 countries in which he shows that there is a slowdown in the rate of increase in social security spending; the average ratio of social security to GNP for the richest 16 countries is only slightly higher than that for the second sixteen.

Pryor's (1968, pp. 179–181) times series analysis of economic development and social welfare effort also shows a slowdown in the rate of social security spending at higher levels of development. Pauker (1968, pp. 105–110) finds that the percentage of the Gross Domestic Product allotted to social security ranged from 2 percent for the poorest nations to 12 percent for the 15 richest. However, countries with a Gross Domestic Product of over $1,500 per capita allot a smaller percentage of GNP to social security than do countries in the $1,000-$1,499 range.

While Jackman (1975, p. 32) restricts his definition of the convergence theory to the assumption of a linear relationship as outlined in our first interpretation, he does present results which support what we have described as the curvilinear interpretation of the convergence theory. In an analysis based on a 60 nation sample, he finds that a curvilinear (semilogarithmic) model fits the data better both for the relationship between level of economic development and social equality (pp. 27–43) and for the relationship between what we are calling egalitarian political movements and social equality (pp. 125–131).

If our goal is to predict social welfare effort using a regression model in which level of economic development and strength of egalitarian political movements are the predictors, to be consistent with the curvilinear interpretation of convergence theory we would have to use a logarithmic specification of the economic development indicator. But a plausible case could be made for either a linear or a logarithmic specification for the political predictor. The linear specification would be the most obvious choice and would not need any special justification. The case for a curvilinear specification of a political predictor such as strength of egalitarian political movements would be similar to that used to justify a curvilinear specification of the economic development predictor. Just as we would at some point expect evidence of a diminishing marginal return for further increases in economic development, so too we would expect a diminishing marginal return for further increases in the strength of egalitarian political movements. In both instances there would be a ceiling effect; no nation can spend all its GNP on social welfare efforts. With reference to unions Jackman (1975, p. 122) argues that they "realize their major achievements in the early stages of their development as organizations." In a similar vein Michels (1959, p. 392) points out that soon after a popular movement gains power it begins to lose contact with the masses and interest in redistributive efforts; this observation is central to his "iron law of oligarchy."

Statement of the Problem

In the present study we seek to assess the relative efficacy of the linear as contrasted to the curvilinear interpretation of the convergence theory when applied to the issue of whether egalitarian political movements (i.e., movements committed to a greater redistribution of society's material rewards) have an impact on a nation's social welfare effort. Based on the linear interpretation of the convergence theory one would be led to hypothesize that in linear models political factors such as egalitarian political movements, mainly socialist parties and unions, will have little if any impact on a nation's social welfare effort. If there were any impact at all, we would anticipate its being minor in comparison with that of economic and industrial development. Based on the curvilinear interpretation of the convergence theory we would hypothesize that in the curvilinear (semilogarithmic) specification of the models, political factors will have little if any impact on a nation's social welfare effort; and we would expect the relative impact of these factors to be even less than with the corresponding linear models.

METHODS

Sample

Our analysis is based on a sample of 39 countries. We have restricted the sample to those countries for which data are available for each of the variables used in the analysis. For several of these variables the data are available for a disproportionate number of the highly industrialized countries. Consequently our sample is biased in the direction of the more economically developed nations. The nations included in our sample are: Australia, Austria, Belgium, Bulgaria, Canada, Colombia, Costa Rica, Czechoslovakia, Denmark, Ecuador, El Salvador, Finland, France, Germany (F.R.), Greece, Honduras, Hungary, India, Ireland, Italy, Israel, Japan, Mexico, Netherlands, New Zealand, Norway, Panama, Paraguay, Poland, Sri Lanka, Sweden, Switzerland, Syria, Turkey, the United Kingdom, U.S.S.R., the United States, Venezuela, and Yugoslavia.

Description of Variables

Each of the six variables used in the present analysis is described below. The first is the major dependent variable, the next four are independent variables, and the last is used as both a dependent and an independent variable.

Our measure of *social welfare effort* is social security expenditure as a percent of GNP of 1966; see pp. 317–323 of International Labour Organization (1972).[2] This variable is more appropriately considered a measure of social welfare effort than outcome; there is no assurance that an increase in social welfare expenditures necessarily increases real welfare.

We consider two measures of *level of development*. The first is *level of economic development* as measured by Gross National Product per capita, circa 1960 (U.S. Arms Control and Disarmament Agency, 1975, pp. 20–66). The second is *level of technological development* (or indus- trialization) as measured by energy consumption per capita in kilograms of coal equivalents, 1960 (Taylor and Hudson, 1972, pp. 291, 326–328).

We also consider two measures of *strength of egalitarian political movements*. The first is *socialist party strength* as measured by votes for socialist parties as a percentage of total vote, circa 1960 (Russett *et al.*, 1964, pp. 93–94). The second is *labor union strength* as measured by the ratio of labor union membership to the non-agricultural labor force, circa 1960 (Gurr, 1966, pp. 91–110).

Our measure of the *institutionalization of welfare bureaucracy* is an index that measures the total number of years of social security program experience a nation has had with each of five types of social security programs between 1934 and 1960 (see Cutright, 1965).[3] The five major types of social security programs include: (1) work injury; (2) sickness and/or maternity; (3) old age, invalidism, and death; (4) family allowance; and (5) unemployment insurance. We are assuming that the longer these various social insurance programs have been in operation the more institutionalized they have become.

RESULTS

On the basis of the linear interpretation of the convergence theory as illustrated by Kerr *et al.* (1964) we would expect our indicators of strength of egalitarian political movements to be poor predictors of social welfare effort. The relevant data are presented in Table 1. The correlations for socialist party strength (.46) and labor union strength (.32) are moderately strong. Together these variables have a multiple correlation of .57 and account for 32 percent of the variance in social welfare effort. While the indicators of level of development account for a bit more variance (35 percent), the difference is small.

The argument is sometimes made that after indicators of economic and technological development are taken into consideration, there is little if any additional variance which can be accounted for by political factors. But we find that when all four predictors are included in the same equation, the amount of variance accounted for increases from 35 percent (for the level of development indicators alone) to 48 percent; this represents a substantial increase.

It is reasonable to conclude on the basis of the preceding analysis that political factors, particularly those relating to the strength of egalitarian

Table 1. Linear models:[a]
Social welfare effort as predicted by level of development and strength
of egalitarian political movements (N=39).

	Social Welfare Effort		
	Pearson Correlation	Multiple Correlation	Explained Variance R^2 x 100
Predictor[a]			
Level of Development			
Technological Development	.54**		
Economic Development	.54**		
Both Development Predictors		.59**	.35%
Strength of Egalitarian Political Movements			
Socialist Party Strength	.46**		
Labor Union Strength	.32*		
Both Political Predictors		.57**	.32%
All Four Predictors		.69**	48%

[a]This table presents results for three separate multiple regression models. The first model includes only the two level of development predictors. The second includes only the two strength of egalitarian political movements predictors. The third includes all four of these predictors.

*Significant at the .05 level.
**Significant at the .01.

political movements, are almost as important as level of economic and technological development in predicting social welfare effort. This conclusion is not consistent with the linear interpretation of the convergence theory and it is not consistent with Kerr's "logic of industrialization" thesis.

So far we have considered only linear models. But evidence from previous studies suggests that the relationship between our predictors and various measures of social equality effort would be better represented using curvilinear models. In view of this, it is reasonable to ask how our conclusions based on the linear models would be modified in light of results for curvilinear models. On the basis of the curvilinear interpretation of the convergence theory we would hypothesize a better fit for the curvilinear models. The data relevant to this hypothesis are presented in Table 2. All of the independent variables have undergone logarithmic transformations.

If the curvilinear interpretation of the convergence theory were

Table 2. Semi-logarithmic models:[a,b]
Social welfare effort as predicted by level of development and strength
of egalitarian political movements (N=39).

	Social Welfare Effort		
	Pearson Correlation r	Multiple Correlation R	Explained Variance R^2 x 100
Predictor			
Level of Development			
1n Technological Development	.70**		
1n Economic Development	.68**		
Both Development Predictors		.73**	53%
Strength of Egalitarian Political Movements			
1n Socialist Party Strength	.52**		
1n Labor Union Strength	.52**		
Both Political Predictors		.67**	45%
All Four Predictors		.80**	64%

[a]This table presents results for three separate multiple regression models. The first model includes only the two level of development predictors. The second includes only the two strength of egalitarian political movements predictors. The third includes all four of these predictors.

[b]For all models in this table the independent variables have undergone a natural logarithmic transformation.

**Significant at the .01 level.

superior to the linear interpretation, then we would expect a semi-logarithmic specification of the economic development indicators to yield models which account for more variance than do the corresponding linear models. Consistent with this expectation we find that the amount of variance accounted for by the level of development indicators increases from 35 percent (Table 1) to 53 percent (Table 2). Similarly, the amount of variance accounted for by all four predictors increases from 48 to 64 percent.

If the curvilinear interpretation were better than the linear, we would expect the superiority of the level of development predictors over the political predictors to be more evident when a curvilinear specification of our models is used. Consistent with this hypothesis we find that the gap in variance accounted for increases from only 3 percent (35 −32 percent) in Table 1 to 8 percent (53 −45 percent) in Table 2.

Based on our analysis to this point it would be reasonable to conclude that the curvilinear interpretation is superior to the linear interpretation; however, this purely relative comparison is of somewhat limited utility in assessing the efficacy of the curvilinear interpretation because our data fail to support the linear interpretation. For this reason we now turn to the original hypothesis derived from the curvilinear interpretation of the convergence theory, that in the semi-logarithmic specification of the models political factors will have little if any impact on a nation's social welfare effort. As we have seen in Table 2 the difference between the amount of variance accounted for by the level of development indicators (53 percent) and that accounted for by the political indicators (45 percent) is more substantial than was the case in the linear specification of the models presented in Table 1. However, this difference of 8 percent is still too small to lend support to the conclusion that political factors are not important as predictors of social welfare effort. The level of development indicators are definitely stronger predictors, but the strength of egalitarian political movements indicators remain at least moderately strong predictors even when we consider a curvilinear specification of our models.

The evidence presented so far supports the contention that political factors, such as the strength of socialist parties and the strength of labor unions, do affect a nation's social welfare effort. But we have not as yet explored the causal mechanism involved. The path analysis to which we now turn is addressed to this issue.

Causal Models

In previous efforts to model the causal process by which political and economic factors influence social equality efforts, a measure of what we refer to as *institutionalization of welfare bureaucracy* has proven to be an important intervening variable. Cutright (1965) has presented evidence that economic and technological development are important determinants of what we are calling the institutionalization of welfare bureaucracy. Nations must have money to spend before welfare bureaucracies can be established. Elsewhere he (Cutright, 1967) points out that the general population becomes a constituency supporting the bureaucracy and its demands for higher benefits and more extensive coverage. Socialist party strength and labor union strength are causally prior to the institutionalization of welfare bureaucracy since historically these egalitarian political movements have exerted pressure on governments to expand welfare programs. Wilensky (1975) shows the importance of what we are calling institutionalization of welfare bureaucracy as an intervening variable mediating the effect of GNP (and a variety of other factors including political structure) on social security spending. Jackman (1975) makes

Figure 1. Path model showing institutionalization of welfare
bureaucracy as an intervening variable.[a]

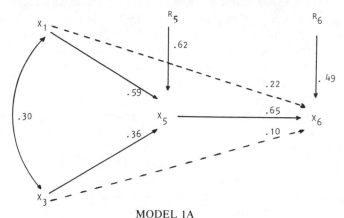

MODEL 1A

X₁ In level of technological development
X₂ In level of economic development
X₃ In Socialist Party strength

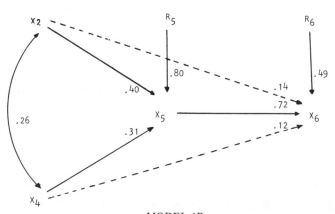

MODEL 1B

X₄ In labor union strength
X₅ Institutionalization of welfare bureaucracy
X₆ Social welfare effort

[a]Solid line indicates path coefficient is significant at the .05 level; dotted line indicates path
coefficient is not significant.

extensive use of this measure as an intervening variable between level of development and various measures of social equality.

In view of the above we have constructed a pair of causal models (see Figure 1) in which institutionalization of welfare bureaucracy is tentatively included as an intervening variable mediating the effect of level of development and strength of egalitarian political movements on social welfare effort. Our assumptions as to causal ordering are implicit in these models.

We have constructed two separate models differing only in the choice of indicators for measuring level of development and strength of egalitarian political movements. We have done this so we can demonstrate that the same basic conclusions follow independently of which one of the indicators is selected. Had we attempted to include all the variables in the same model, this would have complicated efforts to specify a causal ordering among them and it would have introduced serious multicollinearity problems.

The basic issue to be resolved on the basis of the path analysis is whether or not the institutionalization of welfare bureaucracy can be viewed as an intervening variable through which level of development and strength of egalitarian political movements affect social welfare efforts.

For both models the indirect effect of the political variable through the institutionalization variable is greater than is the direct effect of the political variable on social welfare effort. In Model 1A the direct effect is .10 and the indirect effect through the institutionalization variable is .23; in Model 1B the corresponding effects are .12 and .22. The results are similar for the level of development variables. Taken together our path analysis results strongly support the conclusion that egalitarian political movements and level of development have substantial indirect effects on social welfare effort as a result of the impact they have on the development of a social welfare bureaucracy.

CONCLUSION

Our major objective has been to re-examine two of the most common interpretations of the convergence theory, with particular emphasis on assessing the importance of political factors in the shaping of the welfare state toward which all industrial societies are alleged to be converging. In previous research the conclusion has generally been that political factors, particularly structure of government and ideology of governing elites, have little impact on social equality effort. Our study is in part motivated by the belief that the door has been prematurely shut with respect to the potential relevance of political factors as predictors of a nation's social welfare effort.

In an analysis based on linear models we find that political factors such as socialist party and labor union strength have a substantial impact on social welfare effort. This finding leads us to reject what we refer to as the linear interpretation of the convergence theory.

The results from our analysis of the curvilinear interpretation of the theory are mixed. When the models are given a semi-logarithmic specification, the level of development predictors account for more variance than is the case in the corresponding linear models.[4] We also find that in these semi-logarithmic models the level of development predictors account for substantially more variance than do the political predictors. These findings are consistent with and lend support to the curvilinear interpretation of the convergence theory. But even in the curvilinear models the political predictors continue to account for a substantial amount of the variance in social welfare effort.

Where does this leave us? Our results suggest that the curvilinear interpretation of the convergence theory is useful for describing the functional form of the relationship between level of development and social welfare effort. It is also useful to the extent to which it points to level of development as a major determinant of social welfare effort. But our results also suggest that it is not appropriate to use it as a single factor theory. More specifically, it is not appropriate to use the theory to exclude political variables in efforts to account for variation between nations in social welfare effort. The path analysis results suggest that a substantial portion of the effect that egalitarian political movements have on a nation's social welfare effort is a consequence of the effect such movements have on the development and institutionalization of a welfare bureaucracy.

FOOTNOTES

*The authors would like to thank Robert Lay for his valuable comments on an earlier draft of this chapter.

1. For the interpretation we have outlined, the mathematically ideal model is the hyperbola, and hyperbolic transformations would be appropriate in the subsequent analysis. However, we have decided to use the more familiar natural logarithmic transformation which provides an adequate approximation for our purposes.

2. This same variable has been referred to as *social equality effort* by Cutright (1967) and *social security effort* by Wilensky (1975). It includes compulsory social insurance, family allowances, public health services, public assistance (welfare), as well as other related programs such as benefits granted to war victims.

3. Cutright (1965) was the first to propose the variable referring to it as *social insurance program experience* (SIPE); it was subsequently used by Jackman (1975). Wilensky (1975) used the natural logarithm of the variable referring to it as *age of social security system*.

4. A case can be made that the superiority of the semi-logarithmic model over the linear model can in part be accounted for in purely statistical terms (Russett *et al.*, 1964).

REFERENCES

Baum, Ramer (1974) "Beyond Convergence: Toward Theoretical Relevance in Quantitative Modernization Research." *Sociological Inquiry* 44:225–240.

Cutright, Phillips (1965) "Political Structure, Economic Development, and National Social Security Programs." *American Journal of Sociology* 70: 537–550.

—— (1967) "Income Redistribution: A Cross-national Analysis." *Social Forces* 46: 180–190.

Fuguitt, Glenn V. and Stanley Lieberson (1974) "Correlations of Ratios or Difference Scores Having Common Terms." Pages 128–144 in Herbert L. Costner (ed.), *Sociological Methodology 1973-1974.* San Francisco: Jossey-Bass.

Gurr, Ted R. (1966) *New Error-Compensated Measures for Comparing Nations.* Princeton, NJ: Center of International Studies, Princeton University.

International Labour Organization (1972) *The Cost of Social Security: Seventh International inquiry, 1964–66.* Geneva: I.L.O.

Jackman, Robert W. (1974) "Political Democracy and Social Equality: A Comparative Analysis." *American Sociological Review.* 39: 29–45.

—— (1975) *Politics and Social Equality: A Comparative Analysis.* New York: Wiley.

Kerr, Clark *et al.* (1964) *Industrialism and Industrial Man: Problems of Labor and Management in Economic Growth.* New York: Oxford University Press.

Lewis, H. Greg (1963) *Unionism and Relative Wages in the United States, an Empirical Inquiry.* Chicago: University of Chicago Press.

Maine, Henry Sumner (1964) *Ancient Law.* Boston: Beacon Press.

Meyer, John, John Boli-Bennett and Christopher Chase-Dunn (1975) "Convergence and Divergence in Development." Pages 223–246 in Alex Inkeles (ed.), *Annual Reviews of Sociology,* Vol. 1. Palo Alto, CA: Annual Review Inc.

Michels, Robert (1959) *Political Parties: A Sociological Study of the Oligarchical Tendencies of Modern Democracy.* New York: Dover Publications.

Mishra, Ramesh (1973) "Welfare and Industrial Man." *Sociological Review* 21: 535–560.

Paukert, Felix (1968) "Social Security and Income Redistribution: Comparative Experience." Pages 101–128 in Everett M. Kassalow (ed.), *The Role of Social Security in Economic Development.* Washington, DC: Social Security Administration.

Pryor, Frederick L. (1968) *Public Expenditures in Communist and Capitalist Nations.* Homewood, IL: Irwin.

Russett, Bruce M. *et al.* (1964) *World Handbook of Political and Social Indicators.* New Haven, CT: Yale University Press.

Taylor, Charles L. and Michael C. Hudson (1972) *World Handbook of Political and Social Indicators,* 2nd edition. New Haven, CT: Yale University Press.

Tocqueville, Alexis de (1952) *Democracy in America,* translated by Henry Reeve. New York: Oxford University Press.

Toennies, Ferdinand (1963) *Community and Society,* translated by Charles P. Loomis. New York: Harper and Row.

U.S. Arms Control and Disarmament Agency (1975) *World Military Expenditures and Arms Trade, 1963-1966*. Washington, DC: Government Printing Office.

Weinberg, Ian (1969) "The Problem of Convergence of Industrial Societies: A Critical Look at the State of a Theory." *Comparative Studies in Society and History* 11: 1–15.

Wilensky, Harold L. (1975) *The Welfare State and Equality: Structural and Ideological Roots of Public Expenditures*. Berkeley: University of California Press.

Williamson, John B. and Jeanne J. Fleming (1977) "Convergence Theory and the Social Welfare Sector: A Cross-National Analysis." *International Journal of Comparative Sociology* 18: 242–253.

INEQUALITY AND POLITICAL CONFLICT*

Peter G. Sinden

Social inequality has long been regarded as a primary source of political conflict and instability. It has generally been assumed that the relationship is simple and direct,the greater the inequality the greater the conflict. Research on this question has attempted to test this assumption. Yet it has perhaps done more to confuse than to clarify the issue; findings of a direct (Gurr and Duvall, 1973; Paige, 1970; Paranzino, 1972; Russett, 1964), inverse (Mitchell, 1968; Parvin, 1973), curvilinear (Nagel, 1974), and nonexistent (Russo, 1972; Sigelman and Simpson, 1977) relationship between inequality and instability has been reported. I suggest that this confusion exists because these studies have failed, for the most part, to take

Comparative Social Research, Vol. 2. pp. 303—320.
Volume 1 published as Comparative Studies in Sociology
Copyright © 1979 JAI Press, Inc.
All rights of reproduction in any form reserved.
ISBN 0-89232-112-1

into account the pertinent theoretical literature which suggests that the relationship is more complex than is apparent. Different outcomes occur dependent upon the type of inequality present and the economic and social structural characteristics of a society. This chapter will develop three divergent arguments and examine their validity in a sample of fifty-nine Western and Third World countries.

INEQUALITY AND INSTABILITY: THEORY

One view of the relationship between inequality and instability revolves around the nexus of poverty, inequality, and conflict. Central to this thesis is the notion that the disruptive effect of inequality is mediated by a country's overall level of economic development. According to Russett (1964), the creation of diversified, industrial economies, which are no longer dependent upon agriculture and land holdings as the primary source of wealth, *reduces* tensions created by existing social inequalities, especially by those which exist in the distribution of the land. He goes on to suggest

> . . . extreme inequality of land distribution leads to political instability only in those poor, predominantly agricultural societies where limitation to a small plot of land almost unavoidably condemns one to poverty. In a rich country, the modest income a farmer can produce from even a small holding may satisfy him. Or, if that is not the case, at least in wealthy countries there are, besides agriculture, many alternative sources of wealth [Russett, 1964, p. 452].

A directly contrasting view of the consequences of gross inequalities is found in the works of Marx (1971) and Durkheim (1933). Both discounted the possibility of large-scale political conflict in predominantly agricultural countries. Marx assumed those who worked the land were too isolated from one another to organize and mobilize for sustained political action. Consequently, Marx (1971, pp. 320–321) thought they would remain inactive even in the face of gross inequalities. In a different vein, Durkheim (1933, pp. 379–380) attributed passivity in this group to its mechanical social organization and enhanced collective conscience which exists to constrain behavior within the group.

*Peter G. Sinden is an Assistant Professor of Sociology at the State University of New York at Fredonia. He combines interests in deviance and social control with continuing efforts to deliniate factors associated with political conflict. His papers have been presented at meetings of the Society for the Study of Social Problems, Eastern Sociological Society, and the American Sociological Association, and he has published in the journal *Ethnicity*.

However, both suggested that conflict, especially between unequally situated classes, would occur in those societies which had already experienced a great deal of economic development. Marx reasoned that a necessary precondition of collective action, especially revolutionary action, is the development of a social and economic organization which brings together people with common interests. Such is the case with the development of a capitalist-industrial society. He predicted that the proletariat would eventually develop as a class working for itself to destroy the institution of private property, because, as the foundation of bourgeois economic and political power, it is the immediate source of working class oppression. In fact Marx (1971, p. 33) argued that the more developed the capitalist society, the greater the oppression, for " . . . nowhere does inequality appear more harshly . . . because nowhere else is it less whitewashed by political inequality."

In a different argument, Durkheim suggests that the critical issue is the manner in which occupational roles and positions are filled in societies with extensive divisions of labor. Problems arise, in Durkheim's view, when the inheritance of great wealth conveys unequal advantages to some and labor becomes divided on the basis of sponsorship and not of ability. It is this "injustice" which, he argues, is a source of "dissension" in society. "The lower classes, not being or no longer being satisfied with the role which has developed upon them from custom or law, aspire to functions which are closed to them and seek to dispossess those who are exercising these functions. Thus civil wars arise . . ." (Durkheim, 1933, p. 374). Moreover, Durkheim suggests that these problems posed by inequalities increase as the division of labor becomes more complex. Thus it is expected that the association between social inequality and conflict will be strongest only in those societies which have developed the most extensive divisions of labor.

Finally, a third theme on this relationship has appeared in a number of studies in recent years (Freiderich, 1970; Moore, 1966; Paige, 1970; Tilly, 1964; and Wolf, 1969). As presented in Moore's work, this theme is critical of the assumption, which both Marx and Durkheim make, that peasant societies are inherently passive. He maintains that, in the face of certain economic changes, an unequal distribution of land is a major source of sustained conflict in a society where agriculture is a dominant economic form. However, taking a cue from Marx, Moore argues that the necessary critical changes are those associated with economic modernization, specifically the introduction of agricultural production for a commercial market.

The intrusion of this market economy is thought to be particularly unsettling in peasant societies because it undermines a way of life based upon distinct patterns of land use and, in Moore's (1966, p. 497) words, upon a specific set of "mores" and "moral standards." The essence of these standards is a crude notion of equality, stressing the justice and necessity of a minimum of land for the performance of essential social tasks." To accomplish these, land was divided and redivided so that all the families of a village or estate had land to till. Furthermore, each had equal access to an undivided commons.

The development of market agriculture had disastrous consequences for these arrangements. In order to be successful in the marketplace, the landowners or their agents found it necessary to increase productivity and reduce costs. As a result, some of the peasants were required to work harder for less, as they were made to pay the landowner higher rents and/or a greater share of their produce. Other peasants were displaced from the land completely as their subsistence level plots were consolidated into larger and more productive acreage, and the commons was placed into production.

In Moore's view, when these conditions occur, particularly if they are brought about by rapid changes in the organization of agricultural production, the potential for political conflict has increased. This, in turn, suggests that in those countries where land tenure is important to the economic well-being of large numbers of a society's population and where the modernization process has begun, one would expect to find a strong positive correlation between inequality in the distribution of land and political conflict and instability.

In sum, this review suggests that there are three distinct hypotheses about this relationship between inequality and instability. One posits that inequality, especially in the distribution of land, will be particularly unsettling only in the poorest countries where the economy is predominantly agricultural. A second comes to an opposite conclusion as it argues that an unequal distribution of capital wealth is a source of conflict in those countries which have developed a wealthier industrial economy and an extensive division of labor. Finally, the last predicts that disparities in land tenure accompanying the modernization process will become disruptive in those countries undergoing this economic and social transformation.

METHOD

In order to examine these hypotheses, data were collected on all those nonsocialist countries which were politically independent around 1960 and for which data on all variables were available. These necessary limitations produced an inital sample of 59 Western and Third World countries from all the continents except sub-Sahara Africa. Although this is a purposive rather than a probability sample, it is representative enough to provide for informative relationships.

The following analysis uses two different measures of political conflict and instability drawn from two different sets of data on political events. One of these measures was constructed from data originally collected and compiled by Feierabend, Feierabend, and Nesvold (1971). Using *Deadline Data on World Affairs* and the *Encyclopaedia Britannica Yearbooks* as their primary sources, they enumerated all of those events indicative of political and economic disturbances which occurred in the sampled countries during 1947–1965. Twenty-five types of events were counted, including demonstrations, strikes, mass arrests, revolts, and civil wars.[1] In addition to reporting their frequency, the compilers also weighted, on a seven-point scale, the judged seriousness of each event for the society in which it occurred. This was done on the assumption that an event such as a civil war, with a long duration and involving large numbers of people in violent circumstances, would be a more serious disturbance than other events involving fewer people in less turbulent circumstances.

In addition, in order to discount the inflationary effects that population size alone may have on the incidence of events, I modified their data further. I did so on the assumption that one may find a greater number of events, such as strikes, demonstrations, and mass arrests where larger numbers of potential participants or detainees may also be found. Consequently, to discount the effects of population size, the total number of these events in each country was normed to its population before being added into the total instability score for that country.

Other events, however, such as civil wars, coups, and rebellions were not normed. Rather, their weighted scores were added directly into the final measure because these events indicate not only a serious and pervasive disruption but also because they tended to have consequences for and/or potentially to involve a vast number of a country's population. Further, unlike the former, it was assumed the probability these latter events would occur more frequently within a country was not necessarily a function of its population size. The complete instability measure, then, was constructed by summing for each country the weighted, and where appropriate, normed frequency of events which occurred during the years 1957–1965 (cf. Feierabend and Feierabend, 1971 and Sinden, 1974, for a discussion of the reliability and validity of this measure).

Because the validity of such a comprehensive index has been questioned (cf. Snyder and Kelly, 1977) the relationships with conflict are also examined using three measures of civil strife which were initially developed and used by Gurr. One of these, the magnitude of turmoil (MT), represents the total number of spontaneous, unstructured events, such as demonstrations, strikes, and riots which occurred in each country. A second indexes the magnitude of conspiracy (MC) as evidenced by organized but small-scale events such as assassinations, terrorism, coups, plots, and purges. The third is a composite index of the total magnitude of civil strife (TMCS). It combines the first two with each country's score for internal war, i.e., the amount of large-scale, organized conflict such as revolts and civil wars.[2] In constructing these measures, Gurr, like the Feierabends, took the pervasiveness, duration, and intensity of each event into account (see Gurr, 1972, pp. 188–191, 213–215, for details and the scores themselves). In addition, Gurr collected data on all but two of the 59 countries in the sample. However, unlike the Feierabend data, Gurr indexed events which occurred only during the years 1961–1965. More importantly, the two sets of data were collected independently of one another from different original sources. Furthermore, the construction of the individual measures was entirely different. Nevertheless, the correlation between the two indexes is a relatively high .82. This suggests that the results of the empirical tests will be strenghtened in so far as the analysis is consistent using both sets of instability measures.

The major independent variable in this study is social inequality. Because the hypotheses under study emphasize different forms of this phenomenon, it has been operationalized in two ways. One, the Gini index of sectoral income inequality indicates the degree to which a country's Gross Domestic Product around 1960 was equally distributed among workers in its major industrial sectors (cf. Alker and Russett, 1966; Cutright, 1967; and Kuznets, 1963). Clearly, this measure is limited because it accounts for income distribution only across large economic sectors such as agriculture, manufacturing, commerce, etc., and not the distribution of income among individuals within a sector (cf. Paukert, 1973). Nevertheless, it is the only available measure of inequality which is comparable across a large number of nations around 1960 (cf. Kuznets, 1963; Cutright, 1967, Jackman, 1975, for discussions of reliability and validity).[3]

In addition to income, land inequality is also operationalized in this study. Although a number of indices of this form of inequality are available, one which Russett (1964) employed is used here. This is the Gini index of the concentration of land holdings. It calculates the degree to which a country's productive land area is unevenly distributed throughout its whole population around 1960 (data reported in Taylor and Hudson, 1972). Unfortunately, these data are not available for the entire sample. Therefore, the effects of land inequality can only be analyzed in a subset of 45 countries.[4]

Finally, because inequality is predicted to have different consequences dependent upon the economic type and level of a society, it is necessary as well to categorize countries along these critical economic dimensions.

A summary measure, useful for this purpose, is the amount of energy consumption (expressed in kilograms of coal or its equivalent) per capita. For the following analysis the countries in the sample were classified on the basis of their energy consumption in 1960 into one of three groups (data reported in Taylor and Hudson, 1972). One, nominally labeled "premodern-agricultural," includes all those countries where the annual energy consumption was less than 300 kilograms of coal per capita in 1960. The "modernizing" group includes all of those countries where the annual energy consumption ranged between 300 to 2,000 kilograms of coal or its equivalent. Finally the "modern" group includes all of those where more than 2,000 kilograms per capita were consumed per year.

DATA ANALYSIS

That this procedure effectively distinguishes categories of countries on economic as well as a number of other dimensions can be seen from data presented in Table 1. For example, the countries which consume the most energy also average more than seven times as much wealth, as measured by GNP per capita, than do those countries with the lowest levels of energy consumption. In addition, the high-energy consumers also have much larger urban populations, as measured by the percentage of people who live in metropolitan areas of 100,000 or more (Davis, 1969, as presented in Taylor and Hudson, 1972), than do either of the modernizing or premodern group.

A similar pattern is evident when each group's mean industrial diversification score is compared. This measure summarizes the extent to which a country's labor force is evenly distributed through what the United Nations classifies as the nine major industrial sectors of an economy. In this form, this measure has been used in a number of studies to indicate the extent of a country's division of labor (Gibbs and Browning, 1966; Gibbs and Martin, 1962).[5] A score near one on this index indicates that a nation's work force is evenly distributed throughout the industrial sectors, whereas scores closer to zero indicate a greater degree of labor force concentration in only one or a few of these sectors. With the countries sampled here, inspection of the original data shows that labor is predominantly concentrated in agriculture in those countries with lower diversification scores. Countries with the highest scores, on the other hand, have much more diversified industrial economies. Therefore, it is not surprising to find that countries in this group also use much more energy and have more wealth and much larger urban populations.

Finally, Table 1 also presents the average level of inequality for each group of countries. As can be seen, both income and land, in general,

Table 1. Means and standard deviations of inequality and
economic variables by economic category, around 1960.

Variables   Economic Categories

                                          Premodern-agricultural (N=23)

	X̄	SD
GNP/Capita	$ 196.51	106.86
Energy Consumption	161.43	74.21
Percent Urban	14.07	6.61
Industrial Diversification	.6231	.1630
Income Inequality	35.73	16.14
Land Inequality[a]	67.21	15.38

                                          Modernizing (N=19)

	X̄	SD
GNP/Capita	$ 550.46	372.10
Energy Consumption	886.32	430.45
Percent Urban	28.35	9.59
Industrial Diversification	.8324	.0737
Income Inequality	29.67	14.32
Land Inequality[b]	69.28	18.20

                                          Modern-industrial (N=17)

	X̄	SD
GNP/Capita	$1507.39	607.30
Energy Consumption	3570.88	1517.34
Percent Urban	37.38	13.66
Industrial Diversification	.9001	.0268
Income Inequality	17.29	11.27
Land Inequality[c]	66.39	13.08

Source: Taylor and Hudson (1972).

Definitions:
Premodern agricultural—energy consumption less than 300 kilograms/capita/year.
Modernizing—energy consumption between 300 and 2,000 kilograms/capita/year.
Modern—industrial—energy consumption more than 2,000 kilograms/capita/year.

Notes:
[a]N=14
[b]N=16
[c]N=15

become more evenly distributed as one moves from the premodern to the modern group, although land inequality does remain relatively high in all three groups. These particular patterns are important from the point of view of Russett's poverty thesis. The latter predicts inequality will be a greater source of disruption in the poorer countries precisely because they experience a greater disparity in the distribution of wealth and resources.

To test this hypothesis, zero-order correlations were computed between income inequality and instability for both the total sample and each economic subgroup. If Russett is correct, we should expect to find a strong positive relationship between the two variables in the premodern group. By way of contrast, recall that both Marx and Durkheim predict this association will be found only in the richer, more industrially developed countries.

Data related to these hypotheses are presented in Table 2. It should be noted first that income inequality manifests a low but significant positive relationship with instability across the entire sample. However, once controls for type of society are introduced, it can be seen that this finding is misleading. In fact, reading down the table, one finds that the relationship between the two variables is different depending upon the economic type and level of the society.

On the one hand, the strong and significant positive correlations which exist between income inequality and instability only in the modern-industrial group of countries provide clear support for the hypothesis derived from the work of both Marx and Durkheim. This is especially the case with the Feierabend index which manifests a very strong association of .85 with inequality. Similar correlations with the Gurr indexes, with the exception of turmoil, are of the same magnitude, significance, and direction. While the relationship with turmoil is not significant, the fact that its moderate size and positive direction occur only among this group of countries makes it consistent with this hypothesis as well.

Table 2. Pearson correlations between income inequality and measures of political conflict for the total sample and within economic categories.

Inequality	Feierabend Total	TMCS	Gurr MC	MT	Country Categories
Income	.25*	.25*	.31**	-.04	Total sample
Income	.86**	.69**	.78**	.34	Modern (N=17 or 16)
Income	.19	.10	.43*	.40	Modernizing (N=19 or 18)
Income	-.31	-.16	-.07	-.05	Premodern (N=23)

* = p ⟨ .05
** = p ⟨ .01

On the other hand, contrary to Russett (1964) and the poverty thesis, one finds no significant relationship between income and inequality and any of the instability measures in the premodern group of countries. Furthermore, what little relationship does appear is negative rather than the predicted positive. However, this analysis can be challenged as a refutation of Russett's thesis because it does not directly consider the issue of land tenure. For him, this was the critical form of imbalance because there are so few economic alternatives to farming in this group of countries. Therefore, the Gini land inequality index was correlated with instability, again within the total sample and each of the three categories.

From the results presented in Table 3, it can be seen that this form of inequality does manifest a significant but moderate positive relationship with all the indicators of conflict across all the countries. Clearly, however, these effects are not uniform in all the categories of countries. Again, Russett's hypothesis, with one exception, is not supported as the association is negative in the premodern group. The exception is with the conspiracy measure which does have a moderate, positive relationship with the uneven distribution of land. Although not significant, it does suggest this form of inequality may play some role in generating small-scale but highly organized reactions, including assassinations, terrorism, and small-scale guerrilla wars.

Recall that Moore (1966) and others have suggested that disparities in the distribution of land would be disruptive where the modernization process, especially the introduction of production for a market, disrupts traditional ways of life and land use patterns. Because these countries occupy middle ranges on such development indicators as energy consumption, urbanization, and industrial diversification suggests that they are undergoing this transition process. Consequently this finding is entirely consistent with Moore's argument.

To this point this analysis has not considered the question of spurious

Table 3. Pearson correlations between land inequality and measures of political conflict for the total sample and within economic categories.

Inequality	Conflict Measures				Country Categories
	Feierabend Total	TMCS	Gurr MC	MT	
Land	.43**	.47**	.51**	.29*	Total sample
Land	.50*	.52*	.54*	.33	Modern (N=15 or 14)
Land	.72**	.72**	.63**	.52*	Modernizing (N=16)
Land	-.17	-.08	.42	-.04	Premodern (N=14)

* = p < .05
** = p < .01

relationships, an issue which is critical to the problem under study. This is so because it is known that indicators of development and wealth generally have negative relationships with both inequality and instability. In fact, in their prior research Nagel (1974), Parvin (1973), Russo (1972), and Sigelman and Simpson (1976) all report what little relationship there was between inequality and instability diminished when a control for each country's GNP per capita was introduced into the analysis.

Because these past studies show that the wealth factor has an important effect on this relationship, partial correlations were computed between both forms of inequality and all the conflict measures while controlling for GNP per capita in 1960. Given the fact that the countries have already been categorized on one measure of economic development, energy consumption, it may seem redundant to proceed with an additional control for wealth which is highly correlated with the former. This is not the case, however, because the question being raised is whether or not within each category some countries are wealthier than the others and, further, whether these varying levels of absolute wealth affect the relationship between inequality and instability. The amount of variation, as indicated by the ranges of GNP per capita $2,687.20, $1,579.50, and $458.10, in the modern, modernizing, and premodern groups, is substantial and therefore sufficient to allow for a meaningful analysis.

Tables 4 and 5 present the results of these partial operations computed for the entire sample as well as within each category. If the initial zero-order correlations between inequality and instability had been spurious, they would now be reduced to near-zero. By the same token, if, in the previous analysis, imputed relationships were being suppressed in the premodern group, they should now become manifest in this new operation. A check of the partial correlations indicates that neither a substantial

Table 4. Partial correlations between income equality and measures of political conflict with controls for GNP per capita; for the total sample and within economic categories.

| Inequality | Feierabend Total | Conflict Measures | | | Country Categories |
		TMCS	Gurr MC	MT	
Income	.06	.08	.13	-.15	Total sample
Income	.84**	.68**	.69**	.37	Modern
Income	.04	-.04	.30	-.43	Modernizing
Income	-.20	.12	-.24	-.17	Premodern

* = p .05
** = p .01

Table 5. Partial correlations between land inequality and measures
of political conflict with controls for GNP per capita;
for the total sample and within economic categories.

| Inequality | Feierabend | | Gurr | | Country Categories |
	Conflict Measures				Country Categories
	Total	TMCS	MC	MT	
Land	.41**	.46**	.51**	.23*	Total sample
Land	.51*	.51*	.57*	.34	Modern
Land	.68**	.68**	.58*	.52*	Modernizing
Land	.04	.11	.47	.04	Premodern

* = p .0 5
** = p .0 1

reduction in the initial relationships nor an uncovering of hidden relationships occurs. The original analysis has been substantiated. Regardless of
the level of wealth within categories, both income and land inequality
remain strong predictors of instability and conflict only in the modern and
modernizing countries.

SUMMARY DISCUSSION

It would be a mistake to assume that inequality is the single necessary and
sufficient cause of political conflict. In fact, various investigators have
examined a number of additional factors, including political mobilization,
repression, and relative deprivation, which have not been presented in
this chapter (Snyder and Tilly, 1972; Gurr, 1972).

Clearly this chapter has not attempted to evaluate these issues. Rather,
it has focused upon only one factor, social inequality and its imputed
relationship or lack thereof, to political instability. In general, the findings
presented here contradict a number of important and widely held notions
concerning the role it plays in the generation of this type of conflict. First,
higher levels of inequality have neither uniform nor universal effects on
instability. Rather, a strong positive relationship occurs only in certain
identifiable types of societies. Second, this association does not appear,
as is commonly assumed, among the poorer nations. This does not mean
that these countries are more stable than the others. In fact, as a group,
they averaged higher instability scores than either of the other two
groups. What it does mean is that, at the national level at least, inequality
does not differentiate the more stable from the less stable of these premodern countries.

Finally, the findings do support contentions that social inequality becomes increasingly important as a source of disruption as countries begin to modernize and remains so even after modern, industrial economies have been achieved. This, perhaps, is the most important finding, because it brings into question a set of assumptions which have obtained a formidable stature. As articulated in the logic of industrialism thesis (Kerr, *et al.*, 1964), they have influenced not only academia but, more importantly, those who make and administer social policy. The central point of this thesis maintains the industrialization process, in and of itself, is inherently beneficial and stabilizing because it creates those conditions that promote social order. It is argued that this occurs not just because of improved capacities for providing necessary goods and services, but primarily because industrial development reduces the social inequities which divide a society. Consequently, it is assumed that all forms of economic assistance which promote the industrial development of the less developed countries would be entirely beneficial. At the same time, it is also assumed that a developed country warrants no similiar active intervention in its social and economic organization because it already receives the inherent benefits of an industrial economy.

It is precisely assumptions such as these which are challenged by the theories of Marx, Durkheim, Moore, and others. What these studies point to is not simply the distribution of land, or occupations, or income and wealth, but primarily to the behavior of elites who control the patterns of distribution which take place. For it is where actions are taken to perpetuate elite power and privilege that one finds displacement from the land (Moore), occupational opportunities closed (Durkheim), and workers being exploited (Marx). It is these inequities which, in turn, become major sources of conflict and instability.

This suggests, then, that policies of economic assistance to a premodern or modernizing country would have serious consequences for it if the policy does nothing to reduce inequality at the same time that the modernization process advances, especially in market agriculture and industrial development. As these theories imply, if inequality is not reduced, then those policies, in whatever form, have a greater probability of *increasing* rather than decreasing conflict and disorder within these societies. This is so because the development process creates those social conditions in which inequality becomes especially problematic.

Equally disturbing, from the same point of view, are those policies of inaction and complacency which the logic of industrialism implies are appropriate for the developed countries. It is suggested that, partly because of this thesis, there is a tendency to react passively to existing problems. Even more important, however, there is also a tendency to stifle the development of creative and constructive policies to meet problems within these countries, when such activities are warranted. As Durkheim makes clear, while societies develop extensive divisions of labor in order to resolve conflicts brought on by increased competition for scarce resources, this development by itself is not sufficient to remove another source of conflict, social inequality. Positive action is required as well. "The task of the most advanced societies," he wrote, "is . . . a work of justice . . . to make social relations always more equitable, so as to assure the free development of all our socially useful forces" (Durkheim, 1933, p. 387). To do otherwise would threaten not only the social "harmony" of those societies but the very "existence" of their people as well.

APPENDIX 1

The Sample

Modern	Modernizing	Premodern
*Australia	*Argentina	Cambodia
*Austria	*Brazil	*Costa Rica
*Belgium	Chile	*Ecuador
Canada	*Colombia	*Egypt
*Denmark	+Cyprus	*El Salvador
France	*Finland	*Guatemala
+*Luxembourg	Greece	*Honduras
*Netherlands	*Iran	Indonesia
*New Zealand	*Iraq	*India
*Norway	*Ireland	Jordan
**Poland	Israel	*Libya
Portugal	*Italy	Morocco
*South Africa	*Japan	*Nicaragua
*Sweden	*Mexico	*Pakistan
*United Kingdom	*Panama	Paraguay
*United States	*Peru	*Philippines
*Venezuela	*Spain	*South Korea
*West Germany	*Taiwan	Sri Lanka
	*Uruguay	Sudan
	**Yugoslavia	Syria
		*Thailand
		Tunisia
		*Turkey

*Countries for which land inequality data are available.
**These countries were included only in the sample in which land inequality was analyzed.
+Countries omitted from the analysis with Gurr data.

APPENDIX 2

One problem with correlations is that, as standardized measures, they are sensitive to artificial changes in the ratio of the standard deviations of the two variables being correlated as well as to changes in "true" effects. Thus differences in the size of correlations between the same variables computed within two or more subgroups may only be a function of statistical artifact and not of factors suggested by theory. As a result, misleading or incorrect inferences may be drawn. This problem can be overcome by use of analysis of covariance in the form of a multiple regression using dummy variables. In this procedure one tests for equality of slopes (in this case the slope of inequality and conflict within each category of countries) through a test of statistical interaction in the multiple regression (cf. Wright, 1976). The data were subjected to this analysis which confirmed the results of the correlational analysis; that is, the slope of the inequality and instability variable do differ across the different categories of countries. The results with the Feierabend data are presented in Tables 6 and 7 while the more familiar correlations are presented in the body of the text under the assumption that they are more comprehensible to a wider audience.

Table 6. Regression models of relationships between income inequality and the Feierabend measure of conflict and economic category.

Model	Equations*	R^2
Model I	$Y = a + b_1 X$	
	$Y = 32.7 + (.559)X + e$	.06
Model II	$Y = a + b_1 X + b_2 M + b_3 N$	
	$Y = 44.1 + (.363)X + (-15.7)M + (-3.8)N + e$	.09
Model III	$Y = a + b_1 X + b_2 M + b_3 N + b_4 O + b_5 P$	
	$Y = 78.7 + (-.606)X + (-94.3)M + (-41.6)N + (3.5)O + (1.1)P + e$	.34

Tests for significance of difference between models

Model contrasts: Test for statistical interaction

II vs. III	df 2, 53	$F = 10.04$ ($p < .01$)

* Y = Feierabend Instability Measure
  X = Gini Index of Income Inequality
  M = 1 if a modern country; 0 otherwise
  N = 1 if a modernizing country; 0 otherwise
  O = Inequality among Modern Countries; 0 otherwise
  P = Inequality among Modernizing Countries; 0 otherwise

Table 7. Regression models of relationships between land inequality and the Feierabend measure of conflict and economic category.

Model	Equations*	R^2
Model I	$Y = a + b_1 X$	
	$Y = -18.5 + (.899)X + e$	.16
Model II	$Y = a + b_1 X + b_2 M + b_3 N$	
	$Y = -10.3 + (.878)X + (-18.5)M + (-3.9)N + e$	.22
Model III	$Y = a + b_1 X + b_2 M + b_3 N + b_4 O + b_5 P$	
	$Y = 65.6 + (-.252)X + (-152.7)M + (-109.5)N + (1.99)O + (1.54)P + e$	.35

Tests for significance of difference between models

Model contrasts: Test for statistical interaction

II vs. III   df 2, 37 $F = 3.70$ ($p < .05$)

* Y = Feierabend Instability Measure
  X = Gini Index of Land Inequality
  M = 1 if a modern country; 0 otherwise
  N = 1 if a modernizing country; 0 otherwise
  O = Land Inequality among Modern Countries; 0 otherwise
  P = Land Inequality among Modernizing Countries; 0 otherwise

FOOTNOTES

*A revision of a paper presented at the 72nd Annual Meeting of the American Sociological Society, September, 1977, Chicago. The data used in this paper were made available, in part, by the Inter-University Consortium for Political Research. The data were originally collected by Charles Lewis Taylor and Michael C. Hudson and by Ivo K. Feierabend, Rosalind L. Feierabend, and Betty A. Nesvold. Neither the original collectors of the data nor the consortium bear any responsibility for the analysis or interpretations presented here.

1. The complete list included: strikes, demonstrations, boycotts, arrests, suicides of significant political persons, martial law, executions, assassinations, terrorism, sabotage, guerrilla warfare, civil war, coups d'état, revolts, exiles, dissolution of legislatures, resignations of politically important persons, organization of new governments, reshuffle of governments, severe trouble within a nongovernmental organization, organization of oppoition parties, and governmental actions of specific groups (Feierabend, Feierabend, and Nesvold, 1971).

2. Separate correlations were computed for Gurr's other measure, the magnitude of internal war, as well. While the results were consistent with the reported analysis, they are not included in this discussion because only eleven of the countries had scores greater than zero on this measure. Because so few countries do vary on this index, it is difficult to interpret what any computed correlation means. Therefore, they were left out of the following analysis.

3. The majority of Gini income index scores were taken from Taylor and Hudson (1972). In addition, I computed a Gini index for five nations (Ceylon, Iran, Iraq, Indonesia, and Taiwan) from data reported in the *Yearbook of Labour Statistics* (I.L.O.) and the *Yearbook of National Account Statistics* (United States).

4. In order to make this sample of 4 countries as comparable as possible with the one Russett (1964) used, two socialist states, Poland and Yugoslavia, were included for the analysis of the effects of land inequality. In addition whenever there is a loss of cases the possibility always exists that bias will be introduced into one's sample. In fact, bias was minimized as a comparison of those countries removed with those which remain in the analysis showed the two groups to be similiar on all dimensions of inequality, instability, and economy.

5. Most countries report employment data using the United Nations' nine-category International Standard Industrial Classification. These categories include: agriculture; forestry, hunting, and fishing; mining and quarrying; manufacturing; construction; electricity, gas, water, and sanitary services; commerce; transport, storage, and communications; and services. The industrial diversification scores were computed from data reported in the *Yearbook of Labour Statistics*.

REFERENCES

Alker, Hayward R. and Bruce M. Russett (1966) "Indices for Comparing Inequality." Pages 349–372. In Richard L. Meritt and Stein Rokkan (eds.), *Comparing Nations: The Uses of Quantitative Data in Cross-National Research*. New Haven: Yale University Press.

Cutright, Phillips (1967) "Inequality: A Cross-National Analysis" *American Sociological Review* 32 (August): 562–578.

Davis, Kingsley (1969) *The World's Metropolitan Areas*. Berkeley: University of California Press.

Durkheim, Emile (1933) *The Division of Labor in Society*, trans. by George Simpson. New York: Free Press.

Feierabend, Ivo K. and Rosalind L. Feierabend (1971) "Aggressive Behaviors within Politics, 1948–1962: A Cross-National Study." Pages 141–166 in J. W. Gillespie, and B. A. Nesvold (eds.), *Macro-Quantitative Analysis*. Beverly Hills, CA: Sage.

——— Rosalind L. Feierabend, and Betty A. Nesvold (1971) *Political Events Project 1948–1965*. Ann Arbor, MI: Inter-University Consortium for Political Research.

Freiderich, Paul (1970) *Agrarian Revolt in a Mexican Village*. Englewood Cliffs, NJ: Prentice-Hall.

Gibbs, Jack P. and Harley L. Browning (1966) "The Division of Labor, Technology, and the Organization of Production in Twelve Countries." *American Sociological Review* 31 (February): 81–92.

——— and Walter T. Martin (1962) "Urbanization Technology and the Division of Labor: International Patterns." *American Sociological Review* 27 (October): 667–677.

Gurr, Ted R. (1972) "A Causal Model of Civil Strife: A Comparative Analysis Using New Indices." Pages 184–222 in Ivo K. Feierabend, Rosalind L. Feierabend, and Ted R. Gurr (eds.), *Anger, Violence, and Politics*. Englewood Cliffs, NJ: Prentice-Hall.

——— and Raymond Duvall (1973) "Civil Conflict in the 1960s." *Comparative Political Studies* 6 (July): 136–169.

International Labour Office (Various years) *Yearbook of Labour Statistics*. London: International Labour Office.

Jackman, Robert W. (1975) *Politics and Social Equality: A Comparative Analysis*. New York: Wiley.

Kerr, Clark *et al.* (1964) *Industrialism and Industrial Man: The Problems of Labor and Management in Economic Growth*. New York: Oxford University Press.

Kuznets, Simon (1963) "Quantitative Aspects of the Economic Growth of Nations: VIII. The Distribution of Income by Size." *Economic Development and Cultural Changes* 11 (January): part 2.

Marx, Karl (1971) *On Revolution*. Ed. and trans. by Saul K. Padover, New York: McGraw-Hill.

Mitchell, Edward J. (1968) "Inequality and Insurgency: A Statistical Study of South Vietnam." *World Politics*, 20 (April): 421–438.

Moore, Barrington, Jr. (1966) *Social Origins of Dictatorship and Democracy: Lord and Peasant in the Making of the Modern World*. Boston: Beacon Press.

Nagel, Jack (1974) "Inequality and Discontent: A Non-linear Hypothesis." *World Politics* 26 (July): 453–472.

Paige, Jeffery M. (1970) "Inequality and Insurgence in Vietnam: A Re-Analysis." *World Politics* 23 (October): 24–37.

Paranzimo, Dennis (1972) "Inequality and Insurgency in Vietnam: A Further Re-Analysis." *World Politics*, 24 (July): 565–578.

Parvin, Manoucher (1973) "Economic Determinants of Political Unrest." *Journal of Conflict Resolution* 17 (June): 271–296.

Paukert, Felix (1973) "Income Distribution at Different Levels of Development." *International Labour Review*, 108 (August–September): 97–125.

Russett, Bruce M. (1964) "Inequality and Instability: The Relation of Land Tenure to Politics." *World Politics*, 16 (April): 442–454.

Russo, Anthony J., Jr. (1972) "Economic and Social Correlates of Government Control in South Vietnam." Pages 314–324 in Ivo K. Feierabend, Rosalind L. Feierabend, and Ted R. Gurr (eds.), *Anger, Violence, and Politics*, Englewood-Cliffs, NJ: Prentice-Hall.

Sigelman, Lee and Miles Simpson (1977) "A Cross-National Test of the Linkage Between Economic Inequality and Political Violence." *Journal of Conflict Resolution*, 21 (March): 105–128.

Sinden, Peter G. (1974) *Durkheim's Division of Labor and Political Stability: A Cross-National Investigation*. Unpublished Ph.D. dissertation. Amherst: University of Massachusetts.

Snyder, David and William R. Kelly (1977) "Conflict Intensity, Media Sensitivity, and the Validity of Newpaper Data." *American Sociological Review* 42 (February): 105–123.

―――― and Charles Tilly (1972) "Hardship and Collective Violence in France, 1830 to 1960." *American Sociological Review* 37 (October): 520–532.

Taylor, Charles L. and Michael C. Hudson (1972) *World Handbook of Political and Social Indicators*. New Haven: Yale University Press.

Tilly, Charles (1964) *The Vendee*. Cambridge, MA: Harvard University Press.

United Nations (Various years) *Yearkbook of National Account Statistics*. New York: United Nations.

Wolf, Eric R. (1969) *Peasant Wars of the Twentieth Century*. New York: Harper and Row.

Wright, Gerald C., Jr. (1976) "Linear Models for Evaluating Conditional Relationships." *American Journal of Political Science*. 20 (May): 349–373.

INTERORGANIZATIONAL RELATIONS: A COMPARISON OF WESTERN AND MAOIST APPROACHES*

Bariman Taraki and David L. Westby

INTRODUCTION

Approaches to the study of formal organization in Western social science are generally rooted in certain presuppositions associated with liberal thought, particularly the liberal premise of the primacy of the social actor's interests and the moral presumtion of his or its right to pursue such interests under relatively unfettered conditions. These presuppositions are the deeply embedded "domain assumptions" of organization theory and have profound ramifications for all aspects of theory building: they are both a foundation for creative work and a limitation on the conceptual apparatus.

Comparative Social Research, Vol. 2, pp. 321–345.
Volume 1 published as Comparative Studies in Sociology
Copyright © 1979 by JAI Press, Inc.
ISBN 0-89232-112-1

More recently, the Maoist movement and revolution have given rise to extensive concern with organizational process in good part, at least, as a foundation for resolving the critical practical questions centering around the shape and function of an entirely new organizational matrix.

Concretely, this has been manifested most significantly in the universal collectivization of agriculture, "a result which no other postwar communist revolution has achieved" (Gray and Cavendish, 1968, p. 23) in the spread of elaborate organizational networks over the largest nation on earth and in the countrywide diffusion of scientific, educational, medical, and industrial networks of organizations. The theoretical study of the Maoist approach, however, has so far eluded the attention of Western observers. The few available works (Barnett, 1967; Schurmann, 1968) either stop short of arriving at theoretical generalizations in a way meaningful to the student of organization theory as the latter is understood in the West, or focus on the micro-organizational processes to the neglect of marco- and inter-organizational relations (Harding, 1971; Whyte, 1973; Andors, 1974b). Since the latter, as will be seen, is of much greater theoretical relevance, one purpose of this study is to throw some light on this subject.

Viewed in cross-cultural perspective, the character of interorganizational relations may be regarded, in preliminary fashion, as a function of the nature of organizational goals and the processes by which goals are defined and clarified.[1] Insofar as goals are determined by the internal dynamics of the organization, the interorganizational arena is one in which *diverse* goals are promoted and in which more or less autonomous organizations constitute *relatively* differentiated universes of information and resources; the flows of information and resources in society exhibit sharp discontinuities at the boundary of each organization.[2] If, on the other hand, goals are determined by processes other than the internal dynamics of each organization (e.g., the political process), and organizations are charged with realizing *delegated* goals, the interorganizational network becomes a sphere in which *uniform* goals and interests are pursued and in which the subordination of each organization to the external goal-setting agency theoretically gives rise to relatively open universes of information and resources. In the latter instance, the flow of information

*Bariman Taraki is a research analyst with the Department of Community and Family Medicine of the College of Medicine of the University of Arizona. His present research interests include work on the barriers to interorganizational cooperation in the delivery of health services to rural Arizona. He is also a student of the assumptions behind Western organizational theory on which he has published several recent articles. David L. Westby teaches sociology at Pennsylvania State. His major interests are in theory, social movements, and political sociology. He recently published (1976) *The Clouded Vision: The Student Movement in the United States in the Sixties.*

and resources within the organization is ideally continuous with that in the interorganizational network. It should be noted at this point that these alternative models are *not* descriptive of what Blau and Scott (1963, p. 57), for example, call "commonweal" organizations and "business concerns." In the West, organizational behavior (and the theory derived therefrom) is so deeply implanted in the pluralist premise of the actor's autonomy that researchers (Hoover Commission, 1952, p. 291; Randall, 1973) have found little difference between private and public agencies in this respect.

Related to the above distinction is another important difference: the relative salience or the primacy of the interorganizational network. In Western theories, interorganizational relations, though considered important, are still regarded as theoretically subordinate to the study of internal organizational dynamics; the latter continues to receive a much larger share of attention (Zeit, 1974, p. 132). Most theorists study interorganizational relations essentially from the perspective of the focal organization (Thompson and McEwen, 1958, p. 29; Evan, 1966, p. 178; Van de Ven, Emmet, and Koenig, 1974, p. 122; Mindlin and Aldrich, 1975, p. 390). The Maoist approach, by contrast, shifts the emphasis from any given organization to the interorganizational network as a whole, and this dictates a different method and analytic approach.

BASIC CONTRASTS

As we noted at the outset, Western organization theory, in its broadest underlying theoretical structure, incorporates the essential feature of the liberal pluralist social environment—the existence as well as legitimacy of *autonomous* entities of social behavior. In an early study of the subject, Hemphill and Westie (1950, p. 326) found that "autonomy," defined as "the degree to which a group functions independently of other groups and occupies an independent position in society" emerged as a reliable dimension of organizational behavior. Other researchers (Gouldner, 1959, p. 258; Litwak and Hylton, 1962, p. 413; Levine *et al.*, 1963, p. 1183; Guetzkow, 1966, p. 25; Aiken and Hage, 1968; Alford, 1974, p. 485; Hage, 1974) have, in one way or another, retained the assumption of organizational autonomy.

Although a significant strand in organization theory (Emery and Trist, 1965; Evan, 1966; Terreberry, 1968) emphasizes interdependence more than autonomy, even here the assumption of autonomy is retained with respect to the organization's definition of interests and goals, if not with regard to the organization's actual activity.[3] The organization's autonomous definition of goals and interests is the precondition for interdependence, for interests and goals, though autonomously *defined,* cannot be autonomously *promoted.*

This primacy of the actor's interests also implies that from the point of view of any particular organization, the character and content of inter-organizational relations are largely a function of, and dependent upon, the internal dynamics of that organization, its definition of goals, the constancy or elusiveness of its goals, and the type of resources needed for the fulfillment of these goals. The quality and content of cooperative exchange relationships into which the organization ought to enter are determined by these factors. In an early study, Form and Nosow (1958, p. 244) discovered that the integration of organizations participating in rescue operations in times of disaster becomes difficult because of the differences in their structures, the varying conditions characterizing their community performance, the differences in their perception of each other, and the tendency for each organization to preserve its self-identity over its cooperative identity. Levine and White (1961, p. 593) view interorganizational relations as exchange relations made necessary by scarcity, and in a later study of health and welfare agencies, Levine, White, and Paul (1963, p. 1197) discovered that various barriers to greater interorganizational cooperation had developed because the function of each agency had taken shape in a laissez faire manner as each attempted to meet its own objectives independently. This dependency of the interorganizational relations upon the internal processes of interacting organizations is also asserted, explicitly or implicity, in findings by Form and Miller (1960, p. 6), Litwak and Hylton (1962), Emery and Trist (1965), Turk (1973, p. 40), Randall (1973, p. 236) and Allen (1974, p. 393).

By asserting the primacy of collective (as opposed to constituent) interests, the Maoist position reverses the relationship between intra- and interorganizational relations. The latter becomes the key factor affecting the quality of *intra*organizational relations. Although this point is acknowledged (Richman, 1969, p. 767), and although it derives from the basic political premises of the regime, as in the practice of "unified planning" (Mao, 1957, p. 197) and in the role of the Communist Party and the Trade Unions (Harper, 1969, p. 84), its implications with respect to organization theory and practice are as yet to be worked out. For example, the fact that organizational goals are delegated by an agency external to the organization itself gives rise to a fundamentally different conception of *organizational rationality.* Rationality and efficiency are not measured on the basis of the performance of a single enterprise but of the interorganizational network as a whole. Economic accounting is practiced in the sphere of the society as a whole: "Every industrial enterprise should start from the common interests of the national economy and subordinate its partial interests to those of the whole" (Tan Hsi, 1975, p. 52). This means that an enterprise ought to *incur losses* if these contribute to the efficiency of the total network of interorganizational activities. The Shanghai Wrist Watch Factory, for example, reportedly opted for the manufacturing of less profitable but more urgently needed variety of watches "in consideration of the purchasing power of the majority of the people" (Union Research Service, 1974, p. 304).

The preference for small and medium sized (as opposed to large scale) enterprises is also informed by this interorganizational focus of rationality and efficiency:

> Small and medium-sized enterprises . . . need less investment and are easier to equip, and their techniques can be mastered more quickly. They can be built in a short time and both the turnover of funds and accumulation are fast. Local authorities can make full use of these advantages and, in the light of available conditions, including manpower and material resources, set up their own enterprises. Thus all positive factors can be brought into play and local resources fully utilized, resulting in a more rational distribution of industries. Viewed apart, the small and medium-sized enterprises are insignificant both in scale and ouput, but together, their output is quite a large amount. Take chemical fertilizer for instance. The output of synthetic ammonia by small chemical fertilizer plants in Kiangsu Province today is four times the total produced by its large plants [*Peking Review*, 1974d, p. 24].

In Western theories, the primacy of the actor's interests, of necessity, leads to the recognition of conflict in interorganizational relations. After a brief dalliance during the earlier hegemony of functionalism (Parsons, 1956), organization theory has gravitated toward accepting the reality of conflict—a view which even Parsons (1974, p. 9) has recently come to acknowledge. Conflictual relationships are the logical result of the presence of autonomous interests in the liberal pluralist context. A representative case in point is the dispute over the Kings River project in California. According to the Hoover Commission (1952, p. 291) two separate projects, one by the Corp of Engineers and another by the Bureau of Reclamation, were proposed to the Congress in February 1940. Each wanted to construct a multipurpose reservoir on the Kings River, but each had quite different approaches, philosophies, and clientele. Among other factors, the conflict was said to be caused by their divergent definition of interests (Hoover Commission, 1952, pp. 296–297).

Understanding interorganizational relations as basically conflictual is one of those issues on which Western theories have arrived at a broad consensus (Dimock, 1952, pp. 290–291; Form and Nosow, 1958, p. 236; Miller, 1958; Black and Kase, 1963; Reid, 1964; Litwak and Hylton, 1962,

p. 397; Levine, White and Paul, 1963, p. 1197; Turk, 1973, p. 47). Paradoxically, the reality of conflict and the resultant need to enhance one's power also creates an imperative for interorganizational cooperation as well. Perrucci and Pilisuk (1970, p. 1056) conceptualize power as "interorganizational ties which result in the creation of resource networks which can be mobilized and brought to bear upon particular community issues." These resource networks could be identified through the overlapping executive positions held by persons in different organizations. Allen's (1974, p. 393) study of the 50 largest financial corporations reveals that the uncertainties resulting from the potentially disruptive unilateral actions of other corporations creates the need for "corporate interlocking" as a means of anticipating and controlling such uncertainty. A similar view of interorganizational cooperation is to be found also in many of the "power elite" theories (Hunter, 1953; Presthus, 1964; Mills, 1956), the literature on oligopolies and monopolies (Pfeffer and Leblebici, 1973, p. 459) and the so-called "ecologists" (e.g., Duncan, 1972).

In the Maoist model, rivalry and conflict between organizations are regarded as evidence of incipient capitalism (*Peking Review*, 1975a, p. 16). The "unified plan" of the state is predicated on the possibility of harmonious interorganizational relations[4] (*Peking Review*, 1976, p. 24). In Western theories, the enhancement of an organization's combative capacities is essential for the attainment of maximum efficiency. In the Maoist model—in which rationality is defined within a societal focus— the goal of efficiency is considered a function of maximum interorganizational cooperation. This is exemplified by the experience of four communes around the Fan-chia embankment of the Haihao River. The communes and their brigades reportedly joined their forces to dig up 43 large ditches and canals more than 250 *li* in length (one *li* is equal to one-third of a mile), built more than 23,000 *mu* of terraced and striped fields (one *mu* is equal to one-sixth of an acre), and laid more than 42,000 *mu* of garden fields. In 1972, when over 200 milimeters of continuous rainfall had occurred, they drained all the water first into Hsuan-hui River and then into the sea, and thus achieved a bumper harvest in agriculture (*Union Research Service*, 1973m, p. 203). In the Canton Iron and Steel Works, a system of handing over and taking shifts was organized among three work sections in order to improve efficiency. The result was that the workshops reportedly achieved the highest record of daily output during 1973 (*Union Research Service*, 1973k, p. 43). The Party committees of the Chinghai Petroleum Administration Bureau and the Transport Department subordinate to it joined their forces and, in cooperation with other units, overfulfilled the September quota for the transport of pipes and equipment in only seven days (*Union Research Service*, 1973l, pp. 191–192.

THE DIFFERING FOCI OF INTEGRATION

In Western theories, the relative autonomy of organizations and the discontinuity in the flow of information and resources at organizational boundaries confine the focus of integration to the processes within the organization: integration acquires a micro-focus. The relations within organizations" (March and Simon, 1958, p. 190). Whereas interorganizacoordination" as opposed to "diffuse and variable relations among organizations" (March and Simon, 1958, p. 190.) Whereas interorganizational relations are viewed as conflictual, intraorganizational analysis assumes that conflict beyond a certain level will lead to a breakdown in organizational structure (Litwak and Hylton, 1962, p. 397).

Intraorganizational integration has been traditionally expressed in the concept of "span of control" (Hamilton, 1921, p. 229; Urwick, 1956); that is, the relationship between the optimum number of hierarchical levels and the optimum number of units within the same hierarchical level (Urwick, 1956; Simon, 1957, p. 26). The problem of integration is seen as one of reconciling the need for downward delegation with the necessity for outward dispersion. The optimization of both is said to yield the optimum degree of integration. Recent studies of the subject (Crazo and Yanouza, 1969; Hummon, 1970) also stress the relevance of the size of the span to the degree of integration. The size of the span is found related to organizational size, complexity, and coordination (Klatzky, 1970); the span of control is used as a measurement of the closeness of contact between a superior and his subordinate (Ouchi and Dowling, 1974, p. 357). In their study of colleges and small companies, Entwisle and Walton (1961, p. 523) discovered a small positive correlation between the size of the organization and the size of the span.

When the focus of integration is shifted from the micro- to the macro-level, the problem of horizontal and vertical integration must be confronted at the level of inter- as well as intraorganizational analysis. In the Maoist approach, the political determination of societal goals leads to an identity between organizational integration and political development. One result is that "micro-management," that is, the management of individual productive enterprises (Richman, 1969, p. 30) becomes an extension of "macro-management," the management of the economy as a whole (Richman, 1976, pp. 12–13). The microcosm which a single organization represents may be viewed as a replica of similar microcosms, each part of an integrated whole (Richman, 1969, p. 767). Whereas in Western theories the span of control is a conceptual device which summarizes the concurrent optimization of both horizontal and vertical integration, in the Maoist model this optimization takes the form of what will here be described as linear integration.

Linear integration is a sociological type meant to capture *one common aspect* of a number of *otherwise diverse* techniques, procedures, and processes. It may be defined as those processes and devices used to link up two horizontally and vertically differentiated units of organization, either inter- or intraorganizationally. The simplest model of linear integration may be represented as follows:

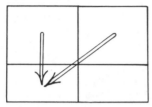 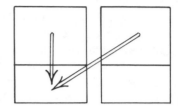

Intra-organizational   Interorganizational

With regard to Chinese social organization, linear integration has had many empirical facets. The most important contributory factor is the relatively greater authority of the Communist Party, its fractions and branches in various organizations, as compared to other units at the same level. The principle was elucidated by Wang Hung-wen in his "Report on the Revision of Party Constitution" to the Tenth National Congress of the Chinese Communist Party:

> Organizationally, the Party's centralized leadership should be given expression in two respects: First, as regards the relationship between various organizations at the same level, of the seven sectors—industry, agriculture, commerce, culture and education, the Army, the Government and the Party—it is the Party that exercises overall leadership, the Party is not parallel to the others and still less is it under the leadership of any other. Second, as regards the relationship between higher and lower levels, the lower level is subordinate to the higher level, and the entire party is subordinate to the Central Committee [*Peking Review*, 1973, p.32].

One manifestation of this pattern is the Party control of government agencies and enterprises both on a functional and a regional basis. In 1961, the Ninth Plenary Session of the Eighth Central Committee recreated the six bureaus of the Central Committee: Northeast, North, East, Central South, Southwest, and Northwest bureaus. Whereas the aim of these regional bureaus in the fifties was the deconcentration of power to the regions (Chang, 1975, p. 57), this time they were expected to "act for the Central Committee in strengthening leadership over the Party committees in the provinces, municipalities and autonomous regions'' (Union Research Institute, 1971, p. 178).

In the relationship between the Party and the government hierarchies, Barnett (1967, p. 18) observes, the Central Committee departments and committees form a kind of ''shadow government'' with each department or committee responsible for one of the several fields into which most government work falls, providing continuous policy guidance to all the government agencies within that field. Although this study was made in the sixties (Barnett, 1967), and the functional differentiation among the ''general systems'' into which government work was divided is now considerably more fluid and diffused, the principle of the linear integration of the Party with the government remains the same.

Another instance of linear integration is known as ''dual rule.''[5] As Schurmann (1968, p. 189) says, this means multiple rather than single channels of command and information. A lower level agency receives commands from more than one higher agency and must report to more than one. The theoretical ground for the principle of dual rule was implied by Mao's (1967, III, pp. 120–121) statement to the effect that:

> In relaying to subordinate units any task . . . a higher organization and its departments should in all cases go through the leader of the lower organization concerned so that he may assume responsibility; in this way both division of labor and unified centralized leadership are achieved. A department at a higher level should not go solely to its counterpart at the lower level (for instance, a higher department concerned with organization, propaganda, or anti-espionage should not go solely to the corresponding department at the lower level), leaving the person in overall charge of the lower organization (such as secretary, the chairman, the director of the school principal) in ignorance or without responsibility. Both the person in overall charge and the person with specific responsibility should be informed and given responsibility.

Dual rule is different from other varieties of linear integration in one crucial respect: The *content* of command and information received from *both* higher levels and of the reports submitted to them are qualitatively identical. They may be either matters of policy, or of task or supervisory functions, or a mixture of these; the duality of rule serves as a countervailing check for purposes of accountability. For this reason, the most clearcut example of dual rule, as Schurmann (1968, p. 189) indicates, is the use of coordinating agencies as supplementary supervisory bodies. An example of dual rule in the late 1950s and early 1960s was the relationship between the State Planning Commission and the State Economic Commission on the one hand, and on the other, the various departments and agencies delivering reports to, and receiving information from, these agencies (Schurmann, 1968, p. 189). At present, an instance of dual rule at lower levels is the dual control exercized both by the First Ministry of Machine Building and the municipality of Shenyang over the Shenyang Heavy Machinary Factory (Donnithorne, 1974, p. 774).

In other forms of linear integration, the responsibility of the lower echelon to each one of the higher echelon organs may differ in accordance with the latter's respective functions and jurisdiction. A lower organ may be accountable to one jurisdiction in policy matters and to another in operational matters, and in each case, the content and quality of information and command being exchanged may vary. Such is the relationship, for example, between the state organs and the Party committees at higher or similar levels (Bettelheim, 1974, p. 35).

In addition to the relatively greater authority of Party branches and committees, the institution of "political directorates" and "political departments" are avenues of linear integration most extensively utilized in the Army. At each level, the command structure is paralleled by a structure of political officers, supplementing the hierarchy of Party branches and Party committees (Starr, 1973, p. 223). A resolution of 1960 which still seems to be in effect clarified this relationship by stipulating that "the political director of a company is the agent of the political organ assigned to the company to conduct Party and mass work" (Union Research Institute, 1971, p. 372). Through the political directors, the Army is kept under civilian control, and the strictly hierarchical structure of command is mitigated by the countervailing chain of authority knitting the Army with the Party. Political departments are also in charge of registering compliance to the political line within the Army, providing an added counterpoise to the drift of the military toward professionalism. In the "Learn from the PLA (People's Liberation Army)" movement launched in 1964, hierarchies of political departments were also transplanted into the Party and state organizations (Joffe, 1971, p. 364).

Linear integration would have been impossible had it not been due to the overriding importance of the Party "fraction" and the Party "branch." Mao (1967, I, p. 84) recognized as early as 1928 that the principal reason the Red Army had been able to carry on such arduous fighting without falling apart was the organization of the Party on a company basis within the Army. In recent years, the "Party branch" has come to designate all of the Party members within any governmental, industrial, military, or agricultural organ. The size of the branch varies with the size of the organ and is a relatively large group in many government agencies. The "Party fraction," on the other hand, is a small group of half a dozen or so of the leading Party members of an agency (Starr, 1973, p. 204; Barnett,

1967, p. 19). The Party "branch" and "fraction" should not be mistaken for the Party committees. The latter are units in the Party's own organization; the former are assemblages of Party members within *other* organizations, although the membership of the committee may overlap and, on occasions, be identical with the branch and fraction. Nevertheless, as an instrument of linear integration, the Party committee has the same role as the branch and fraction. This role is specifically consequential in the administration of factories and enterprises. The system of the responsibility of the director of each factory and enterprise under the leadership of the Party committee, created during the Great Leap Forward (Liu Lan-t'ao, 1959), is still in force, although the factory and enterprise director has vacated his seat to the revolutionary committee. During the early sixties,

> . . . the Party committee at the enterprise level became a kind of executive committee of the plant, with overall support and enforcement powers over a hierarchical organizational structure. Its main role was as political and economic mediator between the enterprise and the higher levels of economic administration [Andors, 1974a, pp. 439–440].

Recent reports indicate that "branch agencies are subordinate to a revolutionary committee at the same level, and that their own Party organization is led by the Party committee at the same level" (Bastid, 1973, p. 188). Bastid also cites the Shanghai Metallurgy Industry Bureau as an example. The Bureau is subordinate to the Shanghai Revolutionary committee and the Party Committee of the Shanghai Metallurgy Industry Bureau is led by the Shanghai Party Committee. And it is from the Shanghai Revolutionary Committee, not from a Peking ministry, that the Bureau receives assignments, although it is also in contact with Peking ministries for contracts. In this example, linear integration is achieved by the status of the Shanghai Party Committee and Revolutionary Committee, both of which are outside agencies, but both of which control the Bureau *in conjunction* with the Bureau's own Party Committee. Similarly, Donnithorne (1974, p. 773) reports that the Anshan Iron and Steel corporation is now jointly controlled by the Ministry of Metallurgy and the Province of Liaoning, while politically, it is under the Anshan Municipal Party Committee. Likewise, the Dalin Locomotive and Carriage Plant is said to be a centrally controlled enterprise under the Ministry of Communications, but the enterprise's Party Committee—which has jurisdiction over political matters and labor problems within the plant—reports directly to the Dalin Municipal Party Committee.

THE DIFFERING PRINCIPLES OF INTEGRATION

In the previous section, interorganizational integration in the Maoist model was compared with the process of intraorganizational integration in Western theories. Because of the formal similarities between the two, this comparison should help illuminate—at least indirectly—the different patterns of integration in interorganizational relations.[6]

One corollary of the functional autonomy of organizations is that interorganizational integration acquires a *functional* character: As each organization pursues its own goals and interests, its activities produce functional consequences which some other organization might find relevant to *its* aims and interests. As Levine, White, and Paul *et al* (1963, p. 1190) discovered in their study of local health and welfare systems, the flow of elements is not centrally coordinated but rests upon voluntary agreements between autonomous organizations. The accent on the functional aspect of interdependence is so great that Randall (1973, p. 236) could extend the "market theory of private organizations" to the study of Human Resources Development program of the Wisconsin State Employment Service in relations to other employment agencies. According to Hage (1974, p. 36), the basis of organizational coalition is, first of all, a functional necessity, "a complex problem that could only be solved by a system of organizations," and, second, "a technological imperative, requiring joint programming or technological interdependence."

Functional interdependence must be distinguished from *political* interdependence. The former arises from mutual need to regulate competition and institutionalize conflict (Emery and Trist, 1965; Terreberry, 1968; Turk, 1973,). Political interdependence, on the other hand, arises from collective orientation to a politically fixed goal. The coordinating mechanisms arising from political interdependence must, likewise, possess supraorganizational status. It appears that Mao (1969, p. 67) often assigned such a supraorganizational role to committees. In the River Commune in Kwangtung Province after the Great Leap Forward, two parallel agencies—one Party and another government—served as headquarters organizations at both the Commune and brigade levels. Both operated as coordinating agencies in matters pertaining to policy and operation (Pelzel, 1972, p. 400). After the Cultural Revolution, the role of Party committees as the overseers of policy in interenterprise relations has been made more precise and institutionalized (Bettelheim, 1974, p. 37; Ahn, 1975). Schurman (1968, p. 128) notes that important coordinating functions are performed by committees which bring together individuals from different agencies and permit decision making in a context in which broad knowledge is available. Andors (1974a, p. 440) observes that in the years after the Great Leap Forward, China seems to have experienced a conflict between the functional and the political styles of interorganizational integration. The Maoist position saw the issue of interenterprise coordination essentially in political terms. Party committees were to act as coordinating agencies between enterprises and higher authorities. Coordination was characterized by the face-to-face bargaining in which not only the question of cost, scarcity, and fixing prices but also the ultimate social goals of organizational activity were considered. The "functional" approach, on the other hand, saw interenterprise relationships in "economic" terms and stressed the role of prices and the importance of profit maximization at the participant and the enterprise levels. Enterprise managers were to react to their environment in making economic decisions while higher order goals were articulated by the prices determined by the planning authorities. When this latter scenario came under attack during the Cultural Revolution, interenterprise relations were accurately seen as resonant of capitalist free enterprise (Dittmer, 1974, p. 250).

On the basis of the preceding discussion, we may distinguish between two principles of interorganizational relations, the confederative and the federative. The *confederative principle* is one in which interorganizational relations are mediated at the level of the interacting organizations themselves and in which, though mediating bodies might exist, organizational interaction is regulated chiefly through the functional consequences of the promotion of autonomously defined goals and interests. The *federative principle* is one in which interorganizational relations are mediated at the supraorganizational level by bodies possessing binding authority on all the interacting units and in which organizational interaction is politically regulated.

The most important element in which the two models differ is the role of mediating bodies. In Western theories, such bodies almost invariably possess an advisory or adjudicative role; their decisions are either not binding, or, as in the case of courts, affect only cases related to the violation of law and discipline. The confederative principle, as noted, rests on the recognition of interorganizational conflict. The role of adjudicative bodies is seen as one of regulating conflicts under conditions of unstructured authority (Litwak and Hylton, 1962, p. 410). Examples are various forms of interjurisdictional agreements in metropolitan areas between different levels of government (Friesema, 1970, p. 240), interorganizational committees serving as quasi-coordinating bodies (Aiken and Hage, 1972), a supracorporate board to protect the public interest as proposed by Hage[7] (1974, p. 31), and the informal and nonbureaucratic style of mediation, as in the U.S. educational establishment, where private groups serve as connectors between public organizations and levels of government (Clark, 1965, p. 232). And finally, Parsons (1974, p. 9) is "deeply convinced that the problem of integration of complex organizations is very heavily dependent on *procedural institutions*," such as those dealing with law "where it is presumed that parties to litigation have divergent and often conflicting interests."

The federative principle, as implied earlier, is informed by the assumption of interorganizational harmony. Here, the role of the mediating agent is to foster and consolidate such harmony. One broadcast (Union Research Service, 1973i, p. 4) urged that "the provincial military district, the military subdistricts, and the various departments of the people's armed forces at various levels should direct their main energy to militia work," and that this should be done under the leadership of the Party committees. A typical instance of the federative principle is the convocation of periodic "telephone conferences" designed to strengthen interorganizational cooperation through an ad hoc supraorganizational device. Thus, the Telephone conference on Cotton field management, arranged by the Hupeh Provincial Party Committee in July 1973, sought to coordinate production efforts of communes engaged in cotton growing and achieve maximum efficiency and cooperation (Union Research Service, 1973h, p. 249). Another report from Hunan Province (Union Research Service, 1973b, p. 78) suggested that since "grain and cotton are mutually supporting, success in grain production would create better conditions for developing cotton production, while success in cotton production would provide more capital and manure for gain production." To achieve this rational balance, the report went on, Party organizations and revolutionary committees at all levels must play their leadership role by paying "attention to suitable concentration and rational management."

THE EXTENT AND SCOPE OF INTERORGANIZATIONAL RELATIONS

The functional character of interorganizational relations implies that the interactions of an organization are limited to, or at least occur more frequently with, those others with which it is functionally interdependent and with which exchange of information and resources is more beneficial or important. One important result is the segmentation of the interorganizational universe into clusters of interdependent networks. Hunter (1953, p. 62) was one of the first to recognize that the *several* pyramids of power in the city of Atlanta were analytically more relevant than *a* pyramid of power. Evan (1966, p. 178) has developed the notion of "organization set," a cluster of organizations with which a given organization, the "focal organization," interacts more than with any other, as measured by the role sets of the boundary personnel, the flow of information, products and services, and the flow of personnel. Osborn and Hunt (1974, p. 244) define an organization's "task environment" as "the set of organizations with which a given organization must interact," and Van de Ven, Emmet, and Koenig (1974, p. 119) speak of an "interorganizational collectivity" in which two or more organizations join together as an action system to attain similar objectives. Other instances of the segmented nature of interorganizational relations are the formation of oligopolies (Pfeffer and Leblebici, 1973, p. 459), "domain consensus" among health and welfare agencies (Levine, White, and Paul, 1963, p. 1191), and the concept of "organizational network" as developed by Hage (1974, p. 18).

As opposed to this, the ideal-typical Maoist model opts for *comprehensiveness* in interorganizational relations; these relations involve the totality of the interorganizational network. This comprehensiveness is exemplified by the building of the Chinhuangtao–Peking Oil Pipeline:

> The building of this pipeline is also the result of socialist cooperation on a big scale. Apart from the mobilization of the masses in Peking, Tientsin and Hopei Provinces to take part in the work, more than 240 factories and mines throughout the country supplied the necessary steel pipes, electric motors, oil pumps, transformers and other main installations as well as complete sets of equipment [*Peking Review*, 1975b, p. 29].

The spread of "scientific networks" during the Great Leap and renewed emphasis on them after the Cultural Revolution are other instances of this comprehensiveness. In mid-1958, branches of the Chinese Academy of Sciences were extended into provinces and counties. Science committees and associations of science and technology paralleling the science committees as well as "scientific research groups" devoted to popularization of science were established with branches in factories and villages (Suttmeier, 1975, p. 217). In 1975, it was urged, "each county must set up agricultural, scientific experimental organizations at the county, commune, production brigade and production team levels and weld them into a complete network." The masses were also encouraged to "carry out widespread scientific experiments, and bring into full play the function of professional, scientific and technical personnel" (*Peking Review,* 1975c, p. 10). Similar relations are reported to exist among units of the medical and health network, as well as between these and other organizations (Union Research Service, 1973f, p. 6).

Departure from comprehensiveness resulting in the formation of clusters of organizations along functional lines are denounced as deviant cases of "departmentalism"; those along geographical lines are dismissed as "localism" (Taraki, 1977). The tendency toward functional segmentation which came under attack during the Cultural Revolution had led to a divorce between economic integration and local (government or Party) political authority. Integration was sought in functionally coordinated corporations or trusts *(hsi-t'ung)* arranged around the marketing or production of related commodities (Andors, 1974a, p. 442). Barnett (1967) drew attention to this segmentation of organizational network in the early sixties. Functional "systems," each forming a distinct chain of command were organized on a nationwide basis. In some functional areas there were two or three different clusters of vertical, functional chains of command (Barnett, 1967, p. 6).

Another instance of this segmentation is the bifurcation of organizational elites into "red" and "expert," the political and the technocratic leaders (Schurmann, 1968, p. 163). Sometimes the drift of a major organizational sector, such as the Army, toward professionalism produces such a segmentation and the complaints about it (Nelson, 1972). In the circumstances surrounding the purge of Lin Piao, the Army, or at least a significant part of it, was believed to be gravitating toward "departmentalism." This was evident from the observation that 80 percent of the military leaders purged along with Lin Piao came from his Fourth Field Army (Domes, 1973, p. 639). In these and other manifestations of the bi- or multi-furcation of the interorganizational network into separate and relatively discontinuous clusters, the ideal of comprehensiveness and open organizational boundaries is lost. The interorganizational network approaches the pattern of Western organization theory and practice. Hence, the Maoists see these symptoms as capitalist in nature (Dittmer, 1974).

In addition to the extent of interorganizational relations discussed above, the functional accent in Western theories also has implications for the scope of these relationships.[8] The interaction among organizations is confined to *situationally* relevant areas, activities, and resources which the interacting organizations need most. In the "pyramid of power" which Hunter (1953, p. 65) discovered in Atlanta, the constituency of the pyramid would change according to the project at hand. Form and Nosow (1958) point out the situational and selective nature of interorganizational cooperation which increases in times of disaster. The "primary function" of an organization, according to Levine and White (1961, p. 593), determines its need for exchange elements and, hence, for the type of resources being exchanged. Levine, White, and Paul (1963, p. 1190) noted that in the welfare and health agencies they studied the kind and degree of interaction were affected by the agency's function, which determined the elements they needed, their access to elements from outside the system of health and welfare, and the degree of "domain consensus" within the system. The situational and selective aspect of interorganizational relations is also underscored by the factors which, according to Guetzkow (1969, p. 14), creates the need for interaction. These are: (1) those developing by virtue of interpenetration of groups, (2) those deriving from the specialized roles and teams assigned to handle interaction across organizational boundaries, and (3) those growing from indirect mediations of supraorganizational processes. Finally, Pfeffer and Nowak (1976, p. 399) found that patterns of joint ventures undertaken by large domestic corporations with other American companies engaged in manufacturing or oil and gas extraction tended to follow the exchange of resources across industrial sectors.

In the Maoist model, interorganizational relations are open-ended and *diffuse*. Although accentuated in areas in which relevant resources and information are mutually needed, they are not restricted to these. In one commune, "in the light of the special features of more concentrated

Chart 1. Basic differences between the Western and Maoist positions on interorganizational relations.

Western	*Maoist*
Organizations are relatively autonomous	Organizations are dependent upon the political process
Organizations have relatively closed boundaries	Organizations have relatively open boundaries
Interorganizational relations are conflictual	Interorganizational relations are harmonious
Interdependence is functional	Interdependence is political
Integration has an intraorganizational focus	Integration has intra- as well as interorganizational focus
Interorganizational relations are based on the confederative principle	Interorganizational relations are based on the federative principle
Interorganizational relations are segmented	Interorganizational relations are comprehensive
Interorganizational relations are situational and selective	Interorganizational relations are open-ended and diffuse
The purpose of self-sufficiency is to enhance the organization's power	The purpose of self-sufficiency is to enhance the potential to cooperate

double-rush work and greater demand for labor," a leading member of the County Party Committee mobilized the labor force to put aside sideline production, and by bringing in women's organizations and auxiliary labor, labor attendance was raised by 50 percent (Union Research Service, 1973g, p. 76). In Canton, the Fatshan Municipal Party Committee together with the Party Committees of various industrial bureaus drew out more than 100 office cadres and sent them to 18 key enterprises. The aim of this open-ended exchange was to carry out "measures for tapping the potentialities in every trade and at each unit, one by one, and further unfolding the mass movement of increasing production and practicing economy" (Union Research Service, 1973k, p. 45). Similarly unrestricted and diffuse patterns of interaction are reported among scientific and health organizations (Union Research Service, 1973d, p. 157; 1973f, p. 4). These comparisons are summarized in Chart 1.

CONCLUSION

These differences stem from the basic socio-political premises underlying organizational activity and the significance of interorganizational relations. The two theoretical approaches have arisen from two diametrically opposite sets of social conditions which Thomas (1975) describes as competitive and cooperative group interdependence. If the actor's interests are autonomously defined and promoted, interorganizational relations aim at minimizing an otherwise escalating state of conflict. If organizations are charged with the fulfillment of goals sanctioned and legitimized by the social imperatives guiding their actions, the purpose of interorganizational relations is to enhance an already presumed state of cooperation. Thus, Western organization theory follows the Hobbesian logical sequence and deduces the need for cooperation from the reality of conflict; the Maoist position follows the Kantian logical sequence and deduces the need for cooperation from the presumed existence of transcendental interests. Or stated differently, in the one school, interorganizational relations are rooted in the liberal conception of right; in the other, they are embedded in a Kantian type of conception of duty. Whereas in the former, an organization must improve its extractive capabilities (Eisenstadt, 1965, p. 187; Hill, 1974, p. 1075), in the latter it must enhance its potential to provide. The two positions may be further contrasted by juxtaposing the following passages:

> When a jurisdictional fight is to be undertaken, you first look around you for your natural allies. Then you try to estimate the possible strength of your opponent. Finally,

you outline your tactical campaign, keeping always in mind the importance of the right kind of timing |Dimock, 1952, p. 285|.

|As a result of overcoming departmentalism|, when one team has difficulties, the other teams take the initiative by sending their own men to help. Unity and coordination between teams and individuals in each brigade also have been enhanced |*Peking Review*, 1974, p. 13|.

This conception of interorganizational relations finds a paradoxical expression in the Chinese notion of "self-reliance." Communes and factories are urged to be "self-reliant" in order to minimize their dependence for resources on other organizations and improve their own capacity to provide such resources. Thus contrary to Donnithorne's (1972, pp. 605–606) contention, self-reliance is not meant to lead to "cellularization" and regional autarky, but to more active and effective interorganizational cooperation (Snead, 1975, p. 306). In the city of Changchow plans to set up a large comprehensive tractor plant for making walking-tractors fell through on two occasions. Then the city reportedly "made self-reliance and tapping the potential of old factories the basis of its work." Self-reliance meant that "more than a score of small factories coordinated in manufacturing different tractor parts and accessories, with each factory working to the best of its ability." The reported result:

In two years, their combined annual production capacity rose to 3,000 walking tractors, and this has been further increased through technical innovations to 15,000 today. Changchow's experience points to a quicker way of industrial development. Under a unified plan, it has made full use of what factories and resources it originally had, used simple indigenous methods, organized various factories and coordinated their efforts to form a serial production line and turn out some major products (*Peking Review*, 1975d, p. 25).

We have argued that the rejection of the primacy of the constituent interests in the Maoist model yields an entirely new set of organizational principles. The approach to interorganizational relations is heavily conditioned by the Maoist "world hypothesis" regarding the necessity of transcendent definition of interests and the possibility that the participating individual or organization could be intrinsically motivated to work for those interests. Just as Western approaches are, for the most part, rooted in Hobbesian assumptions concerning human motivation, the alternative to them is a challenge to these assumptions. The Maoist approach is one concrete form which such a challenge is taking.

FOOTNOTES

*A revised version of "From Prussia to Yenan: A Comparison of Modern Western and the Maoist Views on Interorganizational Relations," presented at the Seventy-first Annual Meeting of the American Sociological Association, New York City, August-September 1976.

1. It is possible to regress further and assert that the conception of organizational goal is affected by the prevailing conception of *interest*. The liberal conception of interest, which affirms the legitimacy and priority of constituent interest for the constituent actor leads to imprecision and elusiveness in organizational goals. For a study of this subject from this perspective, see Etzioni (1962), Cohen, March, and Olsen (1972) and Mohr (1973). In these and other authors, the liberal conception of interest is asserted implicitly.

2. This could be best understood in terms of Deutsch's (1966) theory of organization as a social system within which the internal flow of communication is more intense and frequent than between it and the outside world. The recent "open system" approach to interorganizational relations (Baker, 1973; Katz and Kahn, 1970; Miller and Rice, 1967) seems to recognize the interdependence of organizations for resources and support. However, organizational boundaries are still considered selectively open to environmental currents. Katz and Kahn (1970, p. 154), for example, say that the "reception of inputs into a system is selective. . . . Systems can react only to those information signals to which they are attuned. The general term for the selective mechanisms of a system by which incoming materials are rejected or accepted and translated for the structure is coding. The nature of the functions performed by the system determines its coding mechanisms, which in turn perpetuates this type of functioning."

3. For a detailed discussion of the assumption of conflict as the core assumption in organization theory, see Randall Collins (1975, pp. 286ff).

4. Interorganizational cooperation does not preclude *social* conflict. In the latter respect, Mao is certainly a conflict theorist as implied by his doctrine of permanent revolution. However, social conflict is not supposed to follow organizational boundaries pitting one organization against another. The medium of conflict is the "political line." The "struggle between restoration and counter-restoration" (Taraki, forthcoming) is one in which the old and the new patterns of values and habits are in conflict with organizations serving as arenas of such conflicts. In terms of Western organization theory, conflict is a feature of the institutional sphere. The organizational applications of this view makes it clear that the Chinese recognize the utility of *institutional* conflict in building cooperative *organizational* relations, a possibility to which Coser (1956) has also drawn attention.

5. Andors (1974a, p. 435) counterposes dual rule against "two participations, one renovation and triple combination," that is, workers' participation in management, management's participation in labor, renovation of rules and regulations, and the combination of workers, technicians and administrative cadres into decision-making bodies. However, dual rule is a device for macro-integration and interorganizational relations, while "2-1-3" is a principle of intraorganizational participation. Although Liu Shao-ch'i, Mao's opponent during the Cultural Revolution, is known to have favored the former, the two could quite conceivably be put into practice simultaneously. Although an ardent champion of "2-1-3," Mao is not known to have objected to dual rule. In fact, this was instituted in the mid-fifties in opposition to the Soviet model of "one-man management," prevalant until that time.

6. The fact that the focus of integration in the Maoist model is intra- as well as interorganizational, introduces some formal similarities between the Western approaches to *micro*-integration and the Maoist approach to *macro*-integration. Hence, the difference between the two schools over the style of macro-integration.

7. Aiken (1974, p. 18) considers interdependence "less than a merger or some system of hierarchical control among organizations . . . a network that is more than a confederation and less than a federation." We will nevertheless use the term "confederate" as defined here for semantic convenience.

8. The difference between extent and scope is that the former refers to the number of *organizations* involved, while the latter designates the number of *functions and activities* carried along interorganizational lines.

REFERENCES

Ahn, Byung-Joon (1975) "The Political Economy of the People's Communes." *Journal of Asian Studies* 24 (May): 631–658.

Aiken, Michael and Jerald Hage (1968) "Organizational Interdependence and Intra-organizational Structure." *American Sociological Review* 33 (December): 912–930.

———— (1972) "Organizational Permeability, Boundary Spanners and Organizational Structure." Paper presented at the 1972 Annual Meeting (September) of the American Sociological Association, New Orleans, LA.

Alford, Robert R. (1974) "Problems of Data and Measurement in Interorganizational Studies of Hospitals and Clinics: Research Notes." *Administrative Science Quarterly* 19 (December): 485–490.

Allen, Michael P. (1974) "The Structure of Interorganizational Elite Cooptation: Interlocking Corporate Directorates." *American Sociological Review* 39 (June): 393–406.

Andors, Stephen (1974a) "Factory Management and Political Ambiguity: 1961–1963." *China Quarterly* 59 (July–September): 435–476.

———— (1974b) "Beyond Hobbes and Weber: The Political Economy of Decentralization in Chinese Industry: A Theoretical Inquiry." *Journal of Comparative Administration* 5 (February): 487–427.

Baker, Frank (ed.) (1973) *Organizational Systems: General Systems Approaches to Complex Organization.* Homewood, IL: R. D. Irwin.

Barnett, A. Doak (1967) *Cadres, Bureaucracy, and Political Power in China.* New York: Columbia University Press.

Bastid, Marianne (1973) "Levels of Economic Decision Making." Pages 159–198 in Stuart R. Schram (ed.), *Authority, Participation and Cultural Change in China.* London: Cambridge University Press.

Benson, J. Kenneth (1975) "The Interorganizational Network as a Political Economy." *Administrative Science Quarterly* 20 (June): 229–249.

Bentley, Arthur F. (1967) *The Process of Government.* Cambridge, MA: Belknap Press of Harvard University Press.

Bettelheim, Charles (1974) *Cultural Revolution and Industrial Organization in China.* New York: Monthly Review Press.

Black, Bertram J. and Harold M. Kase (1963) "Interagency Cooperation in Rehabilitation and Mental Health." *Social Service Review* 37 (March): 26–32.

Blau, Peter M. and W. Richard Scott (1963) *Formal Organizations: A Comparative Approach.* London: Routledge and Kegan Paul.

Chang, Parris (1975) *Power and Policy in China.* University Park, PA: Penn State Press.

Clark, Burton (1965) "Interorganizational Patterns in Education." *Administrative Science Quarterly* 10 (September): 224–237.

Cohen, Michael D., James G. March, and John P. Olsen (1972) "A Garbage Can Model of Organizational Choice." *Administrative Science Quarterly* 17 (March): 1–25.

Collins, Randall (1975) *Conflict Sociology: Toward an Explanatory Science*. New York: Academic Press.

Coser. Lewis (1956) *The Functions of Social Conflict*. New York: Free Press.

Crazo, Rocco, Jr. and John M. Yanouza (1969) "Effects of Flat and Tall Organization Structure." *Administrative Science Quarterly* 14 (June): 178–191.

Crozier, Michael (1964) *The Bureaucratic Phenomenon*. Chicago: University of Chicago Press.

Deutsch, Karl (1966) *The Nerves of Government*. New York: J ee Press.

Dimock, Marshall E. (1952) "Expanding Jurisdictions: A Case ɔtudy in Bureaucratic Conflict." Pages 282–290 in Merton, *et al.* (ed)., *Reader in Bureaucracy*, Glencoe, IL: Free Press.

Dittmer, Lowell (1974) *Liu Shao-ch'i and the Chinese Cultural Revolution: The Politics of Mass Criticism*. Berkeley: University of California Press.

Domes, Jurgen (1973) "New Course in Chinese Domestic Politics: The Anatomy of Readjustment." *Asian Survey* 13 (July): 633–646.

Donnithorne, Audrey (1972) "China's Cellular Economy: Some Economic Trends Since the Cultural Revolution." *China Quarterly* 52 (October–December): 605–619.

——— (1974) "Recent Economic Development." *China Quarterly* 60 (October–December): 772–774.

Duncan, Robert A. (1972) "Characteristics of Organizational Environments and Perceived Environmental Uncertainty." *Administrative Science Quarterly* 17 (September): 313–327.

Eisenstadt, S. N. (1965) "Bureaucracy, Bureaucratization, and Power Structure." Pages 117–215 in S. N. Eisenstadt (ed.), *Essays on Comparative Institutions*. New York: Wiley.

Emery, F. E. and E. L. Trist (1965) "The Causal Texture of Organizational Environment." *Human Relations* 18 (February): 21–23.

Entwisle, Doris R. and John Walton (1960) "Observations on the Span of Control." *Administrative Science Quarterly*. 5 (March): 522–533.

Etzioni, Amitai (1960) "Two Approaches to Organizational Analysis" *Administrative Science Quarterly* 5 (September): 257–278.

Evan, William M. (1966) "The Organization Set: Toward a Theory of Interorganizational Relations." Pages 173–192 in James Thompson (ed.), *Approaches to Organizational Design*. Pittsburgh: University of Pittsburgh Press.

Form, William H. and Delbert Miller (1960) *Industry, Labor, and Community*. New York: Harper.

——— and Sigmund Nosow (1958) *Community in Disorder*. New York: Harper and Row.

Friesema, H. Paul (1970) "Interorganizational Agreements in Metropolitan Areas." *Administrative Science Quarterly* 15 (June): 242–252.

Gouldner, Alvin W. (1959) "Reciprocity and Autonomy in Functional Theory." Pages 241–270 in Llewellyn Gross (ed.), *Symposium on Sociological Theory*. Evanston, IL: Row and Peterson.

Gray, Jack and Patrick Cavendish (1968) *Chinese Communism in Crisis: Maoism and the Cultural Revolution*. New York: Praeger.

Guetzkow, Harold (1966) "Relations Among Organizations." Pages 13–44 in Raymond Bowers (ed.), *Studies on Behavior in Organizations*. Athens: University of Georgia Press.

Hage, Jerald (1974) "A Strategy for Creating Interdependent Delivery Systems to Meet Complex Needs." *Organization and Administrative Sciences* 5 (Spring): 17–44.

Hamilton, Sir Ian (1921) *The Soul and Body of an Army*. London: Faber and Faber.

Harding, Harry (1971) "Mao's Theories of Organization and Policy Making." Pages 112–164 in Thomas W. Robinson (ed.), *The Cultural Revolution in China.* Berkeley: University of California Press.

Harper, Paul (March 1969) "The Party and the Unions in Communist China." *China Quarterly* 37 (March): 84–119.

Hemphill, J. K. and C. M. Westie (1950) "The Measurement of Group Dimensions." *Journal of Psychology* 29 (April): 325–342.

Hill, Larry B. (1974) "Institutionalization, the Ombudsman, and Bureaucracy." *American Political Science Review* 68 (September): 1075–1085.

Hoover Commission (1952) "Duplication of Functions: A Case Study in Bureaucratic Conflict." Pages 291–297 in Merton *et al.* (eds.), *Reader in Bureaucracy.* Glencoe, IL: Free Press.

Hummon, Norman P. (1970) "Criticism of Effects of Flat and Tall Organization Structure." *Administrative Science Quarterly* 15 (June): 230–234.

Hunter, Floyd (1953) *Community Power Structure: A Study of Decision Makers.* Chapel Hill: University of North Carolina Press.

Joffe, Ellis (1971) "The Chinese Army under Lin Piao: Prelude to Political Intervention." Pages 343–376 in John M. H. Lindbeck (ed.), *China: Management of a Revolutionary Society.* Seattle: University of Washington Press.

Katz, Daniel and Robert L. Kahn (1970) "Open System Theory." Pages 149–160 in Oscar Grusky and George a. Miller (eds.), *The Sociology of Organizations: Basic Studies.* New York: Free Press.

Klatzky, S. R. (1970) "Relationship of Organizational Size to Complexity and Coordination." *Administrative Science Quarterly* 15 (December): 428–438.

Kochan, Thomas A. (1975) "Determinants of the Power of Boundary Units in an Interorganizational Bargaining Relations." *Administrative Science Quarterly* 20 (September): 434–452.

Levine, Sol and Paul White (1961) "Exchange as a Conceptual Framework for the Study of Interorganizational Relationships." *Administrative Science Quarterly* 5 (March): 583–601.

———, ———, and Benjamin D. Paul (1963) "Community Interorganizational Problems in Providing Medical Care and Social Services." *American Journal of Public Health* 53 (August): 1183–1195.

Litwak, Eugene and Lydia R. Hylton (1962): "Interorganizational Analsyis: A Hypothesis on Coordinating Agencies." *Administrative Science Quarterly* 6 (March): 395–420.

Liu Lan-t'ao (1959) "The Chinese Communist Party Is the Supreme Commander of the Chinese People in Building Socialism." Pages 95–106 in Union Research Institute (ed.), *The Case of Peng Teh-huai,* Hong Kong: Union Research Institute.

Mao Tse-tung (1962) "On the Correct Handling of Contradictions Among the People." Pages 273–295 in Robert R. Bowie and John K. Fairbank, (eds.), *Communist China: Policy Documents with Analysis,* Cambridge, MA: Harvard University Press.

——— (1967) *Selected Works,* Volumes I, II and III. Peking: Foreign Languages Press.

——— (1969) *Selected Works,* Volume IV. Peking: Foreign Languages Press.

March, James and Herbert Simon (1958) *Organizations.* New York: Wiley.

Merton, Robert K. *et al.* (eds.) (1952) *Reader in Bureaucracy.* Glencoe, IL: Free Press.

Miller, Eric and A. K. Rice (1967) *Systems of Organization: The Control of Task and Sentient Boundaries.* London: Tavistock Publications.

Miller, Walter B. (1958) "Inter-Institutional Conflict: A Major Impediment in Delinquency Prevention." *Human Organization* 17 (Fall): 20–23.

Mills, C. Wright (1956) *The Power Elite.* New York: Oxford University Press.

Mindlin, Sergio E. and Howard Aldrich (1975) "Interorganizational Dependence: A Review of the Concept and a Re-examination of the Findings of the Aston Group," *Administrative Science Quarterly* 20 (September): 382–392.

Mohr, Lawrence B. (1973) "The Concept of Organizational Goal." *American Political Science Review* 67 (June): 470–481.

Nebeker, Delbert M. (1975) "Situational Favorablity and Perceived Environmental Uncertainty: An Integrative Approach." *Administrative Science Quarterly* 20 (June): 281–294.

Nelson Harvey (1972) "Military Forces in the Cultural Revolution." *China Quarterly* 51 (July–September): 44–474.

New China News Agency (1970) translated in *Survey of China Mainland Press*, No. 4643. Hong Kong: Union Research Institute, p. 17.

Osborn, Richard N. and James G. Hunt (1974) "Environment and Organizational Effectiveness." *Administrative Science Quarterly* 19 (June): 231–246.

Ouchi, William G. and John B. Dowling (1974) "Defining the Span of Control" *Administrative Science Quarterly* 19 (September): 357–365.

Parsons, Talcott (1956) "Suggestions for a Sociological Approach to the Theory of Organizations." *Administrative Science Quarterly* 1 (June): 63–85.

——— (1974) "The Institutional Function in Organization Theory." *Organization and Management Sciences* 5 (Spring): 3–16.

——— (1970) in *Survey of China Mainland Press* No. 4751: (September 21): 11–12.

Peking Review (Peking) (1973) September 7: 32.

——— (1974) April 26: 13.

——— (1975a) January 3: 16.

——— (1975b) July 18: 7.

——— (1975c) October 31: 10.

——— (1975d) 7 November: pp. 24–25.

——— (1976) April 16: 24.

People's Daily (Peking) (1959) in Union Research Institute (ed.), *The Case of Peng Teh-huai* (August 14): 105.

Pelzel, John C. (1972) "Economic Management of a Production Brigade in Post-Leap China." Pages 387–416 in W. E. Ellmott (ed.), *Economic Organization in Chinse Society*. Stanford: Stanford University Press.

Perrucci, Robert and Marc Pilisuk (1970), "Leaders and Ruling Elites: The Interorganizational Basis of Community Power." *American Sociological Review* 35 (December): 1040–1057.

Pfeffer, Jeffrey and Huseyin Leblebici (1973) "Executive Recruitment and the Development of Interfirm Organizations." *Administrative Science Quarterly* 18 (December): 449–461.

——— and Philip Nowak (1976) "Joint Ventures and Interorganizational Interdependence." *Administrative Science Quarterly* 21 (September): 398–418.

Randal, Ronald (1973) "Influence of Environmental Support and Policy Space on Organizational Behavior." *Administrative Science Quarterly* 18 (June): 236–247.

Reid, William (1964) "Interagency Coordination in Delinquency Prevention and Control." *Social Service Review* 38 (December): 418–428.

Richman, Barry (1967) *Management Development and Education in the Soviet Union.* East Lansing, MI: Michigan State University Press.

Schurmann, Franz (1968) *Ideology and Organization in Communist China.* Berkeley: University of California Press.

Selznick, Philip (1957) *Leadership in Administration: A Sociological Interpretation.* New York: Harper.

Simon, Herbert (1970) *Administrative Behavior: A Study of Decision-Making Process in Administrative Organization.* New York: Macmillan.

Snead, William G. (1973) "Self-Reliance, Internal Trade and China's Economic Structure." *China Quarterly* 62 (June): 302–308.

Starr, John Bryan (1973) *Ideology and Culture: An Introduction to the Dialectic of Comtemporary Chinese Politics.* New York: Harper and Row.

Suttmeier, Richard P. (1975) "Science Policy Shifts, Organizational Change, and China's Development." *China Quarterly* 62 (June): 207–241.

Tan Hsi (1975) "Adhere to the Socialist Principle of Economic Accounting." *Chinese Economic Studies* 9 (Fall): 48–49.

Taraki, Bariman (1977) "The Chinese Communist View of Organizational Pathologies." *Asia Quarterly* 1 (March): 76–97.

—— (forthcoming) "Institutionalization and Bureaucracy in China: The Relevance of the Maoist Experience." *Studies in Comparative International Development.*

Terreberry, Shirley (1968) "The Evolution of Organizational Environment." *Administrative Science Quarterly* 12: 590–613.

Thomas, Edwin J. (1959) "Effects of Facilitative Role Interdependence on Group Functioning." *Human Relations* 19 (June): 347–366.

Thompson, James D. and William J. McEwen (1958) "Organizational Goal and Environment." *American Sociological Review* 23 (February): 23–31.

Turk, Herman (1973) "Comparative Urban Structure from an Interorganizational Perspective." *Administrative Science Quarterly* 18 (March): 37–55.

Udy, Stanley H. Jr. (1970) "Technical and Institutional Factors in Productive Organizations: A Preliminary Model." Pages 47–57 in Henry A. Landsberger (ed.), *Comparative Perspectives on Formal Organization.* Boston: Little, Brown.

Union Research Institute (ed.) (1968) *The Case of Peng Teh-huai* Hong Kong: Union Research Institute.

—— (1971) *Documents of the Chinese Communist Party Central Committe,* Volume I: Hong Kong: Union Research Institute.

Union Research Service. Hong Kong: Union Research Institute: (1973a) April 13: 49; (1973b) April 20: 78; (1973c) April 27: 114; (1973d) May 11: 157; (1973e) May 22: 201; (1973f July 3: 4, 6; (1973g) July 23: 76; (1973h) August 31: 249; (1973i) October 2: 4; (1973j) October 5: 17; (1973k) October 13: 43, 45; (1973l) November 20: 191; (1973m) November 23: 205; (1973n) December 7: 262; (1974) September 20: 304.

Urwick, Luther (1956) "The Manager's Span of Control." *Harvard Business Review* 34 (May–June): 39–47.

Van de Ven, Andrew H., Dennis Emmet, and Richard Koenig Jr. (1974) "Frameworks for Interorganizational Analysis." *Organization and Administrative Sciences* 5 (Spring): 113–130.

Whyte, Martin King (1973) "Bureaucracy and Modernization in China: The Maoist Critique." *American Sociological Review* 38 (April): 149–163.

Zeit, Gerald (1974) "Interorganizational Relationships and Social Structure: A Critique of Some Aspects of the Literature." *Organization and Administrative Sciences* 5 (Spring): 131–140.

CUMULATIVE INDEX TO AUTHORS, Volumes 1 and 2

(Volume 1 published as *COMPARATIVE STUDIES IN SOCIOLOGY*)

OTHER SERIES OF INTEREST FROM JAI PRESS INC.

Consulting Editor for Sociology: Rita J. Simon, Director, Program in Law and Society, University of Illinois

COMPARATIVE SOCIAL RESEARCH
(Formerly: Comparative Studies in Sociology)
Series Editor: Richard F. Tomasson, University of New Mexico

POLITICAL POWER AND SOCIAL THEORY
Series Editor: Maurice Zeitlin, University of California—Los Angeles

RESEARCH IN COMMUNITY AND MENTAL HEALTH
Series Editor: Roberta Simmons, University of Minnesota

RESEARCH IN LAW AND SOCIOLOGY
Series Editor: Rita J. Simon, Director, Program in Law and Society, University of Illinois

RESEARCH IN RACE AND ETHNIC RELATIONS
Series Editors: Cora B. Marrett, University of Wisconsin, and Cheryl Leggon, University of Illinois—Chicago Circle

RESEARCH IN SOCIAL MOVEMENTS, CONFLICTS AND CHANGE
Series Editor: Louis Kriesberg, Syracuse University

RESEARCH IN SOCIAL PROBLEMS AND PUBLIC POLICY
Series Editor: Michael Lewis, University of Massachusetts

RESEARCH IN SOCIAL STRATIFICATION AND MOBILITY
Series Editor: Donald J. Treiman, National Academy of Sciences

RESEARCH IN SOCIOLOGY OF EDUCATION AND SOCIALIZATION
Series Editor: Alan C. Kerckhoff, Duke University

RESEARCH IN SOCIOLOGY OF KNOWLEDGE, SCIENCES AND ART
Series Editors: Robert Alun Jones, University of Illinois, and Henrika Kuklick, University of Pennsylvania

RESEARCH IN THE INTERWEAVE OF SOCIAL ROLES: WOMEN AND MEN
Series Editor: Helena Z. Lopata, Center for the Comparative Study of Social Roles, Loyola University of Chicago

RESEARCH IN THE SOCIOLOGY OF HEALTH CARE
Series Editor: Julius A. Roth, University of California—Davis

RESEARCH IN THE SOCIOLOGY OF WORK
Series Editor: Ida Harper Simpson, Duke University, and Richard Lee Simpson, University of North Carolina, Chapel Hill

STUDIES IN COMMUNICATIONS RESEARCH
Series Editor: Thelma McCormack, York University—Toronto

STUDIES IN SYMBOLIC INTERACTION
Series Editor: Norman K. Denzin, University of Illinois

ALL VOLUMES IN THESE ANNUAL SERIES ARE AVAILABLE AT
INSTITUTIONAL AND INDIVIDUAL SUBSCRIPTION RATES.
PLEASE ASK FOR DETAILED BROCHURE ON EACH SERIES.

A 10 percent discount will be granted on all institutional standing orders placed directly with the publisher. Standing orders will be filled automatically upon publication and will continue until cancelled. Please indicate with which volume Standing Order is to begin.

 **JAI PRESS INC.**
P.O. Box 1678
165 West Putnam Avenue
Greenwich, Connecticut 06830

(203) 661-7602   Cable Address: JAIPUBL

Comparative Studies in Sociology

A Research Annual

Series Editor: **Richard F. Tomasson, Department of Sociology, The University of New Mexico.**

REVIEW: "...this collection should be a valuable asset to a college or university library ... they should be valuable resource material for sociologists, economists, historians, and political scientists...each article has an adequate bibliography." — *Choice*

Volume 1.   Published 1978   Cloth   348 pages   Institutions: $ 26.50
ISBN 0-89232-025-7   Individuals: $ 13.00

CONTENTS:

INTRODUCTION.
Comparative Sociology: The State of the Art, *Richard F. Tomasson, The University of New Mexico.*

MODERNIZATION.
Modernization and Other Determinants of National Birth, Death, and Growth Rates 1958-1972, *Phillips Cutright and William R. Kelly, Indiana University.* **National Differences in Individual Modernity,** *Alex Inkeles, Stanford University.* **Cities and Homicide: A New Look at an Old Paradox,** *Dane Archer, Robin Akert and Tim Lockwood, University of California — Santa Cruz and Rosemary Gartner, University of Wisconsin.* **Domestic Service and Industrialization,** *David Chaplin, Western Michigan University.* **Revolution as Cataclysm and Coup: Political Transformation and Economic Development in Mexico and Brazil,** *Susan Eckstein, Boston University and Peter Evans, Brown University.* **The Ethnic Systems of Premodern Spain,** *Thomas F. Glick, Boston University.*

SOCIAL INDICATORS AND THE QUALITY OF LIFE.
Value Priorities, Life Satisfaction, and Political Dissatisfaction Among Western Publics, *Ronald Inglehart, University of Michigan.* **The Relationship Between Objective and Subjective Indicators in the Light of a Comparative Study,** *Erik Allardt, University of Helsinki.* **Government Pensions for the Aged in 19 Industrialized Countries: Demonstration of a Method for Cross-National Evaluation,** *Lincoln H. Day, The Australian National University.*

TWO-CASE STUDIES.
An Index of Evaluated Equality: Measuring Conceptions of Social Justice in England and the United States, *Wendell Bell and Robert V. Robinson, Yale University.* **A Formula for Genocide: Comparison of the Turkish Genocide (1915) and the German Holocaust (1939-1945),** *Helen Fein, New Paltz, New York.* **Imperfectly Unified Elites: The Cases of Italy and France,** *G. Lowell Field, University of Connecticut and John Higley, The Australian National University.* **Imperial Development: The Cases of American Puerto Rico and Soviet Georgia,** *Barry B. Levine and Ralph S. Clem, Florida International University.* **Index.**

Series continued as: **Comparative Social Research**

A 10 percent discount will be granted on all institutional standing orders placed directly with the publisher. Standing orders will be filled automatically upon publication and will continue until cancelled. Please indicate with which volume Standing Order is to begin.

JAI PRESS INC., P.O. Box 1678, 165 West Putnam Avenue, Greenwich, Connecticut 06830.
Telephone: 203-661-7602   Cable Address: JAIPUBL

Political Power and Social Theory

A Research Annual

Series Editor: **Maurice Zeitlin, Department of Sociology, University of California — Los Angeles.**

Volume 1.	December 1979 Cloth	Ca. 350	Institutions: $ 26.50
ISBN 0-89232-115-6			Individuals: $ 13.50

Political Power and Social Theory is a new scholarly annual devoted to the class analysis of political relations and historical development. It will appear at a moment when the old paradigms — functionalist, neoclassicist, empiricist and democratic elitist alike — are under sustained intellectual attack from the left and a new body of empirical work guided by class theory is emerging in the social sciences. The aim of the annual, then, is to spur and enrich this emergent intellectual current by providing a regular annual compilation of exemplary historical materialist political studies. Obviously, it will not be limited by disciplinary boundaries or sectarian perspective, and it will strive also to be international in its authorship. This is clear from the table of contents of the inaugural volume of **Political Power and Social Theory.** Scholarly excellence, theoretical relevance, and a Socialist political commitment typify the work of these writers — and it is precisely this combination of qualities that studies appearing in the annual will strive to embody.

CONTENTS: Political Action, Determinism and Contingency, *Ralph Miliband, Leeds University, England.* **Material Bases of Consent: Economics and Politics in a Hegemonic System,** *Adam Przeworski, University of Chicago.* **Two Logics of Collective Action: Theoretical Notes on Social Class and Organizational Form,** *Claus Offe and Helmut Wiesenthal, University of Bielefeld, West Germany.* **Social Policy and the Formation of Political Consciousness,** *Frances Piven, Boston University and Richard Cloward, Columbia University. (Comment: Julia Wrigley, University of California, Los Angeles. Reply: Frances Piven and Richard Cloward.)* **State and Society, 1130-1815: An Analysis of English State Finances,** *Michael Mann, London School of Economics and Political Science.* **Stalinism: A Study of Internal Colonialism,** *Alvin W. Gouldner, Washington University, St. Louis.* **The Politics of Production and the Production of Politics: A Comparative Analysis of Piecework Machine Shops in the United States and Hungary,** *Michael Burawoy, University of California, Berkeley.* **Strikes, Power and Politics in the Western Nations, 1900-1976.** *Walter Korpi, Swedish Institute for Social Research, and Michael Shalev, University of Wisconsin, Madison.*

Volume 2.	Fall 1980	Cloth	Ca. 350 pages	Institutions: $ 26.50
ISBN 0-89232-143-1			Individuals: $ 13.50

TENTATIVE CONTENTS: Corporatist Compromise and the Re-Emergence of Class Conflict: Labor-Capital Relations and the Collapse of the Weimar Republic, *David Abraham, Princeton University.* **Capitalism and Race Relations in South Africa: A Split Labor Market Analysis,** *Edna Bonacich, University of California - Riverside.* **Class, Race, and Capitalism in the South African State: A Marxian Analysis,** *Michael Burawoy, University of California - Berkeley.* **Towards a Marxian Theory of 'Local Government,' Class Relations and the State,** *Manual Castells, Ecole des Hautes Etudes en Sciences Sociales, Paris.* **Political Contradictions of Welfare State Expansion: From Social Democracy to 'Economic Democracy,'** *Gosta Esping-Andersen, Harvard University.* **The Welfare State, Capitalism and Crisis,** *Ian Gough, University of Manchester.* **Race and Business Enterprise in Alabama,** *Stanley Greenberg, Yale University.* **From Riot to Mass Strike: Working Class Consciousness and Community in 19th C. Andalusia,** *Temma Kaplan, University of California - Los Angeles.* **State, Party, and Class in Italy,** *Guido Martinotti, University of Milan.* **From Electoral to Bureaucratic Politics in the Capitalist Class: Class Conflict and the Emergence of the Financial-Industrial Class Segment in the United States, 1886-1905,** *William G. Roy, University of California - Los Angeles.*

A 10 percent discount will be granted on all institutional standing orders placed directly with the publisher. Standing orders will be filled automatically upon publication and will continue until cancelled. Please indicate with which volume Standing Order is to begin.

Research in Political Economy

A Research Annual

Series Editor: **Paul Zarembka, Department of Economics, State University of New York — Buffalo.**

This series of annual volumes develops an approach to understanding society that completely breaks with any approach via separate social science disciplines. The approach here, consistent with classical Marxism, treats society as an integrated whole, the separate parts of which make little sense when studied in isolation. The essential tool is class struggle within a mode of production and the relation between modes of production. With emphasis on the capitalist mode of production, some attention is also given to pre-capitalist modes, as well as to socialism as a structural break from the capitalist mode. Both theoretical abstraction and case studies are and will be included.

A 10 percent discount will be granted on all institutional standing orders placed directly with the publisher. Standing orders will be filled automatically upon publication and will continue until cancelled. Please indicate which volume Standing Order is to begin with.

JAI PRESS INC., P.O. BOX 1678, 165 West Putnam Avenue, Greenwich, Connecticut 06830

Telephone: 203-661-7602 Cable Address: JAIPUBL